STUDY GUIDE
VOLUME 1: CHAPTERS 1-14

INTERMEDIATE ACCOUNTING

TENTH EDITION

Douglas W. Kieso, J.D., M.A.S., C.P.A.
University of California—Irvine
Irvine, California

Donald E. Kieso, Ph.D., C.P.A.
KPMG Peat Marwick Emeritus Professor of Accountancy
Northern Illinois University
DeKalb, Illinois

Jerry J. Weygandt, Ph.D., C.P.A.
Arthur Andersen Alumni Professor of Accounting
University of Wisconsin
Madison, Wisconsin

Terry D. Warfield, Ph.D., C.P.A.
University of Wisconsin
Madison, Wisconsin

JOHN WILEY & SONS, INC.
New York • Chichester • Weinheim
Brisbane • Singapore • Toronto

COVER PHOTO © James Rudnick/The Stock Market.

To order books or for customer service call 1-800-CALL-WILEY (225-5945).

ISBN 0-471-37606-X

Printed in the United States of America

10 9 8 7 6 5 4 3 2 1

Printed and bound by Courier Stoughton, Inc.

CONTENTS

VOLUME I

NOTE TO STUDENTS

This Study Guide is provided as an aid to your study of *Intermediate Accounting,* by Donald E. Kieso and Jerry J. Weygandt, and Terry Warfield. If used wisely, it can supplement and reinforce your understanding of the concepts and techniques presented in the textbook. **Never rely on the Study Guide as a substitute for a thorough reading of the textbook material.** This Study Guide merely highlights the in-depth presentation in the textbook.

An approach that combines use of the Study Guide and textbook material is suggested below.

1. Read the textbook presentation of the chapter.

2. Read the chapter review paragraphs in the Study Guide.

3. Answer the questions and review exercises appearing at the end of the chapter review paragraphs and compare your answers with those found at the end of each chapter. The extent of your success in answering these questions and exercises will indicate your understanding of the chapter. If you were unsuccessful in answering a large percentage of these questions correctly, you should read the textbook again.

4. Work the problems assigned from the textbook.

Solutions to the review questions and exercises are found at the end of each chapter. In addition to identifying the correct answer to each true-false and multiple choice question, an explanation is provided indicating why the answer is false and why a particular alternative (for multiple choice questions) is correct. This approach is designed to aid you in gaining a complete understanding of the material in each chapter.

When preparing for examinations, the Study Guide material may be used to determine your recall of the information presented in specific chapters. Once you have identified those subject areas in need of further review, return to the textbook material for a complete discussion of the subject matter involved. Remember, the Study Guide merely highlights the textbook material; it cannot be relied upon as a comprehensive treatment of a subject area.

In the study of accounting, there is no substitute for hard work and a desire to learn. A proper attitude and a willingness to work will go a long way toward ensuring your success in intermediate accounting.

The following supplemental items are also available from your bookstore, or the publisher, for use in conjunction with this Study Guide and with the textbook, *Intermediate Accounting,* Tenth Edition.

Student Active Learning Aids Working Papers. Working Papers are partially completed accounting forms for all end-of-chapter exercises, problems, and cases. A convenient resource for organizing and completing homework assignments, they demonstrate how to correctly set up solution formats and are directly tied to textbook assignments.

The Problem Solving Survival Guide. This Problem Solving tutorial is designed to improve students' success rates in solving intermediate accounting homework assignments and exam questions. The Problem Problem Solving Survival Guide also provides additional insight and tips on how to study accounting. Each chapter includes an overview of key chapter topics and a review of chapter learning objectives; purpose statements for each question, case, or exercise and a direct link to learning objectives; and tips to alert students to common pitfalls and misconceptions, as well as reminders of concepts and principles to help solve problems. A selection of multiple-choice exercises and cases representative of common exam questions or homework assignments enhance student proficiency, and detailed solutions and explanations assist students in the approach, setup, and completion of problems.

Solving Intermediate Accounting Problems Using Excel. These electronic spreadsheet templates allow students to complete selected end-of-chapter exercises and problems, identified by a spreadsheet icon in the margin of the text. The manuals, which include the disks, guide students step-by-step from an introduction to Excel, to completing preprogrammed spreadsheets, to designing their own spreadsheets. Prepared for students with a range of experience in spreadsheet applications, these templates and tutorials help students develop and hone their computer skills and expose them to software packages often used in real-world business environments.

Rockford Corporation: An Accounting Practice Set. This practice set can be used at or near the beginning of Intermediate Accounting, and provides material that can be assigned in conjunction with Chapter 3, "A Review of the Accounting Process." The practice set has been designed as a student review and update of the accounting cycle and the preparation of financial statements that are covered in the traditional first-year principles of financial accounting. Completion of this practice set requires the student to (1) analyze transactions, (2) journalize transactions, (3) post to the general ledger and to subsidiary ledgers, (4) prepare year-end adjusting entries, (5) use a 10-column work sheet, (6) prepare financial statements (including the optional preparation of a statement of cash flows), and (7) close the accounts. This practice set is estimated to take between 10 and 14 hours to work. This practice set is also available computerized, with an accompanying diskette and documentation.

ACKNOWLEDGEMENTS

The authors (Donald E. Kieso, Douglas W. Kieso, Jerry J. Weygandt, and Terry Warfield) wish to acknowledge the following individuals for their assistance in this study guide: Mary Ann Benson, compositor; Julie Kerr of John Wiley & Sons, Inc., supplements editor; Monica Frizzell, Western Conneticut State University, reviewer and proofer; and Dick Wasson, Southwestern College, supplements coordinator.

Douglas W. Kieso

1

Financial Accounting and Accounting Standards

CHAPTER STUDY OBJECTIVES

1. Describe the essential characteristics of accounting.
2. Identify the major financial statements and other means of financial reporting.
3. Explain how accounting assists in the efficient use of scarce resources.
4. Identify some of the challenges facing accounting.
5. Identify the objectives of financial reporting.
6. Explain the need for accounting standards.
7. Identify the major policy-setting bodies and their role in the standard-setting process.
8. Explain the meaning of generally accepted accounting principles.
9. Describe the impact of user groups on the standard-setting process.
10. Understand issues related to ethics and financial accounting.

CHAPTER REVIEW

1. Chapter 1 describes the environment that has influenced both the development and use of the financial accounting process. The chapter traces the development of financial accounting standards, focusing on the groups that have had or currently have the responsibility for developing such standards. Certain groups other than those with direct responsibility for developing financial accounting standards have significantly influenced the standard-setting process. These various pressure groups are also discussed in Chapter 1.

Nature of Financial Accounting

2. (S.O. 1) **Accounting** may best be defined by describing the three essential characteristics of accounting: (1) identification, measurement, and communication of financial information about (2) economic entities to (3) interested persons. **Financial accounting** is the process that culminates in the preparation of financial reports on the enterprise as a whole for use by parties both internal and external to the enterprise.

3. (S.O. 2) **Financial statements** are the principal means through which financial information is communicated to those outside an enterprise. The financial statements most frequently provided are (1) the balance sheet, (2) the income statement, (3) the statement of cash flows, and (4) the statement of owners' or stockholders' equity. Other means of financial reporting include the president's letter or supplementary schedules in the corporate annual report, prospectuses, and reports filed with government agencies.

4. (S.O. 3) Accounting is important for markets, free enterprise, and competition because it assists in providing information that leads to capital allocation. The better the information, the more effective the process of capital allocation and then the healthier the economy.

5. (S.O. 4) The challenges facing financial accounting are the following:

a. **Non-financial measurements** such as customer satisfaction indexes, backlog information, and reject rates on goods purchased.
b. **Forward-looking information.**
c. **Soft assets.**
d. **Timeliness.**

6. (S.O. 5) The objectives of financial accounting are to provide information:

a. that is useful to present and potential investors and creditors and other users in making rational investment, credit, and similar decisions;
b. to help present and potential investors and creditors and other users in assessing the amounts, timing, and uncertainty of perspective cash receipts from dividends or interest and the proceeds from the sale, redemption, or maturity of securities or loans; and
c. about the economic resources of an enterprise, the claims to those resources, and the effects of transactions, events, and circumstances that change its resources and claims to those resources.

7. (S.O. 6) The accounting profession has developed a common set of standards and procedures known as **generally accepted accounting principles (GAAP).** These principles serve as a general guide to the accounting practitioner in accumulating and reporting the financial information of a business enterprise. Although the adoption of some generally accepted accounting principles has caused controversy among accountants as well as members of the financial community, a majority of the members in each group recognize the ultimate benefit an accepted set of accounting principles can bring to the financial reporting process.

Accounting Organizations

8. (S.O. 7) Financial accounting standards in use at this time in the United States are primarily a result of the accounting profession's efforts during the past 75 years. Prior to that time accounting practices were relatively unsophisticated owing to the lack of extensive economic development in the United States. The **American Institute of Certified Public Accountants (AICPA),** the national professional organization of practicing Certified Public Accountants (CPAs), has been a catalyst in the development of GAAP in the United States. Although the responsibility for setting accounting standards now rests with the FASB, the Securities and Exchange Commission (SEC), the Governmental Accounting Standards Board (GASB), and other organizations can and do influence the standards-setting process.

9. The **SEC** takes a great deal of interest in the standards developed by the accounting profession. The SEC is an agency of the federal government that monitors the activities of corporate enterprises whose stock is publicly held. The SEC requires each corporate entity under its jurisdiction to **file a set of annual audited financial statements.** The SEC has the mandate to establish accounting principles; however, the SEC's involvement in the development of accounting standards has varied. In general, the SEC has supported the development of accounting standards by the private sector; however, there have been times when they have stepped in and prodded the private sector into a different direction.

10. The first group appointed by the AICPA to address the issue of uniformity in accounting practice was the **Committee on Accounting Procedure (CAP).** This group served the accounting profession from 1939 to 1959. During that period it issued 51 **Accounting Research Bulletins (ARBs)** that narrowed the wide range of alternative accounting practices then in existence. Even though the work of the Committee on Accounting Procedure was a valuable aid to accounting practitioners, the authority for its pronouncements rested solely on general acceptance by the accounting profession.

11. In 1959, the AICPA created the **Accounting Principles Board (APB)**. The major purposes of this group were (a) to advance the written expression of accounting principles, (b) to determine appropriate practices, and (c) to narrow the areas of difference and inconsistency in practice. The APB was designated as the AICPA's sole authority for public pronouncements on accounting principles. Its pronouncements, known as **APB Opinions,** were intended to be based mainly on research studies and be supported by reasons and analysis. The APB Opinions constituted GAAP until superseded by subsequent pronouncements of the body designated by the accounting profession to issue such pronouncements. Although the AICPA recognized other sources as providing substantial authoritative support for accounting practices, the burden for justifying a departure from financial accounting standards rests with the reporting member.

The FASB

12. The APB operated in a somewhat hostile environment for 13 years. Early in its existence it was criticized for overreacting to certain issues. A committee, known as the **Study Group on Establishment of Accounting Principles (Wheat Committee),** was set up to study the APB and recommend changes in its structure and operation. The result of the Study Group's findings was the demise of the APB and the creation of the Financial Accounting Standards Board (FASB). The FASB represents the current rule-making body within the accounting profession.

13. The mission of the FASB is to establish and improve standards of financial accounting and reporting for the guidance and education of the public, which includes issuers, auditors, and users of financial information. The FASB differs from the predecessor APB in the following ways:

a. Smaller membership (7 versus 18 on the APB).
b. Full-time remunerated membership (APB members were unpaid and part-time).
c. Greater autonomy (APB was a senior committee of the AICPA).
d. Increased independence (FASB members must sever all ties with firms, companies, or institutions).
e. Broader representation (it is not necessary to be a CPA to be a member of the FASB).

Two basic premises of the FASB are that in establishing financial accounting standards: (a) it should be responsive to the needs and viewpoints of the entire economic community, not just the public accounting profession, and (b) it should operate in full view of the public through a "due process" system that gives interested persons ample opportunity to make their views known.

14. The FASB issues **Statements of Financial Accounting Standards** and **Interpretations.** Both the Standards and the Interpretations are considered GAAP and must be followed in practice in the same manner as APB Opinions. The FASB also issues **Statements of Financial Accounting Concepts (SFAC)** and **Technical Bulletins.** The SFAC represent an attempt to move away from the problem-by-problem approach to standard setting that has been characteristic of the accounting profession. The Concept Statements are intended to form a cohesive set of interrelated concepts, a body of theory, or conceptual framework, that will serve as a tool for solving existing and emerging problems in a consistent, sound manner. Unlike FASB Statements, the Concept Statements do not establish GAAP. Technical Bulletins provide answers to specific questions related to the application and implementation of FASB Statement or Interpretations, APB Opinions, and ARBs. Technical Bulletins do not alter GAAP; they merely provide guidance on questions related to existing GAAP.

15. In 1984, the FASB created the **Emerging Issues Task Force (EITF)**. The purpose of the Task Force is to reach a consensus (15 of 17 members must agree) on how to account for new and unusual financial transactions that have the potential for creating diversity in financial reporting practices. The EITF can deal with short-term accounting issues by reaching a consensus and thus avoiding the need for deliberation by the FASB and the issuance of an FASB Statement. The Governmental Accounting Standards Board (GASB) was created in 1984 to address state and local governmental reporting issues. The operational structure of the GASB is similar to that of the FASB.

16. There are other professional groups and agencies that have influenced accounting theory and the development of accounting standards. These groups include: The **American Accounting Association (AAA),** the **Institute of Management Accountants (IMA),** the **Financial Executives Institute (FEI),** and the **Internal Revenue Service (IRS).** These groups influence the standard-setting process because of their expressed interest in accounting, their extensive use of the reports generated by the accounting process, or both.

17. Even though the FASB has assumed primary responsibility for the development of accounting and reporting standards, the AICPA has remained quite active in making known its views on major issues. The **Accounting Standards Executive Committee (AcSEC)** informs the FASB of financial reporting problems that are emerging in practice through the development of **issue papers.** Issue papers identify the problem, suggest alternative treatments, and recommend preferred solutions. The AICPA's **Auditing Standards Board** remains the leader in the development of auditing standards and other issues related to the practice of public accounting.

18. (S.O. 8) Generally accepted accounting principles (GAAP) are those principles that have **substantial authoritative support.** Accounting principles that have substantial authoritative support are those found in FASB Statements and Interpretations, APB Opinions, and Accounting Research Bulletins (ARBs). If an accounting transaction is not covered in any of these documents, the accountant may look to other authoritative accounting literature for guidance.

19. (S.O. 9) Although accounting standards are developed by using careful logic and empirical findings, a certain amount of pressure and influence is brought to bear by groups interested in or affected by accounting standards. The FASB does not exist in a vacuum, and politics and special-interest pressures remain a part of the standard-setting process.

20. (S.O. 10) In accounting ethical dilemmas are encountered frequently. The whole process of ethical sensitivity and selection among alternatives can be complicated by pressures that may take the form of time pressures, job pressures, client pressures, personal pressures, and peer pressures. Throughout the textbook, ethical considerations are presented to sensitize you to the type of situations you may encounter in your profession.

GLOSSARY

Accounting. The identification, measurement, and communication of financial information about economic entities to interested users.

Accounting Principles Board (APB). An accounting rule-making board which provided official pronouncements, called APB Opinions, from 1959 through 1973.

Accounting Research Bulletins (ARBs). Pronouncements issued by CAP dealing with a variety of timely accounting problems during the years 1939 to 1959.

Accounting Standards Executive Committee (AcSEC). The senior technical committee authorized to speak for the AICPA in the area of financial accounting and reporting.

American Accounting Association (AAA). An organization, whose members are primarily accounting academics, which encourages the development of accounting theory by encouraging and sponsoring accounting research.

American Institute of Certified Public Accountants (AICPA). The national professional organization of practicing Certified Public Accountants.

APB Opinions. The APB's official pronouncements issued from 1959 through 1973 which were intended to be based mainly on research studies and be supported by reasons and analysis.

Committee on Accounting Procedure (CAP). An organization composed of practicing CPAs which issued Accounting Research Bulletins dealing with a variety of accounting problems during the years 1939 to 1959.

Emerging Issues Task Force (EITF). Created by the FASB with the purpose of having 15 of 17 members reach a consensus on how to account for new and unusual financial transactions that have the potential for creating differing financial reporting practices.

Emerging Issues Task Force Statements. Pronouncements issued by the EITF which examine emerging financial reporting issues and state how to account for new and unusual accounting transactions.

FASB Technical Bulletins. Pronouncements issued by the FASB which are guidelines on implementing or applying FASB Standards or Interpretations, APB Opinions, and Accounting Research Bulletins.

Financial Accounting Concepts. A series of pronouncements issued by the FASB with the purpose of setting forth fundamental objectives and concepts that the FASB will use in developing future standards of financial accounting and reporting.

Financial Accounting Foundation. The organization that selects the members of the FASB and the FASAC, funds their activities, and generally oversees the FASB's activities.

Financial Accounting Interpretations. Pronouncements issued by the FASB which represent modifications or extensions of existing standards.

Financial Accounting Standards. Pronouncements issued by the FASB which are considered generally accepted accounting principles.

Financial Accounting Standards Advisory Council (FASAC). A council responsible for consulting with the FASB on both major policy and technical issues.

Financial Accounting Standards Board (FASB). A seven member board created in 1973 which currently establishes and improves standards of financial accounting and reporting for the guidance and education of the public.

Financial Executives Institute (FEI). An organization, whose members are primarily financial executives, which is interested in research studies on the impact of financial reporting at the corporate level.

Generally accepted accounting principles (GAAP). A common set of standards and procedures adopted by the accounting profession.

Governmental Accounting Standards Board (GASB). Created in 1984 by the Financial Accounting Foundation to address state and local governmental reporting issues.

Institute of Management Accountants (IMA). An organization, whose members are primarily internal accountants, which is primarily interested in cost and managerial accounting issues.

Internal Revenue Service (IRS). A federal government agency which enforces the Internal Revenue Code.

Securities and Exchange Commission (SEC). An agency of the federal government that administers the Securities Exchange Act of 1934.

CHAPTER OUTLINE

Fill in the outline presented below.

(S.O. 1) The Environment of Financial Accounting

(S.O. 2) Financial Statements and Financial Reporting

(S.O. 3) Accounting and Capital Allocation

(S.O.4) The Challenges Facing Financial Accounting

(S.O. 5) Objectives of Financial Reporting

(S.O. 6) The Need to Develop Standards

(S.O. 7) Parties Involved in Standard Setting

The Securities and Exchange Commission

The American Institute of Certified Public Accountants

The Financial Accounting Standards Board

Chapter Outline *(continued)*

Standards and Interpretations

Financial Accounting Concepts

FASB Technical Bulletins

Emerging Issues Task Force Statements

The Governmental Accounting Standards Board

Other Influential Organizations

(S.O. 8) Generally Accepted Accounting Principles

(S.O. 9) Standard Setting in a Political Environment

International Accounting Standards

(S.O. 10) Ethics in Financial Accounting

REVIEW QUESTIONS

TRUE-FALSE

Indicate whether each of the following is true (T) or false (F) in the space provided.

_____ 1. (S.O. 1) The purpose of accounting is to provide quantitative financial information about an economic entity to persons interested in the activities of that entity.

_____ 2. (S.O. 2) Financial accounting is the process that culminates in the preparation of financial reports that are relative to the enterprise as a whole and that are used by parties both internal and external to the enterprise.

_____ 3. (S.O. 3) The environment of accounting is unaffected by social-economic-political-legal conditions, restraints, and influences that vary from time to time.

_____ 4. (S.O. 3) The principal role of accounting is to furnish investors and lenders information that is useful in assessing the prospective risks and returns associated with an investment.

_____ 5. (S.O. 5) Accounting is responsible for providing standards that ensure accurate financial information that cannot be manipulated or improperly reported.

_____ 6. (S.O. 5) Accounting provides measures of the changes in economic resources, economic obligations, and residual interests of a business enterprise as a basis for comparison and evaluation.

_____ 7. (S.O. 5) One of the objectives of financial reporting is to provide information that is useful in assessing cash flow prospects of the entity being reported on.

_____ 8. (S.O. 6) The difference between generally accepted accounting principles (GAAP) and specifically accepted accounting principles concerns the degree of authority each possess.

_____ 9. (S.O. 7) The American Institute of Certified Public Accountants (AICPA) is the national professional organization of practicing Certified Public Accountants (CPAs).

_____ 10. (S.O. 7) The SEC has been the principal organization in the development of accounting standards.

_____ 11. (S.O. 7) The Securities and Exchange Commission (SEC) sets accounting standards for companies that do work for the government.

_____ 12. (S.O. 7) The Accounting Principles Board (APB) replaced the Committee on Accounting Procedure (CAP) and was designated as the AICPA's sole authority for public pronouncements on accounting principles.

_____ 13. (S.O. 7) The difference between Accounting Research Bulletins (ARBs) and Accounting Principles Board Opinions is that ARBs deal with accounting theory and the APB Opinions deal with accounting practice.

_____ 14. (S.O. 7) The major purpose of the APB during its 13-year existence was to develop a single set of accounting standards useful to all business entities.

_____ 15. (S.O. 7) The Accounting Principles Board (APB) was replaced in 1973 by the Financial Accounting Standards Board (FASB), which now is responsible for setting accounting standards.

_____ 16. (S.O. 7) All those who serve on the FASB must be Certified Public Accountants.

_____ 17. (S.O. 7) FASB Interpretations represent modifications or extensions of existing FASB Standards and have the same authority as Standards.

_____ 18. (S.O. 7) FASB Technical Bulletins are designed to provide guidance on the implementation or application of FASB Statements or Interpretations.

_____ 19. (S.O. 7) A major role of the Accounting Standards Executive Committee (AcSEC) is to inform the FASB of financial reporting problems that are developing in practice.

_____ 20. (S.O. 8) Generally accepted accounting principles (GAAP) are defined, in part, as those principles that have substantial authoritative support.

SOLUTIONS TO REVIEW QUESTIONS

TRUE-FALSE

1. (T)

2. (T)

3. (F) Accounting standards are as much a product of political action as they are of careful logic or empirical findings. Standard-setting is part of the real world and, as such, cannot escape politics and political pressure. Also, accounting objectives and practices are not the same today as they were in the past because accounting theory has evolved to meet changing demands and influences.

4. (T)

5. (F) Accounting standards are designed to act as a general guide in developing financial information about an economic entity. Such standards can always be misinterpreted or intentionally violated, thus producing unreliable financial information.

6. (T)

7. (T)

8. (F) The term "specifically accepted accounting principles" has no meaning in accounting.

9. (T)

10. (F) The SEC has the mandate to establish accounting principles but has acted with remarkable restraint in the area of developing accounting standards. Generally, it has relied on the AICPA and FASB to regulate the accounting profession and develop and enforce accounting standards.

11. (F) The SEC is empowered to administer the 1933 and 1934 Securities Acts. The SEC was given broad powers to prescribe the accounting practices and standards to be employed by companies that issue securities to the public or are listed on a stock exchange.

12. (T)

13. (F) Both ARBs and APB Opinions represent authoritative pronouncements designed to establish principles of accounting. The major difference is that ARBs were issued by the Committee on Accounting Procedure (CAP) and APB Opinions were issued by the Accounting Principles Board.

14. (F) The major purposes of the APB were (a) to advance the written expression of accounting principles, (b) to determine appropriate practices, and (c) to narrow the areas of difference and inconsistency in practice.

15. (T)

16. (F) At the present time it is not necessary to be a CPA to be a member of the FASB.

17. (T)

18. (T)

19. (T)

20. (T)

2

Conceptual Framework Underlying Financial Accounting

CHAPTER STUDY OBJECTIVES

1. Describe the usefulness of a conceptual framework.
2. Describe the FASB's efforts to construct a conceptual framework.
3. Understand the objectives of financial reporting.
4. Identify the qualitative characteristics of accounting information.
5. Define the basic elements of financial statements.
6. Describe the basic assumptions of accounting.
7. Explain the application of the basic principles of accounting.
8. Describe the impact that constraints have on reporting accounting information.

CHAPTER REVIEW

1. Chapter 2 outlines the development of a conceptual framework for financial accounting and reporting by the FASB. The entire conceptual framework is affected by the environmental aspects discussed in Chapter 1. It is composed of basic objectives, fundamental concepts, and operational guidelines. These notions are discussed in Chapter 2 and should enhance your understanding of the topics covered in intermediate accounting.

Conceptual Framework

2. (S.O. 1) A **conceptual framework** in accounting is important because it can lead to consistent standards and it prescribes the nature, function, and limits of financial accounting and financial statements. The benefits its development will generate can be characterized as follows: (a) it should be easier to promulgate a coherent set of standards and rules; and (b) practical problems should be more quickly solved.

3. (S.O. 2) The FASB recognized the need for a conceptual framework upon which a consistent set of financial accounting standards could be based. The FASB has issued five Statements of Financial Accounting Concepts (SFAC) that relate to financial reporting. They are listed and described briefly below:

SFAC No. 1. "Objectives of Financial Reporting by Business Enterprises" presents the goals and purposes of accounting.
SFAC No. 2. "Qualitative Characteristics of Accounting Information" examines the characteristics that make accounting information useful.
SFAC No. 3. "Elements of Financial Statements of Business Enterprises" defines the broad classifications of items found in financial statements.

SFAC No. 5. "Recognition and Measurement in Financial Statements of Business Enterprises" gives guidance on what information should be formally incorporated into financial statements and when.

SFAC No. 6. "Elements of Financial Statements" replaces ***SFAC No. 3*** and expands its scope to include not-for-profit organizations.

Basic Objectives

4. (S.O. 3) *SFAC No. 1* describes the objectives of financial reporting as the presentation of information that is useful (a) in making investment and credit decisions, (b) in assessing cash flow prospects, and (c) in learning about economic resources, claims to those resources, and changes in them. *SFAC No. 2* identifies the primary and secondary qualitative characteristics of accounting information that distinguish better (more useful) information from inferior (less useful) information for decision-making purposes.

Primary Qualities

5. (S.O. 4) The **primary qualities** that make accounting information useful for decision making are **relevance** and **reliability**.

Relevance. Accounting information is relevant if it is capable of making a difference in a decision. For information to be relevant, it should have predictive or feedback value, and it must be presented on a timely basis.

Reliability. Accounting information is reliable to the extent that it is verifiable, is a faithful representation, and is reasonably free of error and bias. To be reliable, accounting information must possess three key characteristics: (a) verifiability, (b) representational faithfulness, and (c) neutrality.

Secondary Qualities

6. The **secondary qualities** identified are **comparability** and **consistency**.

Comparability. Accounting information that has been measured and reported in a similar manner for different enterprises is considered comparable.

Consistency. Accounting information is consistent when an entity applies the same accounting treatment to similar events from period to period.

Basic Elements

7. (S.O. 5) An important aspect of developing an accounting theoretical structure is the body of elements or definitions. However, the specific meanings that accountants attach to these basic elements sometimes differ from their meanings in a nonaccounting context. Ten basic elements that are most directly related to measuring the performance and financial status of an enterprise are formally defined in *SFAC No. 6*. These elements, as defined below, are further discussed and interpreted throughout the text.

Assets. Probable future economic benefits obtained or controlled by a particular entity as a result of past transactions or events.

Liabilities. Probable future sacrifices of economic benefits that arise from present obligations of a particular entity to transfer assets or provide services to other entities in the future as a result of past transactions or events.

Equity. Residual interest in the assets of an entity that remains after deducting its liabilities. In a business enterprise, the equity is the ownership interest.

Investment by Owners. Increases in net assets of a particular enterprise resulting from transfers to it from other entities of something of value to obtain or increase ownership interests (or equity) in it. Assets are most commonly received as investments by owners, but that which is received may include services or satisfaction or conversion of liabilities of the enterprise.

Distribution to Owners. Decreases in net assets of a particular enterprise that result from transferring assets, rendering services, or incurring liabilities by the enterprise to owners. Distributions to owners decrease ownership interests (or equity) in an enterprise.

Comprehensive Income. Change in equity (net assets) of an entity during a period from transactions and other events and circumstances from nonowner sources. It includes all changes in equity during a period, except those resulting from investments by owners and distributions to owners.

Revenues. Inflows or other enhancements of assets of an entity or settlement of its liabilities (or a combination of both) during a period from delivering or producing goods, rendering services, or other activities that constitute the entity's ongoing major or central operations.

Expenses. Outflows or other using up of assets or incurrences of liabilities (or a combination of both) during a period from delivering or producing goods, rendering services, or carrying out other activities that constitute the entity's ongoing major or central operations.

Gains. Increases in equity (net assets) from peripheral or incidental transactions of an entity and from all other transactions and other events and circumstances affecting the entity during a period except those that result from revenues or investments by owners.

Losses. Decrease in equity (net assets) from peripheral or incidental transactions of an entity from all other transactions and other events and circumstances affecting the entity during a period except those that result from expenses or distributions to owners.

Basic Assumptions

8. (S.O. 6) In the practice of financial accounting, certain basic assumptions are important to an understanding of the manner in which data are presented. The following four basic assumptions underlie the financial accounting structure:

Economic Entity Assumption. The economic activities of an entity can be accumulated and reported in a manner that assumes the entity is separate and distinct from its owners or other business units.

Going-Concern Assumption. In the absence of contrary information, a business entity is assumed to remain in existence for an indeterminate period of time. The current relevance of the historical cost principle is dependent on the going-concern assumption.

Monetary Unit Assumption. In the United States, economic activities of an entity are measured and reported in dollars. These dollars are assumed to remain relatively stable over the years in terms of purchasing power. In essence, this assumption disregards any inflation or deflation in the economy in which the entity operates.

Periodicity Assumption. The life of an economic entity can be divided into artificial time periods for the purpose of providing periodic reports on the economic activities of the entity.

As you progress through the remaining chapters in the text, the reasoning behind these assumptions should become more apparent.

Basic Principles

9. (S.O. 7) Certain **basic principles** are followed by accountants in recording the transactions of a business entity. These principles relate basically to how assets, liabilities, revenues, and expenses are to be **identified, measured,** and **reported**. The following is a brief review of the basic principles considered in Chapter 2 of the text:

Historical Cost Principle. Acquisition cost is the most objective and verifiable basis upon which to account for assets and liabilities of a business enterprise. Cost has been found to be more definite and determinable than other suggested valuation methods.

Revenue Recognition Principle. Revenue is recognized when the earning process is virtually complete and an exchange transaction has occurred. Generally, this takes place when a sale to another individual or independent entity has been confirmed. Confirmation is usually accomplished by a transfer of ownership in an exchange transaction. Certain variations in the revenue recognition principle include: the **percentage-of-completion** approach, **end-of-production** recognition, and recognition upon **receipt of cash.**

Matching Principle. Accountants attempt to match expenses incurred while earning revenues with the related revenues. Use of **accrual accounting procedures** assists the accountant in allocating revenues and expenses properly among the fiscal periods that compose the life of a business enterprise.

Full Disclosure Principle. In the preparation of financial statements, the accountant should include sufficient information to permit the knowledgeable reader to make an informed judgment about the financial condition of the enterprise in question.

Constraints

10. (S.O. 8) Although accounting theory is based upon certain assumptions and the application of basic principles, there are some exceptions to these assumptions. These exceptions, often called constraints, sometimes justify departures from basic accounting theory. The constraints presented in Chapter 2 are the following:

Cost-Benefit Relationship. This constraint relates to the notion that the benefits to be derived from providing certain accounting information should exceed the costs of providing that information. The difficulty in cost-benefit analysis is that the costs and especially the benefits are not always evident or measurable.

Materiality. In the application of basic accounting theory, an amount may be considered less important because of its size in comparison with revenues and expenses, assets and liabilities, or net income. Deciding when an amount is material in relation to other amounts is a matter of judgment and professional expertise.

Industry Practices. Basic accounting theory may not apply with equal relevance to every industry that accounting must serve. The fair presentation of financial position and results of operations for a particular industry may require a departure from basic accounting theory because of the peculiar nature of an event or practice common only to that industry.

Conservatism. When in doubt, an accountant should choose a solution that will be least likely to overstate assets and income. The conservatism constraint should be applied only when doubt exists. An intentional understatement of assets or income is not acceptable accounting.

11. The basic theory outlined in Chapter 2 is critical for a thorough understanding of the financial accounting process. In subsequent chapters many problem areas are examined that build upon and expand the framework developed in Chapter 2. One's ability to grasp and apply the information related to those problem areas is greatly aided by a familiarity with this framework.

GLOSSARY

Assets. Probable future economic benefits obtained or controlled by a particular entity as a result of past transactions or events.

Comparability. Ability to compare accounting information of different companies because they use the same accounting principles.

Comprehensive income. Change in equity (net assets) of an entity during a period from transactions and other events and circumstances from nonowner sources.

Conceptual framework. A coherent system of interrelated objectives and fundamentals that can lead to consistent standards.

Conservatism. The approach of choosing an accounting method when in doubt that will least likely overstate assets and net income.

Consistency. An entity applies the same accounting treatment to similar events from period to period.

Cost-benefit relationship. The constraint that states that information should be provided only if the benefits of providing such information outweigh the costs of providing it.

Economic entity assumption. An assumption that states economic activity can be identified with a particular unit of accountability.

Equity. Residual interest in the assets of an entity that remains after deducting its liabilities.

Expenses. Outflows or other using up of assets or incurrences of liabilities (or a combination of both) during a period from delivering or producing goods, rendering services, or other activities that constitute the entity's ongoing major or central operations.

Feedback value. Information that confirms or corrects prior expectations.

Full disclosure principle. The principle that information should be provided if it is of sufficient importance to influence the judgment and decisions of an informed user.

Gains.	Increases in equity (net assets) from peripheral or incidental transactions of an entity and from other transactions and other events and circumstances affecting the entity during a period except those that result from revenues or investments by owners.
Going concern assumption.	An assumption that states an enterprise will continue in operation long enough to carry out its existing objectives and commitments.
Historical cost principle.	An accounting principle that states that assets and liabilities should be recorded at their acquisition price.
Industry practices.	The constraint that requires a departure from basic accounting theory because of the peculiar nature of some industries and business concerns.
Liabilities.	Probable future sacrifices of economic benefits arising from present obligations of a particular entity to transfer assets or provide services to other entities in the future as a result of past transactions or events.
Losses.	Decreases in equity (net assets) from peripheral or incidental transactions of an entity and from all other transactions and other events and circumstances affecting the entity during a period except those that result from expenses or distributions to owners.
Matching principle.	The principle that states that efforts (expenses) be matched with accomplishments (revenues).
Materiality.	The constraint of determining if an item is important enough to likely influence the decision of a reasonably prudent investor or creditor.
Monetary unit assumption.	An assumption stating that only transaction data that can be expressed in terms of money be included in the accounting records of the economic entity.
Neutrality.	Information cannot be selected to favor one set of interested parties over another.
Periodicity assumption.	An assumption stating that the economic activities of an enterprise can be divided into artificial time periods.
Predictive value.	Information that helps users make predictions about the ultimate outcome of past, present, and future events.
Qualitative characteristics.	Characteristics that make accounting information useful.
Relevance.	Information capable of making a difference in a decision.

Reliability.	The extent that information is verifiable, is a faithful representation, and is reasonably free of error and bias.
Representational faithfulness.	The numbers and descriptions represent what really existed or happened.
Revenue recognition principle.	The principle that revenue be recognized when (1) realized or realizable and (2) earned.
Revenues.	Inflows or other enhancements of assets of an entity or settlement of its liabilities (or a combination of both) during a period from delivering or producing goods, rendering services, or other activities that constitute the entity's ongoing major or central operations.
Understandability.	Informed users perceive the significance of information.
Verifiability.	The ability to have information confirmed by independent persons.

CHAPTER OUTLINE

Fill in the outline presented below.

(S.O. 1) Nature and Development of a Conceptual Framework

(S.O. 3) First Level: Basic Objectives

Second Level: Fundamental Concepts

(S.O. 4) Primary Qualities

Secondary Qualities

(S.O. 5) Basic Elements

Third Level: Recognition and Measurement Concepts

(S.O. 6) Basic Assumptions

(S.O. 7) Basic Principles of Accounting

(S.O. 8) Constraints

REVIEW QUESTIONS

TRUE-FALSE

Indicate whether each of the following is true (T) or false (F) in the space provided.

_____ 1. (S.O. 1) A conceptual framework is a coherent system of interrelated objectives and fundamentals that can lead to consistent standards and that prescribes the nature, function, and limits of financial accounting and financial statements.

_____ 2. (S.O. 1) A conceptual framework underlying financial accounting is necessary because future accounting practice problems can be solved by reference to the conceptual framework and a formal standard-setting body will not be necessary.

_____ 3. (S.O. 1) Use of a sound conceptual framework in the development of accounting principles will make financial statements of all entities comparable because alternative accounting methods for similar transactions will be eliminated.

_____ 4. (S.O. 2) Accounting theory is developed without consideration of the environment within which it exists.

_____ 5. (S.O. 2) Relevance and reliability are the two primary qualities that make accounting information useful for decision making.

_____ 6. (S.O 2) To be reliable, accounting information must be capable of making a difference in a decision.

_____ 7. (S.O. 4) Information that has been measured and reported in a similar manner for different enterprises is considered comparable.

_____ 8. (S.O. 4) Adherence to the concept of consistency requires that the same accounting principles be applied to similar transactions for a minimum of five years before any change in principle is adopted.

_____ 9. (S.O. 5) The fact that equity represents an ownership interest and a residual claim against the net assets of an enterprise means that in the event of liquidation, creditors have a priority over owners in the distribution of assets.

_____ 10. (S.O. 5) The three elements—assets, liabilities, and equity—describe transactions, events, and circumstances that affect an enterprise during a period of time.

_____ 11. (S.O. 6) The economic entity assumption is useful only when the entity referred to is a profit-seeking business enterprise.

_____ 12. (S.O. 6) The going-concern assumption is generally applicable in most business situations unless liquidation appears imminent.

_____ 13. (S.O. 6) The monetary unit assumption means that money is the common denominator of economic activity and provides an appropriate basis for accounting measurement and analysis.

_____ 14. (S.O. 6) The periodicity assumption is a result of the demands of various financial statement user groups for timely reporting of financial information.

_____ 15. (S.O. 7) If Company A wishes to acquire an asset owned by Company B, the historical cost principle would require Company A to record the asset at the original cost to Company B.

_____ 16. (S.O. 7) Generally, confirmation by a sale to independent interests is used to indicate the point at which revenue is recognized.

_____ 17. (S.O. 7) Recognition of revenue when cash is collected is appropriate only when it is impossible to establish the revenue figure at the time of sale because of the uncertainty of collection.

_____ 18. (S.O. 7) Under the matching principle, it is possible to have an expense reported on the income statement in one period and the cash payment for that expense reported in another period.

_____ 19. (S.O. 7) Period costs such as material, labor, and overhead attach to the product and are carried into future periods if the revenue from the product is recognized in subsequent periods.

_____ 20. (S.O. 7) The full disclosure principle states that information should be provided when it is of sufficient importance to influence the judgment and decisions of an informed user.

_____ 21. (S.O. 7) The notes to financial statements generally summarize the items presented in the main body of the statements.

_____ 22. (S.O. 8) The difficulty in cost-benefit analysis is that the costs and especially the benefits are not always evident or measurable.

_____ 23. (S.O. 8) When an amount is determined by the accountant to be immaterial in relation to other amounts reported in the financial statements, that amount may be deleted from the financial statements.

_____ 24. (S.O. 8) The peculiar nature of some industries and concerns sometimes requires departure from basic theory.

_____ 25. (S.O. 8) The conservatism convention allows for the reporting of financial information in any manner the accountant desires when there is doubt surrounding a particular issue.

MULTIPLE CHOICE

_____ 1. (S.O. 1) Which of the following is not a benefit associated with the FASB Conceptual Framework Project?

A. A conceptual framework should increase financial statement users' understanding of and confidence in financial reporting.
B. Practical problems should be more quickly solvable by reference to an existing conceptual framework.
C. A coherent set of accounting standards and rules should result.
D. Business entities will need far less assistance from accountants because the financial reporting process will be quite easy to apply.

_____ 2. (S.O. 4) Which of the following violates the concept of reliability?

A. The management report refers to new discoveries and inventions made, but the financial statements never report the results.
B. Financial statements included goodwill with a carrying amount estimated by management.
C. Financial statements were issued one year late.
D. An interim report is not issued even though it would provide feedback on past performance.

_____ 3. (S.O. 4) Which of the following is a characteristic describing the primary quality of relevance?

A. Materiality.
B. Predictive value.
C. Verifiability.
D. Understandability.

_____ 4. (S.O. 4) Under Statement of Financial Accounting Concepts No. 2, representational faithfulness is an ingredient of

	Relevance	Reliability
A.	Yes	Yes
B.	Yes	No
C.	No	No
D.	No	Yes

_____ 5. (S.O. 4) If accounting information is verifiable, representationally faithful, and neutral, it can be considered:

A. relevant
B. timely.
C. comparable.
D. reliable.

_____ 6. (S.O. 4) The major objective of the consistency principle is to:

A. provide timely financial information for statement users.
B. promote comparability between financial statements of different accounting periods.
C. match the appropriate revenues and expenses in a given accounting period.
D. be sure the same information is disclosed in each accounting period.

_____ 7. (S.O. 5) Comprehensive income as characterized in *SFAC No. 6* includes all changes in equity during a period except:

A. sale of assets other than inventory.
B. those resulting from investments by or distribution to owners.
C. sales to a particular entity where ultimate payment by the entity is doubtful.
D. those resulting from revenue generated by a totally owned subsidiary.

_____ 8. (S.O. 5) According to the FASB conceptual framework, earnings

A. are the same as comprehensive income.
B. exclude certain gains and losses that are included in comprehensive income.
C. include certain gains and losses that are excluded from comprehensive income.
D. include certain losses that are excluded from comprehensive income.

_____ 9. (S.O. 5) According to the FASB Conceptual Framework, the elements—assets, liabilities, and equity—describe amounts of resources and claims to resources at/during a

	Moment in Time	Period of Time
A.	Yes	No
B.	Yes	Yes
C.	No	Yes
D.	No	No

_____ 10. (S.O. 6) The economic entity assumption in accounting is best reflected by which of the following statements?

A. When a parent and subsidiary company are merged for accounting and reporting purposes the economic entity assumption is violated.
B. The best way to truly measure the results of enterprise activity is to measure them at the time the enterprise is liquidated.
C. The activity of a business enterprise can be kept separate and distinct from its owners and any other business unit.
D. A business enterprise is in business to enhance the economic well being of its owners.

_____ 11. (S.O. 6) Continuation of an accounting entity in the absence of evidence to the contrary is an example of the basic concept of

	Consistency	Going Concern
A.	No	No
B.	Yes	No
C.	No	Yes
D.	Yes	Yes

_____ 12. (S.O. 6) In accounting an economic entity may be defined as:

A. a business enterprise.
B. an individual.
C. a division within a business enterprise.
D. all of the above.

_____ 13. (S.O. 6) Which of the following basic accounting assumptions is threatened by the existence of severe inflation in the economy?

A. Monetary unit assumption.
B. Periodicity assumption.
C. Going-concern assumption.
D. Economic entity assumption.

_____ 14. (S.O. 6) During the lifetime of an entity accountants produce financial statements at artificial points in time in accordance with

	Objectivity	Periodicity
A.	No	No
B.	Yes	No
C.	No	Yes
D.	Yes	Yes

_____ 15. (S.O. 7) Although many objections have been raised about the "historical cost" principle, it is still widely supported for financial reporting because

A. it is an objectively determinable amount.
B. it is a good measure of current value.
C. facilitates comparisons between years.
D. it takes into account price-level adjusted information.

_____ 16. (S.O. 7) Under the revenue recognition principle, revenue is generally recognized when the earning process is virtually complete and:

A. an exchange transaction has occurred.
B. the merchandise has been ordered.
C. all expenses have been identified.
D. the accounting process is virtually complete.

_____ 17. (S.O. 7) Which of the following is an incorrect statement regarding the matching principle?

A. Expenses are recognized when they make a contribution to revenue.
B. Costs are never charged to the current period as an expense simply because no connection with revenue can be determined.
C. In recognizing expenses, accountants attempt to follow the approach of let the expense follow the revenue.
D. If no direct connection appears between costs and revenues, but the costs benefit future years, an allocation of cost on some systematic and rational basis might be appropriate.

_____ 18. (S.O. 7) The concept referred to by the "matching" principle is

A. that current liabilities have the same period of existence as the current assets.
B. that all cash disbursements for a period be matched to cash receipts for the period.
C. that net income should be reported on an quarterly basis.
D. that where possible the expenses to be included in the income statement were incurred to produce the revenues.

_____ 19. (S.O. 7) In complying with the full disclosure principle, an accountant must determine the amount of disclosure necessary. How much disclosure is enough?

A. Information sufficient for a person without any knowledge of accounting to understand the statements.
B. All information that might be of interest to an owner of a business enterprise.
C. Information that is of sufficient importance to influence the judgment and decisions of an informed user.
D. Information sufficient to permit most persons coming in contact with the statements to reach an accurate decision about the financial condition of the enterprise.

_____ 20. (S.O. 8) What is the underlying concept that supports the immediate recognition of a loss?

A. Conservatism.
B. Matching.
C. Consistency.
D. Objectivity.

SOLUTIONS TO REVIEW QUESTIONS

TRUE-FALSE

1. (T)

2. (F) Development of a conceptual framework will not provide a solution to all future accounting problems, nor will it eliminate the need for a formal standard-setting body. However, a soundly developed conceptual framework should enable the FASB to issue more useful and consistent standards resulting in easier solutions to emerging practical problems.

3. (F) Use of a sound conceptual framework will not eliminate alternative accounting methods for similar transactions. However, a sound conceptual framework should allow practitioners to dismiss certain alternatives quickly and focus on a logical and acceptable treatment.

4. (F) The environment within which any discipline exists plays an integral role in shaping the theory of that discipline. The purpose of accounting is to serve the business environment through the issuance of timely and relevant financial information. To present such information, accounting theory must be developed with consideration being given to the business environment.

5. (T)

6. (F) To be relevant, accounting information must be capable of making a difference in a decision. Accounting information is reliable to the extent that it is verifiable, is a faithful representation and is free of error and bias.

7. (T)

8. (F) Consistency means that a company applies the same methods to similar accounting transactions from period to period. It does not mean that companies cannot switch from one method to another. Companies can change to a new method that is considered preferable to the old method as long as financial statement users are made aware to the change.

9. (T)

10. (F) The three elements—assets, liabilities, and equity—describe amounts of resources and claims to resources at a moment of time.

11. (F) The economic entity assumption holds that the activity of a business entity can be kept separate and distinct from its owners and any other business unit. This assumption has nothing to do with the nature of the business organization.

12. (T)

13. (T)

14. (T)

15. (F) The historical cost principle requires that assets be accounted for on the basis of acquisition cost. Whatever it costs a particular entity to acquire an asset is that entity's acquisition cost.

16. (T)

17. (T)

18. (T)

19. (F) Product costs such as material, labor, and overhead attach to the product and are carried into future periods if the revenue from the product is recognized in subsequent periods. Period costs such as officers' salaries and other administrative expenses are charged off immediately, even though benefits associated with these costs occur in the future, because no direct relationship between cost and revenue can be determined.

20. (T)

21. (F) The notes to financial statements generally amplify or explain the items presented in the main body of the statements.

22. (T)

23. (F) Because an item is deemed to be immaterial does not justify its deletion from financial statements. If an amount is so small that it is quite unimportant when compared with other items, application of a particular standard may be considered of less importance.

24. (T)

25. (F) The conservatism convention states that, when in doubt, the accountant should choose the solution that will be least likely to overstate assets and income.

MULTIPLE CHOICE

1. (D) The financial reporting process will always require the expertise of a person trained in accounting. The development of a conceptual framework will aid the accountant because new and emerging practical problems should be more quickly solvable by reference to an existing framework. Alternatives A, B, and C are benefits of the Conceptual Framework Project.

2. (B) Accounting information is reliable to the extent that it is verifiable, is a faithful representation and is reasonably free of error and bias. Because an estimate of goodwill is deemed unreliable, goodwill is only recorded when a company purchases

another company and a determination can be made as to the amount of the purchase price that exceeds the fair market value of the assets acquired.

3. (B) For information to be relevant, it should have predictive or feedback value, and it must be presented on a timely basis. Answer (A), materiality is a constraint which relates to the magnitude of an omission or misstatement that in light of the circumstances, may change or influence the decision of a person relying on the information. Answer (C) is incorrect because verifiability is a characteristic of the primary quality of reliability. Answer (D) is incorrect because understandability is not a characteristic of relevance, but rather, relevance can occur only if the information is understandable.

4. (D) Representational faithfulness means that correspondence or agreement between accounting numbers and descriptions and the resources or events that these numbers and descriptions purport to represent must exist. Thus, accounting information is reliable to the extent that it is reasonably free of error and bias and is a faithful representation. Relevance refers to the fact that accounting information must be capable of making a difference in a decision.

5. (D) To be reliable, accounting information must possess three key characteristics: verifiability, representational faithfulness, and neutrality.

6. (B) Comparability between financial statements of different accounting periods presumes consistent application of GAAP.

7. (B) Comprehensive income, as defined in *SFAC No. 6,* includes net income and all other changes in equity, exclusive of owners' investments and distributions. Items A, C, and D fit into this broad definition.

8. (B) Statement of Financial Accounting Concepts No. 5 addresses this issue by indicating that earnings and comprehensive income include the same broad concepts of revenues, expenses, gains and losses. However, certain classes of gains and losses are excluded from earnings even though they are included in comprehensive income.

9. (A) The FASB classifies the elements of financial statements into two distinct groups. The first group of three elements—assets, liabilities, and equity—describes amounts of resources and claims to resources at a moment in time. The other seven financial statement elements describe transactions, events, and circumstances that affect an enterprise during a period of time. Thus, alternatives B, C, and D are incorrect.

10. (C) The economic entity assumption holds that economic activity can be identified with a particular unit of accountability. Alternative A represents the essence of the economic entity assumption not a violation. Alternative B is related to the periodicity assumption and alternative D is not a basic accounting assumption.

11. (C) The going concern assumption in accounting implies that unless there is evidence to the contrary, an entity will continue to exist in order to carry out its objectives and fulfill its commitments. Consistency describes when an entity applies the same accounting treatment to similar events from period to period.

12. (D) All of the alternatives (A, B, and C) are economic entities for accounting purposes.

13. (A) The monetary unit assumption holds that the unit of measure--the dollar--remains reasonably stable. Severe inflation would cause this assumption to lose its relevance.

14. (C) The concept of periodicity implies that economic activity can be divided into artificial time periods—months, quarters, and years for example.

15. (A) Historical cost is still widely supported for financial reporting because it is an objectively determinable amount. Answer (B) is incorrect because historical cost and current value are generally not the same amount subsequent to the date of acquisition. Answers (C) and (D) are incorrect because it does not facilitate comparisons between years, nor does it take into account price-level adjusted information.

16. (A) Revenue is generally recognized when (a) the earning process is virtually complete and (b) an exchange transaction has occurred.

17. (B) If no definitive connection between costs and revenue can be determined, such costs are charged to the current period as expenses. Examples of such costs include officers' salaries and other administrative expenses. The other alternatives are consistent with the matching principle.

18. (D) Matching is the process of relating expenses with revenues on a cause and effect basis. Answer (A) is incorrect because matching is not related to the period of existence of current assets and current liabilities. Answer (B) is incorrect because the matching principle is not concerned with the timing of cash flows. Answer (C) is incorrect because matching is not concerned with a particular reporting period interval.

19. (C) In deciding what information to report, accountants follow the general practice of providing information that is of sufficient importance to influence the judgment and decisions of an informed user. Alternatives A and D are wrong because they do not assume an informed user. Alternative B would result in disclosing a significant amount of extraneous information.

20. (A) The principle of conservatism reflects a general tendency toward early recognition of unfavorable events. If previously recorded assets lose their capacity to provide future benefits, conservatism would dictate that a loss be recognized immediately.

3

The Accounting Information System

CHAPTER STUDY OBJECTIVES

1. Understand basic accounting terminology.
2. Explain double-entry rules.
3. Identify steps in the accounting cycle.
4. Record transactions in journals, post to ledger accounts, and prepare a trial balance.
5. Explain the reasons for preparing adjusting entries.
6. Prepare closing entries.
7. Explain how inventory accounts are adjusted at year-end.
8. Prepare a 10-column work sheet.

*9. Differentiate the cash basis of accounting from the accrual basis of accounting.

*10. Identify adjusting entries that may be reversed.

**11. Identify (a) the use and types of subsidiary ledgers and (b) the use and types of special journals.

CHAPTER REVIEW

1. Chapter 3 presents a concise yet thorough review of the accounting process. The basic elements of the accounting process are identified and explained, and the way in which these elements are combined in completing the accounting cycle is described.

Procedures and the Double-Entry Recording Process

2. (S.O. 1) The accounting process can be described as a set of procedures used in **identifying, recording, classifying,** and **interpreting** information related to the transactions and other events of a business enterprise. To understand the accounting process, one must be aware of the basic terminology employed in the process. The basic terminology includes: **events, transactions, real accounts, nominal accounts, ledger, journal, posting, trial balance, adjusting entries, financial statements,** and **closing entries.** These terms refer to the various activities that make up the **accounting cycle**. As we review the steps in the accounting cycle, the individual terms will be defined.

3. (S.O. 2) **Double-entry accounting** refers to the process used in recording transactions. The terms **debit** and **credit** are used in the accounting process to indicate the effect a transaction has on account balances. Also, the debit side of any account is the left side; the right side is the credit side. Assets and expenses are increased by debits and decreased by credits. Liabilities, owners' equity, and revenues are decreased by debits and increased by credits.

* *Note: All asterisked (*) items relate to material contained in the Appendices to the chapter. All double asterisked (**) items relate to material contained on the Wiley web site.*

The Accounting Cycle

4. In a double-entry system, for every debit there must be a credit and vice-versa. This leads us, then, to the basic equation in accounting: Assets = Liabilities + Stockholders' Equity.

5. (S.O. 3) The first step in the accounting cycle is **analysis of transactions and selected other events.** The purpose of this analysis is to determine which events represent transactions that should be recorded. Two criteria must be met before an event can be considered a transaction and included in the accounting process. The event must be capable of being **objectively measured in financial terms** and it must **affect the financial position** of the enterprise.

6. Events can be classified as **external** or **internal**. External events are those between the enterprise and its environment, whereas internal events relate to transactions totally within the enterprise.

Journalizing

7. (S.O. 4) Transactions are initially recorded in a **journal,** sometimes referred to as **the book of original entry.** A **general journal** is merely a chronological listing of transactions expressed in terms of debits and credits to particular accounts. No distinction is made in a general journal concerning the type of transaction involved. In addition to a general journal, **specialized journals** are used to accumulate transactions possessing common characteristics.

Posting

8. The next step in the accounting cycle involves transferring amounts entered in the journal to the **general ledger**. The ledger is a book that usually contains a separate page for each account. Transferring amounts from a journal to the ledger is called **posting**. Transactions recorded in a general journal must be posted individually, whereas entries made in specialized journals are generally posted by columnar total.

Trial Balance

9. The next step in the accounting cycle is the preparation of a **trial balance.** A trial balance is a list of all open accounts in the general ledger and their balances. An entity may prepare a trial balance at any time in the accounting cycle. A trial balance prepared after posting has been completed serves to check the mechanical accuracy of the posting process and provides a listing of accounts to be used in preparing financial statements.

Adjusting Entries

10. (S. O. 5) Preparation of **adjusting journal entries** is the next step in the accounting cycle. Adjusting entries are entries made at the end of accounting period to bring all accounts up to date on an accrual accounting basis so that correct financial statements can be prepared. Adjusting entries are necessary to achieve a proper matching of revenues and expenses in the determination of net income for the current period and to achieve an accurate statement of the assets and equities existing at the end of the period. One common characteristic of adjusting entries is that they affect at least **one real account** (asset, liability, or equity account) and **one nominal account** (revenue or expense account). Adjusting entries can be classified as: **prepaid expenses, unearned revenues, accrued revenues,** and **accrued expenses.**

11. Prepaid expenses and unearned revenues refer to situations where cash has been paid or received but the corresponding expense or revenue will not be recognized until a future period. Accrued revenues and accrued expenses are revenues and expenses recognized in the current period for which the corresponding payment or receipt of cash is to occur in a future period. Estimated items are expenses such as bad debts and depreciation whose amounts are a function of unknown future events or developments.

Adjusted Trial Balance

12. After adjusting entries are recorded and posted, an **adjusted trial balance** is prepared. This trial balance serves as a basis for the preparation of the financial statements discussed in the next two chapters.

Closing-Basic Process

13. (S.O. 6) After financial statements have been prepared, nominal (revenues and expenses) accounts should be reduced to zero in preparation for recording the transactions of the next period. This **closing process** requires recording and posting of closing entries. All nominal accounts are reduced to zero by closing them through the **Income Summary** account. The net balance in the Income Summary account after closing is equal to net income or net loss for the period. The net income or net loss for the period is transferred to owners' equity by closing the Income Summary account to Retained Earnings.

Post-Closing Trial Balance

14. A third trial balance may be prepared after the closing entries are recorded and posted. This **post-closing trial balance** shows that equal debits and credits have been posted properly to the Income Summary account.

Closing Inventory and Related Accounts

15. (S.O. 7) When inventory records are maintained on other than a perpetual basis, an adjustment is usually needed to reflect the difference between the beginning and ending inventory. This **year-end inventory adjustment** eliminates all nominal accounts related to the purchase of inventory by transferring them to Cost of Goods Sold. The adjustment also eliminates the beginning inventory amount and establishes the amount of ending inventory to be included on the balance sheet. A typical inventory adjusting entry would include debits and credits to the following accounts:

	Dr.	Cr.
Inventory (ending)	XX,XXX	
Purchase Discounts	X,XXX	
Purchase Allowances	XXX	
Purchase Returns	X,XXX	
Cost of Goods Sold	XXX,XXX	
Inventory (beginning)		XX,XXX
Purchases		XXX,XXX
Transportation-In		X,XXX

16. In summary, the steps in the accounting cycle performed every fiscal period are as follows:
    a. Enter the transactions of the period in appropriate journals.
    b. Post from the journals to the ledger (or ledgers).
    c. Take an unadjusted trial balance.
    d. Prepare adjusting journal entries and post them to the ledger(s).
    e. Take a trial balance after adjusting (adjusted balance).
    f. Prepare the financial statements from the second trial balance.
    g. Prepare closing journal entries and post them to the ledger(s).
    h. Take a trial balance after closing (post-closing trial balance).
    i. Prepare reversing entries and post them to the ledger(s). (Optional step-see appendix)

Work Sheet

17. (S.O. 8) A multicolumn (8, 10, 12, etc.) **work sheet** serves as an aid to the accountant in adjusting the account balances and preparing the financial statements. The work sheet provides an orderly format for the accumulation of information necessary for preparation of financial statements. Use of a work sheet does not replace any financial statements, nor does it alter any of the steps in the accounting cycle.

*18. (S.O. 9) **Cash Basis Accounting Versus Accrual Basis Accounting,** is presented in the appendix of Chapter 3 for the purpose of demonstrating the difference between cash basis and accrual basis accounting. Under the **strict cash basis of accounting,** revenue is recognized only when cash is received, and expenses are recorded only when cash is paid. The accrual basis of accounting recognizes revenue when it is earned and expenses when incurred without regard to the time of receipt or payment of cash.

*Reversing Entries

*19. (S.O. 10) Preparation and posting of **reversing entries** is the final step in the accounting cycle. A reversing entry is made at the beginning of the next accounting period and is the exact opposite of the adjusting entry made in the previous period. The recording of reversing entries is an optional step in the accounting cycle that may be performed at the beginning of the next accounting period. The entries subject to reversal are the adjusting entries for accrued revenues and accrued expenses initially entered in expense or income accounts.

20. (S.O. 11) **Specialized Journals and Methods of Processing Accounting Data is presented as a detailed discussion of subsidiary ledgers and the sales journal, cash receipts journal, purchases journal and cash payments journal.

**21. The method used to process accounting information does not alter the steps in the accounting cycle. When sophisticated electronic data processing (EDP) systems are used, the accounting records may change in appearance, but the steps performed are the same as those in a manual system.

GLOSSARY

Account. A systematic arrangement that shows the effect of transactions and other events on a specific asset or equity.

Accrued expenses. Expenses incurred but not yet paid or recorded.

Accrued revenue. Revenues earned but not yet received or recorded.

Adjusted trial balance. A trial balance taken immediately after all adjustments have been posted.

Adjusting entries. Entries made at the end of an accounting period to bring all accounts up to date on an accrual accounting basis.

Balance sheet. The financial statement that shows the financial condition of the enterprise at the end of the period.

***Cash basis of accounting.** Revenue is recorded only when cash is received and an expense is recorded only when cash is paid.

Closing entries. The formal process by which all nominal accounts are reduced to zero and the net income or net loss is determined and transferred to the owners' equity account.

Credit. The right side of an account.

Debit. The left side of an account.

Double-entry system. A system that records the dual effect of each transaction in appropriate account.

Event. A happening of consequence.

External event. A transaction between an entity and its environment.

Financial statements. Statements that reflect the collection, tabulation, and final summarization of the accounting data.

General ledger. A collection of all the asset, liability, owners' equity, revenue, and expense accounts.

Income statement. The financial statement which measures the results of operations during the period.

Internal event. A transaction that occurs within an entity.

Journal. The book of original entry where transactions and selected other events are initially recorded.

Ledger. The book containing the accounts.

Nominal accounts. Nominal (temporary) accounts are revenue, expense and dividend accounts, except for dividends, they appear on the income statement.

Post-closing trial balance. A trial balance taken immediately after closing entries have been posted.

Posting. The process of transferring the essential facts and figures from the book of original entry (journal) to the ledger accounts.

Prepaid expense. An item paid and recorded in advance of its use or consumption, part of it properly represents expense of the current period and part represents an asset on hand at the end of the period.

Real accounts. Real (permanent) accounts are asset, liability, and equity accounts; and they appear on the balance sheet.

***Reversing entries.** Entries at the beginning of the next accounting period that are the exact opposite of the adjusting entries made in the previous period.

****Special journal.** A journal used to group similar types of transactions.

Statement of cash flows. The financial statement which measures the cash provided and used by operating, investing, and financing activities during the period.

Statement of retained earnings. The financial statement which reconciles the balance of the retained earnings account from the beginning to the end of the period.

Subsidiary ledger. Contains the details related to a given general ledger account.

****Summary account.** An account in the general ledger that summarizes the details of the respective subsidiary ledger.

Transaction. An external event involving a transfer or exchange between two or more entities.

Trial balance. A list of all open accounts in the ledger and their balances.

Unearned revenue. Cash received and recorded as a liability because it has not yet been earned by providing goods or services to customers.

***Voucher system.** An extensive series of prescribed control procedures designed to assure that every disbursement by check is a proper payment.

Work sheet. A columnar sheet of paper used to adjust the account balances and prepare the financial statements.

CHAPTER OUTLINE

Fill in the outline presented below.

(S.O. 1) Basic Terminology

(S.O. 2) Double-Entry Recording Process

(S.O. 3) Identifying and Recording of Transactions

(S.O. 4) Journalizing

Posting to the Ledger

Trial Balance

(S.O. 5) Adjustments

Prepaid Expense

Chapter Outline *(continued)*

Unearned Revenue

Accrued Liabilities or Expenses

Accrued Assets or Revenues

(S.O. 6) Closing Entries

Post-Closing Trial Balance

(S.O. 7) End-of-period Procedure for Inventory and Related Accounts

(S.O. 8) Using a Work Sheet

*(S.O. 9) Cash Basis Versus Accrual Basis

*(S.O. 10) Reversing Entries

**(S.O. 11) Specialized Journals

REVIEW QUESTIONS AND EXERCISES

TRUE-FALSE

Indicate whether each of the following is true (T) or false (F) in the space provided.

____ 1. (S.O. 1) Real (permanent) accounts are revenue and expense accounts and are periodically closed.

____ 2. (S.O. 2) In general, debits refer to increases in account balances, and credits refer to decreases.

____ 3. (S.O. 2) An example of an internal event would be a flood that destroyed a portion of an entity's inventory.

____ 4. (S.O. 2) Double-entry accounting is the process that leads to the basic equality in accounting expressed by the formula: assets = liabilities + owners' equity.

____ 5. (S.O. 4) A general journal may be used by any entity in recording its transactions, whereas special journals may be used only by entities whose transactions meet certain requirements.

____ 6. (S.O. 4) If an entity fails to post one of its journal entries to its general ledger, the trial balance will not show an equal amount of debit and credit balance accounts.

____ 7. (S.O. 4) One purpose of a trial balance is to prove that debits and credits of an equal amount are in the general ledger.

____ 8. (S.O. 5) Adjusting entries are an optional step in the accounting process.

____ 9. (S.O. 5) Adjusting entries are used to correct errors that occur during the posting process.

____ 10. (S.O. 5) Adjusting entries result from compliance with the accrual system of accounting.

____ 11. (S.O. 5) An adjustment for wages expense, earned but unpaid at year end, is an example of an accrued liability.

____ 12. (S.O. 5) Proper matching of revenues and expenses requires that bad debts be recorded as an expense of the period in which the sale was made.

____ 13. (S.O. 6) The Income Summary account used during the closing process is shown in the owners' equity section of the balance sheet.

____ 14. (S.O. 6) It is not necessary to post the closing entries to the ledger accounts because new revenue and expense accounts will be opened in the subsequent accounting period.

____ 15. (S.O. 6) The account "interest expense" is credited during the closing process.

____ 16. (S.O. 6) The post-closing trial balance consists of asset, liability, owners' equity, revenue and expense accounts.

_____ 17. (S.O. 7) Under a perpetual inventory system, purchases and issues are recorded directly in the inventory account as the purchases and issues occur.

_____ 18. (S.O. 7) When inventory records are maintained using a periodic inventory system, a purchases account is used and the inventory is unchanged during the period.

_____ 19. (S.O. 7) The computation of Cost of Goods Sold under a periodic inventory system has the characteristics of both an adjusting entry and a closing entry.

_____ 20. (S.O. 8) A work sheet completed through the adjusted trial balance column provides the information needed for preparation of the financial statements without reference to the ledger or other records.

_____ 21. (S.O. 8) The use of a work sheet at the end of each month or quarter permits the preparation of interim financial statements even though the books are closed only at the end of each year.

_____ 22. (S.O. 8) An adjusted trial balance that shows equal debit and credit columnar totals proves the accuracy of the adjusting entries.

_____ *23. (S.O. 10) Because each accrued item involves either a later receipt of cash for income or a later disbursement of cash for expense, a reversing entry is made to offset part of the credit to income or part of the debit to expense.

_____ *24. (S.O. 10) Reversing entries are made at the end of the accounting cycle to correct errors in the original recording of transactions.

_____ *25. (S.O. 10) In general, all adjusting entries for prepaid items for which the original amount was entered in a revenue or expense account and for all accrued items should be reversed.

MULTIPLE CHOICE

Select the best answer for each of the following items and enter the corresponding letter in the space provided.

_____ 1. (S.O. 2) The accounting equation (A = L + OE) must remain in balance:

A. throughout each step in the accounting cycle.
B. only when journal entries are recorded.
C. only at the time the trial balance is prepared.
D. only when formal financial statements are prepared.

_____ 2. (S.O. 2) The difference between the accounting process and the accounting cycle is:

A. the accounting process results in the preparation of financial statements, whereas the accounting cycle is concerned with recording business transactions.
B. the accounting cycle represents the steps taken to accomplish the accounting process.
C. the accounting process represents the steps taken to accomplish the accounting cycle.
D. merely semantic, because both concepts refer to the same thing.

_____ 3. (S.O. 2) A trial balance taken at year end showed Puccineli Co.'s debit total exceeding the credit total by $6,300. This discrepancy could have been caused by:

A. the balance of $47,000 in accounts receivable being entered in the trial balance as $40,700.
B. an error in adding the Sales Journal.
C. the balance of $700 in the Office Equipment account being entered as a debit of $7,000.
D. a net loss of $6,300.

_____ 4. (S.O. 4) Which of the following is not a principal purpose of a trial balance?

A. It proves that debits and credits of equal amounts are in the ledger.
B. It is the basis for any adjustments to the account balances.
C. It supplies a listing of open accounts and their balances.
D. It proves that debits and credits were properly entered in the ledger accounts.

_____ 5. (S.O. 5) Which of the following journal entries is appropriate when a company receives payment in advance for goods or services?

A. Debit cash and credit an expense account.
B. Credit cash and debit a revenue account.
C. Debit cash and credit a liability account or a revenue account.
D. Credit cash and debit a liability or revenue account.

_____ 6. (S.O. 5) During the first year of Wisnewski Co.'s operations, all purchases were recorded as assets. Store supplies in the amount of $6,540 were purchased. Actual year-end store supplies inventory amounted to $2,150. The adjusting entry for store supplies will:

A. increase net income $4,390.
B. increase expenses by $4,390.
C. decrease store supplies by $6,540.
D. debit accounts payable for $2,150.

_____ 7. (S.O. 5) An adjusting entry should never include:

A. a debit to expense and a credit to a liability.
B. a debit to expense and a credit to revenue.
C. a debit to a liability and a credit to revenue.
D. a debit to revenue and a credit to a liability.

_____ 8. (S.O. 5) Which of the following is an example of an accrued liability?

A. Office supplies purchased at the beginning of the year and debited to an expense account.
B. Property taxes incurred during the year, to be paid in the first quarter of the subsequent year.
C. Depreciation expense.
D. Rent earned during the period, to be received at the end of the year.

_____ 9. (S.O. 5) A prepaid expense can **best** be described as an amount:

A. Paid and currently matched with earnings.
B. Paid and **not** currently matched with earnings.
C. **Not** paid and **not** currently matched with earnings.
D. **Not** paid and currently matched with earnings.

_____ 10. (S.O. 5) Rent collected in advance by a landlord is a (an):

A. Accrued liability.
B. Deferred asset.
C. Accrued revenue.
D. Unearned revenue.

_____ 11. (S.O. 5) An accrued expense can **best** be described as an amount:

A. Paid and **not** currently matched with earnings.
B. **Not** paid and currently matched with earnings.
C. **Not** paid and **not** currently matched with earnings.
D. Paid and currently matched with earnings.

_____ 12. (S.O. 5) The Murphy Company sublet a portion of its warehouse for five years at an annual rental of $24,000, beginning on May 1, 2001. The tenant, Sheri Charter, paid one year's rent in advance, which Murphy recorded as a credit to unearned rental income. Murphy reports on a calendar-year basis. The adjustment on December 31, 2001 for Murphy should be:

		Dr.	Cr.
A.	No entry		
B.	Unearned rental income	8,000	
	Rental income		8,000
C.	Rental income	8,000	
	Unearned rental income		8,000
D.	Unearned rental income	16,000	
	Rental income		16,000

_____ 13. (S.O. 6) Which of the following statements best describes the purpose of closing entries?

A. To facilitate posting and taking a trial balance.
B. To determine the amount of net income or net loss for the period.
C. To reduce the balances of revenue and expense accounts to zero so that they may be used to accumulate the revenues and expenses of the next period.
D. To complete the record of various transactions that were started in a prior period.

_____ 14. (S.O. 6) If expenses are greater than revenues, the Income Summary account will be closed by a debit to:

A. Income Summary and a credit to Cash.
B. Income Summary and a credit to Retained Earnings.
C. Cash and a credit to Income Summary.
D. Retained Earnings and a credit to Income Summary.

_____ 15. (S.O. 7) The following account balances (normal balances) were taken from the journal entry used to transfer various merchandise accounts under a periodic inventory system into the Cost of Goods Sold account:

Cost of Goods Sold	$235,000
Inventory (beginning)	62,500
Transportation-In	6,700
Purchase Discounts	4,500
Purchases	214,000
Purchase Allowances	5,700

Based on the above facts, what was ending inventory?

A. $21,000
B. $45,600
C. $38,000
D. $37,900

_____ 16. (S.O. 7) The gross profit of Fordyce Company for 2001 is $75,000, cost of goods manufactured is $320,000, the beginning inventories of goods in process and finished goods are $22,000 and $25,000, respectively, and the ending inventories of goods in process and finished goods are $30,000 and $32,000, respectively. The sales of Fordyce Company for 2001 must have been:

A. $378,000
B. $385,000
C. $388,000
D. $398,000

_____ 17. (S.O. 8) The work sheet for Sharko Co. consisted of eight pairs of debit and credit columns. The dollar amount of one item appeared in both the credit column of the income statement section and the debit column of the balance sheet section. That item is:

A. net income for the period.
B. beginning inventory.
C. cost of goods sold.
D. ending inventory.

_____ 18. Which of the following statements is not true as it pertains to the accounting process?

A. The established system for recording transactions and other events as they occur is referred to as double entry accounting.
B. Events are of two types: (1) external and (2) internal. Accountants record events that affect the financial position of the enterprise.
C. Adjustments are necessary to achieve a proper matching of revenues and expenses to determine net income for the current period and to achieve an accurate statement of the assets and equities existing at the end of the period.
D. Posting is the initial recording of all transactions in chronological order.

_____*19. (S.O. 10) A reversing entry should never be made for an adjusting entry that:

A. accrues unrecorded revenue.
B. adjusts expired costs from an asset account to an expense account.
C. accrues unrecorded expenses.
D. adjusts unexpired costs from an expense account to an asset account.

_____*20. (S.O. 10) If the following journal entry was made for the purchase of a three-year insurance policy in February of the first year, would an adjusting entry and/or a reversing entry be appropriate at the end of the first year?

	Debit	Credit
Unexpired Insurance	3,000	
Cash		3,000

	Adjusting Entry	Reversing Entry
A.	Yes	No
B.	No	Yes
C.	Yes	Yes
D.	No	No

REVIEW EXERCISES

1. (S.O.4) The accounts listed below have been taken from Davies Co.'s general ledger as of December 31, 2002. The accounts all have normal balances. This is the end of Davies Co.'s first year of operations.

Cash	$ 34,000
Buildings (net)	210,000
Note Payable	72,000
Salary Expense	19,000
Inventory	36,000
Accounts Payable	60,000
Common Stock	185,000
Accounts Receivable	48,000
Sales	______
Notes Receivable	22,000
Bonds Payable	75,000
Rent Expense	15,000
Land	125,000
Cost of Goods Sold	165,000
Tax Expense	20,000
Tax Payable	31,000

Determine sales for the year and prepare the following items for Davies Co. as of the year ended December 31, 2002:

a. trial balance,
b. income statement, and
c. balance sheet.

a. ______________________________

b.

c.

2. (S.O.4) The following changes occurred in the account balances of Cihla's Corporation during 2002.

Accounts Increasing	Amount
Cash	$50,000
Inventory	30,000
Building	25,000
Capital Stock	30,000
Additional Paid-in Capital	10,000

Accounts Decreasing	Amount
Accounts Receivable	$10,000
Accounts Payable	20,000

The accounts shown above represent all the balance sheet accounts for Cihla's Corporation with the exception of Retained Earnings. No dividends were declared during 2002.

Instructions

From the changes above, determine the amount of net income or net loss for 2002.

3. (S.O.5) The following data relate to the accounts of Scacco Company.

a. A three-year insurance policy was purchased on March 1, 2002. The $360 insurance premium was fully paid on that date and a debit to prepaid insurance was recorded.

b. Unpaid salaries at year end amount to $650.

c. Service revenue was credited for $816 on May 1, 2002. The amount represents a one-year advance payment for services to be performed by Scacco Company through April 30, 2003.

d. The Office Supplies account shows a balance of $1,250 on December 31, 2002. A physical count of the supplies on hand at this date reveals a total of $480 available.

e. Scacco Company holds bonds of another corporation that pay interest at a rate of $900 per year. These bonds were purchased on August 1, 2002, and the first interest payment will be received on August 1, 2003.

Instructions

Prepare the necessary adjusting journal entries indicated by each item for the year ended December 31, 2002.

General Journal J1

Date	Account Title	Debit	Credit

4. (S.O.2, 4, 5, 6, 7 and 9) The post-closing trial balance of the Pat Callahan Company at January 1, 2002 is shown below.

Account No.	Account	Debit	Credit
101	Cash	$46,000	
102	Investment in Bonds	50,000	
103	Accounts Receivable	28,000	
104	Allowance for Doubtful Accounts		900
105	Interest Receivable		
106	Inventory (perpetual)	24,000	
107	Building (15-year life)	45,000	
108	Accumulated Depreciation-Building		12,000
109	Delivery Truck (5-year life, $3,000 salvage)	18,000	
110	Accumulated Depreciation-Trucks		6,000
200	Accounts Payable		18,000
201	Notes Payable		29,000
202	Wages Payable		
203	Income Taxes Payable		5,000
300	Common Par Value $1.00		85,000
301	Retained Earnings		55,100
400	Sales		
401	Interest Revenue		
500	Operating Expenses		
501	Wages Expense		
502	Depreciation Expense-Building		
503	Depreciation Expense-Trucks		
504	Bad Debt Expense		
505	Cost of Goods Sold		
506	Income Tax Expense		
		$211,000	$211,000

**Ending Inventory (12/31/02) $26,000.*

The following transactions took place during 2002.

1. Collected: Accounts Receivable, $25,000; Interest on Bonds $5,000; Cash Sales, $80,000 (Cost of Goods Sold $14,000).
2. Paid: Accounts Payable, $15,000; Notes Payable, $21,000; Income Taxes Payable, $5,000; Operating Expenses, $37,000.
3. Purchased inventory, $32,000, of which $16,000 was purchased on account. (Assume perpetual inventory.)
4. Made sales on account, $85,000 (Cost of Goods Sold $16,000).
5. On June 30, 2002, purchased a second delivery truck for $15,000, paying cash. The truck has useful life of 10 years and a salvage value of $3,000.

Instructions

a. Journalize each of the transactions above of the Pat Callahan Company. Some items require more than one journal entry.

b. Post the entries to appropriate accounts. (You should set up a T-account for each account noted on the trial balance.)

c. Prepare a trial balance after posting the journal entries and enter the amounts on a 10-column work sheet like the one shown in the text. Enter all the accounts shown on the original trial balance.

d. Enter the following adjustments on the work sheet: (a) Accrued wages at year end total $700; (b) Bad debt expense is estimated at 1% of credit sales; (c) Record straight-line depreciation on the building and trucks; (d) Accrued interest on the investments in bonds is $1,500; (e) Income tax expense for 2002 is $21,065. The tax is not due until 2003.

e. Complete the income statement and balance sheet columns of the work sheet.

f. Prepare closing journal entries.

a.

General Journal

J1

Date	Account Title	Debit	Credit

b.

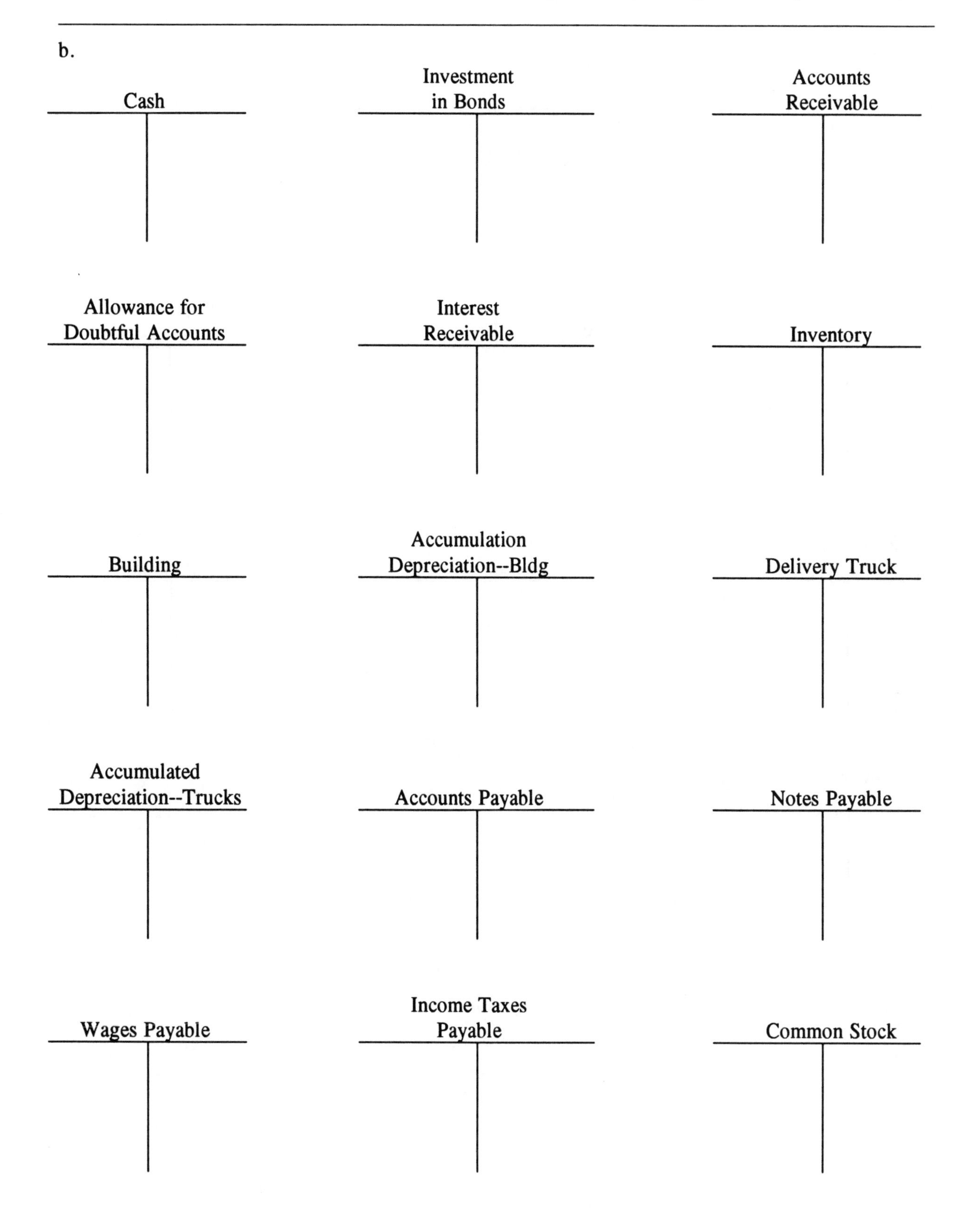
Cash
Investment in Bonds
Accounts Receivable
Allowance for Doubtful Accounts
Interest Receivable
Inventory
Building
Accumulation Depreciation--Bldg
Delivery Truck
Accumulated Depreciation--Trucks
Accounts Payable
Notes Payable
Wages Payable
Income Taxes Payable
Common Stock

b. (continued)

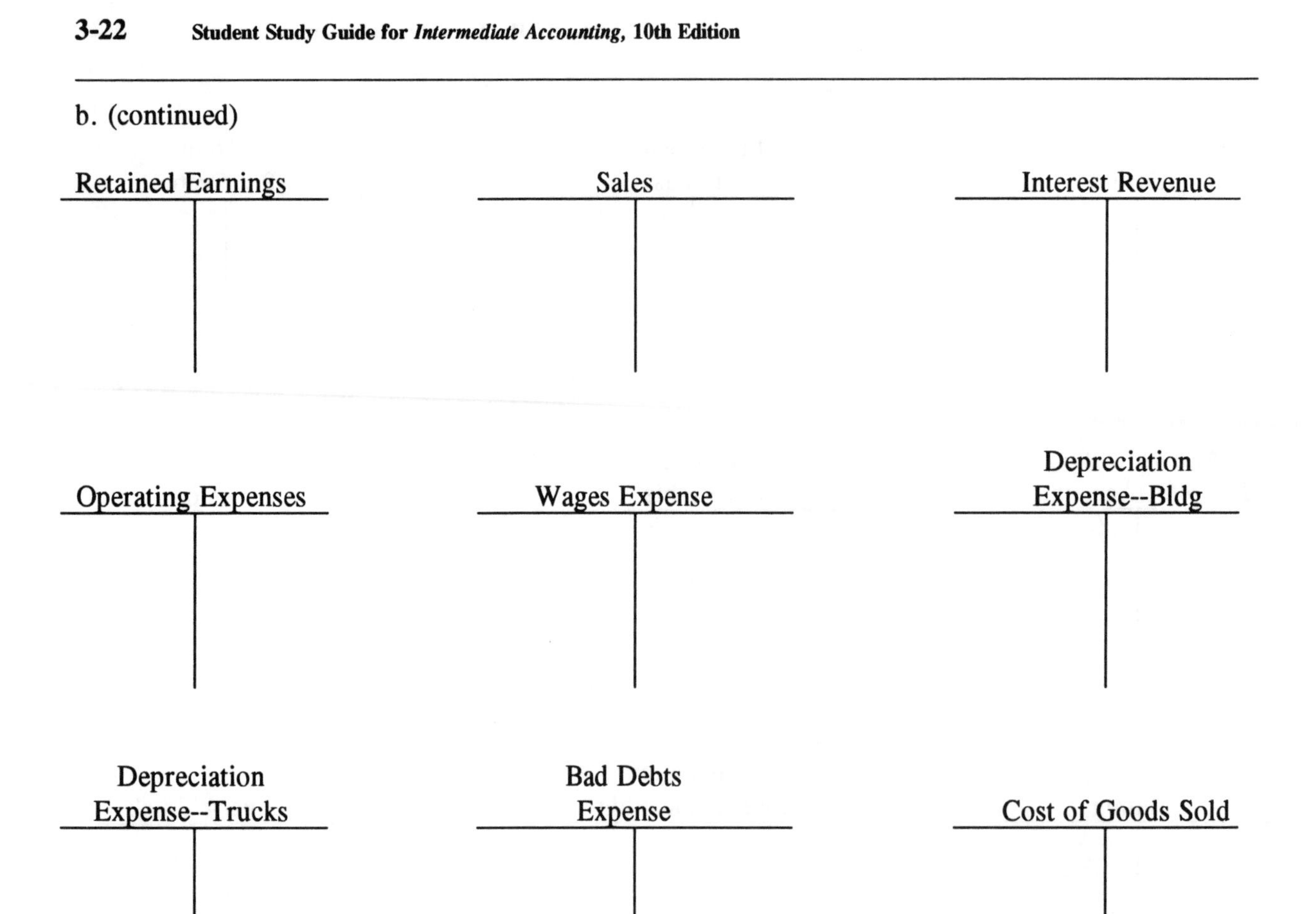
Retained Earnings
Sales
Interest Revenue
Operating Expenses
Wages Expense
Depreciation Expense--Bldg
Depreciation Expense--Trucks
Bad Debts Expense
Cost of Goods Sold

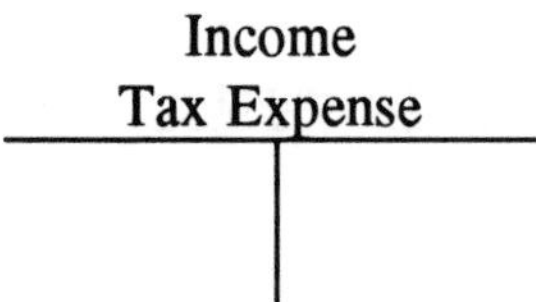
Income Tax Expense

c. d. e.

Pat Callahan Company
Ten-Column Work Sheet
December 31, 2002

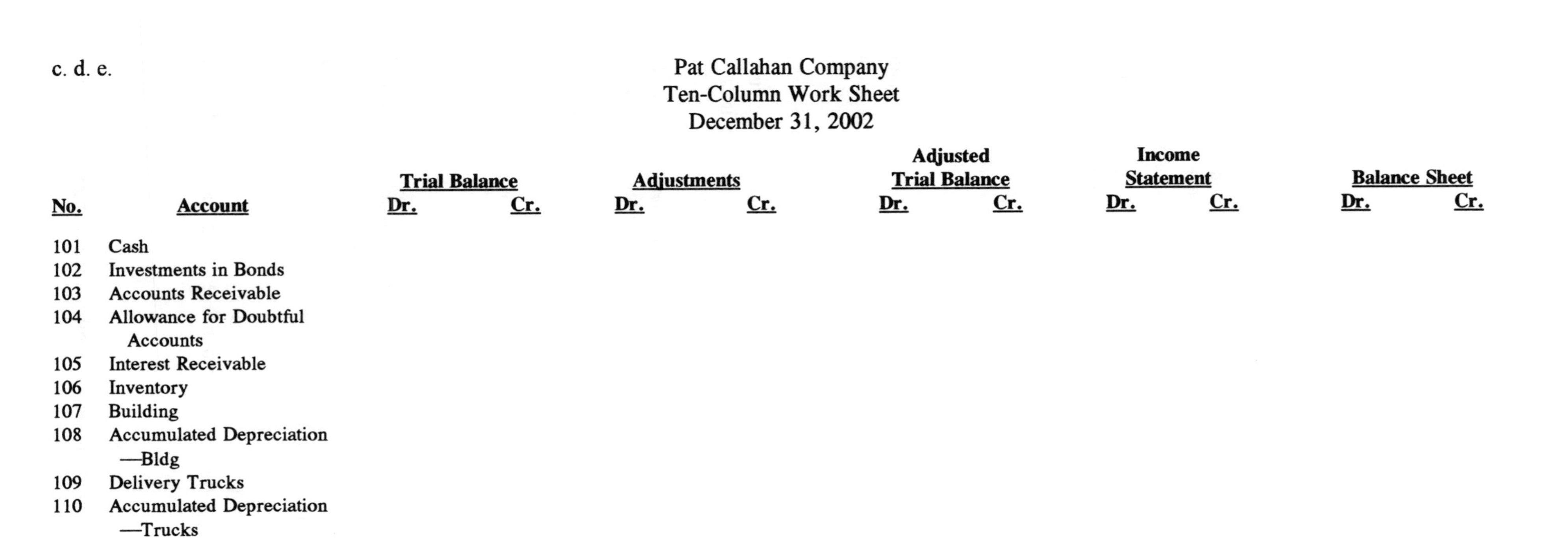

		Trial Balance		Adjustments		Adjusted Trial Balance		Income Statement		Balance Sheet	
No.	Account	Dr.	Cr.	Dr.	Cr.	Dr.	Cr.	Dr.	Cr.	Dr.	Cr.
101	Cash										
102	Investments in Bonds										
103	Accounts Receivable										
104	Allowance for Doubtful Accounts										
105	Interest Receivable										
106	Inventory										
107	Building										
108	Accumulated Depreciation —Bldg										
109	Delivery Trucks										
110	Accumulated Depreciation —Trucks										
200	Accounts Payable										
201	Notes Payable										
202	Wages Payable										
203	Income Taxes Payable										
300	Common Stock										
301	Retained Earnings										
400	Sales										
401	Interest Revenue										
500	Operating Expense										
501	Wages Expense										
502	Depreciation Expense —Bldg										
503	Depreciation Expense —Trucks										
504	Bad Debts Expense										
505	Cost of Goods Sold										
506	Income Tax Expense										
	Net Income										

SOLUTIONS TO REVIEW QUESTIONS AND EXERCISES

TRUE-FALSE

1. (F) Real (permanent) accounts are asset, liability, and owners' equity accounts. Nominal (temporary) accounts are revenue and expense accounts. Nominal accounts are periodically closed; real accounts are not.

2. (F) Debits can be increases or decreases in account balances, depending on the account involved. Debits increase asset and expense accounts; they decrease liability, owner equity, and revenue accounts. Credits result in the opposite effect on account balances.

3. (F) This statement characterizes an external event rather than an internal event. Internal events occur within an entity, whereas external events involve interaction between an entity and its environment.

4. (T)

5. (F) Special journals can be used by any entity for any groups of transactions possessing common characteristics. See **the web site** for a complete discussion of special journals.

6. (F) Failure to post one journal entry to the general ledger will misstate the debit and credit side of a trial balance by the same amount. Thus, the trial balance will show an equal amount of debits and credits.

7. (T)

8. (F) Adjusting entries are necessary to achieve a proper matching of revenues and expenses in determining net income and to achieve an accurate statement of assets and equities at the end of the period.

9. (F) Adjusting entries are necessary to achieve a proper matching of revenues and expenses in the determination of net income for the current period and to achieve an accurate statement of the assets and equities existing at the end of the period. If errors are made in the posting process, they are corrected by means of correcting entries, not adjusting entries.

10. (T)

11. (T)

12. (T)

13. (F) The income summary account is a clearing account through which all revenue and expense accounts are closed at the end of an accounting period. Once the revenue and expense accounts have been closed, any balance existing in the income summary account is closed to retained earnings. Thus, the income summary account never appears on a financial statement.

14. (F) Failure to post closing entries to the general ledger will leave a balance in revenue and expense accounts from a previous period and the retained earnings account will be misstated.

15. (T)

16. (F) The post-cloning trial balance consists only of asset, liability, and owners' equity (the real) accounts.

17. (T)

18. (T)

19. (T)

20. (T)

21. (T)

22. (F) An adjusted trial balance that shows equal debit and credit columnar totals proves nothing more than the fact that each adjusting entry contained an equal amount of debits and credits. Adjusting entries could have included the wrong total dollar amount or an inappropriate account could have been debited or credited. Mistakes such as these would still produce an adjusted trial balance that shows equal debit and credit columnar totals.

*23. (T)

*24. (F) Reversing entries are made to simplify the recording of a subsequent transaction related to an adjusting entry. When an entry is reversed, the related subsequent transaction can be recorded as if the adjusting entry had never been recorded. Reversing entries have nothing to do with the correction of errors.

*25. (T)

MULTIPLE CHOICE

1. (A) If the accounting equation is out of balance at any time during the accounting cycle, then an error has been made.

2. (B) The basic procedures normally used to ensure that the effects of transactions and selected other events are recorded correctly and transmitted to the user are often called the steps in the accounting cycle. The accounting process encompasses all the steps in the accounting cycle.

3. (C)

Recorded debit amount..........................	$7,000
Actual debit balance	700
Excess debit total.................................	$6,300

4. (D) The trial balance accomplishes the things listed in the first three alternatives. However, the purpose of the trail balance is not to prove that the debits and credits were properly entered in the ledger accounts. The fact that the trial balance is in balance proves that an equal amount of debits and credits were made, but there is no assurance that the postings were made to the correct accounts.

5. (C) An advance payment for goods or services requires a debit to cash, but the corresponding credit can be made to a liability or a revenue account. When the goods or services are delivered to the customer, consideration of the account credited in the original entry will dictate the manner in which this event is reflected in the accounts.

6. (B)

Purchased...	$6,540
Year-end inventory	2,150
Used during year................................	$4,390

Adjusting entry:	Supplies Expense	4,390	
	Store Supplies		4,390

7. (B) All adjusting entries include one balance sheet account (asset or liability) and one income statement account (revenue or expense). Thus, all alternatives other than alternative B represent possible adjusting entry descriptions.

8. (B) An accrued liability is an item of expense that has been incurred during the period, but has not been recorded or paid. The property taxes fits this definition, as they are an expense of the period in which they were incurred and represent a liability until they are paid in the subsequent period. The office supplies are a prepaid expense, depreciation is an estimated item, and the rent earned is an accrued revenue item.

9. (B) A prepaid expense can best be described as an amount paid and not currently matched with earnings. The journal entry to record a prepaid expense involves an asset account and crediting cash. The asset is deferred to and expensed in future years. Answer (A) is incorrect because it is not matched with earnings until it is expensed in future years. Answers (C) and (D) are incorrect because a prepaid expense is one that has been paid.

10. (D) Rent collected in advance by a landlord is an unearned revenue. Cash received in advance should not be recognized as revenue until it has been earned as evidenced by providing a product, service, or facility. Answer (A) is incorrect because an accrued liability is the result of an expense which has been incurred but not yet paid. Answer (B) is incorrect because a deferred asset is a cost which has been incurred but the benefits will be received in the future. Answer (C) is incorrect because an accrued revenue is revenue that has been earned but not yet received.

11. (B) An accrued expense can best be described as an amount not paid and currently matched with earnings. The journal entry to record an accrued expense involves debiting an expense account which is deducted from revenues in determining income and crediting a liability account. Accrued expenses are generally incurred as a result of passage of time (e.g., interest, rent, salaries, etc.). Answers (A) and (D) are incorrect because by definition an accrued expense is one that has been incurred but **not** yet paid. Answer (C) is incorrect because the purpose of accruing an expense is to match it currently with earnings.

12. (D) Murphy Company should make an adjusting entry to recognize that two-thirds (8 months) of an annual rental of $24,000 has been earned and should be recognized as rental income in 2001. The journal entry that should be made is:

Unearned rental income	16,000	
Rental income ($24,000 x 2/3)		16,000

13. (C) Closing entries represent the formal process by which all nominal accounts (revenue and expense) are reduced to zero and the net income or net loss is determined and transferred to owners' equity. Even though the amount of net income or net loss is determined through the closing process (alternative B), this is not the primary purpose of closing entries.

14. (D) If expenses are greater than revenues, then the Income Summary account will have a debit balance after closing entries have been made. Thus, to close the Income Summary account the journal entry would include a debit to Retained Earnings and a credit to Income Summary.

15. (C) The journal entry these accounts would have been included in is the following:

Inventory (ending)	38,000	
Purchase Discounts	4,500	
Purchase Allowances	5,700	
Cost of Goods Sold	235,000	
Inventory (beginning)		62,500
Purchases		214,000
Transportation-In		6,700

16. (C) The sales of Fordyce Company for 2001 must have been $388,000. Sales can be computed by determining the cost of goods sold and adding to it the gross profit of $75,000.

Beginning finished goods inventory	$ 25,000
Cost of goods manufactured	320,000
Finished goods available for sale	$345,000
Ending finished goods inventory	32,000
Cost of goods sold	$313,000
Add gross profit	75,000
Sales for 2001	$388,000

17. (D) Ending inventory is the only account that affects the income statement and the balance sheet in the manner indicated. Ending inventory reduced Cost of Goods Sold in the income statement columns (credit) and is an asset (debit) on the balance sheet.

18. (D) Alternatives A, B, and C are statements of fact as they relate to the accounting process. Alternative "D" describes journalization, not the posting process.

*19. (B) The adjusting entry shown in the solution to multiple-choice question 6 above is an example of an adjusting entry that adjusts expired costs from an asset to an expense account. To reverse such an entry would increase the Store Supplies account. This is obviously inappropriate because the only way to increase Store Supplies is to purchase additional supplies. The other three alternatives represent appropriate candidates for reversing entries.

*20. (A) An adjusting entry is necessary because a portion of the insurance has expired as of the end of the first year. However, because this prepaid item was originally entered in an asset account a reversing entry would be inappropriate.

REVIEW EXERCISES

1.

Davies Co.
Trial Balance
December 31, 2002

Cash	$34,000	
Accounts Receivable	48,000	
Notes Receivable	22,000	
Inventory	36,000	
Building	210,000	
Land	125,000	
Accounts Payable		$60,000
Notes Payable		72,000
Tax Payable		31,000
Bonds Payable		75,000
Common Stock		185,000
Sales		271,000
Cost of Goods Sold	165,000	
Rent Expense	15,000	
Salary Expense	19,000	
Tax Expense	20,000	
	$694,000	$694,000

Davies Co.
Statement of Income
Year Ended December 31, 2002

Sales		$271,000
Cost of Goods Sold		165,000
Gross Profit on Sales		$106,000
Rent Expense	$ 15,000	
Salary Expense	19,000	
Tax Expense	20,000	
Total Expenses		54,000
Net Income		$52,000

Davies Co.
Balance Sheet
December 31, 2002

Assets

Current Assets:			
Cash		$ 34,000	
Accounts Receivable		48,000	
Notes Receivable		22,000	
Inventory		36,000	
Total Current Assets			$140,000
Fixed Assets:			
Building		$210,000	
Land		125,000	
Total Fixed Assets			335,000
Total Assets			$475,000

Liabilities and Stockholders' Equity

Current Liabilities:			
Accounts Payable	$60,000		
Notes Payable	72,000		
Taxes Payable	31,000		
Total Current Liabilities		$163,000	
Long-term Liabilities:			
Bond Payable		75,000	$238,000
Stockholders' Equity:			
Common Stock		185,000	
Retained Earnings		52,000	237,000
Total Liabilities and Stockholders' Equity			$475,000

2. **Net change in assets:**

Cash	$50,000	
Accounts Receivable	(10,000)	
Inventory	30,000	
Building	25,000	
Net Change		$ 95,000
Less net change in liabilities and owners' equity:		
Accounts Payable	($20,000)	
Capital Stock	30,000	
Additional Paid-in Capital	10,000	
Net Change		20,000
Net Income for 2002 (Change in Retained Earnings)		$ 75,000

		Account	Debit	Credit
3.	a.	Insurance Expense	100	
		Prepaid Insurance		100
	b.	Salaries Expense	650	
		Salaries Payable		650
	c.	Service Revenue	272	
		Unearned Service Revenue		272
	d.	Supplies Expense	770	
		Office Supplies		770
	e.	Interest Receivable	375	
		Interest Income		375

			Account	Debit	Credit
4.	a.	Item 1:	Cash	25,000	
			Accounts Receivable		25,000
			Cash	5,000	
			Interest Revenue		5,000
			Cash	80,000	
			Sales		80,000
			Cost of Goods Sold	14,000	
			Inventory		14,000
		Item 2:	Accounts Payable	15,000	
			Cash		15,000
			Notes Payable	21,000	
			Cash		21,000
			Income Taxes Payable	5,000	
			Cash		5,000
			Operating Expenses	37,000	
			Cash		37,000
		Item 3:	Inventory	32,000	
			Cash		16,000
			Accounts Payable		16,000
		Item 4:	Accounts Receivable	85,000	
			Sales		85,000
			Cost of Goods Sold	16,000	
			Inventory		16,000
		Item 5:	Delivery Truck	15,000	
			Cash		15,000

b.

Cash

Debit	Credit
46,000	15,000 (2)
(1) 25,000	21,000 (2)
(1) 5,000	5,000 (2)
(1) 80,000	37,000 (2)
	16,000 (3)
	15,000 (5)
47,000	

Investment in Bonds

Debit	Credit
50,000	

Accounts Receivable

Debit	Credit
28,000	25,000 (1)
(4) 85,000	
88,000	

Allowance for Doubtful Accounts

Debit	Credit
	900

Interest Receivable

Debit	Credit

Inventory

Debit	Credit
24,000	14,000 (1)
(3) 32,000	16,000 (4)
26,000	

Building

Debit	Credit
45,000	

Accumulated Depreciation--Bldg

Debit	Credit
	12,000

Delivery Truck

Debit	Credit
18,000	
(5) 15,000	
33,000	

Accumulated Depreciation--Trucks

Debit	Credit
	6,000

Accounts Payable

Debit	Credit
(2) 15,000	18,000
	16,000 (4)
	19,000

Notes Payable

Debit	Credit
(2) 21,000	29,000
	8,000

b. (continued)

Wages Payable

Income Taxes Payable

(2) 5,000	5,000

Common Stock

	85,000

Retained Earnings

	55,100

Sales

	80,000 (1)
	85,000 (3)
	165,000

Interest Revenue

	5,000 (1)

Operating Expenses

(2) 37,000	

Wages Expense

Depreciation Expense--Bldg

Depreciation Expense--Trucks

Bad Debts Expense

Cost of Goods Sold

(1) 14,000	
(4) 16,000	
30,000	

Income Tax Expense

c. d. e.

Pat Callahan Company
Ten-Column Work Sheet
December 31, 2002

No.	Account	Trial Balance Dr.	Trial Balance Cr.	Adjustments Dr.	Adjustments Cr.	Adjusted Trial Balance Dr.	Adjusted Trial Balance Cr.	Income Statement Dr.	Income Statement Cr.	Balance Sheet Dr.	Balance Sheet Cr.
101	Cash	47,000				47,000				47,000	
102	Investments in Bonds	50,000				50,000				50,000	
103	Accounts Receivable	88,000				88,000				88,000	
104	Allowance for Doubtful Accounts		900		(b) 850		1,750				1,750
105	Interest Receivable			(d) 1,500		1,500				1,500	
106	Inventory	26,000				26,000				26,000	
107	Building	45,000				45,000				45,000	
108	Accumulated Depreciation —Bldg		12,000		(c) 3,000		15,000				15,000
109	Delivery Trucks	33,000				33,000				33,000	
110	Accumulated Depreciation —Trucks		6,000		(c) 3,600		9,600				9,600
200	Accounts Payable		19,000				19,000				19,000
201	Notes Payable		8,000				8,000				8,000
202	Wages Payable				(a) 700		700				700
203	Income Taxes Payable				(e) 21,065		21,065				21,065
300	Common Stock		85,000				85,000				85,000
301	Retained Earnings		55,100				55,100				55,100
400	Sales		165,000				165,000		165,000		
401	Interest Revenue		5,000		(d) 1,500		6,500		6,500		
500	Operating Expense	37,000				37,000		37,000			
501	Wages Expense			(a) 700		700		700			
502	Depreciation Expense—Bldg			(c) 3,000		3,000		3,000			
503	Depreciation Expense —Trucks			(c) 3,600		3,600		3,600			
504	Bad Debts Expense			(b) 850		850		850			
505	Cost of Goods Sold	30,000				30,000		30,000			
506	Income Tax Expense			(e) 21,065		21,065		21,065			
		$356,000	$356,000	$ 30,715	$ 30,715	$386,715	$386,715				
								96,215	171,500		
	Net Income							75,285			75,285
								$197,500	$197,500	$290,500	$290,500

	Account	Debit	Credit
f.	Interest Revenue	6,500	
	Sales	165,000	
	Cost of Goods Sold		30,000
	Operating Expenses		37,000
	Wages Expense		700
	Depreciation Expense—Bldg		3,000
	Depreciation Expense—Trucks		3,600
	Bad Debts Expense		850
	Income Tax Expense		21,065
	Income Summary		75,285
	(To close revenues and expenses to income summary)		
	Income Summary	75,285	
	Retained Earnings		75,285
	(To close income summary to retained earnings)		

4

Income Statement and Related Information

CHAPTER STUDY OBJECTIVES

1. Identify the uses and limitations of an income statement.
2. Prepare a single-step income statement.
3. Prepare a multiple-step income statement.
4. Explain how irregular items are reported.
5. Explain intraperiod tax allocation.
6. Explain where earnings per share information is reported.
7. Prepare a retained earnings statement.
8. Explain how other comprehensive income is reported.

*9. Measure and report gains and losses from discontinued operations.

CHAPTER REVIEW

1. Chapter 4 presents a detailed discussion of the concepts and techniques that underlie the preparation of the Income Statement and Statement of Retained Earnings. The requirements for adequate presentation of reported net income are described and illustrated throughout the chapter.

2. (S.O. 1) The income statement helps users of financial statements (1) evaluate the past performance of the enterprise, (2) provide a basis for predicting future performance, and (3) help assess the risk or uncertainty of achieving future cash flows. The limitations of the income statement include (1) items that cannot be measured reliably are not reported in the income statement, (2) income numbers are affected by the accounting methods employed, and (3) income measurement involves judgment.

3. Quality of earnings is important because markets are based on trust and it is imperative that investors have faith in the numbers reported. If that trust is damaged, capital markets will be damaged.

Capital Maintenance Approach vs. Transaction Approach

4. The major elements of net income, as described in Chapter 2, are: **revenues, expenses, gains,** and **losses.** The distinction between revenues and gains and the distinction between expenses and losses depend to a great extent on the typical activities of a business enterprise. When inflows or enhancements of assets result from typical business activities (generally the activities the entity is in business to perform), revenues result. Likewise, outflows or the using up of assets resulting from typical business activities will generate expenses. Nontypical business activities resulting in inflows or outflows of assets will normally generate transactions classified as gains or losses.

* *Note: All asterisked (*) items relate to material contained in the Appendix to the chapter.*

Single-Step vs. Multiple-Step

5. (S.O. 2 and 3) The income statement may be presented in the **single-step format** or the **multiple-step format.** Single-step income statements derive their name from the fact that total costs and expenses are subtracted from total revenues in a "single step" to arrive at net income. Income taxes are normally shown as a separate item among the expenses (usually last) to indicate their relationship to income before taxes. The multiple-step format separates results achieved by regular operations of the entity from those obtained by nonoperating activities. Expenses are also classified by function such as cost of sales, selling, and administrative. The multiple-step format provides more information to financial statement users than does the single-step format; however, both are found in actual practice.

6. An income statement is composed of various sections that relate to different aspects of the earning process. The seven sections identified in the chapter, in the general order of their appearance in the income statement, are:

1. **Operating Section.** Revenues and expenses from the entity's principal operations.
   A. **Sales or revenue section.**
   B. **Cost of goods sold section.**
   C. **Selling expenses.**
   D. **Administrative or general expenses.**
2. **Nonoperating Section.** Revenues and expenses resulting from secondary or auxiliary activities of the company.
   A. **Other revenues and gains.**
   B. **Other expenses and losses.**
3. **Income Tax.** All taxes levied on income from continuing operations.
4. **Discontinued Operations.** Material gains and losses resulting from disposal of a segment of the business.
5. **Extraordinary Items.** Unusual and infrequent material gains and losses.
6. **Cumulative Effect of a Change in Accounting Principle.**
7. **Earnings Per Share.**

The informative content of the income statement may be further enhanced by adding additional subsections to the above major sections.

All-Inclusive Concept vs. Current Operating Performance Concept

7. (S.O. 4) For the most part, accountants tend to agree on the composition of items included on the income statement. However, certain unusual items have stirred controversy in regard to the effect they should have on the presentation of net income. Some accountants favor an **all-inclusive concept** that reports the unusual items directly in the income statement. Those who support the **current operating performance concept** to income measurement believe that the unusual items should be closed directly to retained earnings (not included in computing net income). *APB Opinion No. 9* adopted a modified all-inclusive concept and requires application of this approach in practice.

Reporting Irregular Items

8. In an attempt to provide financial statement users with the ability to better determine the long-range earning power of an enterprise, certain professional pronouncements require that the following irregular items be highlighted in the income statement.

A. **Discontinued operations.**
B. **Extraordinary items.**
C. **Unusual gains and losses.**
D. **Changes in accounting principle.**
E. **Changes in estimates.**

Discontinued Operations

9. An entity is said to have experienced a discontinuance of operations when it **disposes of a segment** of its business. To qualify as discontinued operations, the assets, results of operations, and activities of a segment of a business must be clearly distinguishable, physically and operationally, from the other assets, results of operations, and activities of the entity. When an entity decides to dispose of a segment of its business, certain classification and disclosure requirements must be met. A separate income statement category for gain or loss from disposal of a segment of a business must be provided. In addition, the results of operations of a segment that has been or will be disposed of is reported in conjunction with the gain or loss on disposal—separately from continuing operations.

Extraordinary Items

10. **Extraordinary items** are defined as material items that are **unusual in nature** and **occur infrequently.** Both characteristics must exist for an item to be classified as an extraordinary item on the income statement. Only rarely does an event or transaction clearly meet both criteria and thus gives rise to an extraordinary gain or loss. If an event or transaction meets both tests, it is shown net of taxes in a separate section of the income statement just above net income.

Unusual Gains and Losses

11. Material gains and losses that are **either** unusual **or** occur infrequently, **but not both,** are excluded from the extraordinary item classification. These items are presented with the normal, recurring revenues, costs, and expenses. If material, these items are disclosed separately; if immaterial, they may be combined with other items in the income statement.

Changes in Accounting Principles

12. A **change in accounting principle** results when an entity adopts a new accounting principle that is different from the one previously used. When this type of change is made, the income statement for the year in which the change occurred will include the cumulative effect of the change computed retroactively. The effect of the change (net of tax) should be disclosed as a separate item following extraordinary items in the income statement.

Changes in Estimates

13. Accountants make extensive use of estimates in preparing financial statements. Adjustments that grow out of the use of estimates in accounting are used in the determination of income for the current period and future periods and are not charged or credited directly to Retained Earnings. It should be noted that **changes in estimates** are not considered errors (prior period adjustments) or extraordinary items.

Intraperiod Tax Allocation

14. (S.O. 5) **Intraperiod tax allocation** is the process of relating the income tax effect of an unusual item to that item when it appears on the income statement. Income tax expense related to **continuing operations** is shown on the income statement at its appropriately computed amount. All other items included in the determination of net income should be shown net of their related tax effect. The tax amount may be disclosed in the income statement or in a footnote.

Earnings per Share

15. (S.O. 6) In general, **earnings per share** represents the ratio of net income minus preferred dividends (income available to common shareholders) divided by the weighted average number of common shares outstanding. It is considered by many financial statement users to be the most significant statistic presented in the financial statements, and **must be disclosed on the face of the income statement.** The presentation of earnings per share should include per share data for (a) income from continuing operations, (b) net income before extraordinary items and cumulative effect of changes in accounting principles, and (c) cumulative effect of changes in accounting principles, when such items are included in the determination of net income. Reporting per share amounts for gain or loss on discontinued operations and gain or loss on extraordinary items is optional.

Retained Earnings

16. (S.O. 7) The **statement of retained earnings** serves to reconcile the balance of the retained earnings account from the beginning to the end of the year. The important information communicated by the statement of retained earnings includes: (a) prior period adjustments (income or loss related to corrections of errors in the financial statements of a prior period), (b) the relationship of dividend distributions to net income for the period, and (c) any transfers to and from retained earnings.

Comprehensive Income

17. (S.O. 8) Items that bypass the income statement are included under the concept of comprehensive income. **Comprehensive income** includes all changes in equity during a period except those resulting from investments by owners and distributions to owners. Recently the FASB evaluated approaches to providing more information about other comprehensive income items. It decided that the components of other comprehensive income must be displayed in one of three ways: (1) a second separate income statement; (2) a combined income statement of comprehensive income, or (3) as part of the statement of stockholders' equity.

*18. **The appendix, Accounting for Discontinued Operations,** discusses the more technical aspects of how gains and losses related to discontinued operations are computed, along with related reporting issues.

GLOSSARY

All-inclusive concept. A concept that states that irregular items be included in net income.

Appropriated retained earnings. Retained earnings that are restricted in accordance with contractual requirements, board of directors' policy, or the apparent necessity of the moment.

Change in accounting principle. The use of a principle in the current year that is different from the one used in the preceding year.

Comprehensive income. An income amount that includes all revenues and gains, expenses and losses reported in net income, and, in addition it includes gains and losses that bypass net income but affect stockholders' equity.

Change in estimates. Normal, recurring corrections and adjustments.

Current operating performance concept. A concept that states that the net income figure should show only the regular, recurring earnings of the business.

Discontinued operations. The disposal of a significant segment of a business.

Earnings per share. The net income earned by each share of outstanding common stock.

Extraordinary items. Nonrecurring material items that differ significantly from the entity's typical business activities.

Intraperiod tax allocation. The procedure of associating income taxes with the specific item that directly affects the income taxes for the period.

Multiple-step income statement. An income statement that shows numerous steps in determining net income (or net loss), including operating and nonoperating sections.

Prior period adjustments. Items of income or loss related to corrections of errors in the financial statements of a prior period.

Single-step income statement. An income statement that shows only the one step of deducting expenses from revenues to determine net income (or net loss).

Unusual gains and losses. Items that are unusual or infrequent but not both.

CHAPTER OUTLINE

Fill in the outline presented below.

(S.O. 1) Usefulness and Limitations of the Income Statement

(S.O. 2 and 3) Single-Step Income Statement vs. Multiple-Step Income Statement

(S.O. 4) Reporting Irregular Items

Discontinued Operations

Extraordinary Items

Unusual Gains and Losses

Changes in Accounting Principle

Changes in Estimate

(S.O. 5) Intraperiod Tax Allocation

(S.O. 6) Earnings Per Share

Chapter Outline ***(continued)***

(S.O. 7) Retained Earnings Statement

Prior Period Adjustments

Appropriations of Retained Earnings

(S.O. 8) Other Comprehensive Income

*(S.O. 9) Accounting for Discontinued Operations

REVIEW QUESTIONS AND EXERCISES

TRUE-FALSE

Indicate whether each of the following is true (T) or false (F) in the space provided.

_____ 1. (S.O. 1) One of the limitations of the income statement is that items that cannot be measured reliably are not reported in the income statement.

_____ 2. (S.O. 2) The primary advantage of the single-step format lies in the simplicity of presentation and the absence of any implication that one type of revenue or expense item has priority over another.

_____ 3. (S.O. 3) The multiple-step income statement recognizes a separation of operating transactions from nonoperating transactions and matches costs and expenses with related revenues.

_____ 4. (S.O. 3) From a bank loan officer's point of view, the single-step income statement is preferable to the multiple-step income statement.

_____ 5. (S.O. 4) The advocates of the current operating performance concept include extraordinary items in the calculation of net income.

_____ 6. (S.O. 4) A manufacturer of computer hardware who sells all computer manufacturing facilities located in foreign countries can record the transaction as a disposal of a segment.

_____ 7. (S.O. 4) Phasing out of a product line or class of service is a disposal of assets that qualifies as a disposal of a segment of a business.

_____ 8. (S.O. 4) The results of operations of a segment that has been or will be disposed of need not be separated from the results of continuing operations as long as the gain or loss from the disposal is shown separately.

_____ 9. (S.O. 4) Extraordinary items are events and transactions that are distinguished by their unusual nature and the infrequency of their occurrence.

_____ 10. (S.O. 4) An example of an extraordinary loss, reported as a separate item in the income statement, is a large write-down of accounts receivable caused by the unexpected bankruptcy of a major customer.

_____ 11. (S.O. 4) An example of an extraordinary loss would be when a corporation has received significant losses because of the effects of a strike.

_____ 12. (S.O. 4) The FASB has specifically prohibited a net-of-tax treatment for gains and losses that are either unusual or nonrecurring but not both.

_____ 13. (S.O. 4) Adjustments that grow out of the use of estimates in accounting are not classified as prior period adjustments.

_____ 14. (S.O. 4) The effect on net income of adopting a new accounting principle should be disclosed as a separate item following extraordinary items in the income statement.

____ 15. (S.O. 4) A change in accounting principle is considered appropriate only when it is demonstrated that the newly adopted principle is preferable to the old one.

_____ 16. (S.O. 5) Intraperiod tax allocation causes a reduction in total income tax expense for the period in which it is used.

_____ 17. (S.O. 6) Because of it importance, earnings per share is required to be disclosed on the face of the income statement.

_____ 18. (S.O. 6) The presentation of earnings per share is affected by the existence of prior period adjustments.

____ 19. (S.O. 7) The statement of retained earnings provides a reconciliation of the retained earnings account from the beginning of the year to the end of the year.

_____ 20. (S.O. 7) The statement of retained earnings shows the total change in stockholders' equity for a specified period.

_____ 21. (S.O. 7) A prior period adjustment results from the correction of an error in the financial statements of a prior period discovered subsequent to their issuance.

_____ 22. (S.O. 7) Prior period adjustments should be charged or credited to the opening balance of retained earnings and, thus, excluded from the determination of net income for the current period.

_____ 23. (S.O. 8) According to the FASB, displaying comprehensive income as a part of the statement of stockholders' equity is one of the acceptable ways of presenting comprehensive income items.

_____*24. (S.O. 9) For the period up to the time management commits itself to sell a division, the revenues and expenses of the discontinued operations are included in the aggregate income from operations of the company.

_____*25. (S.O. 9) The reason for aggregating the income (loss) from the measurement date to the disposal date and the gain (loss) on the disposal of the net assets is that the selling company needs a reasonable period to phase out its discontinued operations.

MULTIPLE CHOICE

Select the best answer for each of the following items and enter the corresponding letter in the space provided.

_____ 1. (S.O. 1) Which of the following would represent the least likely use of an income statement prepared for a business enterprise?

A. Use by customers to determine a company's ability to provide needed goods and services.
B. Use by labor unions to examine earnings closely as a basis for salary discussions.
C. Use by government agencies to formulate tax and economic policy.
D. Use by investors interested in the financial position of the entity.

_____ 2. (S.O. 1) The primary reason the income statement is so important to investors and creditors relates to its ability to provide information helpful in

A. determining the honesty of those involved in managing the enterprise.
B. assessing the financial position of the entity at a point in time.
C. predicting the amount, timing, and uncertainty of future cash flows.
D. determining the amount of future income the entity may generate from current operations.

_____ 3. (S.O. 1) The income statement reveals:

A. resources and equities of a firm at a point in time.
B. resources and equities of a firm for a period of time.
C. net earnings (net income) of a firm at a point in time.
D. net earnings (net income) of a firm for a period of time.

_____ 4. (S.O. 3) During the year 2002, Siska Corporation had the following information available related to its income statement:

Disbursements for purchases	$630,000
Increase in trade accounts payable	80,000
Decrease in merchandise inventory	25,000

Cost of goods sold for 2002 amounted to

A. $735,000
B. $685,000
C. $575,000
D. $525,000

_____ 5. (S.O. 3) The occurrence that most likely would have no effect on 2002 net income is the:

A. sale in 2002 of an office building contributed by a stockholder in 1956.
B. collection in 2002 of a dividend from an investment.
C. correction of an error in the financial statements of a prior period discovered subsequent to their issuance.
D. stock purchased in 1988 deemed worthless in 2002.

____ 6. (S.O. 3) One of the primary benefits of the multiple-step income statement over the single-step income statement is that the

A. multiple-step income statement shows gross margin and recognizes different types of costs and expenses.
B. multiple-step income statement shows last year's figures in comparison with the current year.
C. multiple-step income statement discriminates between administrative and selling expenses.
D. multiple-step income statement recognizes no distinction in types of costs or expenses.

____ 7. (S.O. 4) Any gain or loss experienced by a concern, whether directly or indirectly related to operations, contributes to the long-run profitability and should be included in the computation of net income. Those who favor such a philosophy adhere to the

	Current Operating Performance Concept	All-Inclusive Concept
A.	Yes	Yes
B.	No	No
C.	Yes	No
D.	No	Yes

____ 8. (S.O. 4) Which of the following asset disposals would qualify as a disposal of a segment?

A. Phasing out of a product line or class of service.
B. Changes occasioned by a technological improvement.
C. Sale by an auto parts manufacturer of one of its five parts-manufacturing subsidiaries.
D. Sale by a transportation company of its bus operations but not its airline operations.

____ 9. (S.O. 4) Material gains or losses resulting from the disposition of a segment of the business should be reported separately as a component of income

A. after cumulative effect of accounting changes and before extraordinary items.
B. after results from continuing operations and before extraordinary items.
C. before cumulative effect of accounting changes and after extraordinary items.
D. before results from continuing operations and after cumulative effect of accounting changes.

____ 10. (S.O. 4) To be classified on an income statement as an extraordinary item, the transaction or event must be material in nature and

	Unusual	Occur Infrequently
A.	Yes	Yes
B.	No	Yes
C.	Yes	No
D.	No	No

_____ 11. (S.O. 4) An income statement shows "income before income taxes and extraordinary items" in the amount of $685,000. The income taxes payable for the year are $360,000, including $120,000 that is applicable to an extraordinary gain. Thus, the "income before extraordinary items" is:

A. $445,000.
B. $205,000.
C. $465,000.
D. $225,000.

_____ 12. (S.O. 4) Which of the following should not be reported on the income statement as an extraordinary item?

A. The write-off of major assets as a result of new environmental laws prohibiting their use.
B. The write-off of a large receivable resulting from a customer's bankruptcy proceedings.
C. A large loss as a result of an earthquake.
D. Expropriation of assets by a foreign government.

_____ 13. (S.O. 4) In order to be classified as an extraordinary item in the income statement, an event or transaction should be

A. unusual in nature and infrequent; but it need **not** be material.
B. unusual in nature and material; but it need not be infrequent.
C. infrequent and material; but it need **not** be unusual in nature.
D. unusual in nature, infrequent, and material.

_____ 14. (S.O. 4) Which of the following should be reported on the income statement as an extraordinary item?

A. The gain on disposal of a segment of a business.
B. The writedown of receivables deemed uncollectible.
C. The loss from volcanic activity.
D. The gain from a sale of equipment.

_____ 15. (S.O. 4) In general, the basic difference between the concepts of revenues and gains concerns:

A. the materiality of the item being considered.
B. whether the event giving rise to the item relates to the typical activity of the enterprise.
C. whether the item is taxable in the current year.
D. the effect on total assets of the enterprise.

_____ 16. (S.O. 4) When a manufacturing company sells one of its plant assets at a price in excess of its book value it should recognize

	Revenue	Gain
A.	No	Yes
B.	No	No
C.	Yes	No
D.	Yes	Yes

____ 17. (S.O. 4) When a company changes from one accounting principle to another accounting principle, the income statement for the year of change:

A. will normally not be affected, as this event is taken directly to Retained Earnings.
B. should include only footnote disclosure so readers will be aware of the change.
C. should include the cumulative effect, based on a retroactive computation, disclosed as a separate-line item.
D. should include the effect of the change related to the current year only and be disclosed as a separate line item.

____ 18. (S.O. 4) Which of the following items would be presented in the income statement only in the account affected (not in a separate section)?

A. Changes in estimates.
B. Changes in principle.
C. Extraordinary items.
D. Discontinued operations.

____ 19. (S.O. 4) Changing the basis of inventory pricing from FIFO to average cost is an example of a(n):

A. Extraordinary item.
B. Change in principle.
C. Change in estimate.
D. Discontinued operation.

____ 20. (S.O. 4) The concept that reports extraordinary items in the income statement is called:

A. phase-out period concept.
B. prior period adjustment concept.
C. current operating performance concept.
D. all-inclusive concept.

____ 21. (S.O. 5) A material item which is unusual in nature or infrequent in occurrence, but not both should be shown in the income statement

	Net of Tax	Disclosed Separately
A.	No	No
B.	Yes	Yes
C.	No	Yes
D.	Yes	No

____ 22. (S.O. 6) Earnings per share should always be shown separately for:

A. net income and gross margin.
B. net income and pretax income.
C. income before extraordinary items.
D. extraordinary items and prior period adjustments.

_____ 23. (S.O. 6) Which of the following is **not** a generally practiced method of presenting the income statement?

A. The consolidated statement of income.
B. The multiple-step income statement.
C. Including gains and losses from discontinued operations of a segment of a business in determining net income.
D. Including prior-period adjustments in determining net income.

_____ *24. (S.O. 9) On April 30, 2001, Sonoda Corporation, whose fiscal year end is September 30, adopted a plan to discontinue the operations of Kaori Division on November 30, 2001. Kaori contributed a major portion of Sonoda's sales volume. Sonoda estimated that Kaori would sustain a loss of $460,000 from May 1, 2001, through September 30, 2001, and would sustain an additional loss of $220,000 from October 1, 2001, to November 30, 2001. Sonoda also estimated that it would realize a gain of $600,000 on the sale of Kaori's assets. At September 30, 2001, Sonoda determined that Kaori had actually lost $1,120,000 for the fiscal year, of which $420,000 represented the loss from May 1 to September 30, 2001.

Ignoring income tax effects, how much should Sonoda report in its September 30, 2001, financial statements as gain or loss on disposal of Kaori?

A. $ 40,000 loss.
B. $ 80,000 loss.
C. $180,000 gain.
D. $600,000 gain.

_____ *25. (S.O. 9) When a segment of a business has been discontinued during the year, the gain or loss on disposal should

A. be an extraordinary item.
B. exclude operating losses during the phase-out period.
C. include operating losses of the current period up to the measurement date.
D. be net of applicable income taxes.

REVIEW EXERCISES

1. (S.O. 3 and 4) Kubitz Co. had the following amounts in its income statements:

	2001	2002	2003
Sales	46,800	_____	78,000
Beginning Inventory	_____	14,200	16,400
Purchases (Net)	20,050	50,200	_____
Ending Inventory	14,200	_____	18,600
Cost of Goods Sold	_____	48,000	_____
Gross Margin	10,800	14,400	18,000
Operating Expenses	_____	_____	6,000
Income Before Tax	8,800	_____	_____
Tax Expense (40%)	_____	2,560	_____
Net Income (Net Loss)	_____	3,840	_____

Instructions: Complete the tabulation by filling in the missing amounts.

2. (S.O. 4) Schmitt, Inc., a retail store, has the following data for the year ended December 31, 2002:

Sales	$90,000
Extraordinary loss due to hurricane	5,000
Income tax saving on extraordinary loss	(1,100)
Cost of goods sold	55,000
Interest expense	1,000
Selling expenses	11,000
Income tax expense on operations	4,400
General and administrative expenses	3,000
Shares of capital stock outstanding, 10,000	

Instructions:
Develop an income statement for Schmitt, Inc. for the year ended December 31, 2002.

3. (S.O. 5) The following items are presented on financial statements:

   A. Extraordinary items.
   B. Material gains or losses, not considered extraordinary items.
   C. Prior period adjustments.
   D. Changes in estimates.
   E. Changes in principle.
   F. Discontinued operations.

   Instructions: For each of the items listed above, describe (a) the criteria used to identify the item and (b) its placement on the financial statements. Assume that each item is material.

4. (S.O. 4) The following accounts are taken from the adjusted trial balance of Tamara Company as of December 31, 2002.

Common Stock (100,000 shares)	$ 300,000	Purchases	$ 485,600
Transportation-in	12,600	Sales Returns	15,900
Rent Revenue	28,500	Purchase Discounts	12,100
Administrative Expense (Total)	145,800	Gain on Sale of Land	18,300
Merchandise Inventory (12/31)	117,500	Selling Expense (Total)	186,800
Sales Discounts	9,500	Merchandise Inventory (1/1)	96,200
Bond Interest Expense	14,300	Retained Earnings (1/1)	226,900
Sales	1,265,000	Dividend Income	17,700

The gain on the sale of the land is not an extraordinary item. All income is taxed at a uniform rate of 42% except for the gain on the sale of the land, which is taxed at 25%.

Instructions:
Prepare a multiple-step income statement for Tamara Company for the year ended December 31, 2002.

5. (S.O. 4, 5, 6, 7 and 8) Presented below is financial information of the Mickey Corporation for 2002.

Beginning Retained Earnings, 1/1/02	$ 950,000
Gain on the sale of investments (normal recurring)	110,000
Sales for the year	30,000,000
Loss due to flood damage (unusual & infrequent)	125,000*
Cost of goods sold	21,000,000
Loss on disposal of retail division	450,000*
Interest revenue	70,000
Loss on operations of retail division	460,000*
Selling and administrative expenses	5,500,000
Dividends declared on common stock	230,000
Write off of goodwill	520,000
Dividends declared on preferred stock	80,000
Federal income tax for 2002	1,600,000

Mickey Corporation decided to discontinue its retail operations and to retain their manufacturing operations. On August 15, Mickey sold the retail operations to Schoen Company. During 2002, there were 250,000 shares of common stock outstanding all year.

**net of tax*

Instructions:
Prepare a multi-step income statement and retained earnings statement.

5. *(continued)*

SOLUTIONS TO REVIEW QUESTIONS AND EXERCISES

TRUE-FALSE

1. (T)

2. (T)

3. (T)

4. (F) The multiple-step income statement allows a user the opportunity to observe numerous relationships among revenue and expense data. Thus, it is more suitable for use by a bank loan officer than is the single-step income statement.

5. (F) Advocates of the current operating performance concept argue that the net income figure should show only the regular recurring earnings of the business based on its normal operations. Extraordinary items are financial gains or losses that are not expected to recur frequently and would not be considered as recurring in the normal operating process of the business.

6. (F) To qualify as a disposal of a segment, the entity must completely divest itself of operations in a particular line of business. The entity depicted in this question is still in the computer business, so the sale of the foreign manufacturing facilities does not qualify as a disposal of a segment.

7. (F) Phasing out of a product line or class of service is a disposal of assets that does **not** qualify as disposals of a segment of a business.

8. (F) According to generally accepted accounting principles, the assets, results of operations, and activities of a segment of a business must be clearly distinguishable from the other assets, results of operations, and activities of the entity to qualify for discontinued operations treatment.

9. (T)

10. (F) To be classified as an extraordinary item, an event must (a) be unusual in nature and (b) occur infrequently. The write-off of a large account receivable due to the unexpected bankruptcy of a major customer is an event that is neither unusual nor infrequent. Any business that extends credit to a customer risks loss due to the insolvency of the customer.

11. (F) The APB specified various gains and losses which are **not** extraordinary items, of which effects of a strike is included.

12. (T)

13. (T)

14. (T)

15. (T)

16. (F) Intraperiod tax allocation is a method designed to relate the income tax expense of the fiscal period to the items that affect the amount of the tax provision. Use of this method does not affect the income tax expense for the period, merely the manner in which the income tax expense is presented.

17. (T)

18. (F) Because prior period adjustments are carried directly to retained earnings, the presentation of earnings per share, which is included in the income statement, is unaffected.

19. (T)

20. (F) The statement of retained earnings presents a reconciliation of the balance of the retained earnings account from the beginning to the end of the year. This statement does not include information about the other accounts that appear in an entity's equity section.

21. (T)

22. (T)

23. (T)

*24. (F) The revenues and expenses of the discontinued operations up to the time management commits itself to sell a division would be reported on the income statement in the discontinued operations section. The time management commits itself to sell a division is the **measurement date** and income (loss) from the measurement date to the disposal date would be included in the gain or loss on disposal.

*25. (T)

MULTIPLE CHOICE

1. (D) Customers, labor unions, and government agencies may well make use of the income statement for the reasons noted in alternatives A, B, and C respectively. However, the income statement reports results of operations, not financial position. To determine financial position of an entity the investor would have to refer to the information in a balance sheet.

2. (C) Investors and creditors are most interested in the ability of the entity to generate cash flows into the future. Accurate predictions of future cash flows help investors assess the economic value of the enterprise and creditors determine the probability of repayment of their claims against the enterprise. The honesty of management or future income from current operations are not items primarily measured by the income statement. Also, financial position is a balance sheet concept.

3. (D) The income statement is defined as the financial statement of a business entity that reveals net earnings for a period of time.

4. (A) Cash payments for purchases totaled $630,000, but the amount of merchandise purchased in 2002 exceeded this amount by the $80,000 increase in trade accounts payable. Merchandise inventory decreased by $25,000, which means beginning inventory exceeded ending inventory by this amount. Thus, this amount would have to be added to the cash payment amount to arrive at cost of goods sold as follows:

Amount paid for purchases..........................	$630,000
Add increase in trade payables	80,000
Add decrease in inventory...........................	25,000
2002 Cost of goods sold	$735,000

5. (C) Prior period adjustments should be charged or credited to the opening balance of retained earnings and, thus, excluded from the determination of net income.

6. (A) One of the primary benefits of the multiple-step over the single-step income statement is that the multiple-step income statement shows gross margin and recognizes different types of costs and expenses. Analysts often find the multiple-step income statement useful in computing ratios and distinguishing operating and nonoperating activities. A single-step income statement generally has just two categories: (1) revenues and (2) expenses.

7. (D) This statement reflects a philosophy of net income known as the All-Inclusive Concept. Advocates of the all-inclusive concept to net income presentation insist that both regular earnings of the business and irregular gains and losses be included in net income because they reflect the long-range income producing ability of the enterprise.

8. (D) The only disposal that qualifies as a disposal of a segment is the disposal by the transportation company of its entire bus operations. This company remains in the transportation business, but an entire segment of the business has been terminated. Items (A), (B), and (C) are specific examples of asset disposals that do not qualify as disposals of a segment.

9. (B) The effects of discontinued operations are shown net of tax as a separate category in the income statement after continuing operations but before extraordinary items.

10. (A) Extraordinary items are events and transactions that are distinguished by their unusual nature and by the infrequency of their occurrence. **Both** of these criteria must be met to classify an event or transaction as an extraordinary item.

11. (A)

Income before tax and extraordinary item..................	$685,000
Income tax ($360,000 - $120,000)..........................	240,000
Income before extraordinary item...........................	$445,000

12. (B) The criteria for treating an item as extraordinary are: (a) the item must be unusual in nature and (b) its occurrence should not reasonably be expected to recur in the foreseeable future. Alternatives (A), (C), and (D) clearly meet the two criteria. Alternative (B) is not unusual in the business world, and it is always possible that such an event could recur.

13. (D) APB No. 30 describes the criteria to be used in classifying an event as extraordinary, an event or transaction must be material and meet **both** of the following criteria: The event must be (1) unusual in nature, and (2) characterized by its infrequency of occurrence. Answer (A) is incorrect because Opinions of the Accounting Principles Board need not be applied to immaterial items. Answers (B) and (C) are incorrect because material events must meet **both** the criteria of being unusual **and** infrequent to be classified as extraordinary.

14. (C) The loss from volcanic activity would be considered unusual in nature and occur infrequently and therefore should be classified as an extraordinary item. Alternatives (A), (B) and (D) do not meet the criteria of being unusual in nature and occurring infrequently.

15. (B) Revenues represent inflows from activities that constitute the entity's ongoing major or central operations. Gains, on the other hand, represent increases in equity from peripheral or incidental transactions of an entity. The concepts of materiality (A) or taxability (C) have nothing to do with distinguishing revenues from gains.

16. (A) Gains are increases in equity (net assets) resulting from peripheral or incidental transactions of an entity. The sale of plant assets by a manufacturing company is not a part of its regular operations and thus results in a gain rather than revenue.

17. (C) The effect on net income of a change from one accounting principle to another should be disclosed as a separate item following extraordinary items in the income statement. These types of changes are recognized by including in the income statement of the current year the cumulative effect (net of tax), based on a retroactive computation, of changing to a new accounting principle.

18. (A) Changes in estimates are presented in the income statement only in the account affected. Alternatives (B), (C) and (D) are all items that would be presented in a separate section of the income statement.

19. (B) Changing the basis of inventory pricing from FIFO to average cost is an example of a change in principle.

20. (D) The all-inclusive concept of income holds that any gain or loss experienced by a concern, whether directly or indirectly related to operations contributes to its long-run profitability and should be included in the computation of net income.

21. (C) A material item that is unusual in nature or infrequent in occurrence, but not both must be disclosed separately above extraordinary items, but may not be shown net-of-tax. The reason the Board prohibited net-of-tax treatment is so statement users could easily differentiate extraordinary items from material items that are unusual or infrequent, but not both.

22. (C) Earnings per share must be disclosed on the face of the income statement. In addition to net income per share, per share amounts should be shown for income from continuing operations, income before extraordinary items and cumulative effect of changes in accounting principles, and cumulative effect of changes in accounting principles. Reporting per share amounts for gain or loss on discontinued operations and gain or loss on extraordinary items is optional.

23. (D) FASB No. 16 stipulates that prior period adjustments are to be excluded from the determination of income for the current period. Answers (A), (B), and (C) are incorrect because it is generally accepted practice to prepare a consolidated statement of income, multiple-step income statement, and to include gains and losses from discontinued operations of a segment in determining net income.

*24 (A) APB No. 30 requires that the gain or loss from the disposal of a segment of a business be shown separately as part of a separate category on the income statement immediately after income from continuing operations but before extraordinary items. The calculation of the estimated gain or loss on a segment disposal should include (1) the estimated operating results from the measurement date to the disposal date and (2) the estimated gain or loss on the disposal of the segment's net assets. Following this process, if a loss is estimated, it should be recognized at the measurement date. However, if a gain is estimated, it should not be recognized until the disposal date. Since Sonoda Corporation estimates a $40,000 loss on disposal of Kaori Division, it should recognize this loss immediately (in the year ending 9/30/01). This $40,000 loss can be calculated as follows:

Operating loss during phase-out period	
Actual loss sustained 5/1/01 to 9/30/01	$420,000
Estimated operating loss 10/1/01 to 11/30/01	220,000
Total actual and estimated operating loss during phase-out period	$640,000
Less: Estimated gain on sale of Kaori asset	600,000
Loss on disposal of Kaori Division	$ 40,000

*25. (D) APB No. 30 requires that the gain or loss on disposal of a segment of a business be shown as a part of a separate category on the income statement, net of the income tax effects. Answer (A) is incorrect because APB No. 30 specifically excludes gains and losses on segment disposals from the extraordinary classification. Answer (B) is incorrect because operating losses during the phase-out period should be included in the determination of the gain or loss on segment disposal. Answer (C) is incorrect because operating losses of the current period up to the measurement date must be separately disclosed in the income statement immediately before gains and losses on disposal of a segment.

REVIEW EXERCISES

1.

	2001	2002	2003
Sales	46,800	**62,400**	78,000
Beginning Inventory	**30,150**	14,200	16,400
Purchases (Net)	20,050	50,200	**62,200**
Ending Inventory	14,200	**16,400**	18,600
Cost of Goods Sold	**36,000**	48,000	**60,000**
Gross Margin of Profit	10,800	14,400	18,000
Operating Expenses	**2,000**	**8,000**	6,000
Income Before Tax	8,800	**6,400**	**12,000**
Tax Expense (40%)	**3,520**	2,560	**4,800**
Net Income (Net Loss)	**5,280**	3,840	**7,200**

2.

Schmitt Corporation
Income Statement
Year Ending December 31, 2002

Sales	$90,000	
Cost of goods sold	55,000	
Gross margin		$35,000
Operating Expenses		
Selling expenses	$11,000	
General and administrative	3,000	
Total operating expenses		14,000
Income from operations		21,000
Other Expenses and Losses		
Interest expense		1,000
Income before tax		20,000
Income tax		4,400
Income before extraordinary items		15,600
Extraordinary items:		
Loss due to hurricane	5,000	
Less: Income tax saved	1,100	3,900
Net income		$11,700
Earnings per share:		
Income before extraordinary items ($15,600 ÷ 10,000)		$1.56
Extraordinary items ($3,900 ÷ 10,000)		(.39)
Net income ($11,700 ÷ 10,000)		1.17

3.

Item	Criteria	Placement
A. Extraordinary items	Material, unusual *and* non-recurring.	Separate section in the income statement labeled "extraordinary items."
B. Material gains or losses not considered extra-ordinary	Unusual *or* infrequent, but not both. Typical of customary business activity.	Separate section in the income statement above income before extraordinary items.
C. Prior period adjustments	Corrections of errors in previously issued financial statement of a prior period.	Direct adjustment to the begin-ning balance of retained earn-ings.
D. Changes in estimates	Normal, recurring corrections or adjustments to estimate.	Change in income statement only in the account affected.
E. Changes in principle	Change from one accounting principle to another.	Cumulative effect of the adjustment is reflected in the income statement as a separate item following extraordinary items.
F. Discontinued operations	Disposal of a segment of a business constituting a separ-ate line of business or a class of customer.	Separate section in the income statement after continuing operations but before extra-ordinary items.

4.

Tamara Company
Income Statement
For the Year Ended December 31, 2002

Revenues			
Sales			$1,265,000
Less: Sales discounts		$ 9,500	
Sales returns		15,900	25,400
Net sales			1,239,600
Cost of Goods Sold			
Merchandise inventory, 1/1		96,200	
Purchases	$485,600		
Less purchase discounts	12,100		
Net purchases	473,500		
Transportation-in	12,600	$486,100	
Merchandise available for sale		582,300	
Less merchandise inventory, 12/31		117,500	
Cost of goods sold			464,800
Gross profit on sales			774,800
Operating Expenses			
Selling Expenses		186,800	
Administrative Expenses		145,800	332,600
Income from operations			442,200
Other Revenues and Gains			
Rent revenue		28,500	
Dividend income		17,700	
Gain on sale of land		18,300	64,500
			506,700
Other Expenses and Losses			
Bond interest expense			14,300
Income before tax			492,400
Income tax ($474,100 x .42 + $18,300 x .25)			203,697
Net income for the year			$288,703
Earnings per share ($288,703 ÷ 100,000)			$2.89

5.

Mickey Corporation
Income Statement
For The Year Ended December 31, 2002

Sales		$30,000,000
Cost of goods sold		21,000,000
Gross profit		9,000,000
Less selling and administrative expenses		5,500,000
Income from operations		3,500,000
Other revenues and gains:		
Interest revenue	70,000	
Gain on sale of investments	110,000	180,000
Other expenses and losses:		
Write-off of goodwill		520,000
Income from operations before income tax		3,160,000
Income tax		1,600,000
Income from continuing operations		1,560,000
Discontinued operations		
Loss from operations, net of tax	460,000	
Loss from disposition, net of tax	450,000	910,000
Income before extraordinary item		650,000
Extraordinary loss from flood, net of tax		125,000
Net income		$ 525,000

Earnings per share:		
Income from continuing operations		$5.92a
Discontinued operations:		
Loss from operations (net of tax)	$(1.84)	
Loss from disposition (net of tax)	(1.80)	(3.64)
Income before extraordinary item		2.28b
Extraordinary loss (net of tax)		(.50)
Net income		$1.78c

Mickey Corporation
Retained Earnings Statement
For the Year Ended December 31, 2002

Beginning balance of retained earnings		$ 950,000
Add Net income		525,000
Subtotal		1,475,000
Less dividends:		
Preferred stock	80,000	
Common stock	230,000	310,000
Ending balance of retained earnings		$1,165,000

a: $\frac{\$1,560,000 - \$80,000}{250,000 \text{ shares}} = \$5.92$

b: $\frac{\$650,000 - \$80,000}{250,000 \text{ shares}} = \$2.28$

c: $\frac{\$525,000 - \$80,000}{250,000 \text{ shares}} = \$1.78$

5

Balance Sheet and Statement of Cash Flows

CHAPTER STUDY OBJECTIVES

1. Identify the uses and limitations of a balance sheet.
2. Identify the major classifications of the balance sheet.
3. Prepare a classified balance sheet using the report and account formats.
4. Identify balance sheet information requiring supplemental disclosure.
5. Identify major disclosure techniques for the balance sheet.
6. Indicate the purpose of the statement of cash flows.
7. Identify the content of the statement of cash flows.
8. Prepare a statement of cash flows.
9. Understand the usefulness of the statement of cash flows.

*10. Identify the major types of financial ratios and what they measure.

CHAPTER REVIEW

1. Chapter 5 presents a detailed discussion of the concepts and techniques that underlie the preparation and analysis of the balance sheet. Along with the mechanics of preparation, acceptable disclosure requirements are examined and illustrated. A brief introduction to the statement of cash flows is also presented. This explanation serves as a foundation for the more comprehensive discussion of this subject presented in Chapter 24. At the end of Chapter 5, a multi-page illustration of the financial statements and accompanying notes of a corporation is presented. This illustration may be referred to throughout your study of intermediate accounting as it includes information relevant to many of the topics discussed in subsequent chapters.

Uses and Limitations of the Balance Sheet

2. (S.O. 1) For many years financial statement users generally considered the income statement to be superior to the balance sheet as a basis for judging the economic well-being of an enterprise. However, the balance sheet can be a very useful financial statement. If a balance sheet is examined carefully, users can gain a considerable amount of information related to **liquidity, solvency** and **financial flexibility.** Liquidity is generally related to the amount of time that is expected to elapse until an asset is realized or otherwise converted into cash or until a liability has to be paid. Solvency refers to the ability of an enterprise to pay its debts as they mature. Financial flexibility is the ability of an enterprise to take effective action to alter the amounts and timing of cash flow so that it can respond to unexpected needs and opportunities.

* *Note: All asterisked (*) items relate to material contained in the Appendices to the chapter.*

3. Criticism of the balance sheet has revolved around the limitations of the information presented therein. These limitations include: (a) failure to reflect current value information, (b) the extensive use of estimates, and (c) failure to include items of financial value that cannot be recorded objectively.

4. The problem with current value information concerns the **reliability** of such information. The estimation process involved in developing current-value type information causes a concern about the objectivity of the resulting financial information. The use of estimates is extensive in the development of balance sheet data. These estimates are required by generally accepted accounting principles, but reflect a limitation of the balance sheet. The limitation concerns the fact that the estimates are only as good as the understanding and objectivity of the person(s) making the estimates. The final limitation of the balance sheet concerns the fact that some significant assets of the entity are not recorded. Items such as human resources (employee workforce), managerial skills, customer base, and reputation are not recorded because such assets are difficult to quantify.

Classification in the Balance Sheet

5. (S.O. 2) The **major classifications** used in the balance sheet are **assets, liabilities,** and **equity.** These items were defined in the discussion presented in Chapter 2. To provide the financial statement reader with additional information, these major classifications are divided into several **subclassifications.** Assets are further classified as **current** or **noncurrent,** with the noncurrent divided among long-term investments; property, plant, and equipment; intangible assets; and other assets. Liabilities are classified as **current** or **noncurrent.** Owners' equity includes capital stock, additional paid-in capital, and retained earnings. These items are defined as follows:

Assets. Probable future economic benefits obtained or controlled by a particular entity as a result of past transactions or events.

Liabilities. Probable future sacrifices of economic benefits arising from present obligations of a particular entity to transfer assets or provide services to other entities in the future as a result of past transactions or events.

Equity. Residual interest in the assets of an entity that remains after deducting its liabilities. In a business enterprise, the equity is the ownership interest.

Current Assets

6. **Current assets** are cash and other assets expected to be converted into cash, sold, or consumed either in one year or in the operating cycle, whichever is longer. There are some exceptions to a literal interpretation of the current asset definition. These exceptions involve prepaid expenses, investments in common stock, and the subsequent years' depreciation of fixed assets. These exceptions are recognized in the accounting process and are understood by most financial statement users. Current assets are presented in the balance sheet in the order of their liquidity and normally include cash, marketable securities, receivables, inventories, and prepaid expenses.

Long-Term Investments

7. Items classified as **long-term investments** in the assets section of the balance sheet normally are one of four types. These include:

a. Investments in securities, such as stock, bonds, or long-term notes.
b. Investments in tangible fixed assets not currently used in operations.
c. Investments set aside in special funds (sinking, pension, plant expansion, etc.) and cash surrender value of life insurance.
d. Investments in nonconsolidated subsidiaries or affiliated companies.

Long-term investments are rather permanent in nature as they are not normally disposed of for a long period of time. They are shown in the balance sheet below current assets in a separate section called **Investments.**

Property, Plant and Equipment

8. **Property, plant, and equipment** are properties of a durable nature that are used in the regular operations of the enterprise. Examples include land, buildings, machinery, furniture, tools, and wasting resources. **Intangible assets** lack physical substance; however, their benefit lies in the rights they convey to the holder. Examples include patents, copyrights, franchises, goodwill, trademarks, trade names, and secret processes.

Other Assets

9. Many companies include an "**Other Assets**" classification in the balance sheet after Property, Plant, and Equipment. This section includes a wide variety of items that do not appear to fall clearly into one of the other classifications. Some of the more common items included in this section are: deferred charges, noncurrent receivables, intangible assets, assets in special funds, and advances to subsidiaries.

Current Liabilities

10. **Current liabilities** are the obligations that are reasonably expected to be liquidated either through the use of current assets or the creation of other current liabilities. Items normally shown in the current liabilities section of the balance sheet include notes and accounts payable, advances received from customers, current maturities of long-term debt, taxes payable, and accrued liabilities. Obligations due to be paid during the next year may be excluded from the current liability section if the item is expected to be refinanced through long-term debt or the item will be paid out of noncurrent assets.

11. **Working capital** is the excess of current assets over current liabilities. This concept, sometimes referred to as net working capital, represents the net amount of a company's relatively liquid resources. By reference to this amount, a financial statement user is able to assess the entity's margin of safety for meeting financial demands of the operating cycle. While the amount of working capital has a definite relationship to liquidity, the reader must analyze the composition of the current assets to determine their nearness to cash.

Long-Term Liabilities

12. **Long-term liabilities** are obligations whose settlement date extends beyond the normal operating cycle or one year, whichever is longer. Examples include bonds payable, notes payable, lease obligations, and pension obligations. Generally, the disclosure requirements for long-term liabilities are quite substantial as a result of various covenants and restrictions included for the protection of the lenders. Long-term liabilities that mature within the current operating cycle are classified as current liabilities if their liquidation requires use of current assets. Long-term liabilities generally fall into one of the three following categories:

a. Obligations arising from specific financing situations, such as the issuance of bonds, long-term lease obligations, and long-term notes payable.
b. Obligations arising from the ordinary operations of the enterprise such as pensions and deferred income taxes.
c. Obligations that are dependent upon the occurrence or non-occurrence of one or more future events to confirm the amount payable such as warranties and other contingencies.

Owners' Equity

13. The **owners' equity section** of the balance sheet includes information related to capital stock, additional paid-in capital, and retained earnings. Preparation of the owners' equity section should be approached with caution because of the various restrictions imposed by state corporation laws, liability agreements, and voluntary actions of the board of directors.

Balance Sheet Format

14. (S.O. 3) The account format of a classified balance sheet lists assets by sections on the left side and liabilities and stockholders' equity by sections on the right side. The report format lists liabilities and stockholders' equity directly below assets on the same page.

Supplemental Information

15. (S.O. 4) Supplemental information related to **contingencies, valuation methods, and contractual situations** provide for elaboration or qualification of items listed in the balance sheet.

16. A **contingency** is defined as an existing situation involving uncertainty as to possible gain (gain contingency) or loss (loss contingency) that will ultimately be resolved when one or more future events occur or fail to occur. In short, they are uncertain occurrences that may have a material effect on financial position.

17. The methods used to value assets and allocate costs vary considerably among balance sheet accounts. To help users of the financial statements understand and evaluate financial statement components and their relationships, these valuation methods are normally disclosed in a separate **Summary of Significant Accounting Policies** preceding the financial statement notes. In addition to contingencies and valuation methods, any contractual situations of significance should be disclosed. These items include pension obligations, lease contracts, stock options, etc.

Techniques of Disclosure

18. (S.O. 5) Effective communication of the information required to be disclosed in financial statements is an important consideration. Accountants have developed certain methods that have proven useful in disclosing pertinent information. The methods are **parenthetical explanations, notes, cross reference and contra items**, and **supporting schedules**. Numerous examples of the techniques of disclosure are presented in the text. These examples should be reviewed as they represent concepts referred to in subsequent chapter material.

Statement of Cash Flows

19. (S.O. 6) A primary objective of financial reporting is to allow financial statement users the opportunity to assess the amounts, timing, and uncertainty of cash flows. The balance sheet, income statement, and retained earnings statement do not provide a convenient source of information on cash flows. Thus, in an attempt to provide a vehicle to help achieve this objective, the Financial Accounting Standards Board requires the presentation of the **Statement of Cash Flows** as a basic financial statement.

20. (S.O. 7) The primary purpose of the statement of cash flows is to provide relevant information about the cash receipts and cash payments of an enterprise during a period. In accomplishing its purpose, the statement focuses attention on three different activities related to cash flows.

a. **Operating activities** involve the cash effects of transactions that enter into determination of net income.
b. **Investing activities** include making and collecting loans and acquiring and disposing of debt and equity and property, plant, and equipment.
c. **Financing activities** involve liability and owners' equity items and include (1) obtaining capital from owners and providing them with return on (and return of) their investment and (2) borrowing money from creditors and repaying the amounts borrowed.

The basic format of the statement of cash flows is shown below.

Statement of Cash Flows

Cash flows from operating activities	$XXX
Cash flows from investing activities	XXX
Cash flows from financing activities	XXX
Net increase (decrease) in cash	XXX
Cash at beginning of year	XXX
Cash at end of year	$XXX

21. (S.O. 8) The information to prepare the statement of cash flows comes from three sources: (a) comparative balance sheets, (b) the current income statement, and (c) selected transaction data. Preparation of the statement of cash flows involves the following steps.

a. Determine the cash provided by operations.
b. Determine the cash provided by or used in investing and financing activities.
c. Determine the change (increase or decrease) in cash during the period.
d. Reconcile the change in cash with the beginning and the ending cash balances.

The information included in this chapter on the preparation of the statement of cash flows provides a basic introduction to the concepts involved. A complete and detailed presentation of the statement of cash flows is found in Chapter 24 of the text.

Usefulness of the Statement of Cash Flows

23. (S.O. 9) Creditors look for answers to the following questions in the company's cash flow statement:

a. How successful is the company in generating net cash provided by operating activities?
b. What are the trends in net cash flow provided by operating activities over time?
c. What are the major reasons for the positive or negative net cash provided by operating activities?

Financial Liquidity

24. The **current cash debt coverage ratio** is:

$$\frac{\text{Net Cash Provided}}{\text{by Operating Activities}} \div \frac{\text{Average Current}}{\text{Liabilities}} = \frac{\text{Current Cash Debt}}{\text{Coverage Ratio}}$$

Free Cash Flow

25. **Free cash flow** is the amount of discretionary cash flow a company has for purchasing additional investments, retiring its debt, purchasing treasury stock, or simply adding to its liquidity.

*Ratio Analysis

26. **Appendix 5A Ratio Analysis--A Reference** demonstrates various ratios used to analyze financial performance.

GLOSSARY

Additional paid-in capital. The excess of amounts paid in over the par or stated value.

Capital stock. The par or stated value of the shares issued.

Contingencies. Material events that have an uncertain future.

Current assets. Cash and other assets expected to be converted into cash, sold, or consumed either in one year or in the operating cycle, whichever is longer.

Current liabilities. Obligations that are reasonably expected to be liquidated either through the use of current assets or the creation of other current liabilities.

Financial flexibility. The ability of an enterprise to take effective actions to alter the amounts and timing of cash flows so it can respond to unexpected needs and opportunities.

Liquidity. The amount of time that is expected to elapse until an asset is realized or otherwise converted into cash or until a liability has to be paid.

Long-term liabilities. Obligations that are not reasonably expected to be liquidated within a year or the normal operating cycle, whichever is longer, but instead, are payable at some date beyond that time.

Retained earnings. The corporation's undistributed earnings.

Solvency. The ability of an enterprise to pay its debts as they mature.

Valuations and accounting policies. Explanations of the valuation methods used or the basic assumptions made concerning inventory valuations, depreciation methods, investments in subsidiaries, etc..

Working capital. The excess of total current assets over total current liabilities.

CHAPTER OUTLINE

Fill in the outline presented below.

(S.O. 1) Usefulness of the Balance Sheet

Limitations of the Balance Sheet

(S.O. 2) Current Assets

Cash

Short-term Investments

Receivables

Inventories

Prepaid Expenses

Long-term Investments

Chapter Outline *(continued)*

Property, Plant & Equipment

Other Assets

Current Liabilities

Long-term Liabilities

Owners' Equity

Capital Stock

Additional Paid-in Capital

Retained Earnings

(S.O. 4) Supplemental Balance Sheet Information

Chapter Outline *(continued)*

Contingencies

Valuations and Accounting Policies

Contractual Situations

(S.O. 5) Techniques of Disclosure

(S.O. 6) Statement of Cash Flows

*(S.O. 9) Ratio Analysis

REVIEW QUESTIONS AND EXERCISES

TRUE-FALSE

Indicate whether each of the following is true (T) or false (F) in the space provided.

_____ 1. (S.O. 1) The balance sheet reflects a corporation's results of operations for a specified period of time.

_____ 2. (S.O. 1) Liquidity is the ability of an enterprise to take effective actions to alter the amounts and timing of cash flows so it can respond to unexpected needs and opportunities.

_____ 3. (S.O. 2) According to the conceptual framework project, individual balance sheet items should be separately reported and classified in sufficient detail to permit users to assess the amounts, timing, and uncertainty of future cash flows.

_____ 4. (S.O. 2) Price level adjusted information should be disclosed in the balance sheet whenever the inflation rate is above 10%.

____ 5. (S.O. 2) The three general classes of items included in the balance sheet are assets, liabilities, and equity.

____ 6. (S.O. 2) Current assets include only assets expected to be sold within one year or the operating cycle, whichever is longer.

_____ 7. (S.O. 2) If cash is restricted for purposes other than the liquidation of current obligations, it should not be classified as a current asset.

_____ 8. (S.O. 2) Available-for-sale investments are debt securities that the enterprise has the positive intent and ability to hold to maturity.

_____ 9. (S.O. 2) Trading securities are reported at fair value in the current asset section.

_____ 10. (S.O. 2) Proper presentation of inventories for a manufacturing concern includes disclosure of the basis of valuation, the method of pricing, and the stage of completion.

_____ 11. (S.O. 2) Companies often include insurance and other prepayments for 2 or 3 years in current assets even though part of the advance payment applies to periods beyond one year or the current operating cycle.

_____ 12. (S.O. 2) Securities classified as available-for-sale should be reported at cost.

_____ 13. (S.O. 2) The use of an other-asset section varies widely in practice. It should be restricted to unusual items that are different from assets included elsewhere.

_____ 14. (S.O. 2) Current liabilities are the obligations that are reasonably expected to be liquidated either by creation of other current liabilities or through the use of current assets.

_____ 15. (S.O. 2) Long-term liabilities are obligations that are not reasonably expected to be liquidated within one year or the normal operating cycle, whichever is longer.

_____ 16. (S.O. 2) The stockholders' equity accounts used by a corporation are the same as those used in accounting for a partnership or proprietorship.

_____ 17. (S.O. 4) A contingent liability and an estimated liability are treated in the same manner for financial statement reporting purposes.

_____ 18. (S.O. 4) It is recommended that there be a disclosure for all significant accounting principles and methods that involve selection from among alternatives or those that are peculiar to a given industry.

_____ 19. (S.O. 4) Contracts and negotiations of significance, in addition to contingencies, are disclosed in footnotes to the financial statements.

_____ 20. (S.O. 4) Notes are commonly used to disclose the existence and amount of any preferred stock dividends in arrears.

_____ 21. (S.O. 5) The AICPA has recommended that the word "reserve" be used only to describe an appropriation of retained earnings.

_____ 22. (S.O. 6) The primary purpose of the statement of cash flows is to provide relevant information about the cash receipts and cash payments of an enterprise during a period.

_____ 23. (S.O. 8) Determination of cash flows from operating activities requires predicting the amount of cash the entity will collect from customers who purchase the entity's product on account.

_____ 24. (S.O. 8) The sale of 12,000 shares of its common stock by Xerax Company for $22,000 cash would be classified as an investing activity due to the increased investment by company shareholders.

_____ 25. (S.O. 8) To arrive at cash provided by operations, an increase in accounts receivable must be deducted from net income, and an increase in accounts payable must be added back to net income.

MULTIPLE CHOICE

Select the best answer for each of the following items and enter the corresponding letter in the space provided.

____ 1. (S.O. 1) The balance sheet contributes to financial reporting by providing a basis for all of the following except

A. computing rates of return.
B. evaluating the capital structure of the enterprise.
C. determining the increase in cash due to operations.
D. assessing the liquidity and financial flexibility of the enterprise.

____ 2. (S.O. 1) Solvency refers to:

A. the ability of an enterprise to pay its debts as they mature.
B. the amount of time that is expected to elapse until an asset is realized.
C. the amount of time that is expected to elapse until a liability has to be paid.
D. the amount of time that is expected to elapse until an asset is converted into cash.

____ 3. (S.O. 1) One criticism not normally aimed at a balance sheet prepared using current accounting and reporting standards is:

A. failure to reflect current value information.
B. the extensive use of separate classifications.
C. an extensive use of estimates.
D. failure to include items of financial value that cannot be recorded objectively.

____ 4. (S.O. 1) The primary purpose of the balance sheet is to reflect

A. the firm's potential for growth in stock values in the stock market.
B. items of value, debts, and net worth.
C. the value of items owned by the firm.
D. the status of the firm's assets in case of forced liquidation of the firm.

____ 5. (S.O. 2) For accounting purposes the "operating cycle concept"

A. has become obsolete.
B. affects the income statement but not the balance sheet.
C. permits some assets to be classified as current even though they are more than one year removed from becoming cash.
D. causes the distinction between current and noncurrent items to depend on whether they will affect cash within one year.

____ 6. (S.O. 2) If $1,240 cash and a $4,760 note are given in exchange for a delivery truck to be used in a business:

A. assets and liabilities will change by the same amount.
B. owners' equity will be increased.
C. assets will increase and liabilities decrease.
D. assets and liabilities will increase but by different amounts.

_____ 7. (S.O. 2) Which of the following is not a current asset?

A. Prepaid property taxes that relate to the next operating period.
B. The cash surrender value of a life insurance policy carried by a corporation on its president.
C. Marketable securities purchased as a temporary investment of cash.
D. Installment notes receivable due over 15 months in accordance with normal trade practices.

_____ 8. (S.O. 2) Of the following statements, which best illustrates the fact that the formal distinction made between current and noncurrent assets is somewhat arbitrary?

A. Cash in a checking account is a current asset, while cash in a savings account is more permanent and is normally classified as noncurrent.
B. Inventory that may be sold next year, or in the subsequent year as demand dictates may be classified as current or noncurrent.
C. Accounts receivable due in less than one year or the operating cycle are classified as current assets, while accounts receivable due in longer than one year or the operating cycle are classified as noncurrent.
D. An amount equal to the current depreciation charge on buildings should be placed in the current assets section at the beginning of the year, because it will be consumed in the next operating cycle.

_____ 9. (S.O. 2) Which of the following items should never be included in the current section of the balance sheet?

A. Receivable from a customer outstanding for more than a year.
B. Deferred income taxes resulting from interperiod tax allocation.
C. Three-year premium for fire insurance on plant and equipment.
D. A pension fund.

_____ 10. (S.O. 2) Of the following items, the one which should be classified as a current asset is

A. trade installment receivables normally collectible in 20 months.
B. a deposit on equipment ordered, delivery of which will be made within 7 months.
C. cash designated for the redemption of callable bonds.
D. cash surrender value of a life insurance policy of which the company is a beneficiary.

_____ 11. (S.O. 2) Prepaid expenses are included in the current assets section of the balance sheet because

A. they will be converted into cash within one year or the operating cycle, whichever is longer.
B. if they had not been already paid they would require the use of cash during the next year or operating cycle.
C. they were already included in operating expenses on the income statement in the year cash was expended.
D. they reflect payments that were made in a prior period that will not be charged to expense in the current period.

_____ 12. (S.O. 2) One of the main reasons for separating liabilities into current and long-term is:

A. to provide decision makers with information regarding currently maturing debts.
B. to separate large and small debts.
C. to separate capital into its component parts.
D. to separate total equity into its two basic parts.

_____ 13. (S.O. 2) A liability to be paid next year would not be included in the current liability section of the balance sheet if the debt is expected to be refinanced through another long-term issue, or

A. the operating cycle is less than one year.
B. the liability is to be paid with cash that the company expects to earn during the next year.
C. when the debt is retired out of noncurrent assets.
D. the liability is the result of a nonoperating debt instrument due with the next year.

_____ 14. (S.O. 2) A characteristic of all assets and liabilities comprising working capital is that they are

A. monetary.
B. marketable.
C. current.
D. cash equivalents.

_____ 15. (S.O. 2) If a company converted a short-term note payable into a long-term note payable, this transaction would

A. increase both working capital and net income.
B. decrease only working capital.
C. increase only working capital.
D. decrease both working capital and owners' equity.

_____ 16. (S.O. 2) How are the following items handled in computing the total stockholders' equity section of the balance sheet?

	Treasury Stock	Additional Paid-in Capital
A.	Added	Added
B.	Added	Subtracted
C.	Subtracted	Added
D.	Subtracted	Subtracted

_____ 17. (S.O. 4) Which of the following balance sheet classifications would normally require the greatest amount of supplementary disclosure?

A. Current assets.
B. Current liabilities.
C. Plant assets.
D. Long-term liabilities.

_____ 18. (S.O. 5) Which of the following reflects proper use of the term "reserve" in the preparation of financial statements?

A. The term used to describe amounts deducted from assets, such as "reserve for depreciation."
B. The initial term used in connection with an estimated liability, such as "estimated reserve for product warranty."
C. The term used to describe the setting aside of funds for the subsequent payment of an existing liability, such as "reserve for bonds payable."
D. The term used to describe an appropriation of retained earnings in the stockholders' equity section of the balance sheet.

_____ 19. (S.O. 6) The statement of cash flows provides answers to all of the following questions except:

A. Where did the cash come from during the period?
B. What was the cash used for during the period?
C. What is the impact of inflation on the cash balance at the end of the year?
D. What was the change in the cash balance during the period?

_____ 20. (S.O. 7) Which of the following would not be considered a basic source of information useful in preparing a statement of cash flows?

A. Selected transaction data.
B. Comparative balance sheets.
C. An analysis of sales by territory.
D. The current income statement.

_____ 21. (S.O. 9) One of the benefits of the statement of cash flows is that it helps users evaluate financial flexibility. Which of the following explanations is a description of financial flexibility?

A. The nearness to cash of assets and liabilities.
B. The firm's ability to respond and adapt to financial adversity and unexpected needs and opportunities.
C. The firm's ability to pay its debts as they mature.
D. The firm's ability to invest in a number of projects with different objectives and costs.

_____ 22. (S.O. 7) The payment of cash dividends to the common shareholders would be reported on a company's statement of cash flows under the classification of

A. Operating Activities.
B. Financing Activities.
C. Investing Activities.
D. Significant Transactions.

_____ 23. (S.O. 7) How would the two items shown below be handled in arriving at cash provided by operations in the statement of cash flows?

	Increase in Accounts Receivable	Increase in Accounts Payable
A.	Add to net income	Add to net income
B.	Deduct from net income	Deduct from net income
C.	Add to net income	Deduct from net income
D.	Deduct from net income	Add to net income

_____*24. (S.O. 10) Amy Biehl Company had current assets of $12,000, current liabilities of $20,000, net sales of $40,000, cost of goods sold of $24,000, and net income of $8,000. What is Amy Biehl's profit margin on sales?

A. 80%.
B. 60%.
C. 50%.
D. 20%.

_____*25. (S.O. 10) Bodhi Corp. is concerned with measuring its ability to meet interest payments as they come due. Bodhi Corp. would most likely use which following ratio?

A. Payout ratio.
B. Inventory turnover.
C. Times interest earned.
D. Price earnings ratio.

REVIEW EXERCISES

1. (S.O.1) Schwigert Corporation had a balance in accounts receivable on September 1, 2002, of $33,000. All sales are made on account. During September the corporation collected $30,800 from customers, and at the end of September the accountants receivable totaled $27,500.

Instructions: Compute the amount of sales for September.

____
____
____
____
____
____
____
____
____
____

2. (S.O.1 and 2) On December 31, 2002, the total assets of Allen, Inc. were $91,000, and liabilities were $48,000. Allen, Inc. began business January 1, 1998, and had an average net income of $16,000 per year. Total dividends paid for the five-year period were $63,850.

Instructions: Compute Allen, Inc.'s owners' equity balance as of December 31, 2002 and the amount of its original investment.

____

____

____

____

____

____

____

____

____

____

3. (S.O.2) Indicate the most preferred balance sheet classification of each item in Group B by inserting the appropriate letter from Group A in the space provided.

A. Current assets.
B. Property, plant and equipment
C. Long-term investments
D. Intangible assets
E. Other assets
F. Current liabilities
G. Long-term liabilities
H. Capital stock
I. Additional paid-in capital
J. Unappropriated retained earnings
K. Appropriated retained earnings
L. Footnote disclosure
M. Not shown on balance sheet

_____ 1. Cash fund for plant expansion
_____ 2. Preferred stock
_____ 3. Franchise
_____ 4. Accrued interest on customers' notes
_____ 5. Dividend payable in cash
_____ 6. Premium on common stock
_____ 7. Non-fund reserve for possible inventory loss
_____ 8. Advances to suppliers
_____ 9. Accrued employee wages
_____ 10. Unexpired insurance
_____ 11. Ten-year bonds issued to finance plant acquisition
_____ 12. Land
_____ 13. Uncertain outcome of a pending lawsuit
_____ 14. Undistributed portion of current year's net income
_____ 15. Accumulated depreciation
_____ 16. Stock dividend distributable
_____ 17. Discount on bonds payable
_____ 18. Sinking fund for bond retirement
_____ 19. Patent
_____ 20. Purchase commitment (3 years)

4. (S.O.3) The following accounts appeared on the trial balance of Elbert Company at December 31, 2002. All accounts have normal balances.

Account	Amount	Account	Amount
Notes Payable	$ 64,000	Accounts Receivable	$ 172,800
Accumulated Depreciation - Bldg.	261,000	Prepaid Expenses	18,750
Supplies on Hand	12,600	Customers' Deposits	1,250
Accrued Salaries and Wages	11,400	Common Stock***	375,000
Investments in Debt Securities*	93,800	Unappropriated Retained Earnings	?
Cash	56,750	Inventories (average cost)	526,750
Bonds Payable Due 1/1/2006	400,000	Land at Cost	155,000
Allowance for Doubtful Accts.	2,600	Trading Securities****	24,400
Franchise	64,300	Accrued Interest on Notes Payable	650
Notes Receivable	46,000	Buildings at Cost	642,000
Income Taxes Payable	52,000	Accounts Payable	136,650
Preferred Stock**	250,000	Additional Paid-in Capital	54,600
Appropriated Retained Earnings	98,000		

* *The company intends to hold the securities until maturity, which is in ten years.*
** *8% cumulative; $10 par value; 25,000 shares authorized and outstanding.*
*** *$1 par value 400,000 shares authorized; 375,000 shares issued and outstanding.*
**** *The company intends to sell the trading securities in the next year.*

Instructions:
Prepare a classified balance sheet for Elbert Company at December 31, 2002.

4. *(continued)*

5. (S.O.8) The information shown below is taken from the accounts of the Robinson Corporation for the year ended December 31, 2002.

Net income	$209,000
Amortization of intangible (franchise)	12,000
Proceeds from issuance of common stock	103,000
Increase in inventory	18,000
Sale of building at a $10,000 gain	85,000
Increase in accounts payable	15,000
Purchase of computer equipment	125,000
Payment of cash dividends	24,000
Depreciation expense	35,000
Increase in accounts receivable	23,000
Payment of mortgage	52,000
Decrease in short-term notes payable	8,000
Sale of land at a $5,000 loss	26,000
Purchase of delivery truck	33,000
Cash at beginning of year	173,000

Instructions:
Prepare a statement of cash flows for Robinson Corporation for the year ended December 31, 2002.

SOLUTIONS TO REVIEW QUESTIONS AND EXERCISES

TRUE-FALSE

1. (F) The balance sheet reflects a corporation's financial position for a point in time. This accounts for the heading on a balance sheet, which states "December 31, 20X1," rather than "For the year ended December 31, 20X1."

2. (F) Liquidity describes the amount of time that is expected to elapse until an asset is realized or otherwise converted into cash or until a liability has to be paid. Financial flexibility is the ability of an enterprise to take effective actions to alter the amounts and timing of cash flows so it can respond to unexpected needs and opportunities.

3. (T)

4. (F) Historical cost is the basis used to report assets and liabilities on the balance sheet. Price-level adjusted information may be disclosed by an entity as a supplement to the historical cost data. However, there is no accounting requirement to disclose price-level adjusted information when changes in the inflation rate occur.

5. (T)

6. (F) Current assets are cash and other assets that are expected to be converted into cash, sold, or consumed either in one year or in the operating cycle, whichever is longer.

7. (T)

8. (F) Held-to-maturity investments are debt securities that the enterprise has the positive intent and ability to hold to maturity. Trading investments are securities bought and held primarily for sale in the near term to generate income on short-term price differences. Available-for-sale investments are securities not classified as held-to-maturity or trading securities.

9. (T)

10. (T)

11. (T)

12. (F) Securities classified as available-for-sale should be reported at fair value. Securities classified as held-to-maturity are reported at cost.

13. (T)

14. (T)

15. (T)

16. (F) A partnership or proprietorship uses individual capital accounts for each owner in the owners' equity section of the balance sheet. A corporation's owners' equity section shows capital stock accounts representing ownership and a retained earnings account that reflects undistributed earnings of the corporation.

17. (F) The term estimated liability implies that the liability meets the criteria for recording in the accounts. An item that is considered to be a contingent liability may or may not meet both of the criteria necessary for recording it in the accounts. Thus, contingent liabilities are either recorded or disclosed by means of a balance sheet footnote.

18. (T)

19. (T)

20. (T)

21. (T)

22. (T)

23. (F) Cash flow from operating activities refers to the amount of cash inflow and cash outflow which result from the activities an entity enters into for the purpose of generating net income. Because an income statement is prepared on an accrual basis, it includes revenues earned and expenses incurred in earning revenues without regard for the receipt or payment of cash. To compute cash flow from operating activities you must add to or deduct from net income those items in the income statement which did not generate or require the use of cash.

24. (F) When an entity sells its stock for cash it is considered to have entered into a transaction designed to aid in financing the entity's operation. Thus, this transaction would be classified as a financing activity on Xerax Company's statement of cash flows. Investing activities refer to those activities designed to utilize cash to acquire debt and equity investments of other companies (bonds and stocks) as well as property, plant, and equipment.

25. (T)

MULTIPLE CHOICE

1. (C) The balance sheet provides a basis for computing rates of return based on asset growth. The balance sheet also includes information used in evaluating capital structure (equity section) and assessing the liquidity and financial flexibility (assets and liabilities) of the enterprise. However, to determine the increase in cash due to operations one should refer to the statement of cash flows.

2. (A) Solvency refers to the ability of an enterprise to pay its debts as they mature. Alternatives (B), (C) and (D) are all part of the definition of liquidity.

3. (B) The balance sheet is criticized for its failure to reflect current value (A), the extensive use of estimates in its preparation (C), and its failure to include items of financial value that cannot be measured objectively (D). The balance sheet is rarely, if ever, criticized for its division of items into separate classifications.

4. (B) The primary purpose of the balance sheet is to reflect items of value, debts, and net worth. The three classes of items that appear on the balance sheet are assets (items of value measured by historical costs or net realizable values), liabilities (debts and obligations of the firm which represent creditor claims to the assets of the firm), and owners' equity (the net worth of the owners as represented by their claims to the firm's assets). The balance sheet reflects these items as of a particular date.

5. (C) The operating cycle concept is used as a basis for classifying current items. The operating cycle of a firm is the length of time elapsed from the time cash is expended for such items as inventory to the time it converts the inventory back to cash. When the operating cycle is longer than 12 months, the longer period should be used. Therefore, the operating cycle concept does allow some assets to be classified as current even though their conversion into cash will not take place within one year.

6. (A) This transaction causes assets to increase by $4,760. The asset account truck increases by $6,000 (the purchase price), but assets also decrease by $1,240 due to the cash payment. Liabilities increase by $4,760 as a result of the issuance of the note.

7. (B) Generally, the rule is that if an asset is to be turned into cash, sold, or consumed either in one year or the operating cycle, whichever is longer, it is classified as current. The cash surrender value of a life insurance policy is not expected to be turned into cash, etc. within a year or the operating cycle. This item is normally shown in the long-term investments section of the balance sheet.

8. (D) Cash is a current asset whether it is in a checking or savings account. Inventory is a current asset at the time the balance sheet is prepared even though it may not all be sold in the subsequent year, as it is held for sale in the normal course of business. The accounts receivable that are not collectible in the coming year should be classified as a noncurrent asset. However, while the theoretical treatment of next year's depreciation should be shown as a current asset, common practice is to ignore the formal distinction in this case.

9. (D) A pension fund is an investment made by a company for the retirement benefits of its employees. These funds will not be converted to cash for use in the business nor will they be used to liquidate current liabilities. The other three alternatives (A, B, and C) include items that, although somewhat unusual, could be classified as current.

10. (A) A current asset is either cash, something that will be converted into cash or consumed in one year or the operating cycle, whichever is longer. If installment sales are a normal part of operations, they may be classified as current assets because they will be converted into cash within the company's normal operating cycle. Answer (B) is incorrect because the cash deposit is a part of the cost of the machinery ordered and should be classified as a noncurrent asset. Answer (C) is incorrect because cash that is restricted for an indefinite period of time should be classified as a noncurrent asset. Answer (D) is incorrect because a life insurance policy is not likely to be canceled in the near future; therefore, its cash surrender value would be most appropriately reported in the long-term investment section of the balance sheet.

11. (B) Prepaid expenses are expenditures already made for benefits to be received within one year or the operating cycle, whichever is longer. The cash has already been expended, but its inclusion on the income statement will not occur until the benefit has been received by the company.

12. (A) Alternative (B) is incorrect because dividing liabilities between current and long-term has nothing to do with the amount of the debt. Alternative (C) is incorrect because the term "capital" is not a correct term to use in describing debt. Alternative (D) is incorrect because total equity includes both debt and owners' equity.

13. (C) When the operating cycle is less than one year and/or the debt will be paid with cash (alternatives A & B) the item is properly classified as a current liability. Also, all debt acquired or assumed by a company is a liability of that company. However, when the debt is retired out of noncurrent assets it should not be classified as current even if it meets the operating cycle/one year criteria.

14. (C) A characteristic of all assets and liabilities comprising working capital is that they are current. ARB No. 43 defines working capital as the excess of current assets over current liabilities. Answers (A), (B), and (D) are incorrect because not all working capital assets and liabilities are monetary (e.g., inventory), marketable (e.g., federal income taxes payable), or cash equivalents (e.g., prepaid expenses).

15. (C) Conversion of a short-term note payable (current liability) into a long-term note payable (noncurrent liability) would increase working capital. Working capital is the difference between current assets and current liabilities. Conversion of the short-term note payable reduces current liabilities and does not affect current assets. Answers (A) and (D) are incorrect because there is no effect on net income or owners' equity.

16. (C) Treasury stock (the company's own stock reacquired and not canceled) is shown as a reduction of stockholders' equity, while additional paid-in capital is added to the stockholders' equity section of the balance sheet.

17. (D) Long-term liabilities normally require the greatest amount of supplementary disclosure. This is because the terms of all long-term liability agreements, including maturity date or dates, rate of interest, nature of obligation, and any security pledged to support the debt, should be disclosed. The other classifications do require supplementary disclosure, but rarely is it as extensive as that required for long-term liabilities.

18. (D) The profession has recommended that the word "reserve" be used only to describe an appropriation of retained earnings. The term had been used to describe a number of items in the financial statements which has resulted in a great deal of confusion.

19. (C) The statement of cash flows does not adjust the cash balance for the effects of inflation or deflation during the period. Such an amount can be determined by the use of certain indices, but this is not a function of the statement of cash flows.

20. (C) A statement of cash flows deals with gross inflows and outflows of cash. An analysis of sales by territory would generate no information about the cash flow from the sales.

21. (B) Financial flexibility refers to a firm's ability to respond and adapt to financial adversity and unexpected needs and opportunities. Alternative "D" is an indication of flexibility, but does not take into account adversity and unexpected needs. The nearness to cash of assets and liabilities is a firm's liquidity, and the firm's ability to pay its debts refers to solvency.

22. (B) Financing activities involve liability and owners' equity items. They include (1) obtaining capital from owners and providing them with a return on (and a return of) their investment and (b) borrowing money from creditors and repaying the amounts borrowed.

23. (D) To arrive at cash provided by operation, the increase in accounts receivable must be deducted from net income, and the increase in accounts payable must be added back to net income.

*24. (D) The profit margin on sales is 20%. Profit margin on sales is calculated by dividing net income by net sales ($8,000 ÷ $40,000).

*25. (C) The times interest earned ratio measures the ability of a company to meet its interest payments as they come due.

REVIEW EXERCISES

1.

Beginning Receivable balance	$33,000
Ending Receivable balance	27,500
Net change	($5,500)

Collection during September	$30,800
Less decrease in Receivables	5,500
September Sales	$25,300

2. December 31, 2002:

Assets	=	Liabilities	+	Owners' Equity
$91,000	=	$48,000	+	$43,000

Original Investment:

12-31-02 Owners' Equity		$43,000
Net Income 1-1-98—12-31-02 (16,000 x 5)	$80,000	
Less Dividends Paid	63,850	
Increase in Owners' Equity from Operations		16,150
Original Investment		$26,850

3.

1.	(C)	6.	(I)	11.	(G)	16.	(H)
2.	(H)	7.	(K)	12.	(B)	17.	(G)
3.	(D)	8.	(A)	13.	(L)	18.	(C)
4.	(A)	9.	(F)	14.	(J)	19.	(D)
5.	(F)	10.	(A)	15.	(B)	20.	(L) or (M)

4.

Elbert Company
Balance Sheet
December 31, 2002

Assets

Current Assets			
Cash		$ 56,750	
Trading securities		24,400	
Accounts receivable	$172,800		
Less allowance for doubtful accounts	2,600	170,200	
Notes receivable		46,000	
Inventories at average cost		526,750	
Supplies on hand		12,600	
Prepaid expenses		18,750	
Total current assets			$ 855,450
Long-term investments			
Securities to be held-to-maturity			93,800
Property, plant, and equipment			
Land		155,000	
Building	642,000		
Less accumulated depreciation	261,000	381,000	
Total property, plant and equipment			536,000
Intangible assets			
Franchise			64,300
Total assets			$1,549,550

Liabilities and Stockholders' Equity

Current liabilities			
Notes payable		$ 64,000	
Accounts payable		136,650	
Accrued interest on notes payable		650	
Income tax payable		52,000	
Accrued salaries and wages		11,400	
Customers' deposits		1,250	
Total current liabilities			$ 265,950
Long-term debt			
Bonds payable - due 1/1/2006			400,000
Total liabilities			665,950
Stockholders' equity			
Preferred stock, 8% cumulative, $10 par value, 25,000 shares authorized and outstanding		$250,000	
Common stock, $1 par value, 400,000 shares authorized, 375,000 shares issued and outstanding		375,000	
Additional paid-in-capital		54,600	
Earnings retained in the business			
Appropriated	$ 98,000		
Unappropriated	106,000	204,000	
Total stockholders' equity			883,600
Total liabilities and stockholders' equity			$1,549,550

5.

Robinson Corporation
Statement of Cash Flows
For the Year Ended December 31, 2002
Increase (Decrease) In Cash

Cash flows from operating activities		
Net income		$209,000
Adjustments to reconcile net income to net cash provided by operating activities:		
Depreciation expense	$35,000	
Amortization expense	12,000	
Gain on sale of building	(10,000)	
Loss on sale of land	5,000	
Increase in inventory	(18,000)	
Increase in accounts payable	15,000	
Decrease in short-term notes	(8,000)	
Increase in accounts receivable	(23,000)	8,000
Net cash provided by operations		217,000
Cash flows from investing activities		
Sale of building	85,000	
Sale of land	26,000	
Purchase of computer equipment	(125,000)	
Purchase of delivery truck	(33,000)	
Net cash used by investing activities		(47,000)
Cash flows from financing activities		
Issuance of common stock	103,000	
Payment of cash dividends	(24,000)	
Payment of mortgage	(52,000)	
Net cash provided by financing activities		27,000
Net increase in cash		197,000
Cash at beginning of year		173,000
Cash at end of year		$370,000

6

Accounting and the Time Value of Money

CHAPTER STUDY OBJECTIVES

1. Identify accounting topics where the time value of money is relevant.
2. Distinguish between simple and compound interest.
3. Learn how to use appropriate compound interest tables.
4. Identify variables fundamental to solving interest problems.
5. Solve future and present value of 1 problems.
6. Solve future amount of ordinary and annuity due problems.
7. Solve present value of ordinary and annuity due problems.

*8. Use a financial calculator or a spreadsheet to solve time value of money problems.

CHAPTER REVIEW

1. (S.O. 1) Chapter 6 discusses the essentials of compound interest, annuities and present value. These techniques are being used in many areas of financial reporting where the relative values of cash inflows and outflows are measured and analyzed. The material presented in Chapter 6 will provide a sufficient background for application of these techniques to topics presented in subsequent chapters.

2. **Compound interest, annuity, and present value** techniques can be applied to many of the items found in financial statements. In accounting, these techniques can be used to measure the relative values of cash inflows and outflows, evaluate alternative investment opportunities, and determine periodic payments necessary to meet future obligations. Some of the accounting items to which these techniques may be applied are: (a) **notes receivable and payable,** (b) **leases,** (c) **amortization of premiums and discounts,** (d) **pensions,** (e) **long-term assets,** (f) **sinking funds,** (g) **business combinations,** (h) **disclosures,** and (i) **installment contracts.**

<u>Nature of Interest</u>

3. **Interest** is the payment for the use of money. It is normally stated as a percentage of the amount borrowed (principal), calculated on a yearly basis. For example, an entity may borrow $5,000 from a bank at 7% interest. The yearly interest on this loan is $350. If the loan is repaid in six months, the interest due would be 1/2 of $350, or $175. This type of interest computation is known as **simple interest** because the interest is computed on the amount of the principal only. The formula for simple interest can be expressed as **p x i x n** where **p** is the principal, **i** is the rate of interest for one period, and **n** is the number of periods.

4. Selecting an interest rate that is appropriate for a particular financial situation is not an easy task. This is because an interest rate generally has three components: (a) pure rate of interest, (b) credit risk rate of interest, and (c) expected inflation rate of interest. Combining these concepts into

the selection of an appropriate interest rate for a company or investor is an important factor in presenting relevant and reliable accounting information.

Compound Interest

5. (S.O. 2) **Compound interest** is the process of computing interest on the principal plus any interest previously earned. Referring to the example in (2) above, if the loan was for two years with interest compounded annually, the second year's interest would be $374.50 (principal plus first year's interest multiplied by 7%). Compound interest is most common in business situations where large amounts of capital are financed over long periods of time. Simple interest is applied mainly to short-term investments and debts due in one year or less. How often interest is compounded can make a substantial difference in the level of return achieved.

6. In discussing compound interest, the term **period** is used in place of **years** because interest may be compounded daily, weekly, monthly, and so on. Thus, to convert the **annual interest rate** to the **compounding period interest rate,** divide the annual interest rate by the number of compounding periods in a year. Also, the number of periods over which interest will be compounded is calculated by multiplying the number of years involved by the number of compounding periods in a year.

7. (S.O. 4) Certain concepts are fundamental to all compound interest problems. These concepts are:
   a. **Rate of Interest.** The annual rate that must be adjusted to reflect the length of the compounding period if less than one year.
   b. **Number of Time Periods.** The number of compounding periods (a period may be equal to or less than a year).
   c. **Future Amount.** The value at a future date of a given sum or sums invested assuming compound interest.
   d. **Present Value.** The value now (present time) of a future sum or sums discounted assuming compound interest.

8. (S.O. 5) The remaining chapter review paragraphs pertain to **present values** and **future amounts.** The text material covers the following six major time value of money concepts:
   a. Future amount of a single sum.
   b. Present value of a single sum.
   c. Future amount of an ordinary annuity.
   d. Future amount of an annuity due.
   e. Present value of an ordinary annuity.
   f. Present value of an annuity due.

9. Single-sum problems generally fall into one of two categories. The first category consists of problems that require the computation of the **unknown future amount** of a known single sum of money that is invested now for a certain number of periods at a certain interest rate. The second category consists of problems that require the computation of the **unknown present value** of a known single sum of money in the future that is discounted for a certain number of periods at a certain interest rate.

Present Value

10. The concept of **present value** is described as the amount that must be invested now to produce a known future value. This is the opposite of the compound interest discussion in which the present value was known and the future value was determined. An example of the type of question addressed by the present value method is: What amount must be invested today at 6% interest

compounded annually to accumulate $5,000 at the end of 10 years? In this question the present value method is used to determine the initial dollar amount to be invested. The present value method can also be used to determine the **number of years** or the **interest rate** when the other facts are known.

Future Amount of an Annuity

11. (S.O. 6) An **annuity** is a series of equal periodic payments or receipts called **rents.** An annuity requires that the rents be paid or received at equal time intervals, and that compound interest be applied. The **future amount of an annuity** is the sum (future value) of all the rents (payments or receipts) plus the accumulated compound interest on them. If the rents occur at the end of each time period, the annuity is known as an **ordinary annuity.** If rents occur at the beginning of each time period, it is an **annuity due.** Thus, in determining the amount of an annuity for a given set of facts, there will be one less interest period for an ordinary annuity than for an annuity due.

Present Value of an Annuity

12. (S.O. 7) The **present value of an annuity** is a sum of money invested today at compound interest that will provide for a series of equal withdrawals for a specified number of future periods. If the annuity is an **ordinary annuity,** the initial sum of money is invested at the beginning of the first period and withdrawals are made at the end of each period. If the annuity is an **annuity due**, the initial sum of money is invested at the beginning of the first period and withdrawals are made at the beginning of each period. Thus, the first rent withdrawn in an annuity due occurs on the day after the initial sum of money is invested. When computing the present value of an annuity, for a given set of facts, there will be one less discount period for an annuity due than for an ordinary annuity.

Deferred Annuities

13. A **deferred annuity** is an annuity in which two or more periods must pass, after it has been arranged, before the rents will begin. For example, an ordinary annuity of 10 annual rents deferred five years means that no rents will occur during the first five years, and that the first of the 10 rents will occur at the end of the sixth year. An annuity due of 10 annual rents deferred five years means that no rents will occur during the first five years, and that the first of the 10 rents will occur at the beginning of the sixth year. The fact that an annuity is a deferred annuity affects the computation of the present value. However, the **future amount of a deferred annuity** is the same as the amount of an annuity not deferred because there is no accumulation or investment on which interest may accrue.

Time Value of Money Tables

14. Compound interest tables have been developed to aid in the computation of present values and annuities. Examples of the five types of compound interest tables discussed in Chapter 6 are presented at the end of the chapter in this study guide. Careful analysis of the problem as to which compound interest tables will be applied is necessary to determine the appropriate procedures to follow.

15. The following is a summary of the contents of the five types of compound interest tables discussed in the chapter.

"Future amount of 1" table. Contains the amounts to which 1 will accumulate if deposited now at a specified rate and left for a specified number of periods.

"Present value of 1" table. Contains the amount that must be deposited now at a specified rate of interest to amount to 1 at the end of a specified number of periods.

"Future amount of an ordinary annuity of 1" table. Contains the amount to which periodic rents of 1 will accumulate if the rents are invested at a specified rate of interest and are continued for a specified number of periods. (This table may also be used as a basis for converting to the amount of an annuity due of 1.)

"Present value of an ordinary annuity of 1" table. Contains the amounts that must be deposited now at a specified rate of interest to permit withdrawals of 1 at the end of regular periodic intervals for the specified number of periods.

"Present value of an annuity due of 1" table. Contains the amounts that must be deposited now at a specified rate of interest to permit withdrawals of 1 at the beginning of regular periodic intervals for the specified number of periods.

*17. (S.O. 8) Business professionals, after mastering the above concepts, will often use a financial (business) calculator or computerized spreadsheet to solve time value of money problems. When using financial calculators, the five most common keys used to solve time value of money problems are:

N | I | PV | PMT | FV

where:
N = number of periods.
I = interest rate per period (some calculators use I/YR or i).
PV = present value (occurs at the beginning of the first period).
PMT = payment (all payments are equal, and none are skipped).
FV = future value (occurs at the end of the last period).

DEMONSTRATION PROBLEMS

1. Compute the future amount of 10 periodic payments of $5,000 each made at the beginning of each period and compounded at 12%.

Solution:

1.	Future amount of ordinary annuity for 10 periods of 12% (Table 6-3)	17.54874
2.	Factor (1+.12)	x 1.12
3.	Future amount of annuity due for 10 periods of 12%	19.65459
4.	Periodic payment (rent)	$ 5,000
5.	Future amount	$98,272.95

Solution:

Inputs: Set payments to "Begin"

10	12	0	-5,000	?
N	I	PV	PMT	FV

Answer: $98,272.95

2. Compute the present value of 14 receipts of $800 each received at the beginning of each period, discounted at 10% compound interest.

Solution:

This is the present value of an annuity due of $800 payments for 14 periods at 10%.

1.	Present value of an annuity due for 14 periods at 10% (Table 6-5)	8.10336
2.	Periodic receipt (rent)	x $800
3.	Present value	$6,482.69

Solution:

Inputs: Set payments to "Begin"

14	10	?	-800	0
N	I	PV	PMT	FV

Answer: $6,482.69

3. How much must be invested at the end of each year to accumulate a fund of $50,000 at the end of 10 years, if the fund earns 9% interest, compounded annually?

Solution:

Known final amount (a)	$ 50,000
Divide (a) by the amount of an ordinary annuity of $1 for 10 years at 9% (Table 6-3)	÷ 15.19293
The result is the periodic rent that would accumulate $50,000 at the end of 10 years at 9% interest	$ 3,291

Solution:

Inputs: Set payments to "End"

10	9	0	?	50,000
N	I	PV	PMT	FV

Answer: $3,291

4. An asset has a cash price of $9,593.37. The purchaser agrees to pay $2,000 down and 4 annual payments of $2,500 at the end of each year. Assuming compounding on an annual basis, what is the stated interest rate of this transaction?

Solution:

Cash price	$9,593.37
Down payment	2,000.00
Net amount due	$7,593.37

$7,593.37 ÷ $2,500 = 3.03735

Go to Table 6-4 and find the factor 3.03735 in row 4 and read up to the top of the column to find the appropriate interest rate which is **12%**.

Inputs: Set payments to "End"

N	I	PV	PMT	FV
4	?	$7,593.37	-2,500	0

Answer:

$9,593.37 - $2,000 = $7,593.37

5. A fund of $25,000 is deposited in a savings account earning a 12% stated rate but interest is compounded quarterly (3%). What is the maximum amount that could be withdrawn quarterly at the end of each quarter for the next 10 years?

Solution:

$$\begin{aligned} PV &= R\ (PVF - OA_{n,i}) \\ \$25{,}000 &= R\ (PVF - OA_{40,\ 3\%}) \\ \$25{,}000 &= R\ (23.11477) \\ \$1{,}081.56 &= R \end{aligned}$$

Thus, $1,081.56 can be withdrawn at the end of each quarter for the next 10 years. The solution requires that the 12% interest rate be divided by 4 and that the 10 years be multiplied by 4 due to the quarterly compounding. Use the 3% column in Table 6-4 for 40 periods.

Solution:

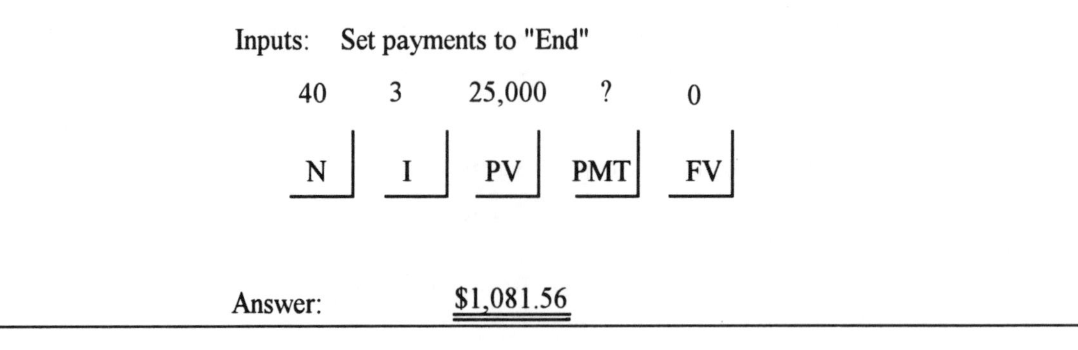

GLOSSARY

Annuity. A series of equal dollar amounts (rents) that are paid or received periodically at equal intervals of time.

Annuity due. An annuity whereby each rent is payable (receivable) at the beginning of the period.

Compound interest. Interest accrues on the unpaid interest of past periods as well as on the principal.

Credit risk rate of interest. The amount of interest that depends on the financial stability, profitability, etc., of a business enterprise.

Deferred annuity. An annuity in which the rents begin after a specified number of periods.

Expected inflation rate of interest. The amount of interest that is based on inflationary or deflationary expectations.

Future value. The value at a future date of a given sum or sums invested assuming compound interest.

Future amount of 1 table. Contains the amounts to which 1 will accumulate if deposited now at a specified rate and left for a specified number of periods.

Future amount of an ordinary annuity of 1 table. Contains the amounts to which periodic rents of 1 will accumulate if the payments are invested at the **end** of each period at a specified rate of interest for a specified number of periods.

Interest. Payment for the use of money.

Ordinary annuity. An annuity whereby each rent is payable (receivable) at the end of the period.

Present value. The value now (present time) of a future sum or sums discounted assuming compound interest.

Present value of 1 table. Contains the amounts that must be deposited now at a specified rate of interest to equal 1 at the end of a specified number of periods.

Present value of an annuity due of 1 table. Contains the amounts that must be deposited now at a specified rate of interest to permit withdrawals of 1 at the **beginning** of regular periodic intervals for the specified number of periods.

Present value of an ordinary annuity of 1 table. Contains the amounts that must be deposited now at a specified rate of interest to permit withdrawals of 1 at the **end** of regular periodic intervals for the specified number of periods.

Principal. The amount borrowed or invested.

Pure rate of interest. The amount at lender would charge if there were no possibilities of default and no expectation of inflation.

Simple interest. Interest on principal only, regardless of interest that may have accrued in the past.

CHAPTER OUTLINE

Fill in the outline presented below.

(S.O. 1) Present Value-Based Accounting Measurements

Nature of Interest

Choosing an Appropriate Interest Rate

(S.O. 2) Simple Interest

Compound Interest

(S.O. 4) Fundamental Variables

(S.O. 5) Future Amount of a Single Sum

Present Value of a Single Sum

Chapter Outline *(continued)*

(S.O. 6) Future Amount of an Ordinary Annuity

Future Amount of an Annuity Due

(S.O. 7) Present Value of an Ordinary Annuity

Present Value of an Annuity Due

Deferred Annuities

REVIEW QUESTIONS AND EXERCISES

TRUE-FALSE

Indicate whether each of the following is true (T) or false (F) in the space provided.

_____ 1. (S.O. 1) Present value techniques can be used in valuing receivables and payables that carry no stated interest rate.

_____ 2. (S.O. 2) The amount of interest on a $1,000, 6%, 6-month note is the same as the amount of interest on a $1,000, 3%, 1-year note.

_____ 3. (S.O. 2) In the formula for compound interest, the number of periods refers to the number of months an obligation will be outstanding.

_____ 4. (S.O. 2)The major difference between compound interest and simple interest lies in the fact that compound interest is computed twice each year, whereas simple interest is computed only once.

_____ 5. (S.O. 2) The growth in principal is the same under both compound and simple interest if only one time period is involved.

_____ 6. (S.O. 3) If interest is compounded quarterly and the annual interest rate is 8%, the compounding period interest rate is 4%.

_____ 7. (S.O. 4) Present value is the amount that must be invested now to produce a known future amount.

_____ 8. (S.O. 6) An annuity requires that periodic rents always be the same even though the interval between the rents may vary.

_____ 9. (S.O. 6) An annuity is classified as an ordinary annuity if the rents occur at the end of the period; it is classified as an annuity due if the rents occur at the beginning of the period.

_____ 10. (S.O. 6) The ordinary annuity table may be used to compute the periodic rents when the desired future amount and the present value of the annuity are not known.

_____ 11. (S.O. 6) Periodic interest earnings under an ordinary annuity will always be lower by one period's interest than the interest earned by an annuity due.

_____ 12. (S.O. 7) The present value of an ordinary annuity is the present value of series of rents to be made at equal intervals in the future.

_____ 13. (S.O. 7) The number of rents exceeds the number of discount periods under the present value of an ordinary annuity.

_____ 14. (S.O. 7) The future amount of a deferred annuity is normally greater than the future amount of an annuity not deferred.

_____ 15. (S.O. 7) The valuation of a sum as of an earlier date involves a determination of present value; the valuation of a sum as of a later date involves a determination of an amount.

MULTIPLE CHOICE

Select the best answer for each of the following items and enter the corresponding letter in the space provided.

_____ 1. (S.O. 3) Which of the following tables would show the largest value for an interest rate of 10% for 8 periods?

A. Future amount of 1 table.
B. Present value of 1 table.
C. Future amount of an ordinary annuity of 1 table.
D. Present value of an ordinary annuity of 1 table.

_____ 2. (S.O. 3) On June 1, 2001, Walsh Company sold some equipment to Fischer Company. The two companies entered into an installment sales contract at a rate of 8%. The contract required 8 equal annual payments with the first payment due on June 1, 2001. What type of compound interest table is appropriate for this situation?

A. Present value of an annuity due of 1 table.
B. Present value of an ordinary annuity of 1 table.
C. Future amount of an ordinary annuity of 1 table.
D. Future amount of 1 table.

_____ 3. (S.O. 3) Which of the following transactions would best use the present value of an annuity due of 1 table.

A. Diamond Bar, Inc. rents a truck for 5 years with annual rental payments of $20,000 to be made at the beginning of each year.
B. Michener Co. rents a warehouse for 7 years with annual rental payments of $120,000 to be made at the end of each year.
C. Durant, Inc. borrows $20,000 and has agreed to pay back the principal plus interest in three years.
D. Babbitt, Inc. wants to deposit a lump sum to accumulate $50,000 for the construction of a new parking lot in 4 years.

_____ 4. (S.O. 5) Bob Geimer plans on going on vacation to Asia in four years. The trip will cost $4,000. He proposes to finance the trip by investing a sum of money now at 9% compound interest. How much should Bob invest now in order to obtain his goal of $4,000?

A. $ 874.67
B. $1,400.00
C. $2,833.72
D. $3,088.72

_____ 5. (S.O. 5) What amount should be deposited in a bank today at an interest rate of 10% to grow to $2,000 four years from today?

A. $2,000/0.68301
B. $2,000 x 0.90909 x 3
C. ($2,000 x 0.90909) + ($2,000 x 0.82645) + ($2,000 x 0.75132) + ($2,000 x 0.68301)
D. $2,000 x 0.68301

_____ 6. (S.O. 5) What amount should Spencer Forman have in his 6% bank account today before withdrawal if he needs $3,000 each year for three years with the first withdrawal to be made today and each subsequent withdrawal at one-year intervals? (He is to have exactly a zero balance in his bank account after the third withdrawal.)

A. $3,000 + ($3,000 x 0.94340) + ($3,000 x 0.89000)
B. ($3,000/0.83962) x 3
C. ($3,000 x 0.94340) + ($3,000 x 0.89000) + ($3,000 x 0.83962)
D. ($3,000/0.94340) x 3

_____ 7. (S.O. 5) If J.J. Morse put $1,000 in a 12% savings account today, what amount of cash would be available 3 years from now?

A. $1,000 x .71178
B. $1,000 x .71178 x 3
C. $1,000/.71178
D. ($1,000/.89286) x 3

_____ 8. (S.O. 6) Kimberly Nelson, a computer programmer, wishes to create her own retirement fund. Kimberly deposits $4,000 today in a fixed rate savings account that earns 5% interest. She plans to deposit $4,000 every year for the next 24 years (total of 25 deposits). How much cash will she have accumulated in her retirement account when she retires in 25 years?

A. $186,908
B. $190,908
C. $194,908
D. $200,454

_____ 9. (S.O. 6) Jeanie Pearson plans to buy a golf course in 10 years. Because of cash flow problems, Jeanie is able to budget deposits of $900,000 that are expected to earn 10% annually only at the end of the seventh, eighth, ninth, and tenth periods. What future amount will Jeanie accumulate at the end of the tenth year?

A. $3,600,000
B. $3,960,000
C. $4,176,900
D. $6,902,631

_____ 10. (S.O. 7) Sharon Walsh has developed and patented a computer chip that allows telecommunications in race cars to become more efficient. She agrees to sell the patent to Pensca for five annual payments of $50,000 each. The payments are to begin three years from today. Given an annual rate of 6%, what is the present value of the five payments?

A. $176,839
B. $187,450
C. $210,618
D. $218,820

REVIEW EXERCISES

1. Listed below are a series of questions. These questions can be answered using the methods presented in Chapter 6.

Instructions:

a. Match each question with the method listed below that would be used in providing a solution.

b. Compute the answer to each of the 10 questions listed below and on the right.

METHOD

A. Present Value or Future Value of a Single Sum
B. Future Amount of an Ordinary Annuity
C. Future Amount of an Annuity Due
D. Present Value of an Ordinary Annuity
E. Present Value of an Annuity Due
F. Present Value of a Deferred Annuity

QUESTIONS

_____ 1. How much will Tom receive if he invests $1,000 for 1 year at 5%?

_____ 2. How much should Bob deposit at the end of each 6-month period to accumulate $20,000 when he graduates in 4 years assuming that he can earn an annual rate of 10% compounded semiannually?

_____ 3. What rate of interest must Connie earn on an investment of $60,000 to be able to withdraw $9,000 at the beginning of each year for the next 10 years?

_____ 4. What amount should Gay invest now at 12% to provide 5 payments of $5,000 at the end of each year, starting 3 years from now?

_____ 5. How many years will it take to accumulate $20,000 if Brent invests $1,845 at 10%?

_____ 6. If Daisy invests $3,000 at 8%, with interest computed on the principal plus undistributed interest, how much will she have at the end of 10 years (annual compounding)?

_____ 7. If Pat has $15,000 in a bank earning 6% interest compounded annually, how much can he withdraw at the end of each year for the next 8 years?

_____ 8. At what annually compounded interest rate must Dave invest $25,331 to provide $50,000 at the end of 6 years?

_____ 9. How much should Karen deposit on each birthday beginning on her twentieth birthday to accumulate $50,000 on her 50th birthday, assuming that she can earn 12% interest compounded annually (no deposit on her fiftieth birthday)?

_____ 10. How much should Mark set aside now, assuming that he can earn 8% interest compounded annually, so he can withdraw $10,000 at the end of each year for the next 10 years?

SOLUTIONS TO REVIEW QUESTIONS

TRUE-FALSE

1. (T)

2. (T)

3. (F) In the formula for compound interest the number of periods refers to the number of times interest is compounded. Interest is generally expressed in terms of an annual rate; however, in many business circumstances, the compounding period is less than a year (daily, monthly, quarterly, semiannually, etc.). In such circumstances the annual interest rate must be converted to correspond to the length of the period. This is done by dividing the annual rate by the number of compounding periods per year.

4. (F) Simple interest is the term used to describe interest that is computed on the amount of the principal only. Compound interest is the term used to describe interest that is compounded on principal and on any interest earned that has not been paid or withdrawn.

5. (T)

6. (F) In this case the compounding interest rate is 2% rather than 4%. This is computed by dividing the annual rate (8%) by the number of compounding periods per year (4).

7. (T)

8. (F) An annuity requires that (a) the periodic payments or receipts (called rents) always be the same, (b) the interval between such rents always be the same, and (c) the interest be compounded once each interval.

9. (T)

10. (F) If the desired future amount or present value of an annuity are not known, the periodic rents cannot be computed.

11. (T)

12. (T)

13. (F) The present value of an ordinary annuity is the present value of a series of equal rents to be withdrawn at equal intervals in the future.

14. (F) Because there is no accumulation or investment on which interest may accrue, the future amount of a deferred annuity is the same as the future amount of an annuity not deferred.

15. (T)

MULTIPLE CHOICE

1. (C) The future amount of an ordinary annuity of 1 table would show the largest value for an interest rate of 10% for 8 periods. Answer (A) is incorrect because the future amount of 1 table only calculates the future amount of a single sum whereas the future amount of an ordinary annuity of 1 table calculates the future amount of a stream of payments. Answer (B) is incorrect because the present value of 1 table includes values of less than 1 whereas the future amount of an ordinary annuity of 1 table includes values greater than 1. Answer (D) is incorrect because the present value of an ordinary annuity of 1 table calculates a stream of payments back to the present whereas the future value of an ordinary annuity of 1 table calculates a stream of payments forward to the future; thus the future amount is greater than the present amount because it is earning more interest.

2. (A) The present value of an annuity due of 1 table would be the appropriate table for this situation. The present value of an annuity due involves the present value of equal future annual payments due **at the beginning** of the annual period. Answer (B) is incorrect because it concerns the present value of equal future annual payments due at the end of the annual period (ordinary annuity). Answers (C) and (D) are incorrect because they involve accumulations of an annuity and of a single amount, respectively, into some future value.

3. (A) The present value of annuity due of 1 table involves equal periodic rents which become due **at the beginning** of regular periodic intervals. Therefore a lease which requires the initial rental payment to be made upon signing the lease would be the correct answer. Answer (B) is incorrect because it would use the present value of an ordinary annuity of 1 table because the rental payments are due at the end of the regular periodic intervals. Answer (C) is incorrect because it involves the future amount of a single sum. Answer (D) is incorrect because it involves the present value of a single sum.

4. (C) This problem involves the present value of a single sum. Using Table 6-2 for 9% at 4 periods, the value of .70843 is multiplied by $4,000 to obtain the amount of $2,833.72.

5. (D) The amount to be deposited today (present value) to grow to $2,000 (future value) four years from now if the bank pays 10% annual compound interest can be calculated by multiplying the desired future value ($2,000) by the present value factor for 4 periods at 10% per period (0.68301). The correct answer is $2,000 x 0.68301.

6. (A) The requirement is to find the amount Spencer Forman should have in his bank account today (present value) if he desires to withdraw $3,000 each year for 3 years with the first $3,000 withdrawal occurring today. Normally the present value of an annuity due table for 1 could be used for this problem; however, such an answer was not provided in the choices given. Instead, the present value of this future series of withdrawals can be calculated by using the present value of 1 table and summing the present value of $3,000 to be received now ($3,000) and, the present value of $3,000 to be received 1 period from now ($3,000 x 0.94340) and the present value of $3,000 to be received 2 periods from now ($3,000 x 0.89000). This series of withdrawals follows the pattern of an annuity due; that is, the withdrawals of the amounts take place at the beginning of an interest period. Consequently the first withdrawal does not earn interest. Answer (C) is incorrect because it describes an ordinary annuity situation where the

withdrawals are made at the end of the interest period; that is, the first withdrawal would have had to be made one interest period from now.

7. (C) The requirement is to determine the calculation needed to find the future value of $1,000 deposited in the bank today. The appropriate table to use would be the future amount of 1 table; however, the answers do not provide that answer so the present value of 1 table can be used to calculate the future value in the following manner:

Present value = Future Value x Present Value Factor for 3 Periods

Let X = Future Value

$1,000 = X(0.71178)

$1,000/0.71178 = X

8. (D) Using the future amount of an ordinary annuity of 1 table, the solution is computed as follows:

Future amount of an ordinary annuity of 1 for 25 periods at 5%	47.72710
Factor (1 + .05)	x 1.05
Future amount of an annuity due of 1 for 25 periods at 5%	50.11350
Periodic payment	x $4,000
Accumulated amount at the end of 25 years	$200,454

9. (C) The amount accumulated is determined by using the standard formula for the future amount of an ordinary annuity for 4 periods at 10%:

X = $900,000 x 4.64100
X = $4,176,900.

10. (B) To compute the present value of a deferred annuity, compute the present value of an ordinary annuity of 1 as if the rents had occurred for the entire period, and then subtract the present value of rents which were not received during the deferral period.

Using only Table 6-4 as follows:

Each periodic rent		$50,000
Present value of an ordinary annuity of 1 for total periods (7) [number of rents (5) plus number of deferred periods (2)] at 6%	5.58238	
Less: Present value of an ordinary annuity of 1 for the number of deferred periods (2) at 6%	1.83339	
Difference		x 3.74899
		$187,449.50

REVIEW EXERCISES

a.

1.	(A)	6.	(A)
2.	(B)	7.	(D)
3.	(E)	8.	(A)
4.	(F)	9.	(C)
5.	(A)	10.	(D)

b. 1. $1,000 x 1.05 = $1,050

2. $20,000 ÷ 9.54911 = $2,094.44 (From Table 6-3, 5% for 8 periods.)

3. $60,000 ÷ $9,000 = 6.667 (From Table 6-5 for 10 periods, the interest rate is between 10% and 12%.)

4.

Each periodic rent		$5,000
Present value of an ordinary annuity of 1 for total periods (8) involved [number of rents (5) plus number of deferred periods (3)] at 12%	4.96764	
Less: Present value of an ordinary annuity of 1 for the number of deferred periods (3) at 12%	2.40183	
Difference		x 2.56581
Present value of 5 rents of $5,000		$12,829.05

5. $20,000 ÷ $1,845 = 10.84010 (From Table 6-1, in the 10% column the number 10.84010 falls between 25 and 26 years.)

6. $3,000 x 2.15892 = $6,476.76 (From Table 6-1, 8% for 10 years).

7. $15,000 ÷ 6.20979 = $2,415.54 (From Table 6-4).

8. $25,331 ÷ $50,000 = .50662 (From Table 6-2, this amount is found for 6 years at 12% interest.)

9.

Future amount of an ordinary annuity of 1 for 30 years at 12%	241.33268
Factor (1+.12)	X 1.12
Future amount of an annuity due for 30 years at 12%	270.29260

$50,000 ÷ 270.29260= $184.98

10. $10,000 X 6.71008 = $67,100.80 (From Table 6-4).

Table 6-1 FUTURE AMOUNT OF 1

$$FVF_{n,i} = (1 + i)^n$$

(n) Periods	2%	2-1/2%	3%	4%	5%	6%
1	1.02000	1.02500	1.03000	1.04000	1.05000	1.06000
2	1.04040	1.05063	1.06090	1.08160	1.10250	1.12360
3	1.06121	1.07689	1.09273	1.12486	1.15763	1.19102
4	1.08243	1.10381	1.12551	1.16986	1.21551	1.26248
5	1.10408	1.13141	1.15927	1.21665	1.27628	1.33823
6	1.12616	1.15969	1.19405	1.26532	1.34010	1.41852
7	1.14869	1.18869	1.22987	1.31593	1.40710	1.50363
8	1.17166	1.21840	1.26677	1.36857	1.47746	1.59385
9	1.19509	1.24886	1.30477	1.42331	1.55133	1.68948
10	1.21899	1.28008	1.34392	1.48024	1.62889	1.79085
11	1.24337	1.31209	1.38423	1.53945	1.71034	1.89830
12	1.26824	1.34489	1.42576	1.60103	1.79586	2.01220
13	1.29361	1.37851	1.46853	1.66507	1.88565	2.13293
14	1.31948	1.41297	1.51259	1.73168	1.97993	2.26090
15	1.34587	1.44830	1.55797	1.80094	2.07893	2.39656
16	1.37279	1.48451	1.60471	1.87298	2.18287	2.54035
17	1.40024	1.52162	1.65285	1.94790	2.29202	2.69277
18	1.42825	1.55966	1.70243	2.02582	2.40662	2.85434
19	1.45681	1.59865	1.75351	2.10685	2.52695	3.02560
20	1.48595	1.63862	1.80611	2.19112	2.65330	3.20714
21	1.51567	1.67958	1.86029	2.27877	2.78596	3.39956
22	1.54598	1.72157	1.91610	2.36992	2.92526	3.60354
23	1.57690	1.76461	1.97359	2.46472	3.07152	3.81975
24	1.60844	1.80873	2.03279	2.56330	3.22510	4.04893
25	1.64061	1.85394	2.09378	2.66584	3.38635	4.29187
26	1.67342	1.90029	2.15659	2.77247	3.55567	4.54938
27	1.70689	1.94780	2.22129	2.88337	3.73346	4.82235
28	1.74102	1.99650	2.28793	2.99870	3.92013	5.11169
29	1.77584	2.04641	2.35657	3.11865	4.11614	5.41839
30	1.81136	2.09757	2.42726	3.24340	4.32194	5.74349
31	1.84759	2.15001	2.50008	3.37313	4.53804	6.08810
32	1.88454	2.20376	2.57508	3.50806	4.76494	6.45339
33	1.92223	2.25885	2.65234	3.64838	5.00319	6.84059
34	1.96068	2.31532	2.73191	3.79432	5.25335	7.25103
35	1.99989	2.37321	2.81386	3.94609	5.51602	7.68609
36	2.03989	2.43254	2.89828	4.10393	5.79182	8.14725
37	2.08069	2.49335	2.98523	4.26809	6.08141	8.63609
38	2.12230	2.55568	3.07478	4.43881	6.38548	9.15425
39	2.16474	2.61957	3.16703	4.61637	6.70475	9.70351
40	2.20804	2.68506	3.26204	4.80102	7.03999	10.28572

8%	9%	10%	12%	15%	(n) Periods
1.08000	1.09000	1.10000	1.12000	1.15000	1
1.16640	1.18810	1.21000	1.25440	1.32250	2
1.25971	1.29503	1.33100	1.40493	1.52088	3
1.36049	1.41158	1.46410	1.57352	1.74901	4
1.46933	1.53862	1.61051	1.76234	2.01136	5
1.58687	1.67710	1.77156	1.97382	2.31306	6
1.71382	1.82804	1.94872	2.21068	2.66002	7
1.85093	1.99256	2.14359	2.47596	3.05902	8
1.99900	2.17189	2.35795	2.77308	3.51788	9
2.15892	2.36736	2.59374	3.10585	4.04556	10
2.33164	2.58043	2.85312	3.47855	4.65239	11
2.51817	2.81267	3.13843	3.89598	5.35025	12
2.71962	3.06581	3.45227	4.36349	6.15279	13
2.93719	3.34173	3.79750	4.88711	7.07571	14
3.17217	3.64248	4.17725	5.47357	8.13706	15
3.42594	3.97031	4.59497	6.13039	9.35762	16
3.70002	4.32763	5.05447	6.86604	10.76162	17
3.99602	4.71712	5.55992	7.68997	12.37545	18
4.31570	5.14166	6.11591	8.61276	14.23177	19
4.66096	5.60441	6.72750	9.64629	16.36654	20
5.03383	6.10881	7.40025	10.80385	18.82152	21
5.43654	6.65860	8.14028	12.10031	21.64475	22
5.87146	7.25787	8.95430	13.55235	24.89146	23
6.34118	7.91108	9.84973	15.17863	28.62518	24
6.84847	8.62308	10.83471	17.00000	32.91895	25
7.39635	9.39916	11.91818	19.04007	37.85680	26
7.98806	10.24508	13.10999	21.32488	43.53532	27
8.62711	11.16714	14.42099	23.88387	50.06561	28
9.31727	12.17218	15.86309	26.74993	57.57545	29
10.06266	13.26768	17.44940	29.95992	66.21177	30
10.86767	14.46177	19.19434	33.55511	76.14354	31
11.73708	15.76333	21.11378	37.58173	87.56507	32
12.67605	17.18203	23.22515	42.09153	100.69983	33
13.69013	18.72841	25.54767	47.14252	115.80480	34
14.78534	20.41397	28.10244	52.79962	133.17552	35
15.96817	22.25123	30.91268	59.13557	153.15185	36
17.24563	24.25384	34.00395	66.23184	176.12463	37
18.62528	26.43668	37.40434	74.17966	202.54332	38
20.11530	28.81598	41.14479	83.08122	232.92482	39
21.72452	31.40942	45.25926	93.05097	267.86355	40

TABLE 6-2 PRESENT VALUE OF 1

$$PVF_{n,i} = \frac{1}{(1+i)^n} = (1+i)^{-n}$$

(n) Periods	2%	2-1/2%	3%	4%	5%	6%
1	.98039	.97561	.97087	.96154	.95238	.94340
2	.96117	.95181	.94260	.92456	.90703	.89000
3	.94232	.92860	.91514	.88900	.86384	.83962
4	.92385	.90595	.88949	.85480	.82270	.79209
5	.90573	.88385	.86261	.82193	.78353	.74726
6	.88797	.86230	.83748	.79031	.74622	.70496
7	.87056	.84127	.81309	.75992	.71068	.66506
8	.85349	.82075	.78941	.73069	.67684	.62741
9	.83676	.80073	.76642	.70259	.64461	.59190
10	.82035	.78120	.74409	.67556	.61391	.55839
11	.80462	.76214	.72242	.64958	.58468	.56279
12	.78849	.74356	.70138	.62460	.55684	.49697
13	.77303	.72542	.68095	.60057	.53032	.46884
14	.75788	.70773	.66112	.57748	.50507	.44230
15	.74301	.69047	.64186	.55526	.48102	.41727
16	.72845	.67362	.62317	.53391	.45811	.39365
17	.71416	.65720	.60502	.51337	.43630	.37136
18	.70016	.64117	.58739	.49363	.41552	.35034
19	.68643	.62553	.57029	.47464	.39573	.33051
20	.67297	.61027	.55368	.45639	.37689	.31180
21	.65978	.59539	.53755	.43883	.35894	.29416
22	.64684	.58086	.52189	.42196	.34185	.27751
23	.63416	.56670	.50669	.40573	.32557	.26180
24	.62172	.55288	.49193	.39012	.31007	.24698
25	.60593	.53939	.47761	.37512	.29530	.23300
26	.59758	.52623	.46369	.36069	.28124	.21981
27	.58586	.51340	.45019	.34682	.26785	.20737
28	.57437	.50088	.43708	.33348	.25509	.19563
29	.56311	.48866	.42435	.32065	.24295	.18456
30	.55207	.47674	.41199	.30832	.23138	.17411
31	.54125	.46511	.39999	.29646	.22036	.16425
32	.53063	.45377	.38834	.28506	.20987	.15496
33	.52023	.44270	.37703	.27409	.19987	.14619
34	.51003	.43191	.36604	.26355	.19035	.13791
35	.50003	.42137	.35538	.25342	.18129	.13011
36	.49022	.41109	.34503	.24367	.17266	.12274
37	.48061	.40107	.33498	.23430	.16444	.11579
38	.47119	.39128	.32523	.22529	.15661	.10924
39	.46195	.38174	.31575	.21662	.14915	.10306
40	.45289	.37243	.30656	.20829	.14205	.09722

8%	9%	10%	12%	15%	(n) Periods
.92593	.91743	.90909	.89286	.86957	1
.85734	.84168	.82645	.79719	.75614	2
.79383	.77218	.75132	.71178	.65752	3
.73503	.70843	.68301	.63552	.57175	4
.68058	.64993	.62092	.56743	.49718	5
.63017	.59627	.56447	.50663	.43233	6
.58349	.54703	.51316	.45235	.37594	7
.54027	.50187	.46651	.40388	.32690	8
.50025	.46043	.42410	.36061	.28426	9
.46319	.42241	.38554	.32197	.24719	10
.42888	.38753	.35049	.28748	.21494	11
.39711	.35554	.31863	.25668	.18691	12
.36770	.32618	.28966	.22917	.16253	13
.34046	.29925	.26333	.20462	.14133	14
.31524	.27454	.23939	.18270	.12289	15
.29189	.25187	.21763	.16312	.10687	16
.27027	.23107	.19785	.14564	.09293	17
.25025	.21199	.17986	.13004	.08081	18
.23171	.19449	.16351	.11611	.07027	19
.21455	.17843	.14864	.10367	.06110	20
.19866	.16370	.13513	.09256	.05313	21
.18394	.15018	.12285	.08264	.04620	22
.17032	.13778	.11168	.07379	.04017	23
.15770	.12641	.10153	.06588	.03493	24
.14602	.11597	.09230	.05882	.03038	25
.13520	.10639	.08391	.05252	.02642	26
.12519	.09761	.07628	.04689	.02297	27
.11591	.08955	.06934	.04187	.01997	28
.10733	.08216	.06304	.03738	.01737	29
.09938	.07537	.05731	.03338	.01510	30
.09202	.06915	.05210	.02980	.01313	31
.08520	.06344	.04736	.02661	.01142	32
.07889	.05820	.04306	.02376	.00993	33
.07305	.05340	.03914	.02121	.00864	34
.06763	.04899	.03558	.01894	.00751	35
.06262	.04494	.03235	.01691	.00653	36
.05799	.04123	.02941	.01510	.00568	37
.05396	.03783	.02674	.01348	.00494	38
.04971	.03470	.02430	.01204	.00429	39
.04603	.03184	.02210	.01075	.00373	40

TABLE 6-3 FUTURE AMOUNT OF AN ORDINARY ANNUITY OF 1

$$FVF\text{-}OA_{n,i} = \frac{(1+i)^n - 1}{i}$$

(n) Periods	2%	2-1/2%	3%	4%	5%	6%
1	1.00000	1.00000	1.00000	1.00000	1.00000	1.00000
2	2.02000	2.02500	2.03000	2.04000	2.05000	2.06000
3	3.06040	3.07563	3.09090	3.12160	3.15250	3.18360
4	4.12161	4.15252	4.18363	4.24646	4.31013	4.37462
5	5.20404	5.25633	5.30914	5.41632	5.52563	5.63709
6	6.30812	6.38774	6.46841	6.63298	6.80191	6.97532
7	7.43428	7.54743	7.66246	7.89829	8.14201	8.39384
8	8.58297	8.73612	8.89234	9.21423	9.54911	9.89747
9	9.75463	9.95452	10.15911	10.58280	11.02656	11.49132
10	10.94972	11.20338	11.46338	12.00611	12.57789	13.18079
11	12.16872	12.48347	12.80780	13.48635	14.20679	14.97164
12	13.41209	13.79555	14.19203	15.02581	15.91713	16.86994
13	14.68033	15.14044	15.61779	16.62684	17.71298	18.88214
14	15.97394	16.51895	17.08632	18.29191	19.59863	21.01507
15	17.29342	17.93193	18.59891	20.02359	21.57856	23.27597
16	18.63929	19.38022	20.15688	21.82453	23.65749	25.67253
17	20.01207	20.86473	21.76159	23.69751	25.84037	28.21288
18	21.41231	22.38635	23.41444	25.64541	28.13238	30.90565
19	22.84056	23.94601	25.11687	27.67123	30.53900	33.75999
20	24.29737	25.54466	26.87037	29.77808	33.06595	36.78559
21	25.78332	27.18327	28.67649	31.96920	35.71925	39.99273
22	27.29898	28.86286	30.53678	34.24797	38.50521	43.39229
23	28.84496	30.58443	32.45288	36.61789	41.43048	46.99583
24	30.42186	32.34904	34.42647	39.08260	44.50200	50.81558
25	32.03030	34.15776	36.45926	41.64591	47.72710	54.86451
26	33.67091	36.01171	38.55304	44.31174	51.11345	59.15638
27	35.34432	37.91200	40.70963	47.08421	54.66913	63.70577
28	37.05121	39.85980	42.93092	49.96758	58.40258	68.52811
29	38.79223	41.85630	45.21885	52.96629	62.32271	73.63980
30	40.56808	43.90270	47.57542	56.08494	66.43885	79.05819
31	42.37944	46.00027	50.00268	59.32834	70.76079	84.80168
32	44.22703	48.15028	52.50276	62.70147	75.29883	90.88978
33	46.11157	50.35403	55.07784	66.20953	80.06377	97.34316
34	48.03380	52.61289	57.73018	69.85791	85.06696	104.18376
35	49.99448	54.92821	60.46208	73.65222	90.32031	111.43478
36	51.99437	57.30141	63.27594	77.59831	95.83632	119.12087
37	54.03425	59.73395	66.17422	81.70225	101.62814	127.26812
38	56.11494	62.22730	69.15945	85.97034	107.70955	135.90421
39	58.23724	64.78298	72.23423	90.40915	114.09502	145.05846
40	60.40198	67.40255	75.40126	95.02552	120.79977	154.76197

8%	9%	10%	12%	15%	(n) Periods
1.00000	1.00000	1.00000	1.00000	1.00000	1
2.08000	2.09000	2.10000	2.12000	2.15000	2
3.24640	3.27810	3.31000	3.37440	3.47250	3
4.50611	4.57313	4.64100	4.77933	4.99338	4
5.86660	5.98471	6.10510	6.35285	6.74238	5
7.33592	7.52334	7.71561	8.11519	8.75374	6
8.92280	9.20044	9.48717	10.08901	11.06680	7
10.63663	11.02847	11.43589	12.29969	13.72682	8
12.48756	13.02104	13.57948	14.77566	16.78584	9
14.48656	15.19293	15.93743	17.54874	20.30372	10
16.64549	17.56029	18.53117	20.65458	24.34928	11
18.97713	20.14072	21.38428	24.13313	29.00167	12
21.49530	22.95339	24.52271	28.02911	34.35192	13
24.21492	26.01919	27.97498	32.39260	40.50471	14
27.15211	29.36092	31.77248	37.27972	47.58041	15
30.32428	33.00340	35.94973	42.75328	55.71747	16
33.75023	36.97371	40.54470	48.88367	65.07509	17
37.45024	41.30134	45.59917	55.74972	75.83636	18
41.44626	46.01846	51.15909	63.43968	88.21181	19
45.76196	51.16012	57.27500	72.05244	102.44358	20
50.42292	56.76453	64.00250	81.69874	118.81012	21
55.45676	62.87334	71.40275	92.50258	137.63164	22
60.89330	69.53194	79.54302	104.60289	159.27638	23
66.76476	76.78981	88.49733	118.15524	184.16784	24
73.10594	84.70090	98.34706	133.33387	212.79302	25
79.95442	93.32398	109.18177	150.33393	245.71197	26
87.35077	102.72314	121.09994	169.37401	283.56877	27
95.33883	112.96822	134.20994	190.69889	327.10408	28
103.96594	124.13536	148.63093	214.58275	377.16969	29
113.28231	136.30754	164.49402	241.33268	434.74515	30
123.34587	149.57522	181.94343	271.29261	500.95692	31
134.21354	164.03699	201.13777	304.84772	577.10046	32
145.95062	179.80032	222.25154	342.42945	644.66553	33
158.62667	196.98234	245.47670	384.52098	765.36535	34
172.31680	215.71076	271.02437	431.66350	881.17016	35
187.10215	236.12472	299.12681	484.46312	1014.34568	36
203.07032	258.37595	330.03949	543.59869	1167.49753	37
220.31595	282.62978	364.04343	609.83053	1342.62216	38
238.94122	309.06646	401.44778	684.01020	1546.16549	39
259.05652	337.88245	442.59256	767.09142	1779.09031	40

TABLE 6-4 PRESENT VALUE OF AN ORDINARY ANNUITY OF 1

$$PVF\text{ - }OA_{n,\,i} = \frac{1 - \frac{1}{(1+i)^n}}{i} = \frac{1 - v^n}{i}$$

(n) Periods	2%	2-1/2%	3%	4%	5%	6%
1	.98039	.97561	.97087	.96154	.95238	.94340
2	1.94156	1.92742	1.91347	1.88609	1.85941	1.83339
3	2.88388	2.85602	2.82861	2.77509	2.72325	2.67301
4	3.80773	3.76197	3.71710	3.62990	3.54595	3.46511
5	4.71346	4.64583	4.57971	4.45182	4.32948	4.21236
6	5.60143	5.50813	5.41719	5.42414	5.07569	4.91732
7	6.47199	6.34939	6.23028	6.00205	5.78637	5.58238
8	7.32548	7.17014	7.01969	6.73274	6.46321	6.20979
9	8.16224	7.97087	7.78611	7.43533	7.10782	6.80169
10	8.98259	8.75206	8.53020	8.11090	7.72173	7.36009
11	9.78685	9.51421	9.25262	8.76048	8.30641	7.88687
12	10.57534	10.25776	9.95400	9.38507	8.86325	8.38384
13	11.34837	10.98319	10.63496	9.98565	9.39357	8.85268
14	12.10625	11.69091	11.29607	10.56312	9.89864	9.29498
15	12.84926	12.38138	11.93794	11.11839	10.37966	9.71225
16	13.57771	13.05500	12.56110	11.65230	10.83777	10.10590
17	14.29187	13.71220	13.16612	12.16567	11.27407	10.47726
18	14.99203	14.35336	13.75351	12.65930	11.68959	10.82760
19	15.67846	14.97889	14.32380	13.13394	12.08532	11.15812
20	16.35143	15.58916	14.87747	13.59033	12.46221	11.46992
21	17.01121	16.18455	15.41502	14.02916	12.82115	11.76408
22	17.65805	16.76541	15.93692	14.45112	13.16300	12.04158
23	18.29220	17.33211	16.44361	14.85684	13.48857	12.30338
24	18.91393	17.88499	16.93554	15.24696	13.79864	12.55036
25	19.52346	18.42438	17.41315	15.62208	14.09394	12.78336
26	20.12104	18.95061	17.87684	15.98277	14.37519	13.00217
27	20.70690	19.46401	18.32703	16.32959	14.64303	13.21053
28	21.28127	19.96489	18.76411	16.66306	14.89813	13.40616
29	21.84438	20.45355	19.18845	16.98371	15.14107	13.59072
30	22.39646	20.93029	19.60044	17.29203	15.37245	13.76483
31	22.93770	21.39541	20.00043	17.58849	15.59281	13.92909
32	23.46833	21.84918	20.38877	17.87355	15.80268	14.08404
33	23.98856	22.29188	20.76579	18.14765	16.00255	14.23023
34	24.49859	22.72379	21.13184	18.41120	16.19290	14.36814
35	24.99862	23.14516	21.48722	18.66461	16.37419	14.49825
36	25.48884	23.55625	21.83225	18.90828	16.54685	14.62099
37	25.96945	23.95732	22.16724	19.14258	16.71129	14.73678
38	26.44064	24.34860	22.49246	19.36786	16.86789	14.84602
39	26.90259	24.73034	22.80822	19.58448	17.01704	14.94907
40	27.35548	25.10278	23.11477	19.79277	17.15909	15.04630

8%	9%	10%	12%	15%	(n) Periods
.92593	.91743	.90909	.89286	.86957	1
1.78326	1.75911	1.73554	1.69005	1.62571	2
2.57710	2.53130	2.48685	2.40183	2.28323	3
3.31213	3.23972	3.16986	3.03735	2.85498	4
3.99271	3.88965	3.79079	3.60478	3.35216	5
4.62288	4.48592	4.35526	4.11141	3.78448	6
5.20637	5.03295	4.86842	4.56376	4.16042	7
5.74664	5.53482	5.33493	4.96764	4.48732	8
6.24689	5.99525	5.75902	5.32825	4.77158	9
6.71008	6.41766	6.14457	5.65022	5.01877	10
7.13896	6.80519	6.49506	5.93770	5.23371	11
7.53608	7.16073	6.81369	6.19437	5.42062	12
7.90378	7.48690	7.10336	6.42355	5.58315	13
8.24424	7.78615	7.36669	6.62817	5.72448	14
8.55948	8.06069	7.60608	6.81086	5.84737	15
8.85137	8.31256	7.82371	6.97399	5.95424	16
9.12164	8.54363	8.02155	7.11963	6.04716	17
9.37189	8.75563	8.20141	7.24967	6.12797	18
9.60360	8.95012	7.36492	7.36578	6.19823	19
9.81815	9.12855	8.51356	7.46944	6.25933	20
10.01680	9.29224	8.64869	7.56200	6.31246	21
10.20074	9.44243	8.77154	7.64465	6.35866	22
10.37106	9.58021	8.88322	7.71843	6.39884	23
10.52876	9.70661	8.98474	7.78432	6.43377	24
10.67478	9.82258	9.07704	7.84314	6.46415	25
10.80998	9.92897	9.16095	7.89566	6.49056	26
10.93516	10.02658	9.23722	7.94255	6.51353	27
11.05108	10.11613	9.30657	7.98442	6.53351	28
11.15841	10.19828	9.36961	8.02181	6.55088	29
11.25778	10.27365	9.42691	8.05518	6.56598	30
11.34980	10.34280	9.47901	8.08499	6.57911	31
11.43500	10.40624	9.52638	8.11159	6.59053	32
11.51389	10.46444	9.56943	8.13535	6.60046	33
11.58693	10.51784	9.60858	8.15656	6.60910	34
11.65457	10.56682	9.64416	8.17550	6.61661	35
11.71719	10.61176	9.67651	8.19241	6.62314	36
11.77518	10.65299	9.70592	8.20751	6.62882	37
11.82887	10.69082	9.73265	8.22099	6.63375	38
11.87858	10.72552	9.75697	8.23303	6.63805	39
11.92461	10.75736	9.77905	8.24378	6.64178	40

TABLE 6-5 PRESENT VALUE OF AN ANNUITY DUE OF 1

$$PVF\text{ - }AD_{n,i} = 1 + \frac{1 - \frac{1}{(1+i)^{n-1}}}{i} = (1+i) + \left(\frac{1-v^n}{i}\right) = (1+i)\left(a_{\overline{n}|i}\right)$$

(n) Periods	2%	2-1/2%	3%	4%	5%	6%
1	1.00000	1.00000	1.00000	1.00000	1.00000	1.00000
2	1.98039	1.97561	1.97087	1.96154	1.95238	1.94340
3	2.94156	2.92742	2.91347	2.88609	2.85941	2.83339
4	3.88388	3.85602	3.82861	3.77509	3.72325	3.67301
5	4.80773	4.76197	4.71710	4.62990	4.54595	4.46511
6	5.71346	5.64583	5.57971	5.45182	5.32948	5.21236
7	6.60143	6.50813	6.41719	6.24214	6.07569	5.91732
8	7.47199	7.34939	7.23028	7.00205	6.78637	6.58238
9	8.32548	8.17014	8.01969	7.73274	7.46321	7.20979
10	9.16224	8.97087	8.78611	8.43533	8.10782	7.80169
11	9.98259	9.75206	9.53020	9.11090	8.72173	8.36009
12	10.78685	10.51421	10.25262	9.76048	9.30641	8.88687
13	11.57534	11.25776	10.95400	10.38507	9.86325	9.38384
14	12.34837	11.98319	11.63496	10.98565	10.39357	9.85268
15	13.10625	12.69091	12.29607	11.56312	10.89864	10.29498
16	13.84926	13.38138	12.93794	12.11839	11.37966	10.71225
17	14.57771	14.05500	13.56110	12.65230	11.83777	11.10590
18	15.29187	14.71220	14.16612	13.16567	12.27407	11.47726
19	15.99203	15.35336	14.75351	13.65930	12.68959	11.82760
20	16.67846	15.97889	15.32380	14.13394	13.08532	12.15812
21	17.35143	16.58916	15.87747	14.59033	13.46221	12.46992
22	18.01121	17.18455	16.41502	15.02916	13.82115	12.76408
23	18.65805	17.76541	16.93692	15.45112	14.16300	13.04158
24	19.29220	18.33211	17.44361	15.85684	14.48857	13.30338
25	19.91393	18.88499	17.93554	16.24696	14.79864	13.55036
26	20.52346	19.42438	18.41315	16.62208	15.09394	13.78336
27	21.12104	19.95061	18.87684	16.98277	15.37519	14.00317
28	21.70690	20.46401	19.32703	17.32959	15.64303	14.21053
29	22.28127	20.96489	19.76411	17.66306	15.89813	14.40616
30	22.84438	21.45355	20.18845	17.98371	16.14107	14.59072
31	23.39646	21.93029	20.60044	18.29203	16.37245	14.76483
32	23.93770	22.39541	21.00043	18.58849	16.59281	14.92909
33	24.46833	22.84918	21.38877	18.87355	16.80268	15.08404
34	24.98856	23.29188	21.76579	19.14765	17.00255	15.23023
35	25.49859	23.72379	22.13184	19.41120	17.19290	15.36814
36	25.98862	24.14516	22.48722	19.66461	17.37419	15.49825
37	26.48884	24.55625	22.83255	19.90828	17.54685	15.62099
38	26.96945	24.95732	23.16724	20.14258	17.71129	15.73678
39	27.44064	25.34860	23.49246	20.36786	17.86789	15.84602
40	27.90259	25.73034	23.80822	20.58448	18.01704	15.94907

8%	9%	10%	12%	15%	(n) Periods
1.00000	1.00000	1.00000	1.00000	1.00000	1
1.92593	1.91743	1.90909	1.89286	1.86957	2
2.78326	2.75911	2.73554	2.69005	2.62571	3
3.57710	3.53130	3.48685	3.40183	3.28323	4
4.31213	4.23972	4.16986	4.03735	3.85498	5
4.99271	4.88965	4.79079	4.60478	4.35216	6
5.62288	5.48592	5.35526	5.11141	4.78448	7
6.20637	6.03295	5.86842	5.56376	5.16042	8
6.74664	6.53482	6.33493	5.96764	5.48732	9
7.24689	6.99525	6.75902	6.32825	5.77158	10
7.71008	7.41766	7.14457	6.65022	6.01877	11
8.13896	7.80519	7.49506	6.93770	6.23371	12
8.53608	8.16073	7.18369	7.19437	6.42062	13
8.90378	8.48690	8.10336	7.42355	6.58315	14
9.24424	8.78615	8.36669	7.62817	6.72448	15
9.55948	9.06069	8.60608	7.81086	6.84737	16
9.85137	9.31256	8.82371	7.97399	6.95424	17
10.12164	9.54363	9.02155	8.11963	7.04716	18
10.37189	9.75563	9.20141	8.24967	7.12797	19
10.60360	9.95012	9.36492	8.36578	7.19823	20
10.81815	10.12855	9.51356	8.46944	7.25933	21
11.01680	10.29224	9.64869	8.56200	7.31246	22
11.20074	10.44243	9.77154	8.64465	7.35866	23
11.37106	10.58021	9.88322	8.71843	7.39884	24
11.52876	10.70661	9.98474	8.78432	7.43377	25
11.67478	10.82258	10.07704	8.84314	7.46415	26
11.80998	10.92897	10.16095	8.89566	7.49056	27
11.93518	11.02658	10.23722	8.94255	7.51353	28
12.05108	11.11613	10.30657	8.98442	7.53351	29
12.15841	11.19828	10.36961	9.02181	7.55088	30
12.25778	11.27365	10.42691	9.05518	7.56598	31
12.34980	11.34280	10.47901	9.08499	7.57911	32
12.43500	11.40624	10.52638	9.11159	7.59053	33
12.51389	11.46444	10.56943	9.13535	7.60046	34
12.58693	11.51784	10.60858	9.15656	7.60910	35
12.65457	11.56682	10.64416	9.17550	7.61661	36
12.71719	11.61176	10.67651	9.19241	7.62314	37
12.77518	11.65299	10.70592	9.20751	7.62882	38
12.82887	11.69082	10.73265	9.22099	7.63375	39
12.87858	11.72552	10.75697	9.23303	7.63805	40

7

Cash and Receivables

CHAPTER STUDY OBJECTIVES

1. Identify items considered cash.
2. Indicate how cash and related items are reported.
3. Define receivables and identify the different types of receivables.
4. Explain accounting issues related to recognition of accounts receivable.
5. Explain accounting issues related to valuation of accounts receivables.
6. Explain accounting issues related to recognition of notes receivable.
7. Explain accounting issues related to valuation of notes receivable.
8. Explain accounting issues related to disposition of accounts and notes receivable.

*9. Explain common techniques employed to control cash.

**10. Prepare a proof of cash (four-column bank reconciliation).

CHAPTER REVIEW

1. (S.O. 1) Chapter 7 presents a detailed discussion of two of the primary liquid assets of a business enterprise, cash and receivables. Cash is the most liquid asset held by a business enterprise and possesses unique problems in its management and control. Receivables are composed of both accounts and notes receivables. Chapter coverage of accounts receivable places emphasis on trade receivables. In covering notes receivables, the chapter includes both short-term and long-term notes.

Nature of Cash

2. (S.O. 2) **Cash** consists of coin, currency, bank deposits, and negotiable instruments such as money orders, checks, and bank drafts. Cash that has been designated for some specific use, other than for payment of currently maturing obligations, is segregated from the general cash account. This amount may be classified as a current asset if it will be disbursed within one year or the operating cycle, whichever is longer. Otherwise, the amount should be shown as a noncurrent asset.

Management of Cash

3. Control over the handling of cash and cash transactions is an important consideration for any business enterprise. Cash presents special management and control problems because: (1) cash enters into a great many transactions; (2) cash is the single asset readily convertible into any other type of asset; and (3) neither too much nor too little should be available at any time. Amongst the control procedures that are used for cash transactions are the use of bank accounts such as a general checking account, imprest bank accounts and lockbox accounts.

* *Note: All asterisked (*) items relate to material contained in the Appendices to the chapter. All double asterisked (**) items relate to material contained on the Wiley web site.*

Petty Cash

4. In an imprest petty cash system, a petty cash custodian is given a small amount of currency from which to make small payments (minor office supplies, taxi, postage, etc.). Each time a disbursement is made, the petty cashier obtains a signed receipt for the payment. When cash in the fund runs low, the petty cashier submits the signed receipts to the general cashier and a check is prepared to replenish the petty cash fund. This process is designed to promote control over small cash disbursements which would be awkward to pay by check.

Compensating Balance

5. It is common practice for an enterprise to have an agreement with a bank concerning credit and borrowing arrangements. When such an agreement exists, the bank usually requires the enterprise to maintain a minimum cash balance on deposit. This minimum balance is known as a **compensating balance**. Compensating balances that result in legally restricted deposits must be separately classified in the balance sheet. The nature of the borrowing arrangement determines whether the compensating balance is classified as a current asset or a noncurrent asset.

6. Bank overdrafts occur when a check is written for more than the amount in the cash account. Bank overdrafts should be accounted for as accounts payable or, if material, separately disclosed. Cash equivalents are short-term, highly liquid investments that are both **(a)** readily convertible to known amounts of cash and **(b)** so near their maturity that they present insignificant risk of changes in interest rates.

Accounts Receivable

7. (S.O. 3) **Receivables** are defined as claims held against customers and others for money, goods, or services. Receivables may generally be classified as **trade** or **nontrade**. Trade receivables (accounts receivable and notes receivable) are the most significant receivables an enterprise possesses. Accounts receivable are oral promises of the purchaser to pay for goods and services sold. Notes receivable are written promises to pay a certain sum of money on a specified future date. Nontrade receivables arise from a variety of transactions and can be written promises either to pay or to deliver. Nontrade receivables are generally classified and reported as separate items in the balance sheet.

8. (S.O. 4) In most receivable transactions, the amount to be recognized is the exchange price (amount due from the debtor) between two parties to a sales transaction. Two elements that must be considered in measuring receivables are **(a)** the availability of discounts and **(b)** the length of time between the sale and the payment due date (the interest factor).

9. Two types of discounts that must be considered in determining the value of receivables are **trade discounts** and **cash discounts**. Trade discounts represent reductions from the list or catalog prices of merchandise. They are often used to avoid frequent changes in catalogs or to quote different prices for different quantities purchased. Cash discounts (also called sales discounts) are offered as an inducement for prompt payment and are communicated in terms that read, for example, 2/10, n/30 (2% discount if paid within 10 days of the purchase or invoice date, otherwise the gross amount is due in 30 days).

10. (S.O. 5) It is highly unlikely that a company that extends credit to its customers will be successful in collecting all of its receivables. Thus, some method must be adopted to account for receivables that ultimately prove to be uncollectible. The two methods currently used are the **direct write-off method** and the **allowance method**. Under the direct write-off method, the receivable account is reduced and an expense is recorded when a specific account is determined to be uncollectible. The direct-write off method is theoretically deficient because it usually does not match costs and revenues of the period, nor does it result in receivables being stated at estimated realizable value on the balance sheet. The direct write-off method is not appropriate if the amount deemed uncollectible is material.

11. Use of the allowance method requires a year-end estimate of expected uncollectible accounts based upon credit sales or outstanding receivables. The estimate is recorded by debiting an expense and crediting an allowance account in the period in which the sale is recorded. Then in a subsequent period when an account is deemed to be uncollectible, an entry is made debiting the allowance account and crediting accounts receivable.

12. Advocates of the allowance method contend that its use provides for a proper matching of revenues and expenses as well as reflecting a proper carrying value for accounts receivable at the end of the period. When the allowance method is used, the estimated amount of uncollectible accounts is normally based upon a percentage of sales or outstanding receivables. The **percentage-of-sales method** attempts to match costs with revenues, and is frequently referred to as the income statement approach. The **percentage-of-outstanding-receivables approach** provides a reasonably accurate estimate of the net realizable value of receivables shown on the balance sheet. This approach is commonly referred to as the balance sheet approach.

13. The method used to determine the amount of bad debts expense each year affects the amount of expense recorded. Under the percentage-of-sales method, the amount recorded as bad debts expense is the amount determined by multiplying the estimated percentage times the credit sales. However, under the outstanding-receivables approach, the unadjusted ending balance in the allowance account must be considered in arriving at bad debts expense for the year.

Special Allowance Accounts

14. To properly match expenses to sales revenues, it is sometimes necessary to establish additional allowance accounts as contra accounts to accounts receivable. The most common allowances are the allowance for sales returns and allowances.

Notes Receivable

15. (S.O. 6) The major differences between trade accounts receivables and **trade notes receivables** are (a) notes represent a formal promise to pay and (b) notes bear an interest element because of the time value of money. Notes are classified as notes bearing interest equal to the effective rate and those bearing interest different than the effective rate. **Interest-bearing notes** have a stated rate of interest, whereas **noninterest-bearing notes (zero-interest bearing)** include the interest as part of their face amount instead of stating it explicitly.

16. (S.O. 7) Short-term notes are generally recorded at face value (less allowances) because the interest implicit in the maturity value is immaterial. A general rule is that notes treated as cash equivalents (maturities of 3 months or less) are not subject to premium or discount amortization. Long-term notes receivable, however, are recorded at the present value of the future cash inflows. Determination of the present value can be complicated, particularly when a zero interest-bearing note

or a note bearing an unreasonable interest rate is involved. There are three important categories discussed in the text for accounting for notes receivable that have an unrealistic stated rate of interest. These categories are (**a**) notes received solely for cash, (**b**) notes received for cash, but with some right or privilege also being exchanged, and (**c**) notes received in a noncash exchange for property, goods, or services.

17. Long-term notes receivable should be recorded and reported at the present value of the cash expected to be collected. When the interest stated on an interest-bearing note is equal to the effective (market) rate of interest, the note sells at face value. When the stated rate is different from the market rate, the cash exchanged (present value) is different from the face value of the note. The difference between the face value and the cash exchanged, either a **discount** or a **premium**, is then recorded and amortized over the life of the note to approximate the effective interest rate. The discount or premium is shown on the balance sheet as a direct deduction from or addition to the face of the note.

18. Whenever the face amount of a note does not reasonably represent the present value of the consideration given or received in the exchange, the accountant must evaluate the entire arrangement to record properly the exchange and the subsequent interest. Notes receivable are sometimes issued with zero interest rate stated or at a stated rate that is unreasonable. In such instances the present value of the note is measured by the cash proceeds to the borrower or fair value of the property, goods, or services rendered. The difference between the face amount of the note and the cash proceeds or fair value of the property represents the total amount of interest during the life of the note. If the fair value of the property, goods, or services rendered is not determinable, estimation of the present value requires use of an **imputed interest rate**. The choice of a rate may be affected specifically by the credit standing of the issuer, restrictive covenants, collateral, payment, and the existing prime interest rate. Determination of the imputed interest rate is made when the note is received; any subsequent changes in prevailing interest rates are ignored.

Assigning and Factoring

19. (S.O. 8) Companies wishing to avoid the 30- to 60-day collection period for accounts receivables can generate cash immediately by either **assigning** or **factoring** their accounts receivable. Assignment is a borrowing-type arrangement in which assigned accounts receivable are pledged as security for the loan received. Factoring of accounts receivable is an outright sale of the receivables to a finance company or bank.

20. The assignment of accounts receivable can be a **general assignment** or a **specific assignment**. In a general assignment, all accounts receivable serve as collateral for the note. Thus, new receivables can be substituted for the ones collected. In a specific assignment, an agreement is reached between the borrower and lender concerning (**a**) who is to receive the collections, (**b**) the finance charges, (**c**) the specific accounts that serve as security, and (**d**) notification or nonnotification of debtors. The accounts assigned in a specific assignment should be transferred to a special ledger control account, and assignment should be clearly noted in the subsidiary ledger.

21. When accounts and notes receivable are factored (sold), the factoring arrangement can be **with recourse** or **without recourse**. If receivables are factored on a with recourse basis, the seller guarantees payment to the factor in the event the debtor does not make payment. When a factor buys receivables without recourse, the factor assumes the risk of collectibility and absorbs any credit losses. Receivables that are factored with recourse should be accounted for as a sale, recognizing any gain or loss, if all three of the following conditions are met: **(a)** transferor surrenders control of the future economic benefits of the receivables, **(b)** transferor's obligation under the recourse provisions can be reasonably estimated, and **(c)** transferee cannot require the transferor to repurchase the receivables. If these conditions are not met, the transfer is accounted for as a borrowing.

22. The presentation of receivables in the balance sheet includes the following considerations: **(a)** segregate the different receivables that an enterprise possesses, if material; **(b)** insure that the valuation accounts are appropriately offset against the proper receivable accounts: **(c)** determine that receivables classified in the current asset section will be converted into cash within the year or the operating cycle, whichever is longer; **(d)** disclose any loss contingencies that exists on the receivables; **(e)** disclose any receivables assigned or pledged as collateral; and **(f)** disclose all significant concentrations of credit risk arising from receivables.

***Bank Reconciliation**

*23. (S.O. 9) A basic cash control is preparation of a monthly bank reconciliation. The bank reconciliation, when properly prepared, proves that the cash balance per bank and the cash balance per book are in agreement. The items that cause the bank and book balances to differ, and thus require preparation of a bank reconciliation, are the following:

a. **Deposits in Transit**. Deposits recorded in the cash account in one period but not received by the bank until the next period.
b. **Outstanding Checks.** Checks written by the company that have yet to be presented at the bank for collection.
c. **Bank Charges.** Charges by the bank for services that are deducted from the account by the bank and which the company learns of when it receives the bank statement.
d. **Bank Credits.** Collections or deposits in the company's account that the company is not aware of until receipt of the bank statement.
e. **Bank or Depositor Errors.** Errors made by the company or the bank that must be corrected for the reconciliation to balance.

*24. Two forms of bank reconciliation may be prepared. One form reconciles from the bank statement balance to the book balance or vice versa. The other form is described as **the reconciliation of bank and book balances to corrected cash balance.** This form is composed of two separate sections that begin with the bank balance and book balance, respectively. Reconciling items that apply to the bank balance are added and subtracted to arrive at the corrected cash balance. Likewise, reconciling items that apply to the book balance are added and subtracted to arrive at the same corrected cash balance. The corrected cash balance is the amount that should be shown on the balance sheet at the reconciliation date.

**25. (S.O. 10) The Wiley web site presents a description of a four-column bank reconciliation. This type of reconciliation is most often used by auditors in connection with their examination of any entity's financial statements.

GLOSSARY

Accounts Receivable. Oral promises of the purchaser to pay for goods and services sold.

Aging Schedule. The analysis of customer balances by the length of time they have been unpaid.

Allowance Method. A method for recording uncollectible receivables where an estimate is made of the expected uncollectible receivables.

Assignment of Receivables. The owner of the receivables borrows cash from a lender by writing a promissory note designating or pledging the accounts receivable as collateral.

Bank Charges. A fee charged by the bank for its services.

Bank Credits. Collections or deposits by the bank for the benefit of the depositor that have not been recorded by the depositor.

Bank Overdrafts. When a check is written for more than the amount in the cash account.

***Bank Reconciliation.** A schedule explaining any differences between the company's record and the bank's record of the company's cash.

Cash. Resources that consist of coin, currency, money orders, certified checks, cashier's checks, personal checks, and bank drafts.

Cash Equivalents. Short-term, highly liquid investments that are both (a) readily convertible to known amounts of cash, and (b) so near their maturity that they present insignificant risk of changes in interest rates.

Cash (Sales) Discounts. Discounts offered as an inducement for prompt payment communicated in terms that read, for example, 2/10, n/30.

Compensating Balances. Minimum cash balances required by a bank in support of bank loans.

Deposits in Transit. Deposits recorded by the depositor that have not been recorded by the bank.

Direct Write-Off Method. A method for recording uncollectible receivables where no entry is made until a specific account has been established as uncollectible.

Dishonored Notes.	A note that is not paid in full at maturity.
Electronic Funds Transfer (EFT).	A process that uses wire, telephone, telegraph, computer, satellite, or other electronic device rather than paper to make instantaneous transfers of funds.
Factoring Receivables.	When a finance company or bank buys receivables from a business for a fee and then collects the remittances directly from the customers.
Imprest Petty Cash System.	A cash fund used to pay relatively small amounts.
Lockbox Account.	An account where customer remittances are mailed to a local post office box and a local bank is authorized to pick up the remittances mailed to it.
Net Realizable Value.	The net amount expected to be received in cash.
Notes Receivable.	Written promises to pay a certain sum of money on a specified future date.
Not-Sufficient-Funds (NSF) Check.	A check that is not paid by a bank because of insufficient funds in a customer's bank account.
Outstanding Checks.	Checks issued and recorded by a company that have not been paid by the bank.
Percentage-of-Receivables (Balance Sheet) Approach.	Management establishes a percentage relationship between the amount of receivables and the expected losses from uncollectible accounts.
Percentage of Sales (Income Statement) Approach.	Management establishes a percentage relationship between the amount of credit sales and expected losses from uncollectible accounts.
Promissory Note.	A negotiable instrument signed by a maker promising to pay a certain sum of money at a specified future date to a designated payee.
Receivables.	Claims held against customers and others for money, goods, or services.
Sales Returns and Allowances.	When a customer returns goods to the seller for credit or cash refund or when a customer has chosen to keep defective merchandise and receive a deduction from the selling price.

Trade Discount. The difference between list or catalog prices and discounted prices which are used to avoid frequent changes in catalogs and to quote different prices for different quantities purchased.

Trade Receivables. Amounts owed by customers for goods sold and services rendered as part of normal business operations.

Transfer Without Recourse. When receivables are sold and the purchaser assumes the risk of collectibility and absorbs any credit losses.

Transfer With Recourse. When receivables are sold and the seller guarantees payment to the purchaser in the event the debtor fails to pay.

Zero Interest Note. A note which has no stated interest rate but has effective interest inherent in the instrument because of the difference in the present value of the note and its maturity value.

CHAPTER OUTLINE

Fill in the outline presented below.

(S.O. 1) Definition of Cash

Items Considered to be Cash

Items Considered to be Temporary Investments

Other Items Not Considered to be Cash

(S.O. 2) Management and Control of Cash

Imprest Petty Cash System

Reporting Cash

Restricted Cash

Bank Overdrafts

Cash Equivalents

Chapter Outline *(continued)*

(S.O. 4) Definitions of the Different Types of Receivables

Recognition of Accounts Receivable

Trade Discounts

Cash (Sales) Discounts

(S.O. 5) Valuation of Accounts Receivable

Direct Write-Off Method

Allowance Method

Percentage-of-Sales Approach

Percentage-of-Receivables Approach

Sales Returns and Allowances

(S.O. 6) Recognition of Notes Receivable

Notes Bearing Interest

Zero Interest or Unreasonable Interest-Bearing Notes

Chapter Outline *(continued)*

(S.O. 7) Valuation of Notes Receivable

(S.O. 8) Assignment of Accounts Receivable

General Assignment

Specific Assignment

Factoring of Accounts Receivable

Factoring Without Recourse

Factoring With Recourse

Balance Sheet Presentation of Receivables

*(S.O. 9) Bank Reconciliation

Reconciling Items for the Balance per Bank Statement

Reconciling Items for the Balance per Books

**(S.O. 10) Four-Column Bank Reconciliation

REVIEW QUESTIONS AND EXERCISES

TRUE-FALSE

Indicate whether each of the following is true (T) or false (F) in the space provided.

_____ 1. (S.O. 1) Cash consists of coin, currency, money market funds, certificates of deposit and other available funds on deposit at the bank.

_____ 2. (S.O. 1) Postage stamps on hand are classified as part of cash.

_____ 3. (S.O. 1) Because the bank has the legal right to demand notice before withdrawal, savings accounts usually are not classified on an entity's balance sheet as cash.

_____ 4. (S.O. 2) The replenishment of the petty cash fund under an imprest system requires a debit to the Petty Cash account for the amount of the replenishment.

_____ 5. (S.O. 2) If cash proves out short in a petty cash fund, the shortage is debited to the Cash Over and Short account.

_____ 6. (S.O. 2) Legally restricted deposits held as compensating balances against short-term borrowing arrangements should be stated separately among the cash and cash items in current assets.

_____ 7. (S.O. 2) Bond sinking fund cash should not be classified as a current asset because its use is restricted.

_____ 8. (S.O. 2) Bank overdrafts occur when a check is written for less than the amount in the cash account.

_____ 9. (S.O. 3) Accounts receivable are frequently accepted from customers who need to extend the payment period of an outstanding note receivable.

_____ 10. (S.O. 4) When a sale and the related receivable are initially recorded at the gross amount, sales discounts will be recognized in the accounts only when payment is received within the discount period.

_____ 11. (S.O. 5) The direct write-off method used in recording uncollectible accounts receivable allows the expense associated with bad debts always to be recorded in the accounting period in which the sale was made.

_____ 12. (S.O. 5) Because the collectibility of receivables is considered a loss contingency, the allowance method for recording bad debts is appropriate only in situations where it is probable that an asset has been impaired and that the amount of the loss can be reasonably estimated.

_____ 13. (S.O. 5) The percentage-of-receivables approach is also referred to as the income statement approach.

_____ 14. (S.O. 5) It is improper to offset assets and liabilities in the balance sheet, except where a right of offset exists.

_____ 15. (S.O. 5) The inclusion in the income statement of all returns and allowances made during the period is not acceptable accounting practice as some of the returns and allowances resulted from sales of a prior period and, thus, the matching concept is violated.

_____ 16. (S.O. 7) The process of interest-rate approximation is called imputation, and the resulting interest rate is called the imputed interest rate.

_____ 17. (S.O. 7) A trade receivable due two years hence should never be classified as a current asset.

_____ 18. (S.O. 8) Factoring is the term used to describe the pledging of receivables as collateral for a loan.

_____ 19. (S.O. 8) If receivables are sold with recourse, the seller guarantees payment to the purchaser in the event the debtor does not pay.

_____ 20. (S.O. 8) The credit balance in Unamortized Discount on Notes Receivable should be classified on the balance sheet as a deferred credit.

_____ 21. (S.O. 8) The present value of a note is measured by the fair value of the property, goods, or services exchanged for the note or by an amount that reasonably approximates the market value of the note.

_____ 22. (S.O. 8) The essence of a transfer of receivables in a borrowing transaction is that the transferor retains the same risks of collectibility on the receivables after the transaction that it had before the transaction.

_____ *23. (S.O. 9) A bank reconciliation is an integral part of the system of internal control over cash.

_____ *24. (S.O. 9) Of the two bank reconciliation formats used by a business entity, the more widely used form reconciles both the bank balance and the book balance to a correct cash balance.

_____ *25. (S.O. 9) When preparing a bank reconciliation for the purpose of arriving at a correct cash balance, NSF (not sufficient funds) checks are subtracted from the balance per books.

DEMONSTRATION PROBLEMS

1. (S.O. 5) The following account balances appeared on the trial balance of Cobb Company at 12/31:

	Dr.	Cr.
Accounts Receivable	$88,500	
Allowance for Doubtful Accounts		2,065
Sales		452,600
Sales Returns	3,200	

Required:

What amount would be debited or credited to Allowance for Doubtful Accounts if the company records bad debts expense based on:

a. 2% of net sales
b. 8% of accounts receivable

Solution:

a. Net sales ([$452,600 - $3,200] x .02) $8,988 — $8,988
(The current balance in the "Allowance account is not considered. Thus, the "Allowance" account would have a balance of $11,053 ($8,988 + $2,065) after the entry)

b.	
$88,500 x.08	$7,080
Less current "Allowance" balance	2,065
Entry amount	$5,015

2. (S.O. 7) On December 31, 2001, Sondgeroth Construction Company accepted a promissory note from Morgan Enterprises for services rendered. The note has a face value of $475,000, is due December 31, 2008, and pays interest annually at a stated rate of 3%. The market rate of interest for a note of similar risk is 9%.

Required:

Compute the present value of the note and the amount of discount.

Solution:

Face value of the note		$475,000
Present value of $475,000 due in 7 years at 9%:		
$475,000 x .54703 (Table 6-2)	$259,839	
Present value of $14,250 payable annually for 7 years at 9%:		
$14,250 x 5.03295 (Table 6-4)	71,720	
Present value of the note		331,559
Discount		$143,441

Demonstration Problems *(continued)*

*3. (S.O. 9) The following information applies to the cash account of the Nick Price Aviation Corporation as of August 31.

Balance per company books	$7,165.84
Bank service charge for August	25.00
Note collected for the company by the bank	1,200.00
August outstanding checks	1,822.17
NSF* check returned with August bank statement	328.45
Balance per August bank statement	8,438.56
Interest on the note collected by the bank	54.00
Receipts recorded on August 31 and sent to the bank that night	1,450.00

* Not sufficient funds.

Required:

A. Prepare a bank reconciliation for Price Aviation Corporation at August 31 that shows the correct cash balance as of that date.
B. Prepare any necessary journal entries.

Solution:

A. Price Aviation Corporation

Bank Reconciliation
August 31

Book balance		$7,165.84	Bank Balance	$8,438.56
Add:			Add:	
Note collected		1,200.00	Deposit in transit	1,450.00
Interest on note		54.00		9,888.56
		8,419.84		
Less:				
Service charge	25.00		Less:	
NSF check	328.45	353.45	Outstanding checks	1,822.17
Correct cash balance		$8,066.39		$8,066.39

B.

Miscellaneous expense	25.00	
Accounts receivable	328.45	
Cash		353.45
Cash	1,254.00	
Notes receivable		1,200.00
Interest income		54.00

MULTIPLE CHOICE

Select the best answer for each of the following items and enter the corresponding letter in the space provided.

_____ 1. (S.O. 1) Which of the following is properly classified as cash?

A. Customer's postdated checks on hand.
B. Certificates of deposit.
C. Savings accounts.
D. Bond sinking fund cash.

_____ 2. (S.O. 1) Kari, Inc.'s book balance on December 31, 2001, was $5,000. In addition, Kari had the following items on its premises on December 31:

Check payable to Kari, Inc., dated January 3, 2002, included in December 31 book balance	$ 200
Postage stamps on hand not included in December 31 book balance	100
Cashier's check payable to Kari, Inc., dated December 28, 2001, not included in December 31 book balance	1,300

The proper amount to be shown as Cash on Kari's balance sheet at December 31, 2001, is

A. $6,100
B. $6,200
C. $6,300
D. $6,400

_____ 3. (S.O. 2) Etheredge Company held an IOU at December 31, 2001. The IOU should be reported as

A. an investment.
B. petty cash.
C. cash.
D. a receivable.

_____ 4. (S.O. 2) Which of the following journal entries is appropriate to establish an imprest petty cash fund?

A.	Petty Cash Fund	500	
	Cash		500
B.	Petty Cash Expense	500	
	Cash		500
C.	Administrative Expense	100	
	Selling Expense	200	
	Operating Expense	200	
	Cash		500
D.	Miscellaneous Expense	500	
	Cash		500

_____ 5. (S.O. 2) A compensating balance as defined by the SEC is best reflected by which of the following?

A. A savings account maintained at the bank equal to the amount of all outstanding loans.
B. An amount of capital stock held in the company's treasury equal to outstanding loan commitments.
C. The portion of any demand deposit, time deposit, or certificate of deposit maintained by a corporation which constitutes support for existing borrowing arrangements of the corporation with the lending institution.
D. A balance held in a time or demand deposit account that is equal to the interest currently due on a loan.

_____ 6. (S.O. 2) A cash equivalent is a short-term, highly liquid investment that is readily convertible into known amounts of cash and

A. is acceptable as a means to pay current liabilities.
B. has a current market value that is greater than its original cost
C. bears an interest rate that is at least equal to the prime rate of interest at the date of liquidation.
D. is so near its maturity that it presents insignificant risk of changes in interest rates.

_____ 7. (S.O. 3) What is the preferable presentation of accounts receivable from officers, employees, or affiliated companies on a balance sheet?

A. As offsets to capital.
B. By means of footnotes only.
C. As assets but separately from other receivables.
D. As trade notes and accounts receivable if they otherwise qualify as current assets.

_____ 8. (S.O. 4) When a customer purchases merchandise inventory from a business organization, she may be given a discount which is designed to induce prompt payment. Such a discount is called a(n)

A. trade discount.
B. nominal discount.
C. enhancement discount.
D. cash discount.

_____ 9. (S.O. 5) The advantage of relating a company's bad debt expense to its accounts receivable is that this approach:

A. gives a reasonably correct measure of receivables in the balance sheet.
B. relates bad debt expense to the period of sale.
C. is the only generally accepted method of valuing accounts receivable.
D. makes estimates of uncollectible accounts unnecessary.

_____ 10. (S.O. 5) Which of the following statements is not correct regarding uncollectible accounts receivable?

A. The direct write-off method records the bad debt in the year that it is determined that a specific receivable cannot be collected.
B. The allowance method is based on the assumption that the percentage of receivables that will not be collected can be predicted from past experiences, present market conditions, and an analysis of outstanding balances.
C. The direct write-off method will provide for a proper matching of costs with revenues of the period when the average monthly accounts receivable balance is consistent throughout the year.
D. An uncollectible account receivable is a loss of revenue that requires—through proper entry in the accounts—a decrease in the asset accounts receivable and a related decrease in income and stockholder's equity.

_____ 11. (S.O. 5) For the month of December 2001, the records of White Corporation show the following information:

Cash sales	$20,000
Cash received on accounts receivable	25,000
Accounts receivable, December 1, 2001	70,000
Accounts receivable, December 31, 2001	64,000
Accounts receivable written off as uncollectible	1,000

The White Corporation uses the direct write-off method in accounting for uncollectible accounts receivable. What are the gross sales for the month of December 31, 1998?

A. $39,000
B. $40,000
C. $45,000
D. $52,000

_____ 12. (S.O. 5) The allowance method is preferable to the direct write-off method because the allowance method

A. relies on estimates which are always accurate and stable among years.
B. reflects the real facts.
C. recognizes the expense of a bad debt in the year in which the account is determined to be uncollectible.
D. recognizes the expense of a bad debt in the same period as the sale.

_____ 13. (S.O. 5) Green Company wrote off a client's account receivable of $400 as uncollectible. What will be the effect on net income under each of the following methods of recognizing bad debt expense?

	Direct Write-Off	Allowance
A.	None	Decrease
B.	Decrease	None
C.	None	None
D.	Decrease	Decrease

_____ 14. (S.O. 5) Gardin Corporation uses the allowance method of accounting for uncollectible accounts. During 2001 Gardin had charges to Bad Debts Expense of $20,000 and wrote off as uncollectible, accounts receivable totaling $16,000. These transactions decreased working capital by:

A. $20,000.
B. $16,000.
C. $ 4,000.
D. $ 0.

_____ 15. (S.O. 5) The basic accounting issues for both accounts receivable and notes receivable would center around which of the following?

	Recognition	Valuation
A.	Yes	No
B.	Yes	Yes
C.	No	Yes
D.	No	No

_____ 16. (S.O. 6) Moluf Corporation receives a 5-year, $20,000 zero interest-bearing note, the present value of which is $11,348.60. What is the implicit interest rate that equates the total cash to be received to the present value of the future cash flows?

A. 8%
B. 9%
C. 10%
D. 12%

_____ 17. (S.O. 7) Pinkowski sold land to Ewell for $100,000 cash and a zero interest-bearing note with a face amount of $400,000. The fair value of the land at the date of sale was $450,000. Pinkowski should value the note receivable at:

A. $450,000.
B. $400,000.
C. $350,000.
D. $500,000.

_____ 18. (S.O. 7) Vonesh Company sold a drill press to Mary Company, taking in exchange a zero interest-bearing note. The drill press had a fair market value of $12,000 and the face amount of the note was $13,000. In a balance sheet prepared immediately after receipt of the note, Vonesh should present the note at its face amount

A. plus implicit interest.
B. plus the anticipated net earnings related to the note.
C. less implicit interest.
D. without adjustment.

_____ 19. (S.O. 8) Which of the following statements is incorrect regarding the classification of accounts and notes receivable?

A. Segregation of the different types of receivables is required if they are material.
B. Disclose any loss contingencies that exist on the receivables.
C. Any discount or premium resulting from the determination of present value in notes receivable transactions is an asset or liability respectively.
D. Valuation accounts should be appropriately offset against the proper receivable accounts.

_____ 20. (S.O. 8) Thresher Corporation sold its accounts receivable outright to Kari Company, a financing company which normally buys accounts receivable of other companies without recourse. The accounts receivable have been

A. collateralized.
B. pledged.
C. factored.
D. assigned.

_____ 21. (S.O. 8) In which of the following accounts receivable assignment arrangements do all receivables serve as collateral for the promissory note given by the assignor?

	General Assignment	Specific Assignment
A.	Yes	Yes
B.	Yes	No
C.	No	Yes
D.	No	No

_____ 22. (S.O. 8) Of the following conditions, which is the only one that is not required if the transfer of receivables with recourse is to be accounted for as a sale?

A. The transferor is obligated to make a genuine effort to identify those receivables that are uncollectible.
B. The transferor surrenders control of the future economic benefits of the receivables.
C. The transferee cannot require the transferor to repurchase the receivables.
D. The transferor's obligation under the recourse provisions can be reasonably estimated.

_____*23. (S.O. 9) When preparing a bank reconciliation for the purpose of arriving at the correct cash balance:

A. outstanding checks can be added to the balance per books.
B. NSF checks should be deducted from the balance per books.
C. deposits in transit are deducted from the balance per bank.
D. notes collected by the bank should be added to the balance per bank.

_____*24. (S.O. 9) In a bank reconciliation that attempts to reconcile the bank balance to the corrected cash balance, the following items would affect the reconciliation in what way?

	Outstanding Checks	Deposits In Transit
A.	Added	Added
B.	Subtracted	Added
C.	Added	Subtracted
D.	Subtracted	Subtracted

_____*25. (S.O. 9) In preparing its bank reconciliation for the month of September 2001, Chudzick Company has available the following information:

Balance per bank statement, 9/30/98	$42,000
Deposits in transit, 9/30/98	7,200
Outstanding checks, 9/30/98	6,500
Bank service charges for September	25

What should be the correct balance of cash at September 30, 2001?

A. $41,275
B. $41,300
C. $42,675
D. $42,700

REVIEW EXERCISES

1. (S.O. 5) A trial balance for Foerch Company shows the following balances at December 31:

	Debit	Credit
Accounts Receivable	$120,000	
Allowance for Doubtful Accounts		$ 200
Sales	360,000	
Sales Discounts	10,000	

Instructions:
Prepare the adjusting entry necessary at December 31 to provide for estimated uncollectibles under each of the following independent assumptions.

a. Foerch Company uses the percentage of sales method of accounting for uncollectible accounts. Company experience indicates that 1% of net sales will prove uncollectible.
b. Foerch bases its estimate of uncollectible accounts on an aging of accounts receivable. The aging at December 31 indicates uncollectible accounts of $4,000.

a.

General Journal

J1

Date	Account Title	Debit	Credit

b.

General Journal

J1

Date	Account Title	Debit	Credit

2. (S.O. 8) The following transactions of Relias Company occurred during 2001.

August 14 -- Sold merchandise on account to Erml Company for $10,000.

September 5 -- Received a $10,000, 6%, 60-day note dated September 5 from Erml Company for the sale made on August 14.

September 5 -- Factored the note receivable from Erml Company at McEllen State Bank. The transfer was without recourse and had a finance charge of 4% of the amount of the note and the Bank retained an amount equal to 5% of the note.

Instructions:
Prepare the journal entries necessary to record the above transactions for Relias Company.

General Journal			J1
Date	Account Title	Debit	Credit

3. (S.O. 6 and 7) DeFilippo Company agreed to loan Morreale Glass Corporation $400,000. Morreale Glass Corporation gave a zero interest-bearing note due in 4 years and also promised to provide DeFilippo Company with glass products at a special discount price. (A 12% interest rate is an appropriate rate for both companies.)

Instructions:

a. Prepare the journal entry DeFilippo Company would make to record this transaction.
b. Prepare an amortization schedule for the note using the effective interest method.

a.

General Journal

J1

Date	Account Title	Debit	Credit

b.

Year	Cash Interest	Effective Interest	Discount Amortized	Unamortized Discount	Note Present Value
1					
2					
3					
4					

4. (S.O. 8) Ehrlich Company factors $175,000 of accounts receivable with Vegas Finance Corporation on a without recourse basis on July 1, 2001. All the records related to the receivables are transferred to Vegas Finance as it will receive the collections. Vegas Finance assesses a finance charge of 2% of the amount of accounts receivable and retains an amount equal to 5% of accounts receivable to cover sales discounts, returns, and allowances.

Instructions:

a. Prepare the journal entry that Ehrlich Company would make to record the sale of these receivables on July 1, 2001.
b. Prepare the journal entry that Vegas Finance Corporation would make to record the purchase of the receivables on July 1, 2001.

a.

General Journal J1

Date	Account Title	Debit	Credit

b.

General Journal J1

Date	Account Title	Debit	Credit

*5. (S.O. 9) You are asked to prepare a bank reconciliation for Malikowski Company as of October 31, 2001. By placing the appropriate letter in the space provided, indicate whether the following items should be:

A. added to the balance per bank statement.
B. deducted from the balance per bank statement.
C. added to the balance per books.
D. deducted from the balance per books.
E. omitted from the bank reconciliation because the bank amount and the book amount are already in agreement with respect to this item.

_____ 1. Outstanding checks of Malikowski Company as of October 31, 2001; the checks were written in October 2001.

_____ 2. Outstanding checks of Malikowski Company as of October 31, 2001; the checks were written in September 2001.

_____ 3. A check of Mankowski Company had been charged by the bank against the account of Malikowski Company.

_____ 4. A certified check by Malikowski Company, dated October 10, 2001, is outstanding as of October 31.

_____ 5. Bank service charges for October.

_____ 6. Discovered that check No. 101 (one of the cancelled checks included with the bank statement) had been made out to Blue Company (a creditor) for $100. Malikowski Company had recorded the check in its Cash Payments Journal in the amount of $1,000.

_____ 7. Malikowski Company understated the amount of a customer's check in its Cash Receipts Journal. The check was received and deposited by Malikowski in October.

SOLUTIONS TO REVIEW QUESTIONS

TRUE-FALSE

1. (F) Cash consists of coin, currency, and available funds on deposit at the bank. Money market funds, money market savings certificates, certificates of deposit (CDs), and similar types of deposits that provide small investors with an opportunity to earn high rates of interest are more appropriately classified as temporary investments.

2. (F) Postage stamps on hand are classified as part of office supplies inventory or as a prepaid expense.

3. (F) Banks rarely exercise the right to demand notice before withdrawal of funds from a savings account. Thus, these funds are normally classified as cash for financial reporting purposes.

4. (F) Entries are made to the Petty Cash account only to increase or decrease the size of the fund. When the petty cash fund is replenished, various expense accounts are debited and the cash account is credited.

5. (T)

6. (T)

7. (T)

8. (F) Bank overdrafts occur when a check is written for more than the amount in the cash account.

9. (F) Notes receivables are frequently accepted from customers who need to extend the payment period of an outstanding accounts receivable.

10. (T)

11. (F) The direct write-off method does not always match costs with revenues of the period. This is because receivables recorded late in one year might be written off in a subsequent year under the direct write-off method.

12. (T)

13. (F) The percentage-of-sales approach is also referred to as the income statement approach. The percentage-of-receivables approach is also referred to as the balance sheet approach.

14. (T)

15. (F) Including all returns and allowances in the current period's income statement is an acceptable accounting practice justified on the basis of practicality and immateriality.

16. (T)

17. (F) The rule about classification of current assets is that the item is classified as a current asset if it will be converted into cash within one year or the operating cycle, whichever is longer. Thus, if a company had an operating cycle of two years or longer, the trade receivable due in two years would be classified as a current asset.

18. (F) Factoring is the sale of accounts receivable to factors. Factors are finance companies or banks that buy receivables from businesses for a fee and then collect remittances directly from the customer.

19. (T)

20. (F) Unamortized discounts and premiums on notes receivable are classified along with the note. Discounts are deducted from notes receivable and premiums are added to notes receivable when shown on the balance sheet.

21. (T)

22. (T)

*23. (T)

*24. (T)

*25. (T)

MULTIPLE CHOICE

1. (C) A customer's postdated check is most appropriately classified as a receivable. Certificates of deposit provide investors with an opportunity to earn high rates of interest and should be classified as temporary investments rather than cash. Bond sinking fund cash is restricted and is classified either in the current asset or in the long-term asset section, depending on the date of disbursement. A savings account is the only item listed that is properly classified as cash.

2. (A) Kari should show cash of $6,100 on its December 31, 2001 balance sheet. This corrected cash balance can be calculated as follows:

Unadjusted cash balance at 12/31/01		$5,000
Add:	Cashier's check	1,300
Less:	Postdated check	(200)
Correct cash balance at 12/31/01		$6,100

3. (D) IOUs should be reported as receivables. Only coin, currency, available funds on deposit at the bank, money orders, certified checks, cashier's checks, personal checks, and bank drafts should be reported as part of the cash balance.

4. (A) The establishment of an imprest petty cash account requires the establishment of a fund that is recorded in an asset account. In an imprest petty cash system the fund is replenished by an entry debiting expense account(s) and crediting cash.

5. (C) The SEC defines the concept of a compensating balance in terms of deposits with a lending institution that support existing borrowing arrangements. The amount is not specified to be equal to outstanding loans nor is the interest due a consideration.

6. (D) A cash equivalent is classified as such due to quick convertibility and nearness to maturity. In fact, only investments with original maturities of three months or less qualify for consideration of cash equivalent status.

7. (C) Notes and accounts receivable from officers, employees, or affiliated companies may have different terms, such as due dates and interest rates, than trade receivables. Therefore, these receivables should be reported separately from other receivables on the balance sheet if they are material.

8. (D) A cash discount (sometimes called a sales discount) is often offered as an inducement to prompt payment. Such discounts may be quoted as 2/10, n/30, which means a 2% discount is given if the price is paid within 10 days, otherwise the gross amount is due in 30 days. A trade discount is an amount taken off the price of merchandise as an inducement for customers to buy the merchandise. The other two terms, nominal and enhancement, have no formal definition as discount terminology.

9. (A) The objective of relating bad debts expense to accounts receivable is to report receivables in the balance sheet at net realizable value. Relating bad debts to accounts receivable is a balance sheet approach. The other commonly used approach to the determination of bad debts expense is to take a percentage of credit sales for the period.

10. (C) The major problem with the direct write-off method is that it does not match costs with revenues of the period nor does it result in receivables being stated at estimated net realizable value on the balance sheet. The other three alternatives reflect accurate statements about uncollectible accounts receivable.

11. (B) White Corporation's gross sales for December 2001 can be calculated as follows:

Gross sales:	
Cash sales	$20,000
Credit sales (see T-account)	20,000
Total	$40,000

Accounts Receivable			
Dec. 1	$70,000		
		Cash received	$25,000
		Written off	1,000
Credit sales	**$20,000**		
Dec. 31	$64,000		

12. (D) It is believed that matching the estimated expenses of bad debts against sales in the period of the sale gives the best matching of revenues and expense. Answer (C) is incorrect because a proper matching of revenues and expenses is not obtained under the direct write-off method.

13. (B) The entries for the write off of an account receivable under each method would be:

Direct write-off method		
(Decrease net income):		
Bad debts expense	400	
Accounts receivable		400
Allowance method		
(No effect on net income):		
Allowance for uncollectible receivable	400	
Accounts receivable		400

From the above example entries, it can be seen that when a specific customer's account receivable is written off as uncollectible there is no effect on income if the allowance method is used. However, when the direct write-off method is used, writing off a specific customer's account decreases net income for the period.

14. (A) The entry to record bad debts expense includes a credit to the Allowance for Doubtful Accounts account. Working capital is reduced by the credit to the account because it is a contra account to the current asset accounts receivable. The subsequent entry to write off $16,000 of accounts deemed uncollectible does not affect working capital because the net amount of accounts receivable (total receivables less the allowance) is unchanged. For example:

	Before Write-off	After Write-off
Accounts Receivable	$120,000	$104,000
Allowance	30,000	14,000
Net	$ 90,000	$ 90,000

15. (B) The basic issues in accounting for notes and accounts receivable are essentially the same—recognition and valuation. When and where the item should be included in the financial statements along with the proper amount to record are the basic accounting issues surrounding the receivables accounts.

16. (D) Present value - Cash to be received = P.V. factor for 5 years. ($11,348.60 ÷ $20,000 = .56743). In Table 6-2 the factor .56743 is the factor for 5 periods at 12%.

17. (C) The note should be valued at the fair value of the asset exchanged. If the land has a fair value of $450,000 and $100,000 in cash is given, then the note is valued at $350,000. The additional $50,000 ($400,000 - $350,000) is an interest factor or discount that should be amortized over the life of the note.

18. (C) The zero interest-bearing note received by Vonesh Company should be valued at the fair market value of the drill press sold according to APB No. 21. This value would equal the face of the note less imputed interest.

19. (C) Premiums or discounts that arise from present value computations for notes receivable transactions are not assets or liabilities. The discount or premium accounts are reported in the balance sheet as a direct deduction from or addition to the notes' face amount.

20. (C) Accounts receivable are said to be factored when they are sold outright without recourse. Answers (B) and (D) are incorrect because accounts receivable are pledged or assigned as collateral for borrowings. These transactions are not sales of the accounts receivable.

21. (B) In a general assignment all receivables serve as collateral for the note. Also, new receivables can be substituted for the ones collected.

22. (A) Alternatives B, C, and D represent the three conditions that must be present for with recourse transfers to be accounted for as sales. These are the conditions that are specified by the FASB.

*23. (B) When preparing a bank reconciliation for the purpose of arriving at a correct cash balance, NSF (not sufficient funds) checks should be deducted from the balance per books. This is because these checks were added to the book balance when received; however, as the maker is unable to pay the check, the cash book balance would be overstated if the amounts were not deducted. The other alternatives reflect the opposite treatment each would receive on a bank reconciliation designed to arrive at a corrected cash balance.

*24. (B) Outstanding checks are checks that have been written by the company and have not cleared the bank as of the date of the reconciliation. Deposits in transit are deposits sent to the bank that have not cleared the bank as of the reconciliation date. Thus, the outstanding checks need to be deducted from the bank balance and the deposits in transit need to be added in arriving at the corrected cash balance.

*25. (D) Chudzick Company's correct cash balance at September 30, 2001, can be calculated as follows:

Balance per bank, 9/30/01		$42,000
Add:	Deposits in transit, 9/30/01	7,200
Less:	Outstanding checks, 9/30/01	(6,500)
Corrected balance per books, 9/30/01		$42,700

The bank service charge would not be deducted since the bank would have already accounted for it in its balance per bank.

REVIEW EXERCISES

1. a.

Bad Debts Expense	$3,500*	
Allowance for Doubtful Accounts		$3,500

*.01 (360,000 - 10,000) = 3,500

b.

Bad Debts Expense	$3,800*	
Allowance for Doubtful Accounts		$3,800

*4,000 - 200 = 3,800

2.

August 14	Accounts Receivable	10,000	
	Sales		10,000
September 5	Notes Receivable	10,000	
	Accounts Receivable		10,000
September 5	Cash	9,100	
	Due from Factor	500*	
	Loss on Sale of Note	400*	
	Notes Receivable		10,000

*(5% x $10,000)
**(4% x $10,000)

3. a.

Deferred Charge (Future Sales Discount)	145,792	
Notes Receivable	400,000	
Cash		400,000
Discount on Notes Receivable		145,792

Calculation of discount:

Amount of loan		$400,000
Face amount of note	$400,000	
P.V.* of 1 at 12%, 4 years	.63552	
Present value of the note		254,208
Discount		$145,792

*Present value.

b.

Year	Cash Interest	Effective Interest	Discount Amortized	Unamortized Discount	Note Present Value
				$145,792	$254,208
1	$0	$30,505	$30,505	115,287	$284,713
2	0	34,166	34,166	81,121	318,879
3	0	38,265	38,265	42,856	357,144
4	0	42,856	42,856	0	400,000*
		$145,792	$145,792		

*Rounded by $1.

4. a.

Cash	162,750	
Due from Factor	8,750	
Loss on Sale of Receivables	3,500	
Accounts Receivable		175,000

(Finance Charge: $175,000 X .02 = $3,500)
(Due from Factor: $175,000 X .05 = $8,750)

b.

Accounts Receivable	175,000	
Due to Ehrlich Company		8,750
Financing Revenue		3,500
Cash		162,750

*5.

1. (B)
2. (B)
3. (A)
4. (E)
5. (D)
6. (C)
7. (C)

8

Valuation of Inventories: A Cost Basis Approach

CHAPTER STUDY OBJECTIVES

1. Identify major classifications of inventory.
2. Distinguish between the perpetual and periodic inventory systems.
3. Identify the effects of inventory errors on the financial statements.
4. Identify the items that should be included as inventory cost.
5. Describe and compare the flow assumptions used in accounting for inventories.
6. Explain the significance and use of a LIFO reserve.
7. Explain the effect of LIFO liquidations.
8. Explain the dollar-value LIFO method.
9. Identify the major advantages and disadvantages of LIFO.
10. Identify the reasons why a given inventory method is selected.

CHAPTER REVIEW

1. Careful attention is given to the inventory account by many business organizations because it represents one of the most significant assets held by the enterprise. Inventories are of particular importance to merchandising and manufacturing companies because they represent the primary source of revenue for the organization. Inventories are also significant because of their impact on both the balance sheet and the income statement. Chapter 8 initiates the discussion of the basic issues involved in recording, classifying, and valuing items classified as inventory.

Inventory Classifications and Control

2. (S.O. 1) Inventories are asset items held for sale in the ordinary course of business or goods that will be used or consumed in the production of goods to be sold. **Merchandise inventory** refers to the goods held for resale by a trading concern. The inventory of a **manufacturing firm** is composed of three separate items: **raw materials, work in process, and finished goods**.

3. Inventory **planning** and **control** is of vital importance to the success of a trading or manufacturing enterprise. If an excessive amount of inventory is accumulated, there is the danger of loss owing to obsolescence. If the supply of inventory is inadequate, the potential for lost sales exists. This dilemma makes inventory an asset to which management must devote a great deal of attention.

4. (S.O. 2) Inventory records may be maintained on a perpetual or periodic inventory system basis. **A perpetual inventory system** provides a means for generating up-to-date records related to inventory quantities. Under this inventory system, data are available at any time relative to the quantity of material or type of merchandise on hand. In a perpetual inventory system, purchases and sales of goods are recorded directly in the Inventory account as they occur. A Cost of Goods Sold account is used to accumulate the issuances from inventory. The balance in the Inventory account at the end of the year should represent the ending inventory amount.

5. When the inventory is accounted for on a **periodic inventory system,** the acquisition of inventory is debited to a Purchases account. Cost of goods sold must be calculated when a periodic inventory system is in use. The computation of cost of goods sold is made by adding beginning inventory to net purchases and then subtracting ending inventory. Ending inventory is determined by a physical count at the end of the year under a periodic inventory system. Even in a perpetual inventory system, a physical inventory count at year-end is normally taken due to the potential for loss, error, or shrinkage of inventory during the year.

6. Reconciliation between the recorded inventory amount and the actual amount of inventory on hand is normally performed at least once a year. This is called a **physical inventory** and involves counting all inventory items and comparing the amount counted with the amount shown in the detailed inventory records. Any errors in the records are corrected to agree with the physical count.

7. The **cost of goods sold** during any accounting period is defined as all the **goods available for sale** during the period less any unsold goods on hand at the end of the period (**ending inventory**). The process of computing cost of goods sold is complicated by the determination of (**a**) the physical goods to be included in inventory, (**b**) the costs to be included in inventory, and (**c**) the cost flow assumption to be used.

COGS=GAAS-EI

Physical Goods to be Included in Inventory

8. Normally, goods are included in inventory when they are received from the supplier. However, at the end of the period, proper accounting requires that all goods to which the company has legal title be included in ending inventory. Goods in transit at the end of the period, shipped **f.o.b. shipping point**, should be included in the buyer's ending inventory. If goods are shipped **f.o.b. destination**, they belong to the seller until actually received by the buyer. Inventory out on **consignment** belongs to the consignor's inventory.

9. In actual practice a few exceptions exist regarding the general rule that inventory is recorded by the company that has legal title to the merchandise. These exceptions are known as **special sale agreements**. Three of the more common special sale agreements are (**a**) sales with buy back agreement, (**b**) sales with high rates of return, and (**c**) installment sales.

Effect of Inventory Errors

10. (S.O. 3) Errors in recording inventory can affect the balance sheet, the income statement, or both, because inventory is used in the preparation of both financial statements. For example, the failure to include certain inventory items in a year-end physical inventory count would result in the following items being overstated (O) or understated (U): ending inventory (U); working capital (U); cost of goods sold (O); and net income (U). If merchandise was not recorded as a purchase nor counted in the ending inventory, the result would be an understatement of inventory and accounts payable in the balance sheet and an understatement of purchases and inventory in the income statement. Net income would be unaffected by this omission as purchases and ending inventory would be misstated by the same amount.

Costs Included in Inventory

11. (S.O. 4) Inventories are recorded at cost when acquired. Cost in terms of inventory acquisition includes all expenditures necessary in acquiring the goods and converting them to a saleable condition. **Product costs** are those costs that "attach" to the inventory and are recorded in the inventory account. These costs include freight charges on goods purchased, other direct costs of acquisition, and labor and other production costs incurred in processing the goods up to the time of sale. **Period costs**, such as selling expenses and general and administrative expenses, are not considered inventoriable costs. The reason these costs are not included as a part of the inventory valuation concerns the fact that, in most instances, these costs are unrelated to the immediate production process.

12. *FASB Statement No. 34*, "Capitalization of Interest Cost," allows for the capitalization of interest costs related to assets constructed for internal use or assets produced as discrete projects (such as ships or real estate projects) for sale or lease. In the case of inventories that are routinely manufactured or produced in large quantities on a repetitive basis, interest costs should not be capitalized.

Manufacturing Costs

13. In a manufacturing firm, the cost of work in process and finished goods is composed of raw material, direct labor, and manufacturing overhead costs. Manufacturing overhead costs include indirect material, indirect labor, and such items as depreciation, taxes, insurance, heat and electricity incurred in the manufacturing process.

14. In analyzing and accounting for inventory costs in a manufacturing firm, use is made of either **variable costing** or **absorption costing**. In a variable costing system (also called a direct costing system), all costs must be classified as variable or fixed. Under variable costing only costs that vary directly with the production volume are charged to products as manufacturing takes place. Fixed costs are charged to expense under variable costing. Variable costing is used extensively by management for decision making, but is not permitted for income tax purposes or for use in preparing published financial statements.

15. Under absorption costing (also known as full costing), all manufacturing costs, variable and fixed, incurred in the production process attach to the product and are included in the cost of inventory. Absorption costing is required by GAAP for use in the preparation of financial statements.

Purchase Discounts

16. Although **purchase discounts** are sometimes recorded as revenue, they are most appropriately treated as a reduction in the purchase price of inventory. When purchases are recorded net of discounts, failure to pay within the discount period results in the treatment of lost discounts as a financial expense. If the **gross method** is used, purchase discounts should be reported as a deduction from purchases on the income statement. If the **net method** is used, purchase discounts lost should be considered a financial expense and reported in the "other expense and loss" section of the income statement.

17. Determining the specific cost of inventory items that have been sold as well as those remaining in ending inventory is sometimes a difficult process. This is due, in part, to the fact that there is no requirement that the cost flow assumption adopted be consistent with the physical flow of the goods through the inventory account. Thus, it is important when accounting for inventory costs that an entity make consistent use of a cost flow assumption. The major objective in selecting a method should be to choose the one which most clearly reflects periodic income.

Cost Flow Assumptions

18. (S.O. 5) Inventory cost flow assumptions include **(a)** specific identification, **(b)** average cost, **(c)** first-in, first-out (FIFO), **(d)** last-in, first-out (LIFO), and **(e)** dollar-value LIFO. It should be remembered that these assumptions relate to the flow of costs and not the physical flow of inventory items into and out of the company.

19. **Specific identification** calls for identifying each item sold and each item in inventory. The costs of the specific items sold are included in the cost of goods sold, and the costs of the specific items on hand are included in the inventory. The **average cost method** prices items in the inventory on the basis of the average cost of all similar goods available during the period.

FIFO

20. Use of the **FIFO inventory method** assumes that the first goods purchased are the first used or sold. In all cases where FIFO is used, the inventory and cost of goods sold would be the same at the end of the month whether a perpetual or periodic system is used. A major advantage of the FIFO method is that the ending inventory is stated in terms of an approximate current cost figure. However, because FIFO tends to reflect current costs on the balance sheet, a basic disadvantage of this method is that current costs are not matched against current revenues on the income statement.

LIFO

21. Use of the **LIFO inventory method** assumes that the most recent inventory costs are the first costs recorded for goods manufactured or sold. When inventory records are kept on a **periodic basis**, the ending inventory would be priced by using the total units as a basis of computation, disregarding the exact dates of purchases. The calculation of ending inventory and cost of sales changes somewhat when the LIFO method is used in connection with **perpetual inventory records**.

LIFO Reserve

22. (S.O. 6) Many companies use LIFO for tax and external reporting purposes, but maintain a FIFO, average cost, or standard cost system for internal reporting purposes. The difference between the inventory method used for internal reporting purposes and LIFO is referred to as the Allowance to Reduce Inventory to LIFO or the **LIFO Reserve.** The change in the allowance balance from one period to the next must be made each year.

LIFO Liquidation

23. (S.O. 7) When the LIFO inventory method is used, many companies combine inventory items into natural groups or **pools.** Each pool is assumed to be one unit for the purpose of costing the inventory. Any increment above beginning inventory is normally identified as a new inventory layer and priced at the average cost of goods purchased during the year. When the inventory is decreased, the most recently added inventory layer is the first layer eliminated (last-in, first-out). The **pooled approach** reduces record keeping and, accordingly, the cost of utilizing the LIFO inventory method.

Dollar-Value LIFO

24. (S.O. 8) Use of the pooled approach can result in problems for companies that often change the mix of their products, materials, and production methods. To overcome these problems, the **dollar-value LIFO method** has been developed. The important feature of the dollar-value LIFO method is that increases and decreases in a pool are determined and measured in terms of total dollar value, not the physical quantity of the goods as is done in the traditional LIFO pool approach.

25. In computing inventory under the dollar-value LIFO method, the ending inventory is first priced at the most current cost. Current cost is then restated to prices prevailing when LIFO was adopted. This is accomplished by using a **price index**. A new inventory layer is formed when the ending inventory, stated in base-year costs, exceeds the base-year costs of beginning inventory. Increases are priced at current cost. If the ending inventory, stated at base-year costs, is less than beginning inventory, the decrease is subtracted from the most recently added layer. A price index for the current year is computed by dividing **Ending Inventory for the Period at Current-Year Costs** by **Ending Inventory for the Period at Base-Year Costs.** The dollar-value method is a more practical way of valuing a complex, multiple-item inventory than the traditional LIFO method. The **Comprehensive Dollar-Value LIFO Illustration** in the text should be studied as it provides an excellent means of understanding the dollar-value LIFO computation.

Advantages and Disadvantages of LIFO

26. (S.O. 9) Proponents of the LIFO method advocate its use on the basis of its (**a**) proper matching of recent costs with current revenue, (**b**) tax benefits, (**c**) improved cash flow, and (**d**) future earnings hedge. Those opposed to the LIFO method claim that it (**a**) lowers reported earnings, (**b**) reports outdated costs on the balance sheet, (**c**) is contrary to normal physical flow, (**d**) fails to measure real income, (**e**) creates involuntary liquidation problems, and (**f**) invites poor buying habits.

GLOSSARY

Average cost method. An inventory costing method that assumes that the goods available for sale are homogeneous.

Consigned goods. Goods shipped by a consignor who retains ownership to another party called the consignee.

Dollar-value LIFO method. An inventory costing method whereby increases and decreases in a pool are determined and measured in terms of total dollar value, not the physical quantity of the goods in the inventory pool.

Finished goods inventory. The costs identified with the completed but unsold units on hand at the end of the fiscal period.

First-In, First-Out method. An inventory costing method that assumes that the costs of the earliest goods acquired are the first to be recognized as cost of goods sold.

F.O.B. destination.	The terms for shipping goods which state that title does not pass until the buyer receives the goods from the common carrier.
F.O.B. shipping point.	The terms for shipping goods which state that title passes to the buyer when the seller delivers the goods to the common carrier who acts as an agent for the buyer.
Last-In, First-Out method.	An inventory costing method that assumes that the costs of the latest units purchased are the first to be allocated to cost of goods sold.
LIFO liquidation.	The erosion of LIFO inventory, which can lead to distortions of net income and substantial tax payments.
Moving-average method.	An inventory costing method that uses the average cost method for perpetual inventory records.
Period costs.	Costs that are not considered to be directly related to the acquisition or production of goods including selling expenses and general administrative expenses.
Periodic inventory system.	An inventory system in which the quantity of inventory on hand is determined periodically.
Perpetual inventory system.	An inventory system in which the quantity and cost of each inventory item is maintained and the records continuously show the inventory that should be on hand at any time.
Product costs.	Costs that are directly connected with the bringing of goods to the place of business of the buyer and converting such goods to a salable condition.
Purchase discounts.	A reduction in the purchase price when the payment of goods is made within a stated period of time.
Raw materials inventory.	The cost of goods and materials on hand but not yet placed into production.
Specific identification method.	An actual physical flow costing method in which items still in inventory are specifically costed to arrive at the total cost of the ending inventory.
Work in process inventory.	The cost of the raw material on which production has been started but not completed, plus the direct labor cost applied specifically to this material and a ratable share of manufacturing overhead costs.

CHAPTER OUTLINE

Fill in the outline presented below.

(S.O. 1) Inventory Classifications and Control

Raw Materials

Work in Process

Finished Goods

(S.O. 2) Perpetual Inventory

Periodic Inventory

Basic Issues in Inventory Valuation

Goods in Transit

Consigned Goods

Special Sales Agreements

Sales with Buyback Agreements

Chapter Outline *(continued)*

Sales with High Rates of Return

Sales on Installment

(S.O. 3) Effect of Inventory Errors

(S.O. 4) Costs Included in Inventory

Product Costs

Period Costs

Manufacturing Costs

Variable Costing versus Absorption Costing

Purchase Discounts

(S.O. 5) Cost Flow Methods

Specific Identification

Average Cost

First-In, First-Out (FIFO)

Chapter Outline *(continued)*

Last-In, First-Out (LIFO)

(S.O. 6) LIFO Reserve

(S.O. 7) LIFO Liquidation

(S.O. 8) Dollar-Value LIFO

(S.O. 9) Major Advantages of LIFO

Major Disadvantages of LIFO

(S.O. 10) Basis for Selection of Inventory Method

REVIEW QUESTIONS AND EXERCISES

TRUE-FALSE

Indicate whether each of the following is true (T) or false (F) in the space provided.

_____ 1. (S.O. 1) In the determination of cost of goods sold, cost of goods manufactured is to a manufacturing concern what cost of goods purchased is to a merchandising concern.

_____ 2. (S.O. 2) A physical inventory should be taken at least annually, even when a perpetual inventory system is used.

_____ 3. (S.O. 2) The perpetual inventory system provides a continuous record of the balances in both the inventory account and the cost of goods sold account.

_____ 4. (S.O. 2) Cost of goods sold is the excess of the cost of goods available for sale during the period less the cost of the goods on hand at the end of the period.

_____ 5. (S.O. 2) When goods are shipped f.o.b. shipping point, title passes only when the seller receives full payment for the merchandise.

_____ 6. (S.O. 2) Goods held on consignment should be included in the consignee's inventory reported on the balance sheet.

_____ 7. (S.O. 2) Interest costs associated with getting inventories ready for sale usually are included in the cost of the inventory.

_____ 8. (S.O. 3) An understatement of the ending inventory will cause cost of goods sold to be understated and net income to be overstated for that period.

_____ 9. (S.O. 4) Period costs and product costs are both inventoriable costs that relate to manufactured rather than purchased inventory.

_____ 10. (S.O. 4) Variable costing, which excludes fixed manufacturing costs from inventory, is not an acceptable accounting practice for general-purpose financial statements.

_____ 11. (S.O. 4) Under absorption costing, all manufacturing costs, variable and fixed, direct and indirect, incurred in the factory or production process attach to the product and are included in the cost of inventory.

_____ 12. (S.O. 4) If the gross method is employed, purchase discounts should be reported as a deduction from purchases on the income statement.

_____ 13. (S.O. 4) The use of a Purchase Discounts Lost account indicates that purchases are being recorded net of purchase discounts.

_____ 14. (S.O. 5) When a company selects a cost flow assumption (FIFO, LIFO, average cost, etc.), it must be consistent with the actual physical movement of goods through the company.

_____ 15. (S.O. 5) Under the average cost method, beginning inventory should be included in the total units available but not in the total cost of goods available in computing the average cost per unit.

_____ 16. (S.O. 5) A major argument in favor of the FIFO method of inventory costing is that current costs are matched against current revenues.

_____ 17. (S.O. 5) The ending inventory under a FIFO periodic inventory system will be the same as under a FIFO perpetual inventory system.

_____ 18. (S.O. 5) If LIFO is used for tax purposes, it must also be used for financial reporting purposes.

_____ 19. (S.O. 5) LIFO comes closer than FIFO to stating inventory on the balance sheet at current costs.

_____ 20. (S.O. 7) To alleviate the LIFO liquidation problems and to simplify the accounting, goods can be combined into pools.

_____ 21. (S.O. 8) Under dollar-value LIFO, there will never be a layer for a particular year unless the quantity of inventory increased during that year.

_____ 22. (S.O. 8) All companies using the dollar-value LIFO method are required to use the same price index.

_____ 23. (S.O. 9) In a period of rising prices, LIFO yields a larger cost of goods sold than does FIFO.

_____ 24. (S.O. 9) Tax benefits are the major reason why LIFO has become popular.

_____ 25. (S.O. 9) A change in inventory methods requires that the change be explained and its effect be disclosed in the financial statements.

MULTIPLE CHOICE

Select the best answer for each of the following items and enter the corresponding letter in the space provided.

_____ 1. (S.O. 2) The amount of inventory purchased during a particular year is accumulated in a Purchases account under a:

	Periodic Inventory System	**Perpetual Inventory System**
A.	Yes	No
B.	Yes	Yes
C.	No	Yes
D.	No	No

_____ 2. (S.O. 2) Valuation of inventories requires the determination of all of the following except:

A. The costs to be included in inventory.
B. The physical goods to be included in inventory.
C. The cost of goods held on consignment from other companies.
D. The cost flow assumption to be adopted.

_____ 3. (S.O. 2) Goods in transit at the balance sheet date should be included in the purchaser's inventory if they are shipped:

	F.O.B. Destination	**F.O.B. Shipping Point**
A.	No	No
B.	No	Yes
C.	Yes	No
D.	Yes	Yes

_____ 4. (S.O. 2) The following items were included in Voigt Corporation's inventory account at December 31, 2001:

Goods held on consignment by Voigt	$ 7,000
Merchandise out on consignment, at sales price, including 30% mark-up on selling price	12,000
Goods purchased, in transit, shipped f.o.b. shipping point	9,000

Voigt's inventory account at December 31, 2001, should be reduced by:

A. $10,600
B. $12,600
C. $16,000
D. $28,000

_____ 5. (S.O. 3) The ending inventory of the Bonie Company is understated in year one by $20,000. This error is not corrected in year one or in year two. What impact will this error have on total net income for years one and two combined?

A. No effect on total net income for the two years.
B. Overstate total income by $20,000.
C. Understate total income by $20,000.
D. Overstate net income for year one by $20,000 and year two by $20,000 for a total overstatement of $40,000.

_____ 6. (S.O. 3) The failure to record a purchase of merchandise on account even though the goods are properly included in the physical inventory results in:

A. an overstatement of assets and net income.
B. an understatement of assets and net income.
C. an understatement of cost of goods sold and liabilities and an overstatement of assets.
D. an understatement of liabilities and an overstatement of owners' equity.

_____ 7. (S.O. 4) Costs which are inventoriable include all of the following except:

A. costs that are directly connected with the bringing of goods to the place of business of the buyer.
B. costs that are directly connected with the converting of goods to a salable condition.
C. buying costs of a purchasing department.
D. selling costs of a sales department.

_____ 8. (S.O. 4) Which of the following is not considered to be an inventoriable cost under variable costing?

A. Raw materials.
B. Direct labor.
C. Variable factory overhead.
D. Fixed factory overhead.

_____ 9. (S.O. 4) The use of a Purchase Discounts Lost account implies that the recorded cost of a purchased inventory item is its:

A. invoice price.
B. invoice price plus the purchase discount price.
C. invoice price less the purchase discount allowable, when taken.
D. invoice price less the purchase discount allowable, whether or not taken.

_____ 10. (S.O. 5) Which of the following inventory methods comes closest to stating ending inventory at replacement costs?

A. FIFO.
B. LIFO.
C. Weighted-average.
D. Base stock.

_____ 11. (S.O. 5) The use of LIFO under a perpetual inventory system (units and costs):

A. may yield a higher inventory valuation than LIFO under a periodic inventory system when prices are steadily falling.
B. may yield a higher inventory valuation than LIFO under a periodic inventory system when prices are steadily rising.
C. always yields the same inventory valuation as LIFO under a periodic inventory system.
D. can never yield the same inventory valuation as LIFO under a periodic inventory system.

_____ 12. (S.O. 5) One argument against the use of the specific identification inventory method is:

A. actual costs are matched against actual revenues.
B. estimated costs are matched against actual revenues.
C. the potential for the manipulation of net income by selecting costs to match against revenues.
D. that it is difficult to understand.

_____ 13. (S.O. 5) Which of the following represents a departure from the historical cost basis of valuing inventories?

A. Dollar-value LIFO.
B. Specific identification.
C. Replacement cost.
D. Absorption costing.

_____ 14. (S.O. 5) The Slowe Company has been using the LIFO cost method of inventory valuation for 8 years. Its 2001 ending inventory was $135,000 but it would have been $180,000 if FIFO had been used. Thus, if FIFO had been used, Slowe's net income before income taxes would have been:

A. $45,000 less in 2001.
B. $45,000 more in 2001.
C. $45,000 greater over the 8-year period.
D. $45,000 less over the 8-year period.

_____ 15. (S.O. 5) The purchase of inventory items on account using the perpetual inventory method:

A. changes working capital and the current ratio.
B. has no effect on working capital but probably changes the current ratio.
C. has no effect on the current ratio but probably changes working capital.
D. has no effect on working capital or the current ratio.

_____ 16. (S.O. 5) In periods of rising prices, use of LIFO rather than the FIFO inventory method will most likely have what effect on the following items?

	Net Income	Cost of Goods Sold	Working Capital
A.	Higher	Lower	Lower
B.	Lower	Higher	Lower
C.	Higher	Higher	Higher
D.	Lower	Higher	Higher

_____ 17. (S.O. 5) Just prior to a period of rising prices, Brooks Company changed its inventory measurement method from FIFO to LIFO. What would be the effect in the next period?

A. Decrease the current ratio and increase inventory turnover.
B. Increase both the current ratio and inventory turnover.
C. Decrease both the current ratio and inventory turnover.
D. Increase the current ratio and decrease inventory turnover.

_____ 18. (S.O. 5) The traditional LIFO approach which tends to emphasize specific goods in costing LIFO inventories is often unrealistic because:

A. it does not result in a proper matching of costs and revenues in a particular period.
B. cash flows are often distorted and can be delayed for one or two subsequent periods.
C. future price declines will adversely affect the ability to accurately report future earnings.
D. erosion of the LIFO inventory can easily occur which often leads to distortions of net income and large tax payments.

_____ 19. (S.O. 5) Assuming no beginning inventory, what can be said about the trend of inventory prices if cost of goods sold computed when inventory is valued using the FIFO method exceeds cost of goods sold when inventory is valued using the LIFO method?

A. Prices increased.
B. Prices decreased.
C. Prices remained unchanged.
D. Price trend cannot be determined from the information given.

_____ 20. (S.O. 8) The dollar-value inventory method is an improvement over the traditional LIFO pool approach because:

A. the mathematical computations are greatly simplified.
B. it is easier to apply where few inventory items are employed and little change in product mix is anticipated.
C. increases and decreases in a pool are determined and measured in terms of total dollar value rather than the physical quantity of the goods in the inventory pool.
D. dissimilar items of inventory can be grouped to form pools under the dollar-value LIFO method.

_____ 21. (S.O. 8) Which of the following statements is not true as it relates to the dollar-value LIFO inventory method?

A. It is easier to erode LIFO layers using dollar-value LIFO techniques than it is with specific goods pooled LIFO.
B. Under the dollar-value LIFO method, it is possible to have the entire inventory in only one pool.
C. Several pools are commonly employed in using the dollar-value LIFO inventory method.
D. Under dollar-value LIFO, increases and decreases in a pool are determined and measured in terms of total dollar value, not physical quantity.

_____ 22. (S.O. 8) Amidei Company adopts dollar-value LIFO inventory on 12/31/01 when its inventory at current price is $45,000. The inventory value on 12/31/02 at current 2002 prices is $65,000. If prices increased by 30% during 2002, what is the dollar-value LIFO inventory at 12/31/02?

A. $65,000.
B. $58,000.
C. $51,500.
D. $48,700.

_____ 23. (S.O. 8) Estimates of price-level changes for specific inventories are required for which of the following inventory methods?

A. Weighted-average cost.
B. FIFO.
C. LIFO.
D. Dollar-value LIFO.

_____ 24. (S.O. 9) Which of the following is not considered an advantage of LIFO when prices are rising?

A. The inventory will be overstated.
B. The more recent costs are matched against current revenues.
C. There will be a deferral of income tax.
D. A company's future reported earnings will not be affected substantially by future price declines.

_____ 25. (S.O. 9) The acquisition cost of a heavily used raw material changes frequently. The inventory amount of this material at year end will be the same if perpetual records (units and costs) are kept as it would be under a periodic inventory method only if the inventory amount is computed under the:

A. weighted-average method.
B. first-in, first-out method.
C. last-in, first-out method.
D. direct costing method.

REVIEW EXERCISES

1. (S.O.3) An examination of the records of Priestley Company revealed that goods costing $1,000 were received on December 31, 2001. The purchase invoice for these goods was not received until January 4, 2002, at which time the purchase and related liability were recorded. Priestley Company incorrectly excluded the cost of the goods from its December 31, 2001 inventory. Indicate whether the following financial statement items were understated (U), overstated (O), or not misstated (N) for the years 2001 and 2002.

	2001	2002
Purchases	________	________
Inventory, December 31	________	________
Cost of goods sold	________	________
Net income	________	________
Assets	________	________
Liabilities	________	________
Retained earnings	________	________

2. (S.O.4) Garth purchased merchandise inventory costing $24,000 with credit terms of 2/10, net 30. Eight days after the purchase, Garth paid one-half of the outstanding obligation. The remaining amount was paid 30 days after the date of purchase.

Instructions:
Prepare the journal entries Garth would make for the purchase and the two subsequent payments using:
a. the gross method.
b. the net method.

a.

General Journal J1

Date	Account Title	Debit	Credit

b.

General Journal

J1

Date	Account Title	Debit	Credit

3. (S.O.5) Doherty Company's records show the following information related to one of its products:

May 1	Balance on hand	300 units @ $5
May 12	Purchased	600 units @ $6
May 30	Purchased	100 units @ $7

Doherty Company uses a periodic inventory system. Assuming that 600 units were sold during May.

Instructions:
Compute the May 31 inventory and the cost of goods sold during May under each of the following methods:

a. FIFO
b. LIFO
c. Weighted-average

a.

b.

c.

4. (S.O. 5) Spelling Company had the following transactions in connection with their inventory account during the month of August.

Purchases					Sales			
Aug. 1	(Goods on hand)	650	@	$8.40	Aug. 4	280	@	$12.60
Aug. 3		770	@	8.20	Aug. 10	350	@	12.60
Aug. 7		1,250	@	8.00	Aug. 12	900	@	13.00
Aug. 11		650	@	8.50	Aug. 17	650	@	13.00
Aug. 16		500	@	8.70	Aug. 20	860	@	13.50
Aug. 23		750	@	8.60	Aug. 25	700	@	13.50
		4,570				3,740		

Instructions:

a. Assuming that the company keeps perpetual records in units only; compute the inventory at August 31, using (1) LIFO; and (2) average cost.

b. Assuming that perpetual records are kept in dollars, compute the inventory at August 31, using (1) FIFO; and (2) LIFO.

c. Calculate the cost of goods sold and gross profit Spelling Company should record for the month of August assuming FIFO and periodic inventory procedures.

a.

b.

c.

5. (S.O.8) Perry Company manufactures a single product. On December 31, 2001, Perry adopted the dollar-value LIFO inventory method. The inventory on that date using the dollar-value LIFO inventory method was $50,000. Inventory data are as follows:

Year	Inventory at Respective Year-End Cost Prices	Price Index at Year End
2001	$50,000	100
2002	73,500	105
2003	71,500	110

Instructions:

Compute the inventory at December 31, 2002 and 2003 using the dollar-value LIFO method.

5. *(continued)*

SOLUTIONS TO REVIEW QUESTIONS

TRUE-FALSE

1. (T)

2. (T)

3. (T)

4. (T)

5. (F) When goods are shipped f.o.b. shipping point, title passes to the buyer when the seller delivers the goods to the common carrier who acts as an agent for the buyer.

6. (F) Goods held on consignment by a consignee remain the property of the consignor until the goods are sold. Thus, goods on consignment are properly included in the consignor's inventory rather than the inventory of the consignee.

7. (F) Interest costs associated with getting inventories ready for sale usually are expensed as incurred.

8. (F) An understatement in ending inventory results in an overstatement of cost of good sold and a corresponding understatement of net income.

9. (F) Product costs are those costs that "attach" to the inventory (whether purchased or manufactured) and are considered to be a part of the total inventory valuation. Period costs are not considered to be directly related to the acquisition or production of goods and therefore are not considered to be a part of the inventories.

10. (T)

11. (T)

12. (T)

13. (T)

14. (F) A company can select any cost flow assumption regardless of the physical flow of its goods.

15. (F) Under the average cost method, beginning inventory is included in both the total units available and in the total cost of goods available in computing the average cost per unit.

16. (F) Under the FIFO method of inventory costing, the first costs into the inventory account which are the oldest costs are the costs matched against the current revenue. Thus, current costs are not matched against current revenue under the FIFO inventory method.

17. (T)

18. (T)

19. (F) LIFO is an inventory valuation method that emphasizes the recording of current costs on the income statement. Under LIFO the most recent inventory costs are charged against revenue; thus the older inventory costs are shown on the balance sheet.

20. (T)

21. (T)

22. (F) Many companies use a general price-level index such as the Consumers Price Index for Urban Consumers (CPI-U) and when a specific index is not readily available, companies use an index computed using the following formula:

$$\frac{\text{Ending inventory for the period at current cost}}{\text{Ending inventory for the period at base-year cost}} = \text{Price index for current year}$$

23. (T)

24. (T)

25. (T)

MULTIPLE CHOICE

1. (A) Purchases of inventory are debited to the inventory account under a perpetual inventory system. The only time the purchases account is used is when a periodic inventory system is in place.

2. (C) The costs, physical goods, and flow assumption are necessary elements in determining inventory valuation. Goods on consignment from other companies do not belong to the consignee and as such are not a part of the consignee's inventory valuation.

3. (B) Goods shipped f.o.b. (free on board) shipping point in transit at the end of the year belong to the buyer and should be shown in the buyer's records.

4. (A) The following reductions should be made in Voigt's inventory:

Goods held on consignment	$ 7,000*
Gross profit included in merchandise out on consignment (.30 x $12,000)	3,600**
	$10,600

* Goods held on consignment should be included in the consignor's inventory, not the inventory of Voigt, the consignee.

** Inventory should be valued at the lower of cost or market. Therefore, the gross profit on merchandise out on consignment should not be included in Voigt's inventory.

Note: The $9,000 of goods purchased f.o.b. shipping point and which were in transit at December 31, 2001, should be included in Voigt's inventory since title to these goods had passed to Voigt at the time of shipment.

5. (A) This is an example of a counterbalancing error. The income in year one will be understated by $20,000 because of the ending inventory error. However, in the second year the beginning inventory will be understated by $20,000 which will cause an overstatement of net income by the same amount. Thus, the effect of the error on total income over the two year period is zero.

6. (D) The failure to record the purchases understates liabilities because the payable was not recorded. The fact that the amount of the purchase was properly included in the physical inventory but omitted from goods available for sale causes cost of goods sold to be understated. This understatement of cost of goods sold causes net income to be overstated resulting in an overstatement of owner's equity.

7. (D) Inventoriable costs include costs that are directly connected with the bringing of goods to the place of business and converting such goods to a salable condition. The buying costs or expenses of a purchasing department are also included in the inventoriable costs. Selling costs of a sales department are considered period costs and are not inventoriable.

8. (D) Under variable costing, only costs that vary directly with the volume of production are charged to products as manufacturing takes place. Fixed costs are not viewed as costs

of the products being manufactured. Alternative (D) represents the only fixed cost listed.

9. (D) The Purchase Discounts Lost account arises when the purchase of inventory is recorded net of the allowable discount and the purchaser does not pay within the discount period.

10. (A) Because the oldest costs in inventory are charged against income under the FIFO inventory method, the inventory valuation shown on the balance sheet represents the most recent inventory costs. Thus, FIFO comes closest to stating inventory at replacement costs when compared to the other three methods listed.

11. (B) In a period of steadily rising prices, LIFO under a periodic inventory system will find the highest inventory cost being charged against revenue. Under the same set of circumstances, the use of LIFO under a perpetual inventory system (units and costs) might find inventory purchases made subsequent to the final sale. If such is the case, the perpetual method would yield a higher ending inventory valuation.

12. (C) Use of the specific identification method allows for the potential manipulation of net income when similar items that have different costs can be selected for sale. Thus, if two identical inventory items have different costs, selecting the item with the lower cost will increase net income. Alternative "A" is an advantage of the specific identification method. Alternatives "B" and "D" are not relevant alternatives.

13. (C) Replacement cost is a future valuation concept and represents a departure from the historical cost basis of valuing inventories.

14. (C) The effect on net income of differences in ending inventory amounts wash out over two years. The reason for this is that the ending inventory for one year is the beginning inventory for the next year. For example, an overstatement of ending inventory at December 31, 2002, will result in an overstatement of 2002's income but an understatement of 2003's income. Therefore, the only difference in the net income before taxes for the 8 year period ending December 31, 2001, would be that net income before taxes computed under FIFO would be $45,000 greater than that computed under LIFO.

15. (B) The purchase of inventory on account increases both current assets (inventory) and current liabilities (accounts payable) by the same amount. This results in no change in working capital. However, if current assets and current liabilities are both increased by the same amount, the current ratio will decrease if the current ratio was greater than one, increase if the current ratio was less than one, and remain the same if the current ratio was exactly one.

16. (B) In periods of rising prices, the LIFO method will find the higher costs being charged to income resulting in a higher cost of goods sold and a lower net income. Also, with the higher costs being charged to net income, the ending inventory will be lower under LIFO then under FIFO. Thus, other things being equal, the working capital (current assets minus current liabilities) should be lower.

17. (A) If prices are increasing, the inventory value determined using LIFO would be less than that determined by using FIFO. This is so because the oldest prices, in this case, would be used to value inventory. A smaller inventory value would result in decreasing the current ratio (current assets/current liabilities) and increasing the inventory turnover ratio (cost of goods sold/average inventory).

18. (D) Alternatives A, B, and C are either advantages of using the LIFO inventory method or are indications of things that can be avoided by its use. However, the traditional LIFO approach does result in the potential for LIFO liquidation which takes away some of the advantages of LIFO and can result in poor earnings results. Using the specific goods pooled LIFO method can help alleviate the liquidation problem and its attendant negative affect on earnings.

19. (B) LIFO charges the most recent purchases to cost of goods sold. Therefore, if cost of goods sold is less under LIFO than FIFO, prices must be decreasing.

20. (C) The dollar-value LIFO method not only allows increases and decreases in a pool to be determined and measured in terms of total dollar value, but also two additional advantages are noted. First, a broader range of goods may be included in a dollar-value LIFO pool than in a regular pool. Second, in a dollar-value LIFO pool, replacement is permitted if it is similar as to type of material, or similarity in use, or interchangeability.

21. (A) A major reason for the use of dollar-value LIFO concerns the difficulty in eroding the LIFO layers. The entire inventory under dollar-value LIFO can be in one pool or in numerous pools. Also, as the name implies, inventory pools are determined and measured in terms of total dollar value.

22. (C) Ending inventory at beginning of the year prices:

$65,000 ÷ 130% = $50,000

Inventory increase in beginning of year prices:

$50,000 - $45,000 = $5,000

Real dollar quantity increase:

$5,000 X 130% = $6,500

12/31/02 inventory valuation:

First layer (Base price 100%)	$45,000
Second layer (2002 increase @ 130%)	6,500
Dollar-value LIFO Inventory 12/31/02	$51,500

23. (D) Under dollar-value LIFO inventories are maintained at current prices. Estimates of price-level changes (index numbers) are used to convert the ending inventory from year-end prices to LIFO prices.

24. (A) The major advantages of LIFO are (1) the more recent costs are matched against current revenues to provide a better measure of current earnings; (2) as long as the price level increases and inventory quantities do not decrease, a deferral of income tax occurs in LIFO; (3) because of the deferral of income tax, there is improvement of cash; and (4) a company's future reported earnings will not be affected substantially by future price declines. A major disadvantage of LIFO when prices are rising is that inventories will be understated because the older (lower) costs are reflected in inventory.

25. (B) Whether inventory is priced under the periodic or perpetual method, the ending inventory valuation and cost of goods sold will be the same as long as the FIFO cost flow assumption is used.

REVIEW EXERCISES

1.

	2001	2002
Purchases	U	O
Inventory, December 31	U	N
Cost of goods sold	N	N
Net income	N	N
Assets	U	N
Liabilities	U	N
Retained earnings	N	N

2a.

PURCHASE:		
Purchases	24,000	
Accounts Payable		24,000
PAYMENTS:		
(1) Accounts Payable	12,000	
Purchase Discounts		240
Cash		11,760
(2) Accounts Payable	12,000	
Cash		12,000

b.

PURCHASE:		
Purchases	23,520	
Accounts Payable		23,520
PAYMENTS:		
(1) Accounts Payable	11,760	
Cash		11,760
(2) Accounts payable	11,760	
Purchase Discounts Lost	240	
Cash		12,000

3.

		May 31 Inventory	Cost of Goods Sold
a.	FIFO	$2,500	$3,300
b.	LIFO	2,100	3,700
c.	Weighted-average	2,320	3,480

4a. LIFO:

Beginning Inventory & Purchases	4,570
Sales for the Period (units)	3,740
Ending Inventory (units)	830

LIFO Costs:	650	@	$8.40	=	$5,460
	180	@	8.20	=	1,476
Ending Inventory					$6,936

Average Cost:

$$\frac{\text{Total Cost}}{\text{Total Units}} \quad \frac{\$38,099}{4,570} \times 830 = \$6,920$$

b. FIFO:

	750	@	$8.60	=	$6,450.00
	80	@	8.70	=	696.00
Total					$7,146.00

LIFO:

Cost of Sales:					
Aug. 4	280	@	$8.20	=	$ 2,296.00
Aug. 10	350	@	8.00	=	2,800.00
Aug. 12 (900)	650	@	8.50	=	5,525.00
	250	@	8.00	=	2,000.00
Aug. 17 (650)	500	@	8.70	=	4,350.00
	150	@	8.00	=	1,200.00
Aug. 20 (860)	500	@	8.00	=	4,000.00
	360	@	8.20	=	2,952.00
Aug. 25	700	@	8.60	=	6,020.00
Cost of Goods Sold					$31,143.00

Ending Inventory:					
	50	@	$8.60	=	$ 430.00
	130	@	8.20	=	1,066.00
	650	@	8.40	=	5,460.00
Ending Inventory					$6,956.00

c.

Total Sales		$49,148.00
Goods available for sale	$38,099.00	
Less Ending Inventory	7,146.00	
Cost of Goods Sold		30,953.00
Gross Profit		$18,195.00

5.

December 31, 2002 inventory at 2002 prices	$73,500
December 31, 2002, inventory at base-year prices ($73,500 ÷ 1.05)	70,000
January 1, 2002 inventory at base-year prices	50,000
2002 inventory increase at base-year prices	20,000
2002 inventory increase at 2002 prices ($20,000 x 1.05)	21,000

December 31, 2002 inventory:

Layer	Base-Year Prices	Price Index	Dollar-Value LIFO
2001	$50,000	100	$50,000
2002	20,000	105	21,000
	$70,000		$71,000

December 31, 2003 inventory at 2003 prices	$71,500
December 31, 2003 inventory at base-year prices ($71,500 ÷ 1.10)	65,000
January 1, 2000 inventory at base-year prices	70,000
2003 inventory decrease at base-year prices	5,000
2003 inventory decreases at prices in existence when most recent layer was added (2003) $5,000 x 1.05	5,250

December 31, 2002 inventory:

Layer	Base-Year Prices	Price Index	Dollar-Value LIFO
2001	$50,000	100	$50,000
2002	15,000	105	15,750
	$65,000		$65,750

9

Inventories: Additional Valuation Issues

CHAPTER STUDY OBJECTIVES

1. Explain and apply the lower of cost or market rule.
2. Identify when inventories are valued at net realizable value.
3. Explain when the relative sales value method is used to value inventories.
4. Explain accounting issues related to purchase commitments.
5. Determine ending inventory by applying the gross profit method.
6. Determine ending inventory by applying the retail inventory method.
7. Explain how inventory is reported and analyzed.

*8. Determine ending inventory by applying the LIFO retail methods.

CHAPTER REVIEW

1. Chapter 9 concludes the discussion of inventories by addressing certain unique valuation problems not covered in Chapter 8. Chapter 9 also includes a description of the development and use of various estimation techniques used to value ending inventory without a physical count.

Lower of Cost or Market

2. (S.O. 1) When the **future revenue-producing ability** associated with inventory is below its **original cost,** the inventory should be written down to reflect this loss. Thus, the historical cost principle is abandoned when the future utility of the asset is no longer as great as its original cost. This is known as the **lower of cost or market (LCM)** method of valuing inventory and is an accepted accounting practice. When inventory declines in value below its original cost, the inventory should be written down to reflect the loss. This loss of utility in inventory should be charged against revenue in the period in which the loss occurs.

3. The term "market" in lower of cost or market generally refers to the **replacement cost** of an inventory item. However, market value should not exceed **net realizable value (NRV)**, nor should it be less than **net realizable value less a normal markup**. These are known as the **upper** (ceiling) and **lower** (floor) limits of market. Market is defined as replacement cost if such cost falls between the upper and lower limits. Should replacement cost be above the upper limit, market would be defined as net realizable value. If replacement cost falls below the lower limit, market is defined as net realizable value less a normal markup.

* *Note: All asterisked (*) items relate to material contained in the Appendix to the chapter.*

4. For example, consider the following illustration.

Inventory at sales value	$800
Less: Cost to complete and sell	200
Net realizable value (NRV)	600
Less: Normal markup	100
NRV less normal markup	$500

To arrive at the final inventory valuation, **market value** must be determined and then compared to **cost.** Market value is determined by comparing replacement cost of the inventory with the upper and lower limits. If replacement cost of the inventory in the example is $550, then $550 is compared to cost in determining lower of cost or market because replacement cost falls between the upper ($600) and lower ($500) limits. If replacement cost of the inventory is $650, it would exceed the upper limit; thus the upper limit ($600) would be compared to cost in determining lower of cost or market. Similarly, if replacement cost of the inventory is $450, it would be lower than the lower limit and thus the lower limit ($500) would be compared to cost in determining lower of cost or market. The amount that is compared to cost, often referred to as **designated market value,** is always the middle value of the three amounts: replacement cost, net realizable value, and net realizable value less a normal profit margin.

5. The cost or market rule may be applied **(a)** directly to each item, **(b)** to each category, or **(c)** to the total inventory. The individual-item approach is preferred by many companies because tax rules require its use when practical, and it produces the most conservative inventory valuation on the balance sheet. When inventory is written down to market, this new basis is considered to be the cost basis for future periods. The method selected should be the one that most clearly reflects income.

Direct vs. Allowance Method

6. Two methods are used to record inventory at market. The two methods are the **direct method** and the **indirect or allowance method**. The direct method substitutes the market value figure for cost when valuing the inventory. Thus, the loss is buried in the cost of goods sold and no individual loss account is reported in the income statement. Under the indirect method, an entry is made debiting a loss and crediting an allowance account for the difference between cost and market. Separately recording the loss and a contra account is preferable as it does not distort the cost of goods sold and clearly displays the loss from market decline.

7. (S.O. 2) Recording inventory at selling price less estimated cost to complete and sell (net realizable value) is acceptable in certain instances. To be accorded this treatment, the item should **(a)** have a controlled market with a quoted price applicable to all quantities and **(b)** have no significant disposal costs. Certain minerals sold in a controlled market and agricultural products that are marketable at fixed prices provide examples of inventory items carried at selling price.

8. (S.O. 3) When a group of varying inventory items is purchased for a lump sum price, a problem exists relative to the cost per item. The **relative sales value method** apportions the total cost to individual items on the basis of the selling price of each item.

Purchase Commitments

9. (S.O. 4) **Purchase commitments** represent contracts for the purchase of inventory at a specified price in a future period. If material, the details of the contract should be disclosed in a note of the buyer's balance sheet. If the contract price is in excess of the market price and it is expected that losses will occur when the purchase is effected, the loss should be recognized in the period during which the market decline took place.

The Gross Profit Method

10. (S.O. 5) The **gross profit method** is used to estimate the amount of ending inventory. Its use is **not** appropriate for financial reporting purposes; however, it can serve a useful purpose when an approximation of ending inventory is needed. Such approximations are sometimes required by auditors or when inventory and inventory records are destroyed by fire or some other catastrophe. The gross profit method should never be used as a substitute for a yearly physical inventory unless the inventory has been destroyed. The gross profit method is based on the assumptions that **(a)** the beginning inventory plus purchases equal total goods to be accounted for; **(b)** goods not sold must be on hand; and **(c)** if sales, reduced to cost, are deducted from the sum of the opening inventory plus purchases, the result is the ending inventory.

The Retail Inventory Method

11. (S.O. 6) The **retail inventory method** is an inventory estimation technique based upon an observable pattern between cost and sales price that exists in most retail concerns. This method requires that a record be kept of **(a)** the total cost and retail of goods purchased, **(b)** the total cost and retail value of the goods available for sale, and **(c)** the sales for the period.

12. Basically, the retail method requires the computation of the **cost-to-retail ratio** of inventory available for sale. This ratio is computed by dividing the **cost** of the goods available for sale by the **retail value** (selling price) of goods available for sale. Once the ratio is determined, total sales for the period are deducted from the retail value of inventory available for sale. The resulting amount represents ending inventory priced at retail. When this amount is multiplied by the cost to retail ratio, an approximation of the cost of ending inventory results. Use of this method eliminates the need for a physical count of inventory each time an income statement is prepared. However, physical counts are made at least yearly to determine the accuracy of the records and to avoid overstatements due to theft, loss, and breakage.

13. To obtain the appropriate inventory figures under the retail inventory method, proper treatment must be given to markups, markup cancellations, markdowns, and markdown cancellations.

14. When the cost to retail ratio is computed after net markups (markups less markup cancellations) have been added, the retail inventory method approximates lower of cost or market. This is known as the **conventional retail inventory method**. If both net markups and net markdowns are included before the cost to retail ratio is computed, the retail inventory method approximates cost.

15. The retail inventory method becomes more complicated when such items as **freight-in, purchase returns and allowances**, and **purchase discounts** are involved. In essence, the treatment of the items affecting the cost column of the retail inventory approach follows the computation of cost of goods available for sale. Freight costs are treated as a part of the purchase cost; purchase returns and allowances are ordinarily considered both a reduction of the price at both cost and retail; and purchase discounts usually are considered as a reduction of the cost of purchases.

16. Other items that require careful consideration include **transfers-in, normal shortages, abnormal shortages,** and **employee discounts**. Transfers-in from another department should be reported in the same way as purchases from an outside enterprise. Normal shortages should reduce the retail column because these goods are no longer available for sale. Abnormal shortages should be deducted from both the cost and retail columns and reported as a special inventory amount or as a loss. Employee discounts should be deducted from the retail column in the same way as sales.

17. The retail inventory method is widely used (**a**) to permit the computation of net income without a physical count of inventory, (**b**) as a control measure in determining inventory shortages, (**c**) in regulating quantities of inventory on hand, and (**d**) for insurance information. The advantages and disadvantages of the lower of cost or market method (conventional retail) versus LIFO retail are the same as for nonretail operations. In the final analysis, the ultimate decision concerning which retail inventory method to use is often based on the method that results in the lower taxable income.

Presentation and Analysis

18. Inventories normally represent one of the most significant assets held by a business entity. Therefore, the accounting profession has mandated certain disclosure requirements related to inventories. Some of the disclosure requirements include: the composition of the inventory, the inventory financing, the inventory costing methods employed, and whether costing methods have been consistently applied. Currently, there is a great deal of interest in the effects of inflation on inventory holdings. Two common financial ratios used to analyze inventory are (1) the inventory turnover ratio and (2) the average days to sell inventory.

LIFO Retail

*19. Many accountants suggest a LIFO assumption be adopted for use with the application of the retail inventory method. Use of LIFO in connection with the retail inventory method is thought to result in a better matching of costs and revenues. The application of **LIFO retail** is made under two assumptions (**a**) **stable prices**, and (**b**) **fluctuating prices**. Because the LIFO method is a cost method, not a cost or market approach, both the markups and markdowns must be considered in obtaining the proper cost to retail percentage. Beginning inventory is excluded from the computation of the cost to retail percentage because of the layer effect that results from the use of the LIFO method.

*20. If changes in the price level occur, the effect of such changes must be eliminated when using the LIFO retail method. If an enterprise wishes to change from conventional retail to LIFO retail, the beginning inventory must be restated to conform with the LIFO assumption. In effecting the change, the inventory of the prior period must be recomputed on the LIFO basis. This amount than serves as the beginning inventory for the LIFO retail method applied in the current period.

GLOSSARY

Cost-to-retail ratio. Total goods available for sale at cost divided by the total goods available at retail.

***Dollar-value LIFO retail method.** A method of estimating the cost of ending inventory by calculating the dollar increase in retail inventory layers with price indexes.

Gross profit method. A method for estimating the ending inventory by applying a gross profit rate to net sales.

***LIFO retail method.** A method of estimating the cost of ending inventory which excludes the beginning inventory in the cost-to-retail ratio.

Lower (floor) limit. In applying the lower of cost of market method, the market cannot be valued less than net realizable value less a normal profit margin.

Lower of cost or market (LCM). A basis whereby inventory is stated at the lower of cost or market (current replacement cost).

Markdown. A decrease below the original retail price.

Markdown cancellation. An increase in the selling price that follows a markdown. A markdown cancellation will never increase the selling price above the original retail price.

Markup. An increase above the original retail price.

Markup cancellation. A decrease in the selling price of an item that had been previously marked up above the original retail price. A markup cancellation will never reduce the selling price below the original retail price.

Net realizable value. The estimated selling price in the ordinary course of business less reasonably predictable costs of completion and disposal.

Original retail price. The price at which the item was originally marked for sale.

Purchase commitments. Agreements to buy inventory weeks, months, or even years in advance.

Retail inventory method. A method used to estimate the cost of the ending inventory by applying a cost to retail ratio to the ending inventory at retail.

Upper (ceiling) limit. In applying the lower of cost or market method, the market cannot be valued more than net realizable value.

CHAPTER OUTLINE

Fill in the outline presented below.

(S.O. 1) Lower of Cost or Market—Ceiling and Floor

(S.O. 3) Valuation Using Relative Sales Value

(S.O. 4) Purchase Commitments

(S.O. 5) The Gross Profit Method of Estimating Inventory

Computation of Gross Profit Percentage

(S.O. 6) The Retail Inventory Method

Conventional Method—With Markups and Markdowns

(S.O. 7) Presentation and Analysis of Inventories

*(S.O. 8) Dollar-Value LIFO Retail Method—Stable Prices

*Dollar-Value LIFO Retail Method—Fluctuating Prices

DEMONSTRATION PROBLEMS

1. (S.O.1 and 2) Determine the lower of cost or market inventory valuation on the basis of the following facts: quantity, 1,500 units; cost per unit, $4.45; replacement cost, $4.40; selling price, $5.75; cost to complete and sell, $.65; normal profit, $1.00.

Solution:

Upper Limit:	Selling price	$5.75	
	Less cost to complete and sell	.65	
	Net realizable value (upper limit)		$5.10
Lower Limit:	Net realizable value (NRV)	$5.10	
	Less normal profit	1.00	
	NRV less profit (lower limit)		$4.10

Decision rule: 1. If replacement cost is *between* the upper ($5.10) and lower ($4.10) limits, compare replacement cost to cost in deciding on the lower of cost or market. In the problem above, replacement cost ($4.40) is between the upper and lower limits, so it would be compared to cost ($4.45) and inventory would be valued at the lower ($4.40) of these two numbers.

2. If replacement cost *exceeds* the upper limit, then the upper limit is used to compare to cost in determining LCM.

3. If replacement cost is *lower* than the lower limit, then the lower limit is used to compare to cost in determining LCM.

2. (S.O.5) Compute the approximate ending inventory for the Fox Department Store assuming: beginning inventory (cost), $85,000; purchases (cost), $226,000; sales at selling price, $345,000; average gross profit rate on selling prices is 38%.

Solution:

Beginning inventory		$ 85,000
Purchases		226,000
Goods available		311,000
Sales	$345,000	
Less gross profit	131,100*	
Sales at cost		213,900
Approximate ending inventory		$ 97,100

*(38% x $345,000)

REVIEW QUESTIONS AND EXERCISES

TRUE-FALSE

Indicate whether each of the following is true (T) or false (F) in the space provided.

_____ 1. (S.O. 1) Inventory should be written down to market when its revenue-producing ability is no longer as great as its cost.

_____ 2. (S.O. 1) As used in the lower of cost or market rule, market should not exceed net realizable value.

_____ 3. (S.O. 1) Net realizable value is the estimated selling price in the normal course of business less the normal profit margin.

_____ 4. (S.O. 1) It is acceptable practice to write down inventory to market when market is lower than cost, but it is not acceptable to write up inventory to market when market is higher than cost.

_____ 5. (S.O. 1) The loss resulting from the write-down of inventory to market normally should be shown in the income statement as an extraordinary item.

_____ 6. (S.O. 1) When inventory is written down to market, this new basis is considered to be the cost basis for future periods.

_____ 7. (S.O. 2) Under the lower of cost or market rule, the income statement may show a larger net income in future periods than would be justified if the inventory were carried forward at cost.

_____ 8. (S.O. 2) Under the lower of cost or market rule, an item of inventory should not be valued at an amount in excess of net realizable value.

_____ 9. (S.O. 2) The application of the lower of cost or market rule to the inventory as a whole would yield a more conservative inventory value than would application of the rule to each individual item.

_____ 10. (S.O. 2) The recognition of inventories at selling price less cost of disposal means that income is usually recognized before the goods are transferred to an outside party.

_____ 11. (S.O. 3) The allocation of a lump sum cost among the individual units on the basis of relative sales value assumes that each individual unit should show the same dollar amount of profit.

_____ 12. (S.O. 4) No asset or liability is recognized at the inception of a purchase commitment because the contract is "executory" in nature.

_____ 13. (S.O. 4) The account Accrued Loss on Purchase Commitments should be included in the stockholders' equity section of the balance sheet.

_____ 14. (S.O. 4) If the contracted price under a purchase commitment is less than market and it is expected that gains will occur when the purchase is effected, gains should be recognized in the period during which such increases in market prices take place.

_____ 15. (S.O. 5) Gross margin is the excess of selling price over cost.

_____ 16. (S.O. 5) The gross margin expressed as a percentage of cost is normally less than the gross margin expressed as a percentage of sales.

_____ 17. (S.O. 5) The use of the gross profit method for interim reports does not preclude the need for a physical inventory to be taken at least annually.

_____ 18. (S.O. 6) Regardless of which version is used, the retail inventory method is sanctioned by the IRS.

_____ 19. (S.O. 6) The retail inventory method is not useful for interim reports.

_____ 20. (S.O. 6) The conventional retail method includes net markdowns but excludes net markups in the computation of the cost to retail percentage.

_____ 21. (S.O. 6) The inclusion of both net markups and net markdowns in the computation of the cost to retail percentage yields an inventory valuation that approximates cost.

_____ 22. (S.O. 6) The retail method assumes that the mix of the ending inventory is the same as the mix of the total goods available for sale.

_____ 23. (S.O. 6) The conventional retail inventory method is designed to approximate the lower of average cost or market.

_____ 24. (S.O. 7) The basis upon which inventory amounts are stated (lower of cost or market) and the method used in determining cost (LIFO, FIFO, average cost, etc.) should be disclosed in the notes of the financial statements.

_____ *25. (S.O. 8) A major assumption of the LIFO retail method is that the markups and markdowns apply only to the goods purchased during the current period, **not** to the beginning inventory.

MULTIPLE CHOICE

Select the best answer for each of the following items and enter the corresponding letter in the space provided.

_____ 1. (S.O. 1) Which of the following represents the best justification for the departure from the historical cost principle that results when lower of cost or market is used?

A. It is easier to keep track of market value than it is to keep track of cost as market value is available from any supplier.
B. Cost loses its relevance for the determination of cost of goods sold if the cost of inventory has been incurred in an earlier accounting period.
C. The balance sheet valuation of inventory is the most important consideration in the preparation of financial statements.
D. The loss in utility that results from a decline in the market value of inventory should be charged against revenues in the period in which it occurs.

_____ 2. (S.O. 1) Replacement cost is the designated market value used to compare to cost in determining lower of cost or market when its relationship to the items shown below is:

	Net Realizable Value	NRV less Normal Profit
A.	Lower	Higher
B.	Higher	Higher
C.	Higher	Lower
D.	Lower	Lower

_____ 3. (S.O. 1) When using the lower of cost or market method, what is the meaning of "market"?

A. Discounted present value.
B. Net realizable value.
C. Current replacement cost.
D. Net realizable value less a normal profit margin.

_____ 4. (S.O.1) A dudad has an original cost of $15 and a replacement cost of $12. The cost of completion and disposal is $2. If the dudad has a net realizable value of $16 and a normal profit margin of $5, its inventory value should be:

A. $15.
B. $12.
C. $16.
D. $14.

_____ 5. (S.O. 1) If a unit of inventory has declined in value below original cost, and the market value is less than the net realizable value less a normal profit margin, the amount to be used for purposes of inventory valuation is:

A. original cost.
B. market value.
C. net realizable value.
D. net realizable value less a normal profit margin.

_____ 6. (S.O. 1) Let A equal the reported inventory value if the lower of cost or market rule is applied to individual items of inventory; B equals the reported inventory value if the lower of cost or market rule is applied to the inventory as a whole. Which of the following best describes the relationship between A and B?

A. A will always be equal to B.
B. A will always be equal to or less than B.
C. A will always be equal to or greater than B.
D. A can never be equal to B.

_____ 7. (S.O. 1) Martinez Corporation has two products in its ending inventory. A profit margin of 30% on selling price is considered normal for each product. Specific data with respect to each product follows:

	Product A	Product B
Historical cost	$22.00	$ 55.00
Replacement cost	20.00	56.00
Estimated cost to dispose	7.00	31.00
Estimated selling price	35.00	110.00

In pricing its ending inventory using the lower of cost or market method, what unit values should Martinez use for products A and B respectively?

A. $17.50 and $55.00
B. $20.00 and $46.00
C. $20.00 and $55.00
D. $28.00 and $56.00

_____ 8. (S.O. 1) Under the lower of cost or market rule, market will be replacement cost except when replacement cost is:

A. higher than cost.
B. less than net realizable value.
C. less than net realizable value less a normal profit margin.
D. less than cost.

_____ 9. (S.O. 1) When the direct method is used to record inventory at market:

A. there is a direct reduction in the selling price of the product that results in a loss being recorded on the income statement prior to the sale.
B. a loss is recorded directly in the inventory account by crediting inventory and debiting loss on inventory decline.
C. only the portion of the loss attributable to inventory sold during the period is recorded in the financial statements.
D. the market value figure for ending inventory is substituted for cost and the loss is buried in cost of goods sold.

_____ 10. (S.O. 1) When recording market value instead of cost for ending inventory, the method which allows identification of inventory cost on the balance sheet is:

	Direct Method	Indirect Method
A.	No	Yes
B.	No	No
C.	Yes	No
D.	Yes	Yes

_____ 11. (S.O. 1) The fact that it is accepted practice to recognize decreases in the value of inventory prior to the point of sale, but not increases, is an illustration of which one of the following accounting concepts?

A. Objectivity.
B. Conservatism.
C. Materiality.
D. Consistency.

_____ 12. (S.O. 2) Recording inventory at net realizable value is permitted, even if it is above cost, when there are no significant costs of disposal involved and:

A. the ending inventory is determined by a physical inventory count.
B. a normal profit is not anticipated.
C. there is a controlled market with a quoted price applicable to all quantities.
D. the internal revenue service is assured that the practice is not used only to distort reported net income.

_____ 13. (S.O. 4) Maricel Company has a noncancelable purchase commitment to buy 10,000 units of a particular product during the next three years. The contract was signed one year prior to the first year in which the purchase commitment must be honored. At the end of the year in which the contract was signed Maricel Company should formally recognize in its balance sheet:

	An Asset	A Liability
A.	Yes	Yes
B.	No	No
C.	Yes	No
D.	No	Yes

_____ 14. (S.O. 5) Which of the following is **not** a basic assumption of the gross profit method?

A. The beginning inventory plus the purchases equal total goods to be accounted for.
B. Goods not sold must be on hand.
C. If the sales, reduced to the cost basis, are deducted from the sum of the opening inventory plus purchases, the result is the amount of inventory on hand.
D. The total amount of purchases and the total amount of sales remain relatively unchanged from the comparable previous period.

_____ 15. (S.O. 5) On January 31, fire destroyed the entire inventory of Mojares Company. The following data are available:

Sales for January	$60,000
Inventory, January 1	10,000
Purchases for January	55,000
Markup on cost	25%

The amount of the loss is estimated to be:

A. $17,000.
B. $20,000.
C. $15,000.
D. $16,250.

_____ 16. (S.O. 5) Devers Company sells its product for $25.00 per unit. This price is set to yield a gross margin on selling price of 25%. What is the cost of the product and what is the markup on cost for the product?

	Cost of Product	Markup on Cost
A.	$ 6.25	40%
B.	$ 9.75	75%
C.	$12.50	20%
D.	$18.75	33%

_____ 17. (S.O. 6) Which of the following is ***not*** required when using the retail inventory method?

A. All inventory items must be categorized according to the retail markup percentage which reflects the item's selling price.
B. A record of the total cost and retail value of goods purchased.
C. A record of the total cost and retail value of the goods available for sale.
D. Total sales for the period.

_____ 18. (S.O. 6) To determine an inventory valuation that approximates lower of average cost or market using the retail method, the computation of the cost to retail percentage should:

A. include markups but not markdowns.
B. include markups and markdowns.
C. include markdowns but not markups.
D. exclude markups but not markdowns.

_____ 19. (S.O. 6) The retail method has been used by a retail department store during its first year of operations. As of the end of the year, compare (A) the markdowns with (B) the markdown cancellations:

A. A will be equal to B.
B. A will be less than or equal to B.
C. A will be greater than or equal to B.
D. A cannot be equal to B.

_____ 20. (S.O. 6) Phair Co., a specialty clothing store, uses the retail inventory method. The following relates to 2002 operations:

Inventory, January 1, 2002, at cost	$14,200
Inventory, January 1, 2002 at sales price	20,100
Purchases in 2002 at cost	32,600
Purchases in 2002 at sales price	50,000
Additional markups on normal sales price	1,900
Sales (including $4,200 of items that were marked down from $6,400)	60,000

The cost of the December 31, 2002 inventory determined by the conventional retail method is:

A. $9,800
B. $6,370
C. $6,743
D. $6,543

_____ 21. (S.O. 6) One of the basic assumptions of the conventional retail method is that:

A. net markups apply to the goods sold.
B. net markdowns apply to the total goods available for sale.
C. net markdowns apply only to the goods sold.
D. the cost to retail percentage is unchanged from that of prior years.

_____ 22. (S.O. 6) Under the retail inventory method, purchase returns and allowances are normally considered a reduction of price at:

	Cost	Retail
A.	No	No
B.	No	Yes
C.	Yes	No
D.	Yes	Yes

Items 23 and 24 are based on the following information:

The Stipes Company uses the retail-inventory method to value its merchandise inventory. The following information is available:

	Cost	Retail
Beginning inventory	$ 30,000	$ 60,000
Purchases	190,000	300,000
Freight-in	1,000	-
Markups (net)	-	2,000
Markdowns (net)		4,000
Employee discounts		1,000
Sales		290,000

_____ 23. (S.O. 6) What is the ending inventory at retail?

A. $66,000
B. $67,000
C. $69,000
D. $71,000

_____ 24. (S.O. 6) If the ending inventory is to be valued at the lower of cost or market, what is the cost-to-retail ratio?

A. $221,000/$362,000
B. $221,000/$360,000
C. $221,000/$358,000
D. $221,000/$357,000

_____ 25. (S.O. 6) Which of the following is **not** a reason the retail inventory method is used widely:

A. as a control measure in determining inventory shortages.
B. for insurance information.
C. to permit the computation of net income without a physical count of inventory.
D. to defer income tax liability.

REVIEW EXERCISES

1. (S.O.1 and 2) You are given the following information regarding four inventory items:

	Inventory Items			
	A	B	C	D
Cost	$62	$41	$46	$85
Replacement cost	48	42	40	80
Net realizable value	59	47	42	78
Normal profit margin	8	4	4	5

Instructions:
In the space provided, indicate the inventory value for each item in accordance with the lower of cost or market rule.

A _____ B _____ C _____ D _____

2. (S.O.1) Josie Bisset Company determines its inventory using the lower of cost or market inventory valuation. For the years ended 12/31/01 and 12/31/02 the data for inventory values at cost and lower of cost or market are as follows:

	Cost	Lower of Cost or Market
12/31/01	$296,000	$272,000
12/31/02	$321,000	$306,000

Instructions:

a. Prepare the journal entries required at 12/31/01 and 12/31/02, assuming that the inventory is recorded at market, and a periodic inventory system (direct method) is used.

b. Prepare the journal entries required at 12/31/01 and 12/31/02, assuming that the inventory is recorded at cost and an allowance account is adjusted at each year-end under a periodic system.

a.

General Journal **J1**

Date	Account Title	Debit	Credit

b.

General Journal

J1

Date	Account Title	Debit	Credit

3. (S.O.5) Leighton Company uses the gross profit method to estimate monthly inventory balances. During recent months, gross profit has averaged 30% of net sales. The following data for January are obtained from the ledger:

Inventory, January 1	$ 30,000
Purchases	100,000
Purchase returns	2,000
Freight-in	3,000
Sales	120,000
Sales returns	4,000

Instructions:

Compute the January 31 inventory.

4. (S.O.5) Calabro Inc. had a majority of its inventory destroyed by a fire just prior to year-end. The company controller had kept the accounting records current and provided you with the following account balances.

Beginning inventory	$ 67,500
Purchases for the year	235,700
Purchase returns	17,500
Sales	526,800
Sales returns	16,200
Gross profit rate on sales	36%

Inventory with a selling price of $18,000 was undamaged by the fire. Damaged inventory with an original selling price of $10,000 had a net realizable value of $4,800.

Instructions:
Compute the amount of the loss caused by the fire, assuming no insurance coverage is carried by the company.

5. (S.O. 6) The following information for the month of April is available from the records of Ireland Department Store:

	At Cost	At Retail
Inventory, April 1	$ 8,400	$12,000
Purchases	48,810	80,000
Freight-in	2,000	
Additional markups		4,300
Markup cancellations		800
Markdowns		6,600
Markdowns cancellations		200
Sales		72,600

Instructions:

Compute the April 30 inventory at the lower of approximate cost or market using the conventional retail method.

*6. (S.O. 8) The following information pertains to the records of the Zuniga Company.

Beginning inventory	$ 46,000	$ 65,000
Net purchases	374,000	535,000
Markups		35,000
Markup cancellations		10,000
Markdowns		26,000
Markdown cancellations		16,000
Net sales		520,000

Instructions:

Compute the ending inventory under each of the following methods.

a. Conventional retail method.

b. LIFO retail method assuming stable prices.

c. Dollar-value LIFO method assuming the price index was 100 at the beginning of the year and 120 at year end.

a.

b.

c.

SOLUTIONS TO REVIEW QUESTIONS AND EXERCISES

TRUE-FALSE

1. (T)

2. (T)

3. (F) Net realizable value is defined as selling price less the estimated cost of completion and disposal. When the normal profit margin is subtracted from net realizable value, the resulting amount is referred to as net realizable value less a normal profit margin.

4. (T)

5. (F) The loss resulting from the write-down of inventory to market is shown as a separate item in the income statement but not as an extraordinary item.

6. (T)

7. (T)

8. (T)

9. (F) The lower of cost or market rule may be applied directly to each item or to the total of the inventory. When the lower of cost or market rule is applied to the inventory as a whole, increases in the market prices of some items offset decreases in the market prices in other items to some extent. Thus, the application of the lower of cost or market rule to individual inventory items gives the most conservative valuation for balance sheet purposes.

10. (T)

11. (F) When the relative sales value method is used, it is used because the items being valued vary in terms of such characteristics as shape, size, attractiveness, and so on. Because of these types of differences, the amount of gross profit generated by each item will be different.

12. (T)

13. (F) If the contracted price of a purchase commitment is in excess of market price and it is expected that losses will occur when the purchase is effected, a loss should be recognized and an Accrued Loss on Purchase Commitments should be credited. The loss is reported on the income statement under other expenses and losses, and the Accrued Loss is reported in the liability section of the balance sheet.

14. (F) If the contracted price is in excess of market and it is expected that losses will occur when the purchase is effected, losses should be recognized in the period during which such declines in market prices take place. Under the conservatism principle, gains are not recognized.

15. (T)

16. (F) Because selling price is greater than cost and the gross margin amount is the same for both, gross margin on selling price will always be less than the related percentage based on cost.

17. (T)

18. (T)

19. (F) Because a fairly quick and reliable measure of inventory value is usually needed, the retail inventory method is particularly useful for any type of interim report.

20. (F) The conventional retail inventory method is designed to approximate the lower of average cost or market. Thus, the cost percentage computation includes markups but not markdowns. When a company has an additional markup, it normally indicates that the market value of that item had increased. If the company has a net markdown, it means that a decline in the utility of that item has occurred. Therefore, if the attempt is to approximate lower of cost or market, markdowns are considered a current loss and are not involved in the calculation of the cost to retail ratio.

21. (T)

22. (T)

23. (T)

24. (T)

*25. (T)

MULTIPLE CHOICE

1. (D) The general rule is that the historical cost principle is abandoned when the future utility (revenue producing ability) of the inventory is no longer as great as its original cost. It is no easier to keep track of market value than it is to keep track of cost, and cost does not lose its relevance if market value remains in excess. The balance sheet valuation is not the most significant reason for lower of cost or market.

2. (A) The amount that is compared to cost is always the middle value of the three amounts: replacement cost, net realizable value, and NRV less a normal profit. Because NRV is greater than NRV less a normal profit, replacement cost can only be the middle value when it is lower than NRV and higher than NRV minus a normal profit.

3. (C) "Market" as used in the lower of cost or market method is the current replacement cost in the acquisition market for the inventory item.

4. (B)

Net Realizable Value	$16
NRV Minus Profit	$11
Replacement Cost	$12

Market is defined in this case as replacement cost because the replacement cost is between the upper limit (NRV) and the lower limit (NRV minus profit). Thus, when the replacement cost ($12) is compared to cost ($15), the inventory is valued at $12.

5. (D) "Market" (replacement cost) cannot go below the floor, net realizable value less a normal profit margin. Therefore, in this question where market is below cost and less than the floor, net realizable value less a normal profit margin is the amount that should be used for purposes of inventory valuation.

6. (B) Increases in the market prices of some inventory items tend to offset decreases in other inventory items when the cost or market rule is applied to the inventory as a whole. Thus, the inventory valuation that results from applying the cost or market method to individual items in inventory (alternative A) will always be equal to or less than the inventory valuation that results from applying the cost or market rule to the inventory as a whole (alternative B).

7. (C) The unit values Martinez should use for products A and B can be determined as follows:

	Market			
	Replacement Cost	Net Realizable Value	Net Realizable Value Less Normal Profit	Amount Selected for Market
Product A	$20.00	$28.00*	$17.50**	$20.00
Product B	$56.00	$79.00*	$46.00**	$56.00

*Computation of net realizable value:

	Product A	Product B
Estimated selling price	$35.00	$110.00
Less: estimated cost to dispose	7.00	31.00
Net Realizable Value	$28.00	$ 79.00

**Computation of net realizable value less normal profit:

Product A: $28.00 - .30($ 35.00) = $17.50

Product B: $79.00 - .30($110.00) = $46.00

Applying lower of cost or market:

	Market	Cost	Amount Selected
Product A	$20.00	$22.00	$20.00
Product B	$56.00	$55.00	$55.00

8. (C) If replacement cost is less than net realizable value less a normal profit margin, then replacement cost is below the lower limit for market value. When this occurs, market is defined as the lower limit (NRV minus a normal profit margin).

9. (D) Under the direct method, no entry for the decline in the value of the inventory is recorded. Merely, the ending inventory value used in computing cost of goods sold is valued at market (which is lower than cost) and the cost of goods sold that results is larger. This results in a lower net income so the loss is technically buried in the cost of goods sold computation.

10. (A) The indirect method does not change the cost amount recorded for inventory, but establishes a separate contra asset account and loss account to record the write-off. Thus, the indirect method permits balance sheet disclosure of inventory at cost and lower of cost or market as a result of using an "allowance" account (the contra asset).

11. (B) The conservatism concept is based on the assumption that in accounting we provide for all losses and anticipate no gains. This is the basis for recognizing decreases in inventory prior to the point of sale, but not increases.

12. (C) With no significant disposal costs and a controlled market, net realizable value is an appropriate inventory valuation approach. For example, inventories of certain minerals are ordinarily reported at selling prices because there is often a controlled market without significant costs of disposal. A similar treatment is given to agricultural products that are immediately marketable at fixed prices. Also, this method proves to be valuable when cost figures are too difficult to obtain.

13. (B) Even with formal, noncancelable purchase contracts, no asset or liability is recognized at the date of inception, because the contract is "executory" in nature; neither party has fulfilled its part of the contract. However, if material, such commitment details should be disclosed in the buyer's balance sheet in a footnote.

14. (D) The gross profit method assumes a constant gross profit percentage, but makes no assumptions about the total amount of sales or purchases. Alternatively (A), (B), and (C) are basic assumptions of the gross profit method.

15. (A) A 25% markup on cost is equivalent to a 20% markup on selling price:

$$\text{GP on selling price} = \frac{\%\text{ markup on cost}}{100\% + \%\text{ markup on cost}}$$

$$\text{GP on selling price} = \frac{.25}{1.25}$$

$$\text{GP on selling price} = .20$$

Sales	$60,000
GP ($60,000 x .20)	12,000
Cost of goods sold	$48,000
Goods available for sale	65,000
Inventory loss	$17,000

16. (D) C + .25SP = SP
C = (1 - .25)SP
C = .75SP
C = .75($25)
C = $18.75

SP	$25.00
C	18.75
GP	$ 6.25

Markup on Cost = $6.25 ÷ $18.75 = 33%

17. (A) Inventory items need not be categorized in any manner. The major benefit of the retail inventory method is that inventory items are accumulated without the need to separate them into distinct classifications. Alternatives B, C and D reflect the requirements for use of the retail inventory method.

18. (A) See explanation of True-False question No. 20.

19. (C) Markdown cancellations represent the cancellation of previous markdowns applied to a product. Therefore, markdown cancellations are limited to the total amount of markdowns previously recorded. Thus, for any entity, markdowns will be greater than or equal to markdown cancellations.

20. (B)

	Cost	Retail
Inventory 1/1/02	$14,200	$20,100
Purchase	32,600	50,000
	$46,800	$70,100
Additional Markups		1,900
Totals	$46,800	$72,000

(Cost-to-retail ratio: $46,800 ÷ 72,000 = 65%)

Deduct Markdowns	2,200
Sales Price of Goods Available	$69,800
Deduct Sales	60,000
Ending Inventory at Retail	$ 9,800

Ending Inventory at LCM: $9,800 x .65 = $6,370

21. (C) When the attempt is to approximate lower of cost or market, under the retail inventory method, markdowns are considered a current loss and are not involved in the calculation of the cost to retail ratio.

22. (D) Purchase returns and allowances are ordinarily considered both as a reduction of the price at cost and retail.

23. (B) Stipes Company's ending inventory at retail can be calculated as follows:

		Retail
Beginning inventory		$ 60,000
Purchases		300,000
Available		$360,000
Add:		
Markups, net		2,000
		$362,000
Less:		
Markdowns, net	$4,000	
Employee discounts	1,000	
		5,000
		$357,000
Less: Sales		290,000
Ending inventory at retail		$ 67,000

24. (A) Stipes Company's cost-to-retail ratio approximating lower of cost or market can be determined as follows:

	Cost	Retail
Beginning inventory	$ 30,000	$ 60,000
Purchases	190,000	300,000
Freight-in	1,000	-
	221,000	360,000
Add: Markups, net		2,000
		362,000

The cost-to-retail ratio approximating lower of cost or market includes net markups but not net markdowns: $221,000/$362,000 = 61.05%.

25. (D) The retail inventory method is used widely (1) to permit the computation of net income without a physical count of inventory, (2) as a control measure in determining inventory shortages, (3) in regulating quantities of merchandise on hand, and (4) for insurance information. The retail inventory method does not necessarily cause a decrease in income taxes like LIFO during a period of rising prices.

REVIEW EXERCISES

1. A. **$51** B. **$41** C. **$40** D. **$78**

2. a.

Date	Account	Debit	Credit
12/31/01	Inventory	272,000	
	Cost of Goods Sold (or Income Summary)		272,000
12/31/01	Cost of Goods Sold (or Income Summary)	272,000	
	Inventory		272,000
12/31/02	Inventory	306,000	
	Cost of Goods Sold		306,000

b.

Date	Account	Debit	Credit
12/31/01	Inventory	296,000	
	Cost of Goods Sold		296,000
	Loss Due to Market Decline of Inventory	24,000	
	Allowance to Reduce Inventory to Market		24,000
12/31/02	Cost of Goods Sold (or Inventory Summary)	296,000	
	Inventory		296,000
12/31/02	Inventory	321,000	
	Cost of Goods Sold (or Income Summary)		321,000
	Allowance to Reduce Inventory to Market	9,000*	
	Recovery of Market Decline of Inventory		9,000

*	
Cost of inventory 12/31/01	$296,000
Lower of Cost or Market at 12/31/01	272,000
Allowance amount needed to reduce inventory to market	$ 24,000

Cost of inventory at 12/31/02	$321,000
Lower of cost or market at 12/31/02	306,000
Allowance amount needed to reduce inventory to market	$ 15,000

Recovery of previously recognized loss: $24,000 - 15,000 = $9,000

3.

Inventory, January	$ 30,000
Purchases	100,000
Freight-in	3,000
Purchase returns	(2,000)
Goods available (at cost)	$131,000
Sales	$120,000
Sales returns	4,000
Net sales	$116,000
Less gross profit (30% of 116,000)	34,800
Cost of goods sold	81,200
Inventory, January 31 (at cost) (131,000 - 81,200)	$ 49,800

4.

Sales	$526,800	
Sales returns	(16,200)	
Net sales	510,600	
Gross profit rate	.36	
Gross profit	$183,816	

Cost of goods sold: $510,600 - $183,816 = $326,784

Beginning inventory		$ 67,500
Purchases	235,700	
Purchase returns	17,500	
Net purchases		218,200
Goods available for sale		$285,700
Estimated ending inventory: $326,784 - $285,700 = $41,084		
Inventory loss due to fire:		
Estimated ending inventory		$41,084
Undamaged inventory [$18,000 - ($18,000 X 36%)]		(11,520)
NRV of damaged goods		(4,800)
Loss due to fire		$24,764

5.

	Cost	Retail
Inventory, April 1	$ 8,400	$12,000
Purchases	48,810	80,000
Freight-in	2,000	
Net markups		3,500
Goods available	$59,210	$95,500

Cost to retail ratio 59,210/95,500 = 62.0%

Less:		
Sales	72,600	
Net markdowns	6,400	
		79,000
Inventory, April 30, at retail		$16,500
Inventory, April 30, at lower of cost or market (16,500 x.62)		$10,230

6. a. **Conventional Retail**

	Cost		Retail
Beginning inventory	$ 46,000		$ 65,000
Purchases (net)	374,000		535,000
Totals	420,000		600,000
Add net markups			
Markups		35,000	
Markup cancellations		10,000	25,000
	$420,000		625,000
Deduct net markdowns			
Markdowns		26,000	
Markdown cancellations		16,000	10,000
Sales price of goods available			615,000
Deduct sales			520,000
Ending inventory at retail			$ 95,000

$$\text{Cost-to-retail ratio} = \frac{420,000}{625,000} = 67.2\%$$

Ending inventory at lower of cost or market: $95,000 X .672 = $63,840

b. **LIFO Retail Method (Stable Prices)**

	Cost	Retail
Beginning inventory	$ 46,000	$ 65,000
Purchases (net)	374,000	535,000
Net markups		25,000
Net markdowns		(10,000)
Total excluding beginning inventory	374,000	550,000
Total including beginning inventory	$420,000	615,000
Net sales		$520,000
Ending inventory at retail		$ 95,000

Establishment of cost-to-retail percentage
under assumption of LIFO retail 374,000 ÷ 550,000 = 68%

Ending inventory at cost:		
Beginning inventory (65,000 x .7077*)		$ 46,000
Additional increment	$ 95,000	
Ending inventory	65,000	
Beginning inventory	30,000	
Cost to retail percentage	x .68	20,400
Ending inventory at LIFO cost (stable prices)		$ 66,400

*($46,000 ÷ 65,000)

c. **Dollar-value LIFO (Fluctuating Prices)**

	Cost	Retail
Beginning inventory	$ 46,000	$ 65,000
Purchases (net)	374,000	535,000
Net markups		25,000
Net markdowns		(10,000)
Total excluding beginning inventory	374,000	550,000
Total including beginning inventory	$420,000	615,000
Net sales		$520,000
Ending inventory at retail		$ 95,000

Establishment of cost-to-retail percentage under assumption of LIFO retail 374,000 ÷ 550,000 = 68%

A. Ending inventory at retail prices deflated to base-year prices $95,000 x 100/120 =	$79,167
B. Beginning inventory at base-year prices	65,000
C. Inventory increase from beginning of period	$14,167
D. Increment priced in terms of end-of-year prices $14,167 x 120/100 =	$17,000

Ending inventory at cost:

First layer	$46,000
Second layer (increase at new price level times cost to retail percentage) $17,000 x .68 =	11,560
Ending inventory at LIFO cost (fluctuating prices)	$57,560

10

Acquisition and Disposition of Property, Plant, and Equipment

CHAPTER STUDY OBJECTIVES

1. Describe the major characteristics of property, plant and equipment.
2. Identify the costs included in the initial valuation of land, buildings, and equipment.
3. Describe the accounting problems associated with self-constructed assets.
4. Describe the accounting problems associated with interest capitalization.
5. Understand accounting issues related to acquiring and valuing plant assets.
6. Describe the accounting treatment for costs subsequent to acquisition.
7. Describe the accounting treatment for the disposal of property, plant, and equipment.

CHAPTER REVIEW

1. Chapter 10 presents a discussion of the basic accounting problems associated with the incurrence of costs related to property, plant, and equipment; and the accounting methods used to retire or dispose of these costs. These assets, also referred to as fixed assets, are of a durable nature and include land, building structures, and equipment. Fixed assets are an important part of the operations of most business organizations. They provide the major means of support for the production and/or distribution of a company's product or service.

2. (S.O. 1) **Property, plant, and equipment** possess certain characteristics that distinguish them from other assets owned by a business enterprise. These characteristics may be expressed as follows: **(a)** acquired for use in operations and not for resale, **(b)** long-term in nature and usually subject to depreciation, and **(c)** physical substance. An asset must be used in the normal business operations to be classified as a fixed asset. These assets last for a number of years and their costs must be allocated to the periods which benefit from their use.

Acquisition of Property, Plant, and Equipment

3. (S.O. 2) Property, plant and equipment are valued in the accounts at their **historical cost**. Historical cost is measured by the cash or cash equivalent price of obtaining the asset and bringing it to the location and condition necessary for its intended use. Thus, charges associated with freight costs and installation are considered a part of the asset's cost. The process of allocating the historical cost of property, plant, and equipment to the periods benefited by those assets is known as **depreciation**. The topic of depreciation is presented in Chapter 11.

4. With minor exceptions, use of a method other than historical cost in valuing property, plant, and equipment represents a departure from generally accepted accounting principles. This position is justified on the grounds that: **(a)** cost reflects fair value on the date of acquisition, **(b)** historical cost involves actual, not hypothetical transactions, and **(c)** gains and losses should not be anticipated but should be recognized when assets are sold.

5. The assets normally classified on the balance sheet as property, plant, and equipment include land, buildings, and various kinds of machinery and equipment. The cost of each item includes the acquisition price plus those expenditures incurred in getting the asset ready for its intended use. In the case of **land**, cost typically includes **(a)** purchase price; **(b)** closing costs such as title, attorney, and recording fees; **(c)** cost of grading, filling, draining, and clearing the property; **(d)** assumption of any encumbrances on the property; and **(e)** any land improvements that have an indefinite life. The cost of removing an old building from land purchased for the purpose of constructing a new building is properly charged to the land account. Also, when improvements that have a limited life (fences, driveways, etc.) are made to the land they should be set up in a separate Land Improvements account so they can be depreciated over their estimated useful life.

6. **Building costs** include materials, labor, and overhead costs incurred during construction. Also, any fees such as those incurred for building permits or the services of an attorney or architect are included in acquisition cost. In general, all costs incurred from excavation of the site to completion of the building are considered part of the building costs.

7. With respect to **equipment**, cost includes purchase price plus all expenditures related to the purchase that occur subsequent to acquisition but prior to actual use. These related costs would include such items as freight charges, insurance charges on the asset while in transit, assembly and installation, special preparation of facilities, and asset testing costs.

<u>Self-Constructed Assets</u>

8. (S.O. 3) When machinery and equipment to be used by an entity are constructed rather than purchased, a problem exists concerning the allocation of **overhead costs**. These costs may be handled in one of three ways: **(a)** assign no fixed overhead to the cost of the constructed asset, **(b)** assign a portion of all overhead to the construction process, or **(c)** allocate overhead on the basis of lost production. The second method appears preferable because of its consistency with the historical cost principle. It should be noted that the cost recorded for a constructed asset can never exceed the price charged by an outside producer.

<u>Interest Costs</u>

9. (S.O. 4) Capitalization of interest cost incurred in connection with financing the construction or acquisition of property, plant, and equipment is addressed in **FASB Statement No. 34, "Capitalization of Interest Costs."** The profession generally follows the rule of **capitalizing only the actual interest costs incurred during construction**. While some modification to this general rule occurs, its adoption is consistent with the concept that the historical cost of acquiring an asset includes all costs incurred to bring the asset to the condition and location necessary for its intended use.

10. To qualify for interest capitalization, assets must require a period of time to get them ready for their intended use. Assets that qualify for interest cost capitalization include assets under construction for an enterprise's own use (such as buildings, plants, and machinery) and assets intended for sale or lease that are constructed or otherwise produced as discrete projects (like ships or real estate developments). The period during which interest must be capitalized begins when three conditions are

present: **(a)** expenditures for the asset have been made; **(b)** activities that are necessary to get the asset ready for its intended use are in progress; and **(c)** interest cost is being incurred.

11. The amount of interest that may be capitalized is limited to the **lower** of **(a)** actual interest cost incurred during the period or **(b)** the amount of interest cost incurred during the period that theoretically could have been avoided if the expenditure for the asset had not been made **(avoidable interest).** The potential amount of interest that may be capitalized during an accounting period is determined by multiplying interest rate(s) by the **weighted-average amount of accumulated expenditures** for qualifying assets during the period.

12. Examples which demonstrate computation of the weighted-average accumulated expenditures and selecting the appropriate interest rate are included in the chapter. Also, a comprehensive illustration of interest capitalization is shown in the text. This illustration includes both the computations and the related journal entries that should be made in a situation when an asset is constructed and capitalizable interest is a part of the transaction.

Acquisition and Valuation

13. (S.O. 5) A number of accounting problems are involved in the acquisition and valuation of fixed assets. In general, an asset should be recorded at the fair market value of what is given up to acquire it or its own fair market value, whichever is more clearly evident. This appears to be a rather straight forward approach that can be easily followed. However, determining fair market value is not always as easy as it might appear. Some of the problems one encounters in determining proper valuation are discussed in the paragraphs that follow.

14. The purchase of a plant asset is often accompanied by a **cash discount** for prompt payment. If the discount is taken, it results in a reduction in the purchase price of the asset. However, when the discount is allowed to lapse, should a loss be recorded or should the asset be recorded at a higher purchase price? Currently, while the "loss approach" is preferred, both methods are employed in practice.

15. Plant assets purchased on **long-term credit contracts** should be accounted for at the present value of the consideration exchanged on the date of purchase. When the obligation stipulates no interest rate, or the rate is unreasonable, an imputed rate of interest must be determined for use in calculating the present value. Factors to be considered in imputing an interest rate are the borrower's credit rating, the amount and maturity date of the note, and prevailing interest rates. If determinable, the cash exchange price of the asset acquired should be used as the basis for recording the asset and measuring the interest element.

16. In some instances a company may purchase a group of plant assets at a single lump sum price. The best way to allocate the purchase price of the assets to the individual items is the relative fair market values of the assets acquired. To determine fair market value, an appraisal for insurance purposes, the assessed valuation for property taxes, or simply an independent appraisal by a qualified appraiser might be used. When assets are acquired for an entity's stock, the best measure of cost is the fair market value of the stock issued.

Exchanges of Property, Plant, and Equipment

17. **Nonmonetary assets** such as inventory or property, plant, and equipment are items whose price may change over time. Controversy exists in regard to the accounting for these assets when one nonmonetary asset is exchanged for another nonmonetary asset. A critical element in accounting for the exchange of nonmonetary assets is the type of assets involved. **If the transaction involves the exchange of dissimilar assets, the cost of the nonmonetary asset acquired is normally recorded at the fair value of the asset given up and a gain or loss is recognized.** The only time the fair value of the asset acquired is used to value the transaction is when its fair value is more clearly evident than the fair value of the asset given up.

18. **Similar nonmonetary** assets are assets that are of the same general type, that perform the same function, or that are employed in the same line of business. **When similar nonmonetary assets are exchanged and a loss results, the loss should be recognized immediately.** A loss is indicated when the fair value of the asset given up is less than its book value.

19. When **similar nonmonetary assets** are exchanged and a gain results, the presence or absence of cash **(boot)** as a part of the transaction must be considered before the transaction is recorded. If similar nonmonetary assets are exchanged and no cash is involved, no gain is recognized. When some cash is involved in the transaction, the entity giving the cash may not recognize a gain. However, when cash is **received**, a portion of the gain is recognized by the entity receiving the cash. The portion to be recognized is equal to the ratio of the cash received to the total consideration received times the total gain indicated.

20. To summarize these concepts, when a transaction involves an exchange of nonmonetary assets, losses are always recognized whether the exchange involves dissimilar or similar assets. Gains are recognized if the exchange involves dissimilar assets; gains are deferred (not immediately recognized) if the exchange involves similar assets, unless cash or some other form of monetary consideration is **received**, in which case a partial gain is recognized. Also, a gain or loss on the exchange on nonmonetary assets is computed by comparing the book value of the asset given up with the fair value of that same asset. The examples shown below are designed to demonstrate the various situations where exchanges of nonmonetary assets are included.

Dissimilar Assets

Al Company exchanged a used machine with a book value of $26,000 (cost $54,000 less $28,000 accumulated depreciation) and cash of $8,000 for a delivery truck. The machine is estimated to have a fair market value of $36,000.

Cost of truck:	
Fair value of machine exchanged	$36,000
Cash paid	8,000
Cost of truck	$44,000

Journal entry:		
Truck	$44,000	
Accumulated Depreciation - Machine	28,000	
Machine		54,000
Gain on Machine Disposal		10,000
Cash		8,000

Similar Assets-Loss Situation

Al Company trades a used drill press for a new model. The used press has a book value of $11,000 (cost $32,000 less $21,000 accumulated depreciation) and a fair market value of $8,000. The new drill press has a list price of $38,000, and the seller has allowed a trade-in allowance of $15,000 on the old press.

Cost of new machine:	
List price of new drill press	$38,000
Less trade-in allowance	15,000
Cash payment due	23,000
Fair value of used drill press	8,000
Cost of new drill press	$31,000

Journal entry:		
Equipment	31,000	
Accumulated depreciation	21,000	
Loss on disposal of equipment	3,000	
Equipment		32,000
Cash		23,000

Loss verification:	
Book value of used drill press	$11,000
Fair value of used drill press	8,000
Loss on disposal of used drill press	$ 3,000

Similar Assets-Gain Situation (No Cash)

Al Company contracts with Peg Company to exchange delivery vans. Al Company will trade three Dodge Caravans for four Ford Aerostars owned by Peg Company. The fair value of the Caravans is $51,000 with a book value of $38,000 (cost $65,000 less $27,000 accumulated depreciation). The Aerostars have a fair value of $66,000 and Al Company gives $15,000 in cash in addition to the Caravans.

Computation of Gain:	
Fair value of caravans	$51,000
Book value, of caravans	38,000
Total gain (unrecognized)	$13,000

Basis of new vans to Al Company:	
Fair value of Aerostars	$66,000
Less gain deferred	13,000
Basis of Aerostar vans	$53,000

OR

Book value of caravans	$38,000
Cash paid	15,000
Basis of Aerostar vans	$53,000

Al Company journal entry:

Aerostar vans	53,000	
Accumulated depreciation	27,000	
Caravan vans		65,000
Cash		15,000

Similar Assets-Gain Situation
(Some Cash Received)

From the previous example, assume the book value of the Aerostar Vans exchanged by Peg Company was $52,000 (cost $75,000 less $23,000 of accumulated depreciation). Thus, the total gain on the exchange to Peg Company is as follows:

Fair value of vans exchanged	$66,000
Book value of vans exchanged	52,000
Total gain	$14,000

Recognized gain due to cash received:

$15,000/($15,000 + $51,000) X $14,000 = $3,182

Deferred gain:

$14,000 - $3,182 = $10,818

Basis of new vans to Peg Company:

Fair value of Caravans	$51,000
Less gain deferred	(10,818)
Basis of Caravans	$40,182

Peg Company journal entry:

Cash	15,000	
Caravan vans	40,182	
Accumulated depreciation	23,000	
Aerostar vans		75,000
Gain on disposal of vans		3,182

21. Many companies receive assets through donations from other organizations, individuals, or the federal government. These transactions are known as **nonreciprocal transfers**. When an asset is received through donation, the appraisal or fair market value of the asset should be used to establish its value on the books. The credit for this transaction is made to (1) a Donated Capital account that would appear in stockholders' equity, or (2) revenue. A recent FASB standard states that, in general, contributions received should be recorded as revenue.

Costs Subsequent to Acquisition

22. (S.O. 6) Costs related to plant assets that are incurred after the asset is placed in use are either added to the asset account **(capitalized)** or charged against operations **(expensed)** when incurred. In general, costs incurred to achieve greater future benefits from the asset should be capitalized, whereas expenditures that simply maintain a given level of service should be expensed. For the costs to be capitalized, one of three conditions must be present: **(a)** the useful life of the asset must be increased, **(b)** the quantity of service produced from the asset must be increased, or **(c)** the quality of the units produced must be enhanced. In many instances, a considerable amount of judgment is required in deciding whether to capitalize or expense an item. However, consistent application of a capital/expense policy is normally more important than attempting to provide theoretical guidelines.

23. Generally, expenditures related to plant assets being used in a productive capacity may be classified as: **(a)** additions, **(b)** improvements and replacements, **(c)** reinstallation and rearrangement, and **(d)** repairs. Because **additions** result in the creation of new assets, they should be capitalized.

24. **Improvements** and **replacements** are substitutions of one asset for another. Improvements substitute a better asset for the one currently used, whereas a replacement substitutes a similar asset. The major problem in accounting for improvements and replacements concerns differentiating these expenditures from normal repairs. If an improvement or replacement increases the future service potential of the asset, it should be capitalized. Capitalization may be accomplished by: **(a)** substituting the cost of the new asset for the cost of the asset replaced, **(b)** capitalizing the new cost without eliminating the cost of the asset replaced, or **(c)** debiting the expenditure to accumulated depreciation. The specific facts related to the situation will aid in determining the most appropriate method to use.

25. **Rearrangement and reinstallation** costs are generally carried forward as a separate asset and amortized against future income. **Ordinary repairs** are expenditures made to maintain plant assets in operating condition. They are charged to an expense account in the period in which they are incurred.

Dispositions of Plant Assets

26. (S.O. 7) When a plant asset is disposed of, the accounting records should be relieved of the cost and accumulated depreciation associated with the asset. Depreciation should be recorded on the asset up to the date of disposal, and any resulting gains or losses should be reported in accordance with the provisions of *APB Opinion No. 30*. Plant assets may be retired voluntarily or disposed of by **sale, exchange, involuntary conversion, or abandonment**.

Miscellaneous

27. Valuation of property, plant, and equipment on a basis other than historical cost has been widely discussed by those concerned with the financial reporting process. However, historical cost continues to be recognized as the accepted method for valuing these assets in the financial statements. One valuation approach that is sometimes allowed and not considered a violation of historical cost is a method referred to as **prudent cost**. This concept holds that if for some reason you were ignorant about a certain price and paid too much for an asset originally, it is theoretically preferable to charge a loss immediately.

GLOSSARY

Additions. Expenditures on assets which increase or extend them.

Avoidable interest. The amount of interest cost during the period that theoretically could have been avoided if expenditures for the asset had not been made.

Capital expenditure. An expenditure on an asset whereby (1) the useful life of the asset is increased, (2) the quantity of units produced from the asset is increased, or (3) the quality of the units produced is enhanced.

Capitalization period. The period of time during which interest must be capitalized. It begins when (1) expenditures for the asset have been made, (2) activities that are necessary to get the asset ready for its intended use are in progress, and (3) interest cost is being incurred. The time ends when the asset is substantially complete and ready for its intended use.

Dissimilar nonmonetary assets. Nonmonetary assets that are not of the same general type, do not perform the same function, and are not employed in the same line of business.

Historical cost. The value of an asset measured by the cash or cash equivalent price of obtaining the asset and bringing it to the location and condition necessary for its intended use.

Improvements (betterments). Expenditures that substitute a better asset for an existing asset.

Involuntary conversion. An asset's service is terminated through fire, flood, theft, condemnation or some other manner not intended by the owner of the asset.

Lump sum price. The aggregate price at which a group of assets is acquired.

Major repairs. Expenditures made to maintain plant assets whereby the expenditures benefit more than one year or one operating cycle, whichever is longer.

Nonmonetary assets. Assets whose price in terms of the monetary unit may change over time, whereas monetary assets—cash and short- or long-term accounts and notes receivable—are fixed in terms of units of currency by contract or otherwise.

Nonreciprocal transfers. Transfers of assets in one direction such as contributions (donations or gifts).

Ordinary repairs	Expenditures made to maintain plant assets in operating condition.
Property, plant and equipment.	Assets that (1) are acquired for use in operations and not for resale, (2) are long-term in nature and usually subject to depreciation, and (3) possess physical substance.
Rearrangement and reinstallation costs.	Expenditures intended to benefit future periods that result from rearranging or reinstalling assets.
Replacements.	Expenditures that substitute a similar asset for an existing asset.
Revenue (expense) expenditure.	An expenditure on an asset whereby (1) the useful life of the asset does not increase, (2) the quantity of units produced from the asset does not increase, and (3) the quality of the units produced is not enhanced.
Self-constructed assets.	Assets constructed by a company rather than purchased.
Similar nonmonetary assets.	Nonmonetary assets that are of the same general type, or that perform the same function, or that are employed in the same line of business.
Weighted-average accumulated expenditures.	The construction expenditures that are weighted by the amount of time that interest cost could be incurred on the expenditure.

CHAPTER OUTLINE

Fill in the outline presented below.

(S.O. 1) The three characteristics of property, plant and equipment.

1.

2.

3.

(S.O. 2) The acquisition of property, plant and equipment

The cost of land

The cost of buildings

The cost of equipment

(S.O. 3) Self-constructed assets

(S.O. 4) Interest costs during construction

Qualifying assets

Capitalization period

Chapter Outline *(continued)*

Amount to Capitalize

Special issues related to interest capitalization

(S.O. 5) Acquisition and valuation

Cash discount

Deferred payment contracts

Lump sum purchase

Issuance of stock

Exchanges of property, plant and equipment

Dissimilar assets

Similar assets—loss situation

Similar assets—gain situation (no cash received)

Similar assets—gain situation (some cash received)

Chapter Outline *(continued)*

Accounting for contributions

(S.O. 6) Cost subsequent to acquisition

Additions

Improvements and replacements

Rearrangement and reinstallation

Repairs

(S.O. 7) Dispositions of plant assets

Sale of plant assets

Involuntary conversion

Miscellaneous problems

Other asset valuation methods

DEMONSTRATION PROBLEM (S.O. 5)

Rabillo Co. trades a used printing machine for a new improved model. The old machine has a book value of $12,000 (original cost $30,000 less $18,000 accumulated depreciation) and a fair value of $8,000. The new printing machine has a list price of $42,000, and Rabillo Co. receives a $14,000 trade-in allowance on the old machine. Compute (a) the cost to be recorded in the books of Rabillo Co. for the new machine and (b) the amount of any gain or loss as a result of this transaction.

Solution:

(a) Cost of new printing machine (similar assets)

List price of new machine	$42,000
Less trade-in allowance	14,000
Cash payment due	28,000
Fair value of old machine	8,000
Cost of new machine	$36,000*

*$36,000 represents the value given up by Rabillo Co. to acquire the new machine.

(b) Computation of loss

Book value of old machine	$12,000
Fair value of the old machine	8,000
Loss on trade of old machine	$ 4,000

REVIEW QUESTIONS AND EXERCISES

TRUE-FALSE

Indicate whether each of the following is true (T) or false (F) in the space provided.

_____ 1. (S.O. 2) A building owned by a corporation is always classified as property, plant and equipment.

_____ 2. (S.O. 2) The cash or cash equivalent price of items classified as property, plant and equipment best measures the value of the asset on the date of acquisition.

_____ 3. (S.O. 2) Use of the current replacement cost method to account for property, plant and equipment would most likely result in the recognition of gains and losses prior to the time the asset is sold.

_____ 4. (S.O. 2) The cost of items classified as property, plant, and equipment should include all expenditures related to the asset incurred during the first three months of the asset's useful life.

_____ 5. (S.O. 2) When land has been purchased for the purpose of constructing a new building, all costs incurred in connection with preparing the land for excavation are considered building costs.

_____ 6. (S.O. 3) If the allocation of overhead to self-constructed assets results in an asset cost that is greater than the cost that would be charged by an independent producer, the excess overhead should be recorded as a period loss.

_____ 7. (S.O. 4) The interest costs on funds used to acquire an asset should not be capitalized even if a significant period of time is required to bring the asset to a condition or location necessary for its intended use.

_____ 8. (S.O. 4) Land that is not being developed qualifies for interest capitalization.

_____ 9. (S.O. 4) The amount of interest to be capitalized is the higher of actual interest cost incurred during the period or avoidable interest.

_____ 10. (S.O. 4) The interest incurred on the specific borrowings is used for the portion of weighted-average accumulated expenditures that is less than or equal to any amounts borrowed specifically to finance construction of the assets.

_____ 11. (S.O. 5) An asset should be recorded at the fair market value of the consideration given up to acquire it or at its fair market value, whichever is higher.

_____ 12. (S.O. 5) Equipment purchased through the use of deferred payment contracts should be accounted for at the present value of the contract.

_____ 13. (S.O. 5) The purpose of imputed interest is to approximate the interest rate of a deferred purchase contract when one is not expressly stated.

_____ 14. (S.O. 5) In general, because the exchange of nonmonetary assets does not constitute a sale by either party involved in the transaction, the accounting should be based on the book value of the assets involved.

_____ 15. (S.O. 5) If an exchange of nonmonetary assets occurs and the assets are dissimilar, it is presumed that the earnings process related to these assets is completed.

_____ 16. (S.O. 5) If an exchange transaction involving similar nonmonetary assets results in a loss, the loss is recognized immediately, even when boot is included as a part of the transaction.

_____ 17. (S.O. 5) Gains and losses on the exchange of nonmonetary assets are computed by comparing the book value of the asset given up with the fair value of the asset given up.

_____ 18. (S.O. 5) When an exchange of similar nonmonetary assets results in a gain and insignificant boot is included as a part of the transaction, the gain to be recognized is limited to the amount of the boot received.

_____ 19. (S.O. 5) In an exchange of similar assets where there is a gain situation and cash is received in the amount of $25,000 and the fair value of other assets received is $70,000, the recognized gain is limited by the use of a formula.

_____ 20. (S.O. 5) The recommended accounting treatment for donated property, plant, and equipment represents a departure from the cost principle.

_____ 21. (S.O. 6) Once an asset has been placed into productive use, the major criterion used to determine whether an expenditure should be capitalized or expensed is the significance of that expenditure in relation to the original cost.

_____ 22. (S.O. 6) By definition, any addition to a building or machine is capitalized because a new asset has been created.

_____ 23. (S.O. 6) If a capital expenditure related to a machine increases the useful life but does not improve its quality, the expenditure may be debited to accumulated depreciation rather than to the asset account.

_____ 24. (S.O. 7) According to *APB Opinion No. 30,* gains and losses on the retirement of property, plant, and equipment should be shown in the income statement as extraordinary items.

_____ 25. (S.O. 7) If an asset still can be used even though it is fully depreciated, it may be kept on the books at historical cost less depreciation, or the asset may be carried at scrap value.

MULTIPLE CHOICE

Select the best answer for each of the following items and enter the corresponding letter in the space provided.

_____ 1. (S.O. 2) Historical cost is the basis advocated for recording the acquisition of property, plant, and equipment for all of the following reasons except:

A. at the date of acquisition, cost reflects fair market value.
B. property, plant, and equipment items are always acquired at their original historical cost.
C. historical cost involves actual transactions and, as such, is the most reliable basis.
D. gains and losses should not be anticipated but should be recognized when the asset is sold.

_____ 2. (S.O. 2) Which of the following is not a necessary characteristic for an item to be classified as property, plant, and equipment?

A. Usually subject to depreciation.
B. Characterized by physical substance.
C. Can be used in operations for at least 5 years.
D. Not acquired for resale.

_____ 3. (S.O. 2) Stacia Theater Corporation recently purchased the Robinson Theater and the land on which it is located. Stacia plans to raze the building immediately and build a new modern theater on the site. The cost to raze the Robinson Theater should be:

A. written off as an extraordinary loss in the year the theater is razed.
B. capitalized as part of the cost of land.
C. depreciated over the period from the date of acquisition to the date the theater is to be razed.
D. capitalized as part of the cost of the new theater.

_____ 4. (S.O. 2) On January 15, 2001, Thorne Corporation purchased a parcel of land as a factory site for $100,000. An old building on the property was demolished, and construction began on a new building which was completed on October 18, 2001. Costs incurred during this period are listed below:

Demolition of old building	$ 6,000
Architect's fees	15,000
Legal fees for title investigation and purchase contract	5,000
Construction costs	600,000

(Salvaged materials resulting from demolition were sold for $3,000.)

Thorne should record the cost of the land and new building respectively as:

A. $100,000 and $623,000
B. $105,000 and $618,000
C. $108,000 and $615,000
D. $111,000 and $615,000

_____ 5. (S.O. 3) To be consistent with the historical cost principle, overhead costs incurred by an enterprise constructing its own building should be:

A. allocated on the basis of lost production.
B. eliminated completely from the cost of the asset.
C. allocated on an opportunity cost basis.
D. allocated on a pro rata basis between the asset and normal operations.

_____ 6. (S.O. 4) Which of the following is the recommended approach to handling interest incurred in financing the construction of property, plant, and equipment?

A. Capitalize only the actual interest costs incurred during construction.
B. Charge construction with all costs of funds employed, whether identifiable or not.
C. Capitalize no interest during construction.
D. Capitalize interest costs equal to the prime interest rate times the estimated cost of the asset being constructed.

_____ 7. (S.O. 4) Which of the following is not a condition that must be satisfied before interest capitalization can begin on a qualifying asset?

A. Interest cost is being incurred.
B. Expenditures for the assets have been made.
C. The interest rate is equal to or greater than the company's cost of capital.
D. Activities that are necessary to get the asset ready for its intended use are in progress.

_____ 8. (S.O. 4) If land is purchased as a site for a structure (such as a plant site), interest costs capitalized during the period of construction are part of the cost of the:

	Plant	Land
A.	Yes	Yes
B.	Yes	No
C.	No	No
D.	No	Yes

_____ 9. (S.O. 4) The capitalization of interest costs is justified as being necessary in order to fulfill the:

A. Conservatism concept.
B. Economic entity assumption.
C. Revenue recognition principle.
D. Historical cost principle.

_____ 10. (S.O. 4) On January 1, 2001, Probst, Inc. signed a contract to have MCL construct a major plant facility at a cost of $5,000,000. It was estimated that it would take two years to complete the project. In addition, Probst financed the construction costs on January 1, 2001 by borrowing $5,000,000 at an interest rate of 9%. During 2001 Probst made deposit and progress payments totaling $2,000,000 under the contract; the average amount of accumulated expenditures was $750,000 for the year. The excess borrowed funds were invested in short-term securities, from which Probst realized investment income of $300,000. What amount should Probst report as capitalized interest at December 31, 2001?

A. $ 40,500
B. $ 67,500
C. $180,000
D. $450,000

_____ 11. (S.O. 5) How should assets purchased on long-term credit contracts be accounted for?

A. At net realizable value, less an allowance for any potential increase in interest rates prior to the date of final payment.
B. Present value of the estimated valuation of the assets on the scheduled date of complete payment.
C. Present value of the consideration exchanged between the contracting parties or the future value of the asset when final payment is made, whichever is more readily determinable.
D. Present value of the consideration exchanged between the contracting parties at the date of the transaction.

_____ 12. (S.O. 5)When a group of plant assets are purchased for a lump sum purchase price, it would be appropriate to determine fair market value using:

	An Insurance Appraisal	Assessed Valuation for Property Taxes	Independent Appraisal
A.	Yes	No	Yes
B.	No	Yes	Yes
C.	Yes	Yes	Yes
D.	Yes	Yes	No

_____ 13. (S.O. 5) When a property is acquired by a company by issuance of its actively traded common stock, the cost of the property is properly measured by the:

A. par value of the stock.
B. stated value of the stock if it is in excess of the par value.
C. par value or stated value of the stock whichever is more readily determinable.
D. market value of the stock.

_____ 14. (S.O. 5) Which of the following nonmonetary exchange transactions represents a culmination of the earning process?

A. Exchange of similar productive assets.
B. Exchange of products by companies in the same line of business to facilitate sales to customers other than parties to the exchange.
C. Exchange of dissimilar productive assets.
D. Exchange of an equivalent interest in similar productive assets that causes the companies involved to remain in essentially the same economic position.

_____ 15. (S.O. 5) When boot is involved in an exchange of dissimilar assets:

A. gains or losses are recognized in their entirety.
B. gain or loss is computed by comparing the fair value of the asset received with the fair value of the asset given up.
C. only gains should be recognized.
D. only losses should be recognized.

_____ 16. (S.O. 5) The cost of a nonmonetary asset acquired in exchange for a dissimilar nonmonetary asset is usually recorded at:

A. the fair value of the asset given up, and a gain or loss is recognized.
B. the fair value of the asset given up, and a gain but not a loss may be recognized.
C. the fair value of the asset received if it is equally reliable as the fair value of the asset given up.
D. either the fair value of the asset given up or the asset received, whichever one results in the largest gain (smallest loss) to the company.

_____ 17. (S.O. 5) In an exchange of similar nonmonetary assets that results in a gain, the gain is totally deferred when

	Cash Is Received	No Cash Is Received
A.	Yes	Yes
B.	No	Yes
C.	Yes	No
D.	No	No

_____ 18. (S.O. 5) The Chicago Cubs had a player contract with Mark Grace that was recorded in its accounting records at $1,450,000. The Chicago White Sox had a player contract with Frank Thomas that was recorded in its accounting records at $1,600,000. The Cubs traded Grace to the Sox for Thomas by exchanging each player's contract. The fair value of each contract was $2,000,000. What amount should be shown in the accounting records after the exchange of player contracts?

	Cubs	Sox
A.	$1,450,000	$1,450,000
B.	$1,450,000	$1,600,000
C.	$1,600,000	$1,600,000
D.	$2,000,000	$2,000,000

_____ 19. (S.O. 5) Glen Inc. and Armstrong Co. exchange similar productive assets. The asset given up by Glen Inc. has a book value of $12,000 and a fair market value of $15,000. The asset given up by Armstrong Co. has a book value of $20,000 and a fair market value of $19,000. Boot of $4,000 is received by Armstrong Co.. On the basis of the foregoing facts, what amount should Glen Inc. record for the asset received?

A. $15,000.
B. $16,000.
C. $19,000.
D. $20,000.

_____ 20. (S.O. 5) Assuming the same facts as those listed in question 19, what amount should Armstrong Co. record for the asset received?

A. $15,000.
B. $16,000.
C. $19,000.
D. $20,000.

_____ 21. (S.O. 5) Would either company record a loss on the transaction explained in question 19?

A. Glen Inc. would record a loss.
B. Armstrong Co. would record a loss.
C. Both companies would record a loss.
D. Neither company would record a loss.

_____ 22. (S.O. 5) Hardin Company received $40,000 in cash and a used computer with a fair value of $120,000 from Page Corporation for Hardin Company's existing computer having a fair value of $160,000 and an undepreciated cost of $150,000 recorded on its books. How much gain should Hardin recognize on this exchange, and at what amount should the acquired computer be recorded, respectively?

A. $0 and $110,000.
B. $769 and $110,769.
C. $10,000 and $120,000.
D. $40,000 and $150,000.

_____ 23. (S.O. 5) Elizabeth Company recently accepted a donation of land with a cost to the donor of $200,000 and a fair market value of $250,000. Which of the following journal entries would Elizabeth Company most likely make to record the receipt of the land?

A.	Land	200,000	
	Donated Capital		200,000
B.	Land	200,000	
	Revenue from Donation		200,000
C.	Land	250,000	
	Donated Capital		250,000
D.	Land	250,000	
	Revenue from Donation		250,000

_____ 24. (S.O. 6) An expenditure made in connection with a machine being used by an enterprise should be:

A. expensed immediately if it merely extends the useful life but does not improve the quality.
B. expensed immediately if it merely improves the quality but does not extend the useful life.
C. capitalized if it maintains the machine in normal operating condition.
D. capitalized if it increases the quantity of units produced by the machine.

_____ 25. (S.O. 7) When a plant asset is disposed of a gain or loss may result. The gain or loss would be classified as an extraordinary item on the income statement if it resulted from:

A. an involuntary conversion.
B. a sale prior to the completion of the estimated useful life of the asset.
C. the sale of a fully depreciated asset.
D. an abandonment of the asset.

REVIEW EXERCISES

1. (S.O.2 and 7) Stadnicki Corporation purchased a machine on January 1, 1996, for $25,000. Before the machine was utilized in a productive capacity, the following expenditures were made:

a.	Removal of a wall to accommodate the machine	$1,500
b.	Cost of training an operator	850
c.	Installation of a counting device	500
d.	Premium on a 3-year insurance policy	900

Depreciation on the machine was recorded at the end of each year. The depreciation rate is $3,000 per year. On October 1, 2002, the machine was sold for $8,000.

Instructions:
Prepare the journal entries Stadnicki Company should make for the purchase and sale of the machine.

General Journal J1

Date	Account Title	Debit	Credit

2. (S.O. 4) Ivaylo Company has been constructing an asset for its own use. In connection with the construction, Ivaylo Company has been capitalizing interest on expenditures for this asset since construction began. The following costs relate to the month of June:

Expenditures	
Accumulated Expenditures (June 1)	$2,500,000
Accumulated Expenditures (June 30)	3,000,000

Specific Construction Debt
16%, $1,200,000 note

Other Debt
10%, $750,000 short-term note payable
12%, mortgage payable of $1,500,000

Instructions:

a. Compute the weighted-average accumulated expenditures, avoidable interest, and interest to be capitalized for the month of June.
b. Determine the accumulated expenditure balance at the beginning of July.

a.

b.

3. (S.O.5) Tamara Company acquired a group of plant assets at a cost of $150,000 from a company in financial difficulty. The fair market value of the assets acquired is estimated as follows:

Land	$ 36,000
Buildings	108,000
Machinery	72,000

Instructions:
Prepare the journal entry for Tamara Company to record the purchase.

General Journal J1

Date	Account Title	Debit	Credit

4. (S.O.5) Becky and Bol Company enter into an agreement for the trade of certain nonmonetary assets (machinery). The assets involved perform the same function and are employed in the same line of business. The reason for the exchange involves the size of the product produced by the machines. The machines exchanged by Becky Company have a book value of $245,000 (cost $325,000 less accumulated depreciation of $80,000) and a fair value of $275,000. The machines given up by Bol Company have a book value of $260,000 (cost $350,000 less accumulated depreciation of $90,000) and a fair value of $290,000. In addition to the exchange of the machines, Becky Company agrees to pay Bol Company $15,000 as part of the transaction.

Instructions:
Record the exchange transactions for

a. Becky Company, and
b. Bol Company

a.

General Journal J1

Date	Account Title	Debit	Credit

b.

General Journal			J1
Date	Account Title	Debit	Credit

5. (S.O.6) With respect to each of the following plant asset expenditures, indicate whether the item should be expensed or capitalized. Also, indicate whether the item is best classified as: (1) an addition, (2) an improvement, (3) a replacement, (4) a rearrangement and reinstallation, or (5) an ordinary repair.

	Item	Expense	Capitalize	Classification
A.	A new wing on a factory building.			
B.	Steel beams in an old factory building substituted for wooden beams.			
C.	New tires placed on a delivery truck.			
D.	Fee of consulting firm for improvement of production flow by changing the placement of machinery in the factory.			
E.	A new tile floor in the office building substituted for an old tile floor.			
F.	Repainting the interior of the entire factory building.			
G.	New device attached to machinery that automatically sorts production. Such a device has not previously been available.			
H.	New motor installed in a machine. The old motor burned out unexpectedly.			

SOLUTIONS TO REVIEW QUESTIONS AND EXERCISES

TRUE-FALSE

1. (F) To be classified as property, plant, and equipment, the building (a) must be acquired for use in operations and not for resale, (b) be long-term in nature and generally subject to depreciation, and (c) possess physical substance. The second and third criteria would normally be met by any building owned by a company. However, a company could own a building that was not used in its operations and was held for sale. In this case the building would be classified as an other asset.

2. (T)

3. (T)

4. (F) Any costs related to an asset that are incurred after its acquisition such as additions, improvements, or replacements are added to the cost of the asset if they provide future service potential; otherwise, they are expensed in the period of incurrence.

5. (F) When land has been purchased for the purpose of constructing a building, all costs incurred up to the excavation for the new building are considered land costs. Removal of old buildings, clearing, grading, and filling are considered costs of the land because these costs are necessary to get the land in condition for its intended purpose.

6. (T)

7. (F) To qualify for interest capitalization, assets must require a period of time to get them ready for their intended use. The amount of interest to be capitalized for qualifying assets is that portion of total interest cost incurred during the period that theoretically could have been avoided if expenditures for the asset had not been made.

8. (F) Assets that are not being used in the earnings activities of the enterprise and that are not undergoing the activities necessary to get them ready for use do not qualify for interest capitalization.

9. (F) The amount of interest to be capitalized is limited to the lower of actual interest cost incurred during the period or avoidable interest.

10. (T)

11. (F) An asset should be recorded at the fair market value of what is given up to acquire it or at its own fair market value, whichever is more clearly evident.

12. (T)

13. (T)

14. (F) The book value of assets can sometimes be misleading because of the variety of accounting methods that can be used to account for these items. Thus, when an exchange of nonmonetary assets is involved, the accounting should be based on the fair value of the asset given up or the fair value of the asset acquired, whichever is more clearly evident.

15. (T)

16. (T)

17. (T)

18. (F) In this situation, part of the monetary asset is considered sold and part exchanged; therefore, only a portion of the gain is deferred. The formula to determine the amount of the gain recognized when boot is received is:

$$\frac{\text{Cash received}}{\text{Cash rec'd} + \text{fair value of asset rec'd}} \times \text{total gain} = \text{Gain recognized}$$

19. (F) In an exchange of similar assets where there is a gain situation and cash is received in the amount of $25,000 and the fair value of other assets received is $70,000, the cash payment is considered significant (25% or more of the fair value of the exchange); therefore, the exchange should be considered a monetary exchange with the fair value used to measure the gain which is then recognized in its entirety.

20. (T)

21. (F) For an expenditure to be capitalized, one of three future benefit conditions must be present: (a) the useful life of the asset must be increased, (b) the quantity of units produced from the asset must be increased, or (c) the quality of the units produced must be enhanced.

22. (T)

23. (T)

24. (F) Gains or losses on the retirement of property, plant, and equipment should be shown in the income statement along with other items that arise from customary business activities.

25. (T)

MULTIPLE CHOICE

1. (B) Property, plant, and equipment items are acquired at various times during their useful life. Thus, the original historical cost may be appropriate when the asset is originally acquired by a purchaser. However, if the asset is subsequently acquired by a different purchaser, the cost basis would most likely be something other than its original historical cost. The other alternatives represent reasons the historical cost basis is advocated for recording property, plant, and equipment purchases.

2. (C) Items classified as property, plant, and equipment are characterized as items that are long-term in nature. The concept of long-term is generally considered to be in excess of one year, but no minimum number of years is required for this classification. Alternatives (A), (B), and (D) are appropriate characteristics for an item classified as property, plant, and equipment.

3. (B) All expenditures made to acquire land and to ready it for use should be considered as part of the land cost. The purpose of the purchase was to acquire the land so a new theater could be constructed. The old theater has no economic use so that any portion of the purchase price attributable to the old theater is merely considered cost of the land acquired.

4. (C) Thorne should allocate the costs to land and building as follows:

	Land	Building
Purchase price of land	$100,000	
Demolition of old building	6,000	
Architect's fees		$15,000
Legal fees for title investigation and purchase contract	5,000	
Construction costs		600,000
Cash received from salvaged materials resulting from demolition of old building	(3,000)	
	$108,000	$615,000

5. (D) Based upon the historical cost principle, a portion of overhead cost should be assigned to a constructed asset to obtain that asset's total cost. The amount charged should be based upon a pro rata allocation between the asset and normal operations. The other allocation methods mentioned in alternatives A and C are difficult to measure and also are not consistent with the historical cost principle. Alternative B is not consistent with the historical cost principle.

6. (A) This recommended approach is based on the historical cost concept stating that only actual transactions are recorded. It is argued that interest incurred is as much a cost of acquiring the asset as the cost of the materials, labor, and other resources used. The approaches referred to in alternatives B & C have some support but are not the recommended methods. Alternative D is not an approach to handling interest incurred during construction that has any support.

7. (C) Alternatives A, B, and D reflect the conditions that must exist before the interest capitalization can begin on a qualifying asset. These conditions come from FASB Statement No. 34 which includes no requirements related to interest rates or an entity's cost of capital.

8. (B) When land is purchased with the intention of developing it for a particular use, interest costs associated with those expenditures qualify for interest capitalization. In the situation cited in the question the interest cost is capitalized as part of the plant, not the land. The purchase of the land was for the purpose of constructing a plant. If the land had been purchased for development in terms of lot sales then the interest would be capitalized as part of the land.

9. (D) FASB No. 34 states: "The historical cost of acquiring an asset includes the cost necessarily incurred to bring it to the condition and location necessary for its intended use. If an asset requires a period of time in which to carry out the activities necessary to bring it to that condition and location, the interest cost incurred during that period as a result of expenditures for the asset is a part of the historical cost of acquiring the asset."

10. (B) Probst should report $67,500 as its capitalized interest at December 31, 2001. Its capitalized interest can be calculated as follows:

Average amount of accumulated expenditures	$750,000
Interest rate on specific borrowing	x .09
Interest to be capitalized	$ 67,500

Note: The investment transaction and the asset acquisition transaction are viewed as separate transactions. Therefore, interest income on excess borrowings should not be offset against the interest to be capitalized.

11. (D) To properly reflect cost, assets purchased on long-term credit contracts should be accounted for at the present value of the consideration exchanged between the contracting parties at the date of the transaction. Use of any net realizable value concepts or a valuation based on the date of final payment are inappropriate.

12. (C) To determine fair market value of the individual items in a lump sum purchase of plant assets, an appraisal for insurance purposes, the assessed valuation for property taxes, or simply an independent appraisal by an engineer or other appraiser might be used.

13. (D) When property is acquired by the issuance of common stock, the cost of the property is not properly measured by the par or stated value of such stock. If the stock is actively traded, the market value of the stock issued is a fair indication of the cost of the property acquired because stock is a good measure of the current cash equivalent price.

14. (C) Similar nonmonetary assets are those that are of the same general type or that perform the same function or that are employed in the same line of business. If two entities exchange similar assets, the earnings process is not considered complete. Alternatives (A), (B), and (D) all represent exchanges of similar nonmonetary assets.

15. (A) A nonmonetary asset acquired in exchange for a dissimilar nonmonetary asset is usually recorded at the fair value of the asset given up, and a gain or loss is recognized.

16. (A) The cost of a nonmonetary asset acquired in exchange for a dissimilar nonmonetary asset is usually recorded at the fair value of the asset given up, and a gain or loss is recognized. The fair value of the asset received should be used only if it is more clearly evident than the fair value of the asset given up.

17. (B) If an exchange of similar assets results in a gain, and the exchange does not include the receipt of cash, the gain should be totally deferred. In such a situation, it is assumed that the earnings process is not complete. When cash is received, part of the nonmonetary asset is considered sold and part exchanged; therefore, only a portion of the gain is deferred.

18. (B) This is an exchange of similar productive assets. The Cubs' and Sox's gains which will be deferred can be computed as follows:

	Cubs	Sox
Fair value of contract given up	$2,000,000	$2,000,000
Less: Book value of Grace's contract	1,450,000	
Book value of Thomas's contract		1,600,000
Gain on exchange to be deferred	$ 550,000	$ 400,000

The Cubs and Sox would determine the cost of their new player contracts as follows:

Cost (fair value) of new player's contract	$2,000,000	$2,000,000
Less: Deferred exchange gain	(550,000)	(400,000)
Cost to be recorded for new player's contract	$1,450,000	$1,600,000

19. (B)

Fair market value of Glen Inc. asset	$15,000
Book value of Glen Inc. asset	12,000
Total gain (unrecognized)	$ 3,000

Fair market value of Armstrong Co. asset	$19,000
Less gain deferred	3,000
Basis of acquired asset to Glen Inc.	$16,000

20. (A) When similar nonmonetary assets are exchanged and a loss results, the loss should be recognized immediately.

Book value of Armstrong Co. asset	$20,000
Fair market value of Armstrong Co. asset	19,000
Loss on trade	$ 1,000

Armstrong Co.--Journal Entry

New asset	15,000	
Cash	4,000	
Loss on trade	1,000	
Old asset		20,000

21. (B) See explanation in No. 20 above.

22. (C) This is an exchange of similar productive property at a gain with boot received. The boot received, however, is significant because it is 25% or more of the fair value of the exchange ($40,000/$160,000 = .25). When the boot received is significant, the exchange should be considered a monetary exchange with the fair values used to measure the gain which is then recognized in its entirety. The following entry would therefore be made:

Computer (new)	$120,000	
Cash	40,000	
Computer (old), net		150,000
Gain on disposal of computer		10,000

23. (D) The recording of a donated asset by a credit to a revenue account is required by SFAS 116. The amount of the revenue is measured by the fair value of the asset when the donation is received.

24. (D) Expenditures made in connection with assets being used by an entity should be capitalized if **(a)** the useful life of the asset is increased, **(b)** the quantity of units produced by the assets is increased, or **(c)** the quality of the units produced by the asset is enhanced. All other expenditures of this nature should be expensed when incurred. The only alternative that correctly completes the question is (D).

25. (A) An involuntary conversion refers to events such as fire, flood, theft, or condemnation. The computation of the gain or loss that results from an involuntary conversion is the same as any computation of the gain or loss from any disposal. The major difference is that the gain or loss that results from an involuntary conversion is reported in the extraordinary items section of the income statement.

REVIEW EXERCISES

1. Purchase Price = $25,000 + $1,500 + $850 + $500 = $27,850
   Book Value at 10-1-02= $27,850 - (6 X $3,000) = $9,850 (before 2002 depreciation)
   Journal entries:

Date	Account	Debit	Credit
1-1-96	Machine	27,850	
	Cash		27,850
10-1-02	Depreciation Expense	2,250	
	Accumulated Depreciation		2,250
10-1-02	Cash	8,000	
	Accumulated Depreciation	20,250	
	Machine		27,850
	Gain on Sale		400

2a. Accumulated Expenditures (June 1) $2,500,000
Accumulated Expenditures (June 30) 3,000,000
$5,500,000

Weighted Average Accumulated Expenditures: $5,500,000/2 = $2,750,000

Weighted-Average Accumulated Expenditures	X	Interest Rate	=	Avoidable Interest
$1,200,000		16% x 1/12		$16,000
1,550,000		*11.33% x 1/12		14,635
$2,750,000				$30,635

*Weighted-Average Interest Rate Computation:

	Principal	Interest
10%, note payable	$ 750,000	$ 75,000
12%, mortgage payable	1,500,000	180,000
	$2,250,000	$255,000

Total Interest/Total Principal = Weighted Average Rate
$255,000/$2,250,000 = 11.33%*

Actual Interest:

$1,200,000 x 16% x 1/12 =	$16,000
750,000 x 10% x 1/12 =	6,250
1,500,000 x 12% x 1/12 =	15,000
	$37,250

Interest to be Capitalized: $30,635

b. Accumulated Expenditures (July 1) unadjusted $3,000,000
Add: Capitalized Interest 30,635
$3,030,635

3.

	Fair Market Value	Percent of Fair Market Value	Apportionment of Cost
Land	$ 36,000	16-2/3%	$ 25,000
Building	108,000	50%	75,000
Machinery	72,000	33-1/3%	50,000
Total	$216,000		$150,000

Journal Entry:

Land	25,000	
Building	75,000	
Machinery	50,000	
Cash		150,000

4. **Accounting by Becky Company**

Computation of Gain:

Fair value of Becky machines	$275,000
Book value of Becky machines	245,000
Total gain (unrecognized)	$ 30,000

Basis of New Machines to Becky:

Fair value of Bol machines	$290,000		Book value of Becky machines	$245,000
Less gain deferred	(30,000)	*OR*	Cash paid	15,000
Basis of machines received	$260,000		Basis of machines received	$260,000

Journal Entry:

Machines (from Bol)	260,000	
Accumulated Depreciation	80,000	
Machines		325,000
Cash		15,000

Accounting by Bol Company

Computation of Total Gain:

Fair value of Bol machines	$290,000
Book value of Bol machines	260,000
Total gain	$ 30,000

Portion of Gain Recognized by Bol:

$$\frac{\$15,000}{\$15,000 + \$275,000} \times \$30,000 = \underline{\underline{\$1,552}}$$

Basis of New Machines to Bol:

Fair value of Becky machines	$275,000		Book value of Bol machines	$260,000
Less gain deferred (30,000 - $1,552)	(28,448)	*OR*	Add gain recognized	1,552
			Less cash received	(15,000)
Basis of machines received	$246,552		Basis of machines received	$246,552

Journal Entry:

Cash	15,000	
Machines (from Becky)	246,552	
Accumulated Depreciation	90,000	
Machines		350,000
Gain on disposal of old machines		1,552

5. A. Capitalize—Addition
   B. Capitalize—Improvement
   C. Expense—Repair
   D. Capitalize—Rearrangement
   E. Capitalize—Replacement
   F. Expense—Repair
   G. Capitalize—Addition
   H. Capitalize—Replacement

11

Depreciation, Impairments, and Depletion

CHAPTER STUDY OBJECTIVES

1. Explain the concept of depreciation.
2. Identify the factors involved in the depreciation process.
3. Compare activity, straight-line, and decreasing charge methods of depreciation.
4. Explain special depreciation methods.
5. Identify reasons why depreciation methods are selected.
6. Explain the accounting issues related to asset impairment.
7. Explain the accounting procedures for depletion of natural resources.
8. Explain how property, plant and equipment, and natural resources are reported and analyzed.

*9. Describe income tax methods of depreciation.

CHAPTER REVIEW

1. Chapter 11 presents a discussion of the factors involved in the accounting and recording of depreciation and depletion. Depreciation refers to the decline in value of tangible plant assets. Depletion is the term used to describe the decline in natural resources such as timber, oil, or coal. Amortization is the term used to describe the expiration of intangible assets. In addition to a thorough discussion of the accounting problems involved, the chapter presents a detailed analysis and explanation of the various depreciation methods used in practice.

Depreciation Process

2. (S.O. 1) **Depreciation** is the accounting process of allocating the cost of tangible assets to expense in a systematic and rational manner to those periods expected to benefit from the use of the asset. The **cost allocation approach** is justified because it matches costs with revenues and because fluctuation in market values is difficult to determine.

3. (S.O. 2) To compute depreciation, an accountant must establish (a) the **depreciable base** to be used for the asset, (b) the asset's **useful life,** and (c) the **depreciation method** to be used. Determination of the first two factors requires the use of estimates.

4. The depreciable base is the difference between an asset's cost and its salvage value. **Salvage value** is the estimated amount that will be received at the time the asset is sold or removed from service.

* *Note: All asterisked (*) items relate to material contained in the Appendix to the chapter.*

5. The **useful life** (service life) of a plant asset refers to the number of years that asset is capable of economically providing the service it was purchased to perform. The service life of an asset should not be confused with its physical life. For example, a machine may no longer provide a useful service to an organization even though it remains physically functional. Thus, the estimate of an asset's service life is dependent upon both the economic factors and the physical factors related to its use. **Economic factors** are characterized by inadequacy, supersession, and obsolescence. **Physical factors** relate to wear and tear, decay, and casualties that prevent the asset from performing indefinitely.

Depreciation Methods

6. The depreciation method selected for a particular asset should be **systematic and rational.** Depreciation methods may be classified as:

A. Activity method.
B. Straight-line method.
C. Decreasing charge methods.
   a. Sum-of-the-years'-digits.
   b. Declining-balance method.
D. Special depreciation methods.
   a. Group and composite methods.
   b. Hybrid or combination methods.

7. The following information for a piece of machinery will be used to illustrate some of the depreciation methods discussed in the following paragraphs.

Cost of machine	$260,000
Estimated useful life	10 years
Estimated salvage value	$20,000
Productive life in hours	60,000 hours

8. (S.O. 3) When the **activity method** (units of use or production) is used, depreciation is assumed to be a function of productivity rather than the passage of time. This method is most appropriate for assets such as machinery or automobiles where depreciation can be based on units produced or miles driven. One problem associated with the use of this method concerns a before-the-fact estimation of the total output the asset will achieve during its useful life.

Illustration

Assume the machine was used for 6,800 hours in the first year of its useful life.

$$\frac{\text{(Cost less salvage) X hours this year}}{\text{Total estimated hours}} = \text{Depreciation Charge}$$

$$\frac{(\$260{,}000\ -\ \$20{,}000)\ \text{X}\ 6{,}800}{60{,}000} = \$27{,}200$$

9. Use of the **straight-line method** results in a uniform charge to depreciation expense during each year of an asset's service life. This method is based upon the assumption that the decline in an asset's usefulness is the same each year. Although the straight-line method is easy to use, it rests on an assumption that, in most situations, is not realistic.

Illustration

$$\frac{\text{Cost less salvage}}{\text{Estimated service life}} = \text{Depreciation charge}$$

$$\frac{(\$260{,}000 - \$20{,}000)}{10} = \$24{,}000$$

10. The **decreasing charge (accelerated depreciation) methods** result in a higher depreciation cost during the early years of an asset's service life and lower charges in later years. This approach is justified on the basis that assets lose a greater amount of service potential in earlier years and thus depreciation should be higher.

11. The **sum-of-the-years'-digits** method and the **declining-balance** method are the two most often used decreasing charge methods. The sum-of-the-years' digits method requires multiplication of the **depreciable base** by a fraction that decreases during each year of an asset's service life. The declining-balance method requires use of a constant percentage applied to an **asset's cost less accumulated depreciation.** Salvage value is initially ignored under the declining-balance method.

Illustration
Sum-of-Years' Digits

(Cost - Salvage Value) X Depreciation Fraction = Depreciation Charge
($260,000 - $20,000) X 10/55 = $43,636.36

Declining-Balance

The declining-balance method utilizes a depreciation rate that is some multiple of the straight-line method. One popular method is twice the straight-line rate. Thus, in our example the 10-year asset life would translate into a 20% declining rate.

	Beginning of the Year Book Value	X	Rate on Declining Balance	=	Depreciation Charge
Year 1	$260,000	X	20%	=	$52,000
Year 2	$208,000	X	20%	=	$41,600

12. (S.O. 4) **Group and composite methods** involve averaging the service life of many assets and applying depreciation as though a single unit existed. The composite approach refers to a collection of dissimilar assets, whereas the group approach refers to a collection of assets with similar characteristics. The method of computation for group or composite is essentially the same: find an average and depreciate on that basis. For example, the following assets would have the following composite rate and life.

Asset	Original Cost	Salvage Value	Depreciable Cost	Useful Life	Depreciation (Straight-Line)
A	$ 65,000	$ 5,000	$ 60,000	5 yrs.	$12,000
B	148,000	18,000	130,000	10 yrs.	13,000
C	95,000	11,000	84,000	12 yrs.	7,000
	$308,000	$34,000	$274,000		$32,000

Composite Rate:	$32,000/308,000 = 10.39%
Composite Life:	$274,000/32,000 = 8.56 years

These assets will be depreciated at $32,000 per year for 8.56 years.

13. (S.O. 5) In general, depreciation should be based on the number of months an asset is used during an accounting period. If a decreasing charge depreciation method is used for assets purchased during an accounting period, a slight modification is appropriate. When this situation occurs, determine depreciation expense for the full year and prorate the expense between the two periods involved. This process continues throughout the service life of the asset. For example, assume an asset with a 5-year useful life and a depreciable cost of $45,000 is purchased on October 1. At the end of the first year the depreciation charge under sum-of-the-years'-digits method would be:

1st Full Year:	$45,000 X 5/15 = $15,000
2nd Full Year:	$45,000 X 4/15 = $12,000
Year 1 (9/1 to 12/31):	$15,000 X 1/4 = **3,750.**
Year 2:	($15,000 X 3/4) + ($12,000 X 1/4)
	$11,250 + $3,000 = **$14,250**

14. Depreciation expense reduces net income for the accounting period in which it is recorded even though a current cash outflow is not involved. However, depreciation should not be considered a source of cash. Cash is generated by revenues, not accounting procedures.

15. The estimates involved in the depreciation process are sometimes subject to revision as a result of unanticipated occurrences. Such revisions are classified as **changes in accounting estimates** and should be handled in the current and prospective periods rather than changing previously reported results.

Impairments

16. (S.O. 6) The process to determine an impairment loss is **(a)** review events for possible impairment, **(b)** if events suggest impairment, determine if the sum of the expected future net cash flows is less than the carrying amount, if so, then **(c)** the loss is the amount by which the carrying amount of the asset is greater than the fair value of the asset. If an impaired asset is expected to be disposed of, it should be recorded at the lower of cost or net realizable value, and it is not depreciated.

17. If an asset is considered long-lived, the reduced carrying amount is now considered its new cost basis and no write-up is allowed. If an impaired asset is held for disposal, it can be written up or down as long as the write-up is never greater than the carrying amount of asset at the time of the original impairment.

Depletion

18. (S.O. 7) **Depletion** refers to the process of recording the consumption of **natural resources** (wasting assets). The depletion base for natural resources includes **acquisition costs, exploration costs, intangible development costs,** and **restoration costs** reduced by any residual value related to the land. Tangible assets used in extracting natural resources are normally set up in a separate account and depreciated individually.

19. Depletion is normally based on the number of units extracted during the period, which corresponds to the activity depreciation method discussed earlier. A major problem one faces when computing depletion is **estimating recoverable reserves.**

20. Companies in the oil and gas industry may currently account for the costs using either the **successful efforts approach** or the **full costing approach.** Both successful efforts and full costing are historical cost approaches. The SEC once favored the development of a value-based accounting method for companies in the oil and gas industry known as Reserve Recognition Accounting (RRA). However, the development of RRA was abandoned and the SEC has asked the FASB to develop a comprehensive package of value-based disclosures for oil and gas producers.

21. Unique problems, uncommon to most other types of assets, seem to exist in depletion accounting. Not infrequently, the **estimate of recoverable reserves** has to be changed either because new information has become available or because production processes have become more sophisticated. **Discovery value accounting** and **reserve recognition accounting** are essentially similar. If discovery value is recorded, an asset account would be debited and usually an Unrealized Appreciation account would be credited. Unrealized Appreciation would then be transferred to revenue as the natural resources are sold.

22. The tax law has long provided a deduction for the greater of **cost** or **percentage depletion** against income from oil, gas, and most minerals. The percentage or statutory depletion allows a write-off ranging from 5% to 22% (depending on the natural resource) of gross revenue received. As a result, the amount of depletion may exceed the investment cost that is assigned to a given natural resource.

Disclosures

23. (S.O. 8) The basis for valuing property, plant, equipment, and natural resources, which is normally historical cost, should be disclosed in the financial statements along with any pledges, liens, and other commitments related to these assets. Normally, assets not used in a productive capacity (held for future use or as an investment) should be segregated from assets used in operations and classified as "Other Assets." **Financial statement disclosures** related to depreciation include:

a. Depreciation expense for the period.
b. Balances of major classes of depreciable assets, by nature and function.
c. Accumulated depreciation, either by major classes of depreciable assets or in total.
d. A general description of the method or methods used in computing depreciation with respect to major classes of depreciable assets.

24. Both publicly traded and privately held companies engaged in significant oil and gas producing activities are required to disclose (**a**) the basic method of accounting for those costs incurred in oil and gas producing activities and (**b**) the manner of disposing of costs relating to oil and gas producing activities. Public companies must also disclose information about reserve quantities; capitalized costs; acquisition, exploration, and development activities; and a standardized measure of discounted future net cash flows related to proven oil and gas reserve quantities.

Income Tax Depreciation

*25. (S.O. 9) For assets acquired before 1981, depreciation for income tax purposes is based on straight-line, sum-of-the-years'-digits, and declining-balance methods. For assets purchased in the years 1981 through 1986 the Accelerated Cost Recovery System (ACRS) of depreciation is used. A **Modified Accelerated Cost Recovery System,** known as MACRS, was enacted by Congress in the Tax Reform Act of 1986. It applies to depreciable assets placed in service in 1987 and later. Three major differences exist between the computation of depreciation under MACRS and GAAP: **(a)** a mandated tax life, which is generally shorter than the economic life, **(b)** cost recovery on an accelerated basis, and **(c)** an assigned salvage value of zero. MACRS assigns assets to property classes which indicate the depreciable tax life of the assets in each class. The depreciable tax lives range from 3-year property to 31.5-year property.

GLOSSARY

***Accelerated Cost Recovery System (ACRS).** A tax depreciation method used for assets purchased in the years 1981 through 1986.

Activity method (variable charge approach). A depreciation method in which depreciation is a function of use or productivity instead of the passage of time.

Amortization. The accounting process of allocating the cost of intangible assets (i.e., patents and goodwill) to expense.

Composite approach. A depreciation method that depreciates a collection of assets that are heterogeneous and have different lives.

Composite depreciation rate. Depreciation per year divided by the total cost of the assets.

Declining-balance method. A depreciation method that applies a constant rate to the declining book value of the asset and produces a decreasing annual depreciation amount over the useful life of the asset.

Decreasing charge method (accelerated depreciation). A depreciation method which provides for a higher depreciation cost in the earlier years and lower charges in later periods.

Depletion. The accounting process of allocating the cost of natural resources (i.e., timber, gravel, oil, and coal) to expense.

Depreciation. The accounting process of allocating the cost of tangible assets to expense in a systematic and rational manner to those periods expected to benefit from the use of the asset.

Development costs. The costs incurred to extract natural resources and to get them ready for production or shipment.

Discovery value.	An accounting method which would use reserve recognition accounting to the broader category of all natural resources.
Economic factors.	When an asset is retired because of inadequacy, supersession or obsolescence.
Exploration costs.	The costs incurred to find natural resources.
Full cost concept.	Accounting for exploration costs where unsuccessful ventures are capitalized with successful ventures.
Group method.	A depreciation method that depreciates a collection of assets that are similar in nature.
Impairment.	When the carrying amount of an asset is not recoverable and therefore a writeoff is needed.
Inadequacy.	An economic factor for retiring an asset because the asset ceased to be useful to an enterprise due to the demands of the firm having increased.
Liquidating dividend.	A dividend which is a return of capital to the shareholder.
***Modified Accelerated Cost Recovery System (MACRS).**	A tax depreciation method used for assets placed in service in 1987 and thereafter.
Natural resources.	Wasting assets such as petroleum, minerals, and timber.
Obsolescence.	An economic factor for retiring an asset that does not specifically relate to the factors of inadequacy or supersession.
Physical factors.	Wear, tear, decay, and casualties that make it difficult for an asset to perform indefinitely.
Recoverability test.	A screening device used to determine whether an impairment has occurred.
Reserve Recognition Accounting.	An accounting method whereby as soon as a company discovers oil or gas, it reports the value of the oil or gas on the balance sheet and on the income statement.
Restoration costs.	The costs incurred to restore property to its natural state after extraction of natural resources has occurred.
Salvage value.	The estimated amount that will be received at the time the asset is sold or removed from service.
Straight-line method.	A depreciation method in which periodic depreciation is the same throughout the service life of the asset.

Sum-of-the-years'-digits method. A depreciation method that produces decreasing periodic depreciation by applying a decreasing fraction to the depreciable cost of the asset.

Supersession. An economic factor for retiring an asset due to the replacement of one asset with another more efficient and economical asset.

Successful efforts concept. Accounting for exploration costs where only successful ventures are capitalized.

CHAPTER OUTLINE

Fill in the outline presented below.

(S.O. 1) The Concept of Depreciation

(S.O. 2) Factors Involved in the Depreciation Process

Depreciable Base

Estimation of Service Lives

(S.O. 3) Methods of Depreciation

Activity method

Straight-line method

Sum-of-the-years'-digits method

Chapter Outline *(continued)*

Declining-balance method

(S.O. 4) Special depreciation methods

Group and composite methods

Hybrid or combination methods

(S.O. 5) Special depreciation issues

Depreciation of partial periods

Depreciation and replacement of fixed assets

Revision of depreciation rates

(S.O. 6) Impairments

Recoverability test

Calculation of impairment loss

Restoration of impairment loss

Assets to be disposed of

Chapter Outline *(continued)*

(S.O. 7) Depletion

Establishing a depletion base

Acquisition costs

Exploration costs

Development costs

Restoration costs

Writeoff of resource cost

Controversy of full cost concept vs. successful efforts concept

Special problems in depletion accounting

Financial reporting of natural resources and depletion

(S.O. 8) Presentation and Analysis of Property, Plant, and Equipment, and Natural Resources

*(S.O. 9) Income Tax Depreciation

REVIEW QUESTIONS AND EXERCISES

TRUE-FALSE

Indicate whether each of the following is true (T) or false (F) in the space provided.

_____ 1. (S.O. 1) The accounting concept of depreciation reflects the decline in value associated with a plant asset.

_____ 2. (S.O. 2) An asset's cost less its salvage value is referred to as the depreciable base.

_____ 3. (S.O. 2) Physical factors such as wear and tear set the outside limit for the service life of an asset.

_____ 4. (S.O. 2) Whenever the economic nature of the asset is the primary determinant of service life, maintenance plays an extremely vital role in prolonging service life.

_____ 5. (S.O. 2) Replacing a black and white monitor with a color monitor for a computer is an example of supersession.

_____ 6. (S.O. 2) Estimation and judgment are the primary means through which the service life of an asset is determined.

_____ 7. (S.O. 3) One problem associated with the activity method of depreciation concerns estimating the total units of output an asset will produce.

_____ 8. (S.O. 3) Companies that desire low depreciation during periods of low productivity and high depreciation during high productivity either adopt or switch to a declining-balance method.

_____ 9. (S.O. 3) The straight-line method considers depreciation a function of time rather than a function of usage.

_____ 10. (S.O. 3) The straight-line depreciation method is used most often in actual practice. This is because the assumptions upon which it is based apply to most plant assets.

_____ 11. (S.O. 3) Accelerated depreciation methods accomplish the objective of writing an asset off over a shorter period of time than its useful life.

_____ 12. (S.O. 3) Under the declining-balance depreciation method, salvage value is considered only in computing the amount of depreciation for the final year(s) of an asset's service life.

_____ 13. (S.O. 4) Under the group and composite methods, the term group refers to a collection of assets that are similar in nature; composite refers to a collection of assets that are dissimilar in nature.

_____ 14. (S.O. 4) The composite depreciation rate is determined by dividing the depreciation per year by the total cost of the assets.

_____ 15. (S.O. 5) If one of the estimates used in computing depreciation is subsequently found to require adjustments, no change in prior years' financial statements is required.

_____ 16. (S.O. 6) When determining whether an asset has been impaired, the recoverability test compares discounted future net cash flows to the carrying amount of the asset.

_____ 17. (S.O. 6) The impairment loss is the amount by which the carrying amount of the asset is greater than the market value or present value of the asset.

_____ 18. (S.O. 6) Losses or gains relating to impaired assets intended to be disposed of should be reported as extraordinary items.

_____ 19. (S.O. 7) Depletion is the systematic allocation of the cost of natural resources (wasting assets).

_____ 20. (S.O. 7) Development costs include tangible equipment used for transportation and other heavy equipment necessary to extract natural resources and get it ready for production or shipment.

_____ 21. (S.O. 7) The full costing approach, related to accounting for exploration costs, requires that the full costs of exploration be charged against income in the year it is incurred.

_____ 22. (S.O. 7) The computation of depletion is essentially the same as the activity method of depreciation.

_____ 23. (S.O. 7) Reserve recognition accounting is specifically related to the oil and gas industry, whereas discovery value accounting is a broader term associated with the whole natural resources area.

_____ *24. (S.O. 9) The Internal Revenue Code allows the use of an accelerated depreciation method for tax purposes as long as the use of the method does not cause the company to report a net loss.

_____ *25. (S.O. 9) In recording depreciation for tax purposes, companies can use any method as long as the amount reported on the tax return exceeds the amount recorded for financial statement purposes.

MULTIPLE CHOICE

Select the best answer for each of the following items and enter the corresponding letter in the space provided.

_____ 1. (S.O. 1) Which of the following most accurately reflects the concept of depreciation as used in accounting?

A. The process of charging the decline in value of an economic resource to income in the period in which the benefit occurred.
B. The process of allocating the cost of tangible assets to expense in a systematic and rational manner to those periods expected to benefit from the use of the asset.
C. A method of allocating asset cost to an expense account in a manner which closely matches the physical deterioration of the tangible asset involved.
D. An accounting concept that allocates the portion of an asset used up during the year to the contra asset account for the purpose of properly recording the fair market value of tangible assets.

_____ 2. (S.O. 2) The major difference between the service life of an asset and its physical life is that:

A. service life refers to the time an asset will be used by a company and physical life refers to how long the asset will last.
B. physical life is the life of an asset without consideration of salvage value and service life requires the use of salvage value.
C. physical life is always longer than service life.
D. service life refers to the length of time an asset is of use to its original owner, while physical life refers to how long the asset will be used by all owners.

_____ 3. (S.O. 2) The economic factors related to an asset's service life include:

A. obsolescence.
B. wear and tear.
C. decay.
D. unexpected casualties.

_____ 4. (S.O. 2) The activity method of depreciation (often called the variable charge approach) assumes that depreciation is a function of:

	Productivity	Passage of Time
A.	Yes	Yes
B.	No	No
C.	Yes	No
D.	No	Yes

_____ 5. (S.O. 3) Which of the following is a realistic assumption of the straight-line method of depreciation?

A. The asset's economic usefulness is the same each year.
B. The repair and maintenance expense is essentially the same each period.
C. The rate of return analysis is enhanced using the straight-line method.
D. Depreciation is a function of time rather than a function of usage.

____ 6. (S.O. 3) Which of the following statements is the assumption on which straight-line depreciation is based?

A. The operating efficiency of the asset decreases in later years.
B. Service value declines as a function of time rather than use.
C. Service value declines as a function of obsolescence rather than time.
D. Physical wear and tear are more important than economic obsolescence.

____ 7. (S.O. 3) A graph is set up with "depreciation expense" on the vertical axis and "time" on the horizontal axis. Assuming linear relationships, how would the graphs for declining-balance and straight-line, respectively, be drawn?

A. Sloping down to the right and vertically.
B. Sloping up to the right and vertically.
C. Sloping down to the right and horizontally.
D. Sloping up to the right and horizontally.

____ 8. (S.O. 3) Which of the following depreciation methods does not consider salvage value in computing the depreciable base of the asset?

A. Straight-line.
B. Sum-of-years'-digits.
C. Declining-balance.
D. Activity or production.

____ 9. (S.O. 3) SL and YD Companies purchase identical equipment having an estimated service life of 5 years, with no salvage value. SL Company uses the straight-line depreciation method; YD Company uses the sum-of-the-years' digits method. Assuming that the companies are identical in all other respects:

A. if both companies keep the asset for 5 years, YD Company's 5-year total for depreciation expense will be greater than SL Company's 5-year total.
B. if the asset is sold after 3 years, SL Company is more likely to report a gain on the transaction than YD Company.
C. SL Company's depreciation expense will be higher during the 1st year than YD's.
D. SL Company's net income will be lower during the 4th year than YD Company's.

____ 10. (S.O. 3) Each year Abner Corporation sets aside an amount of cash equal to depreciation expense on its only machine. When the asset is completely depreciated, the cash fund will allow the corporation to buy a new machine if:

A. prices rise throughout the life of the property.
B. an accelerated depreciation method was used.
C. prices remain reasonably constant during the life of the property.
D. the retirement depreciation method is used.

_____ 11. (S.O. 3) When depreciation is computed for partial periods under a decreasing charge depreciation method, it is necessary to:

A. charge a full year's depreciation to the year of acquisition.
B. determine depreciation expense for the full year and then prorate the expense between the two periods involved.
C. use the straight-line method for the year in which the asset is sold or otherwise disposed of.
D. use a salvage value equal to the first year's partial depreciation charge.

_____ 12. (S.O. 4) Composite or group depreciation is a depreciation system whereby:

A. the years of useful life of the various assets in the group are added together and the total divided by the number of items.
B. the cost of individual units within an asset group is charged to expense in the year a unit is retired from service.
C. a straight-line rate is computed by dividing the total of the annual depreciation expense for all assets in the group by the total cost of the assets.
D. the original cost of all items in a given group or class of assets is retained in the asset account and the cost of replacements is charged to expense when they are acquired.

_____ 13. (S.O. 5) The Archer Company purchased a tooling machine in 1992 for $30,000. The machine was being depreciated on the straight-line method over an estimated useful life of 20 years, with no salvage value. At the beginning of 2002, when the machine had been in use for 10 years, the company paid $5,000 to overhaul the machine. As a result of this improvement, the company estimated that the useful life of the machine would be extended an additional 5 years. What should be the depreciation expense recorded for this machine in 2002?

A. $1,000.
B. $1,333.
C. $1,500.
D. $1,833.

_____ 14. (S.O. 5) Thucydides Company purchased a new machine on May 1, 1992, for $25,000. At the time of acquisition, the machine was estimated to have a useful life of 10 years and an estimated salvage value of $1,000. The company has recorded monthly depreciation using the straight-line method. On March 1, 2001, the machine was sold for $800. What should be the loss recognized from the sale of the machine?

A. $ 0.
B. $2,000.
C. $3,000.
D. $3,400.

_____ 15. (S.O. 5) Each year a company has been investing an increasing amount in machinery. Because there are a large number of small items with relatively similar useful lives, the company has been applying straight-line depreciation method at a uniform rate to the machinery as a group. The ratio of this group's total accumulated depreciation to the total cost of the machinery has been steadily increasing and now stands at .75 to 1. The most likely explanation of this increasing ratio is that:

A. the estimated average useful life of the machinery is greater than the actual average useful life.
B. the estimated average useful life of the machinery is equal to the actual average useful life.
C. the estimated average useful life of the machinery is less than the actual average useful life.
D. the company has been retiring fully depreciated machinery that should have remained in service.

_____ 16. (S.O. 5) The estimated life of a building that has been depreciated for 30 of its originally estimated life of 50 years has been revised to a remaining life of 10 years. On the basis of this information the accountant should:

A. continue to depreciate the building over the original 50-year life.
B. depreciate the remaining book value over the remaining life of the asset.
C. adjust accumulated depreciation to its appropriate balance, through net income, based on a 40-year life, and then depreciate the adjusted book value as though the estimated life had always been 40 years.
D. adjust accumulated depreciation to its appropriate balance, through retained earnings, based on a 40-year life, and then depreciate the adjusted book value as though the estimated life had always been 40 years.

_____ 17. (S.O. 5) Plato Corporation purchased a machine with a cost of $165,000 and a salvage value of $9,000 on April 1, 2001. The machine will be depreciated over a 12 year useful life using the sum-of-years'-digits method. The amount of depreciation Plato Corporation would record for the year ended 12/31/02 would be:

A. $22,000.
B. $24,000.
C. $16,500.
D. $22,500.

_____ 18. (S.O. 6) An impairment in the value of property, plant, and equipment is recorded by recognizing a:

	Loss	Reduction in Asset Book Value
A.	Yes	No
B.	Yes	Yes
C.	No	Yes
D.	No	No

_____ 19. (S.O. 6) Maimonides Inc. bought a machine on January 1, 1991 for $100,000. The machine had an expected life of 20 years and was expected to have a salvage value of $10,000. On July 1, 2001, the company reviewed the potential of the machine and determined that its undiscounted future net cash flows totaled $50,000 and its discounted future net cash flows totaled $35,000. If no active market exists for the machine and the company does not plan to dispose of it, what should Maimonides record as an impairment loss on July 1, 2001?

A. $ 0
B. $ 2,750
C. $ 5,000
D. $17,750

_____ 20. (S.O. 6) On December 31, 2000, Aquinas Company had equipment that had a carrying amount of $300,000 which the company wrote down to its $250,000 fair value. At the end of 2001 it was determined that the fair value of the equipment had risen to $320,000. At December 31, 2001, assuming Aquinas does not intend to dispose of the equipment, how should Aquinas record the change in fair value of the equipment?

A. The carrying amount of the equipment should not change except for the depreciation taken in 2001.
B. The equipment should reflect the new cost basis of $300,000.
C. The equipment should reflect the new cost basis of $320,000.
D. The equipment should reflect the new cost basis of $270,000.

_____ 21. (S.O. 7) Of the following costs related to the development of natural resources, which one is not a part of depletion cost?

A. Acquisition cost of the natural resource deposit.
B. Exploration costs.
C. Tangible equipment costs associated with machinery used to extract the natural resource.
D. Intangible development costs such as drilling costs, tunnels, and shafts.

_____ 22. (S.O. 7) The Xenophon Company acquired a tract of land containing an extractable natural resource. Xenophon Company is required by its purchase contract to restore the land to a condition suitable for recreational use after it extracts the natural resource. Geological surveys estimate that recoverable reserves will be 3 million tons and that the land will have a value of $600,000 after restoration. Relevant cost information follows:

Land	$6,000,000
Restoration	900,000
Geological surveys...........................	300,000

If Xenophon Company maintains no inventories of extracted material, what should be the charge to depletion expense per ton of material extracted?

A. $1.80.
B. $1.90.
C. $2.00.
D. $2.20.

_____ 23. (S.O. 7) In January 2001, the Lucky Mine Corporation purchased a mineral mine for $3,400,000 with removable ore estimated by geological surveys at 4,000,000 tons. The property has an estimated value of $200,000 after the ore has been extracted. The company incurred $800,000 of development costs preparing the mine for production. During 2001, 400,000 tons were removed and 375,000 tons were sold. What is the amount of depletion cost that Lucky Mine should record for 2001?

A. $375,000
B. $393,750
C. $400,000
D. $420,000

_____ 24. (S.O. 8) Which of the following disclosures is **not** required in the financial statements regarding depreciation?

A. Accumulated depreciation, either by major classes of depreciable assets or in total.
B. Details demonstrating how depreciation was calculated.
C. Depreciation expense for the period.
D. Balances of major classes of depreciable assets, by nature and function.

_____ *25. (S.O. 9) Which of the following is not one of the differences between the computation of depreciation under GAAP and the computation under the Modified Accelerated Cost Recovery System (MACRS)?

A. The recording of depreciation expense is taken directly to retained earnings under the MACRS method.
B. A mandated tax life is used which is generally shorter than the economic life of the asset.
C. Cost recovery is on an accelerated basis under the MACRS.
D. An assigned salvage value of zero is used under the MACRS.

REVIEW EXERCISES

1. (S.O.2 and 3) Augustine Corporation purchased two separate pieces of equipment in March 1995. Facts related to the two items are noted below. Augustine Corporation follows a policy of recording a full-year's depreciation in the year of acquisition and no depreciation in the year of disposition.

Item	Cost	Salvage Value	Useful Life	Depreciation Method	Annual Repair Cost
A	$113,000	$ 5,000	8 yrs.	Sum-of-year's-digits	$1,500
B	$140,000	$10,000	10 yrs.	Declining-balance	$2,500

Because of a lack of experience, the bookkeeper for the corporation made the following entry for the repair cost each year after depreciation was recorded.

Dr. Accumulated Depreciation
Cr. Cash

As a result, when item A was sold in July 2000 for $25,000, the bookkeeper recorded a loss on the sale. Also, when item B was sold in September 2002 for $40,000, the bookkeeper also recorded a loss. (Assume the bookkeeper ignored the debits to Accumulated Depreciation in computing annual depreciation expense on each asset.)

Instructions:

a. What journal entry did the bookkeeper record for each sale, assuming the only error was improperly charging the repair expense to accumulated depreciation.

b. What entry should have been made for each sale?

a.

General Journal J1

Date	Account Title	Debit	Credit

b.

General Journal

J1

Date	Account Title	Debit	Credit

2. (S.O.3) Aristotle Company acquired a machine on July 1, 2002, at a cost of $32,000. The machine has an estimated salvage value of $2,000 at the end of its 4-year useful life. Aristotle Company uses the calendar year as its accounting period.

Instructions:
Using the depreciation methods indicated, compute the depreciation expense for years 2002 and 2003, and the book value of the machine at December 31, 2003.

Depreciation Method	Depreciation Expense 2002	Depreciation Expense 2003	Book Value December 31, 2003
Straight-line			
Sum-of-the-years'-digits			
Declining-balance (200%)			

3. (S.O.4) For the following group of assets, compute the composite depreciation rate, the composite life, and the amount of depreciation recorded in the first year.

Asset	Original Cost	Salvage Value	Estimated Life (yr.)
A	$11,000	$ 500	5
B	7,000	200	4
C	12,500	800	3
D	16,000	1,000	6

If asset B is sold for $1,000 at the end of 3 years, what journal entry should be recorded?

General Journal J1

Date	Account Title	Debit	Credit

4. (S.O.6) Alfarabi Company has an asset that had an original cost of $560,000 and depreciation taken to date of $240,000. Management of Alfarabi Company has decided that the asset has suffered an impairment and its expected future net cash flows total $80,000. Further, the asset has a remaining useful life of 3 years and a salvage value of $15,000. No active market exists for the asset and its present value of expected future net cash flows is $61,000.

Instructions:

a. Prepare the journal entry Alfarabi Company would make to record the impairment in the value of the asset.

b. How is the gain or loss on this impairment reported in the income statement?

a.

General Journal J1

Date	Account Title	Debit	Credit

b.

____

____

____

____

____

____

____

____

____

____

____

____

____

____

____

____

5. (S.O.7) Cicero Oil Company acquired the rights to explore for oil on a 2,000-acre plot of land in the Oklahoma Panhandle. The rights cost $80,000, and the exploration costs associated with the discovery of a major oil deposit amounted to $125,000. The company incurred $980,000 in developmental costs, of which $250,000 were for tangible equipment. This equipment has useful life of 10 years and should be of use in future exploration ventures. During the first year the company extracted 175,000 of the estimated 2.5 million barrels of oil related to the discovery.

Instructions:
Prepare the journal entry for the first year's depletion and show how the above-mentioned assets would be reported in the balance sheet at the end of the first year.

General Journal J1

Date	Account Title	Debit	Credit

SOLUTIONS TO REVIEW QUESTIONS AND EXERCISES

TRUE-FALSE

1. (F) Depreciation is not a matter of valuation but a means of cost allocation in accounting. The concept is defined as the systematic allocation of the cost of an asset.

2. (T)

3. (T)

4. (F) When the economic nature of the asset is the primary determinant of service life, functional factors rather than physical factors (wear and tear) cause the asset to be retired. Functional factors (inadequacy, supersession, and obsolescence) cannot be reversed by repairs and maintenance.

5. (T)

6. (T)

7. (T)

8. (F) Companies that desire low depreciation during periods of low productivity and high depreciation during high productivity either adopt or switch to an activity method.

9. (T)

10. (F) The straight-line method is widely employed in practice because of its simplicity. The major objection to the straight-line method is that it rests on tenuous assumptions that in most situations are not realistic. The major assumptions are that (a) the asset's economic usefulness is the same each year and (b) the repair and maintenance expense is essentially the same each period.

11. (F) Accelerated depreciation methods provide for a higher depreciation cost in the earlier years and lower charges in later periods. The estimated useful life of an asset is unaffected by the depreciation method used.

12. (T)

13. (T)

14. (T)

15. (T)

16. (F) When determining whether an asset has been impaired, the recoverability test compares expected future net cash flows (undiscounted) to the carrying amount of the asset.

17. (T)

18. (F) Losses or gains relating to impaired assets intended to be disposed of should be reported as part of income from continuing operations.

19. (T)

20. (F) Development costs only include intangible development costs for such items as drilling costs, tunnels, shafts, and wells.

21. (F) Under the full costing approach, all costs, whether related to successful or unsuccessful projects, are capitalized and charged against future operations.

22. (T)

23. (T)

*24. (F) The IRS adopted an accelerated depreciation system known as the modified accelerated cost recovery system (MACRS). Under this method, the taxpayer determines the recovery deduction for an asset by applying a statutory percentage to the historical cost of the property. The use of MACRS is not affected by the reporting of a net loss.

*25. (F) For tax purposes companies are required to use a Modified Accelerated Cost Recovery System (MACRS) in computing depreciation. The rate of acceleration depends upon the useful life of the asset being depreciated. Congress enacted MACRS (a) to help companies achieve faster write-off of fixed assets in the hope of stimulating capital investment, and (b) to eliminate the controversy about useful lives of assets by adopting required recovery periods for most capital investments.

MULTIPLE CHOICE

1. (B) Depreciation is a process of systematic and rational allocation of an asset's cost to the periods benefitted by the use of that asset. A decline in value is not a part of the depreciation process, and depreciation does not necessarily match the physical deterioration of the asset. Also, depreciation is a concept most concerned with allocating cost to expense rather than a focus on recording fair market value of an asset on the balance sheet.

2. (A) Service life is the period of time an asset will provide productive service to a company. Physical life indicates how long an asset may be physically capable of producing a product or being used. The major difference is that an asset with physical life may not be economical to use and, as such, would not be of service to an entity. Salvage value is not a relevant issue in this distinction. Also, while physical life may be longer than service life, it is not necessarily always longer. The distinction of original owner vs. future owners is not a major element of the difference.

3. (A) The economic factors related to an asset's service life include: inadequacy, supersession, and obsolescence. The items listed in alternatives (B), (C), and (D) refer to the physical factors related to an asset's physical life.

4. (C) The activity method assumes that depreciation is a function of productivity rather than the passage of time. The life of the asset is considered in terms of either the output it provides (units of production) or an input measure such as number of hours it works.

5. (D) Alternatives A, B, and C reflect problems with use of the straight-line method of depreciation. An asset's economic usefulness is rarely the same each year, and with most assets, repair and maintenance costs increase as the asset gets older. Also, rate of return analysis is distorted under the straight-line method as well as other methods. The one true statement concerns the fact that the straight-line method is a function of time rather than a function of usage.

6. (B) When the service value of an asset declines as a function of time rather than use, it is rational to allocate the asset's cost using the straight-line method. Answer (A) is incorrect because an accelerated-depreciation method gives a better allocation of an asset's cost when the operating efficiency of the asset decreases in later years. Answer (D) is incorrect because an activity depreciation method gives a better allocation of an asset's cost when physical wear and tear are more important than economic obsolescence. Answer (C) is incorrect because, although straight-line depreciation is commonly used in practice to depreciate assets when their service value declines as a function of obsolescence rather than time, this is done as a practical expedient. This practice does not provide the assumption on which straight-line depreciation is based.

7. (C) Declining-balance depreciation results in the highest depreciation expense the first year of an asset's life and then decreases each year of the asset's life thereafter. Thus, the graph of the declining-balance depreciation would be sloping down to the right. Since straight-line depreciation is the same amount each year of an asset's life, the straight-line depreciation graph would be horizontal.

8. (C) The declining-balance method does not deduct salvage value in the computation of depreciable base. The declining-balance rate is multiplied by the book value (cost less accumulated depreciation) at the beginning of each period. By applying the declining-balance rate to the book value each year, a decreasing charge is recorded each year. Depreciation on the asset continues until the asset's book value is equal to its salvage value.

9. (D) If both companies are identical in all respects other than depreciation, then the company using the straight-line depreciation method (SL) will have a higher depreciation expense in the 4th year of the asset's life than the company using the sum-of-the-year's-digits method (YD). Thus, SL company's net income will be lower during the 4th year.

10. (C) Total depreciation on any asset is limited to the cost of that asset. If an amount of money equal to depreciation expense is set aside, the total accumulation will allow for the purchase of a new machine only if prices remain reasonably constant or decrease. The depreciation method employed has no impact on the total amount of depreciation.

11. (B) Under decreasing charge depreciation methods, depreciation expense is computed for each complete year of an asset's life. If the asset being depreciated under the decreasing charge method is purchased during a year, the depreciation for the entire year is computed and then a portion is allocated to depreciation expense based on the percentage of the year that the asset was used.

12. (C) Composite or group depreciation is defined as a system whereby a straight-line rate is computed by dividing the total of the annual depreciation expense for all assets in the group by the total cost of the assets.

13. (B)

Asset cost	\$30,000
Depreciation at 1/1/02	15,000
Book value	15,000
Overhaul addition	5,000
Depreciable base	\$20,000

Remaining useful life 10 + 5 = 15
Depreciation in 2002: \$20,000 ÷ 15 = \$1,333

14. (C)

Asset cost	\$25,000
Depreciation 5/1/92 to 3/1/01 (\$200/mo.)	21,200
Book value at 3/1/01	\$ 3,800
Sales price	800
Loss on sale	\$ 3,000

15. (C) With a uniform rate of depreciation being charged, a steadily increasing ratio of total accumulated depreciation to total cost would indicate that the estimated average useful life of the machinery is less than the actual average useful life. If the estimated average useful life of the machinery was equal to the actual average useful life, the ratio would remain constant.

16. (B) Whenever the estimated useful life of an asset is changed, the undepreciated book value of the asset should be depreciated over the new estimated useful life. This change is merely a change in an estimate and does not require any special accounting treatment.

17. (D) SYD Denominator = [12 X (12 + 1)] /2 = 78
Depreciable Base: \$165,000 - \$9,000 = \$156,000
1st Full Year Depreciation: 12/78 X \$156,000 = \$24,000
2nd Full Year Depreciation: 11/78 X \$156,000 = \$22,000
2001 Depreciation (April 1 to December 31): \$24,000 X 9/12 = \$18,000
2002 Depreciation (January 1 to December 31):

\$24,000 - \$18,000 =	\$ 6,000
\$22,000 X 9/12 =	16,500
2002 Depreciation	\$22,500

18. (B) A permanent impairment in the value of property, plant, and equipment is recorded by recognizing a loss and reducing the book value of the asset through a credit to accumulated depreciation. If the asset is to continue in use, estimates of the remaining useful life and the salvage value may be revised as well.

19. (D) Under the recoverability test, because the expected future net cash flows (undiscounted) of $50,000 is less than the carrying value of $52,750 [$100,000 - (($100,000 - $10,000)/20) x 10.5] an impairment has occurred. The impairment loss is the amount by which the carrying amount of the asset exceeds its fair value. If no market exists, the present value of expected future net cash flows is used as the fair value. Therefore, the impairment loss is equal to $17,750 ($52,750 - $35,000).

20. (A) Once an impairment loss is recorded, the reduced carrying amount of an asset held for use becomes its new cost basis. As a result, the new cost basis is not changed except for depreciation in future periods or for additional impairments.

21. (C) Tangible equipment costs are normally not considered in the depletion base; instead, separate depreciation charges are employed because the asset can be moved from one drilling or mining site to another. Tangible assets that cannot be moved should be separately depreciated over their useful life or the life of the resource, whichever is shorter.

22. (D)

Land cost	$6,000,000
Restoration	900,000
Geological surveys	300,000
Total cost	$7,200,000
Land residual value	600,000
Depletion base	$6,600,000

Depletion expense per ton $6,600,000 ÷ 3,000,000 = $2.20.

23. (C) Lucky Mine's depletion rate per ton of mined ore can be calculated as follows:

Depletable cost:	
Purchase price of mine	$3,400,000
Development cost	800,000
	$4,200,000
Less: Estimated value of property after ore has been extracted	200,000
Total depletable cost	$4,000,000

$$\frac{\text{Depletable cost}}{\text{Estimated recoverable ore}} = \frac{\$4,000,000}{4,000,000 \text{ tons}} = \$1 \text{ depletion per ton of mined ore}$$

Since Lucky Mine Corporation removed 400,000 tons of ore in 1998, it should record $400,000 (400,000 tons x $1) as its depletion cost. This amount would be charged to the account Inventory of Mined Ore and credited to Accumulated Depletion.

Answer (A) is incorrect because depletion cost would be recorded as the ore is mined, not as it is sold.

24. (B) Only a general description of the method or methods used in computing depreciation with respect to major classes of depreciable assets is required in the financial statements regarding depreciation. In addition, answers (A), (C), and (D) are required disclosures in the financial statements.

*25. (A) Depreciation is still an expense which is shown as a reduction in net income under the MACRS. The data in alternatives B, C, and D represent the basic differences in the depreciation computation under MACRS.

REVIEW EXERCISES

1. (a) **Item A:**

Year	Computation	Depreciation Recorded
1995	$108,000 x 8/36	$24,000
1996	108,000 x 7/36	21,000
1997	108,000 x 6/36	18,000
1998	108,000 x 5/36	15,000
1999	108,000 x 4/36	12,000
	Total Depreciation	$90,000
	Repair Expense Charged to Depreciation (1,500 x 5)	(7,500)
	Depreciation Balance (2000)	$82,500

Entry by bookkeeper for sale of item A:

Account	Debit	Credit
Cash	25,000	
Accumulated depreciation	82,500	
Loss on sale	5,500	
Item A		113,000

Correct entry for sale of item A:

Account	Debit	Credit
Cash	25,000	
Accumulated depreciation	90,000	
Gain on sale		2,000
Item A		113,000

(b) **Item B:**

Year	Computation	Depreciation Recorded
1995	$140,000 x .20	$ 28,000
1996	112,000 x .20	22,400
1997	89,600 x .20	17,920
1998	71,680 x .20	14,336
1999	57,344 x .20	11,469
2000	45,875 x .20	9,175
2001	36,700 x .20	7,340
	Total Depreciation	$110,640
	Repair Expense Charged to Depreciation (2,500 x 7)	(17,500)
	Depreciation Balance (2002)	$ 93,140

Entry by bookkeeper for sale of item B:

Cash	40,000	
Accumulated depreciation	93,140	
Loss on sale	6,860	
Item B		140,000

Correct entry for sale of item B:

Cash	40,000	
Accumulated Depreciation	110,640	
Gain on sale		10,640
Item B		140,000

2.

Depreciation Method	Depreciation Expense 2002	Depreciation Expense 2003	Book Value December 31, 2003
Straight Line	$ 3,750 (a)	$ 7,500 (b)	$20,750 (c)
Sum-of-the-years'-digits	6,000 (d)	10,500 (e)	15,500 (f)
Declining-balance (200%)	8,000 (g)	12,000 (h)	12,000 (i)

(a) $30,000 x 1/4 X 1/2 = $3,750
(b) $30,000 x 1/4 = $7,500
(c) $32,000 - (a + b) = $20,750
(d) $30,000 x 4/10 x 1/2 = $6,000
(e) $6,000 + (9,000 x 1/2) = $10,500
(f) $32,000 - (d + e) = $15,500
(g) $32,000 x .5 x 1/2 = $8,000
(h) $8,000 + (8,000 x 1/2) = $12,000
(i) 32,000 - (g + h) = $12,000

3.

Asset	Original Cost	Salvage Value	Depreciable Cost	Useful Life	Depreciation per year (straight-line)
A	$ 11,000	$ 500	$10,500	5	$ 2,100
B	7,000	200	6,800	4	1,700
C	12,500	800	11,700	3	3,900
D	16,000	1,000	15,000	6	2,500
	$46,500	$2,500	$44,000		$10,200

$$\text{Composite rate} = \frac{\$10,200}{46,500} = .219 \text{ or } 22\%$$

Composite life (44,000 ÷ 10,200) = 4.31 years
1st year's depreciation ($46,500 x .22) = $10,230
Sale of asset B for $1,000 after 3 years:

Cash	1,000	
Accumulated depreciation	6,000	
Asset B		7,000

4. (a) Current Book Value:

Current Book Value:	Cost	$560,000
	Accumulated Depreciation	240,000
	Book Value	$320,000
After Impairment:	Cost	$560,000
	Accumulated Depreciation	499,000
	Book Value	$ 61,000

Journal Entry:

Loss on Impairment	259,000	
Accumulated Depreciation		259,000

*($320,000 - $61,000)

(b) The loss of $259,000 is reported separately in the Other Expenses and Losses section of the income statement. This loss is not considered to be an extraordinary item because write offs of operating assets frequently occur in the normal course of business.

5. Depletion base:

Land rights	$ 80,000
Exploration costs..	125,000
Intangible development costs ($980,000 - 250,000)...	730,000
Depletion base..	$935,000

Depletion rate per barrel: $935,000 ÷ 2,500,000 = $.374
First year's depletion: 175,000 x .374 = $65,450

Depletion expense...	65,450	
Accumulated depletion of natural resource.............		65,450

Balance sheet presentation:

Oil deposit (at cost)...	$935,000	
Less accumulated depletion	65,450	$869,550

Tangible assets should be reported separately with a deduction for the related accumulated depreciation.

12

Intangible Assets

CHAPTER STUDY OBJECTIVES

1. Describe the characteristics of intangible assets.
2. Explain the procedure for valuing and amortizing intangible assets.
3. Identify the types of specifically identifiable intangible assets.
4. Explain the conceptual issues related to goodwill.
5. Describe the accounting procedures for recording goodwill.
6. Identify the conceptual issues related to research and development costs.
7. Describe the accounting procedures for research and development costs.
8. Indicate the presentation of intangibles and related items.

*9. Identify the accounting treatment for computer software costs.

*10. Explain various approaches to valuing goodwill.

CHAPTER REVIEW

1. Chapter 12 discusses the identification, measurement, and disposition of intangible assets. These assets provide the entity that owns them with some kind of preferred position because of certain rights or special privileges they are allowed. Intangible assets are valued at their cost and generally are adjusted downward to reflect their future benefit to the entity as of the end of each fiscal period.

<u>Valuing and Amortizing Intangibles</u>

2. (S.O. 1) The characteristics of an **intangible asset** are: (1) they lack physical existence, (2) they are not a financial instrument, and (3) they are long-term in nature and subject to amortization. The most common types of intangibles reported are patents, copyrights, franchises or licenses, trademarks or trade names, and goodwill.

3. The problem in accounting for intangible assets often stem from the unique characteristics these assets possess. Also, intangible assets may be further characterized by other somewhat unique characteristics such as the following:

A. Identifiability
    1. Separately identifiable
    2. Lacking specific identification

B. Manner of Acquisition
    1. Acquired singly
    2. Acquired in groups
    3. Acquired in business combinations
    4. Developed internally

**Note: All asterisked (*) items relate to material contained in the Appendices to the chapter.*

C. Expected Period of Benefit
   1. Limited by law or contract
   2. Related to human or economic factors
   3. Indefinite or indeterminate duration

D. Separability from an Entire Enterprise
   1. Rights transferable without title
   2. Saleable
   3. Inseparable from the enterprise or a substantial part of it

4. (S.O. 2) **Cost** is the appropriate basis for recording purchased intangible assets. Like tangible assets, cost includes acquisition price and all other expenditures necessary in making the asset ready for its intended use. When intangibles are acquired for consideration other than cash, the cost of the intangible is the fair market value of the consideration given or the intangible asset received, whichever is more clearly evident. Costs incurred to create **internally-created intangibles** are generally expensed as incurred.

5. The cost of an intangible asset is systematically charged to expense through the process of **amortization.** The major problem involved in computing amortization is determination of the intangible's useful life. This problem stems from the high degree of uncertainty that surrounds the future usefulness of many intangible assets. The factors that might be considered in determining useful life include: **(a)** legal life, **(b)** economic conditions, and **(c)** actions of competitors.

6. When an intangible asset ceases to provide future service potential to an enterprise, its cost should be removed from the accounting records. In the case of intangible assets that are considered to have indeterminable useful lives, proper accounting requires amortization over a period not to exceed **40 years.** The entry for amortization includes a debit to an expense account and a credit to either the appropriate intangible asset account or a separate accumulated amortization account. Intangible assets acquired from other enterprises should not be written off at acquisition. Intangibles are normally amortized using the straight-line method (this method is required for income tax purposes). However, there is no requirement that the straight-line method be used in all situations. If the entity can demonstrate that another method is more appropriate, its use is appropriate.

7. (S.O. 3) Intangible assets are **specifically identifiable** (cost of creating the intangible can be identified) or **goodwill-type intangibles.** Goodwill-type intangibles create a right or privilege that is not specifically identifiable; they have an indeterminate life; and their cost is inherent in a continuing business.

<u>**Patents**</u>

8. A **patent** gives the holder an exclusive right to use, manufacture, and sell a product or process for a period of 20 years. The two principal kinds of patents are **product patents,** which cover actual physical products, and **process patents,** which relate to the process by which products are made. **Amortization is recorded over the legal life or useful life, whichever is shorter.** Any legal costs incurred to successfully defend a patent suit may be charged to the Patents account and amortized over the remaining useful life. However, **research and development** costs related to the development of a product, process, or idea that is subsequently patented must be expensed as incurred.

Copyrights

9. A **copyright** is a federally granted right that authors and other artists have in their creations. A copyright is granted for the life of the creator plus 50 years. During this time the owner or heirs have the exclusive right to reproduce and sell an artistic or published work. Normally, the useful life of a copyright is less than its legal life, but, in any case, amortization should not exceed 40 years.

Trademarks or Trade Names

10. A **trademark** or **trade name** is a word, phrase, or symbol that distinguishes or identifies a particular enterprise product. A company that registers a trademark or trade name with the U.S. Patent Office may renew it for an unlimited number of 20 year periods. Thus, a company establishing a trademark or trade name can consider it to have an unlimited life. The cost to be capitalized for a trademark or trade name is the acquisition cost if purchased, or all associated expenditures (other than research and development costs) if the item is developed by the company. Even though the life of a trademark or trade name may be unlimited, its cost must be amortized over the periods benefited or 40 years, whichever is shorter.

Leaseholds

11. A **leasehold** is a contractual right to the use of specific property for a specified period of time. If rent is paid in advance, the amount is most appropriately included in the current or other asset category. Leases that are in substance purchases of assets (capital lease) should be recorded on the basis of substance rather than legal form. Detailed coverage of lease accounting is presented in Chapter 22.

12. Improvements made to leased property by the lessee normally revert to the lessor at the end of the lease. Thus, the cost of **leasehold improvements** should be capitalized by the lessee and depreciated over the life of the lease or the useful life of the improvement, whichever is shorter. Leasehold improvements are generally classified as tangible assets, although some accountants classify them as intangible assets.

Franchises and Licenses

14. A **franchise** provides an entity with the right to conduct a particular business or sell a particular product, usually in a designated geographical area. A **license** is granted by a government entity for the use of public property or a service. Franchises and licenses may be for a definite period of time, for an indefinite period of time, or perpetual. Franchise or license costs that benefit future periods should be recorded in a Franchise or License account. These costs are amortized over the life of the franchise or license or 40 years, whichever is less. Continuing periodic franchise and license payments are expenses of the period and do not represent assets associated with future periods.

Goodwill

15. (S.O. 4) In a business combination, the cost (purchase price) is assigned where possible to the identifiable tangible and intangible net assets, and the remainder is recorded in an intangible asset account called **Goodwill.** The problem of determining the proper cost to allocate to intangible assets in a business combination is complex because of the many different types of intangibles that may be considered.

16. **Goodwill** is recorded only when an entire business is **purchased** because **goodwill is a "going concern" valuation and cannot be separated from the business as a whole.** Goodwill is measured in a business purchase by computing the difference between the fair market value of the net assets purchased and their bargained price.

17. Goodwill, like other intangible assets, should be amortized over its useful life or 40 years, whichever is less. *APB Opinion No. 16* prohibits the complete write-off of goodwill against revenue in the period of purchase. For tax purposes, the amortization of goodwill is over 15 years.

18. **Negative goodwill,** often called **badwill**, arises when the fair market value of the net assets acquired is higher than the purchase price of the asset. When negative goodwill exists, *APB Opinion No. 16* requires that it be applied to a reduction of the values assigned to noncurrent assets.

19. The general rules that apply to impairments of long-lived assets also apply to intangibles. Goodwill impairments involve a grouping of net assets.

20. Intangible assets are normally shown in financial statements at cost less total amortization taken to date. The financial statements should disclose the method of amortization, but a separate Accumulated Amortization account need not be presented.

<u>Research and Development</u>

21. (S.O. 6 and 7) The expenditure for **research and development** is designed to develop new products or processes, improve existing processes, and discover new knowledge. In general, *FASB Statement No. 2* requires that all research and development (R & D) costs be charged to expense when incurred. The reasons for this decision include problems associated with **(a)** identifying the costs associated with particular activities, projects, or achievements and **(b)** determining the magnitude of future benefits and length of time over which such benefits may be realized. The following is a description of the recommended treatment of the costs associated with R & D activities:

a. **Materials, Equipment, and Facilities.** Expense the entire costs, unless the items have alternative future uses (in other R & D projects or otherwise), then carry as inventory and allocate as consumed or capitalize and depreciate as used.
b. **Personnel.** Salaries, wages, and other related costs of personnel engaged in R & D should be expensed as incurred.
c. **Purchased Intangibles.** Expense the entire cost, unless the items have alternative future uses (in other R & D projects or otherwise), then capitalize and amortize.
d. **Contract Services.** The costs of services performed by others in connection with the reporting company's R & D should be expensed as incurred.
e. **Indirect Costs.** A reasonable allocation of indirect costs should be included in R&D costs, except for general and administrative cost, which must be clearly related to be included and expensed.

22. **Start-up costs** and **advertising costs** are also to be expensed as incurred.

23. (S.O. 8) Acceptable accounting practice requires that disclosure be made in the footnotes to the financial statements of the total R & D costs charged to expense in each period for which an income statement is presented.

*24. (S.O. 9) **The appendix, Accounting for Computer Software Costs,** presents the diverse issues related to handling the costs involved in developing computer software. Coverage of the FASB position and answers to the key questions addressed in accounting for computer software are presented.

*25. (S.O. 10) **Appendix 12B, Valuing Goodwill**, states that goodwill can also be measured in a business purchase by discounting the extra earning potential of an enterprise and determining the present value of this extra inflow.

*26. Discounting the extra earning potential is, conceptually, the more appealing approach to the measurement of goodwill. However, this approach depends on a number of factors that are tenuous and subject to negotiation. The factors necessary to compute goodwill under this approach are: **(a)** the **normal rate of return** for the enterprise, **(b)** an estimate of the **future earnings** of the enterprise, **(c)** the **discount rate** that should be applied to excess profits, and **(d)** the **number of periods** over which excess profits should be discounted. For example, one potential valuation of goodwill is to capitalize average earnings at some discount rate. Assume a purchased company has the following financial data:

Average earnings past 5 years	$ 58,000
Discount rate	17%
Fair market value of net assets	$250,000

If goodwill is equal to the difference between FMV of purchased assets and average earnings capitalized at the discount rate, the computation would be the following:

$58,000/17%	$341,176
Less fair market value of net assets	250,000
Goodwill	$ 91,176

GLOSSARY

Capital lease. A lease agreement that transfers substantially all of the benefits and risks incident to ownership of the property so that the economic effect on the parties is similar to that of an installment purchase.

Copyright. A federally granted right that all authors, painters, musicians, sculptors, and other artists have in their creations and expressions, which is granted for the life of the creator plus 50 years.

Development activities. The translation of research findings or other knowledge into a plan or design for a new product or process or for a significant improvement to an existing product or process whether intended for sale or use.

Development stage enterprise. A company that is in the stage of directing its efforts toward establishing a new business and either the principal operations have not started or no significant revenue has been earned.

***Excess earnings approach.** A method of determining goodwill by computing the earning power that a company commands.

Franchise. A contractual arrangement under which the franshisor grants the franshisee the right to sell certain products or services, to use certain trademarks or trade names, or to perform certain functions, usually within a designated geographical area.

Goodwill. The aggregate of many advantageous factors and conditions that might contribute to the value and earning power of an enterprise.

Goodwill-type intangibles. Intangibles where there is a created right or privilege, but it is not specifically identifiable and has an indeterminable life.

Intangible assets. Characteristics include: (1) lack of physical existence, (2) they are not a financial instrument, and (3) they are long-term in nature and subject to amortization.

Leasehold. A contractual understanding between a lessor (owner of property) and a lessee (renter of property) that grants the lessee the right to use specific property, owned by the lessor, for a specific period of time in return for stipulated, and generally periodic, cash payments.

Leasehold improvements. Improvements made to leased property which revert to the lessor at the end of the life of the lease.

License.	A right granted by a government body for the use of public property.
Master valuation approach.	The valuation of goodwill by taking the difference between the cost of the group of assets or enterprise acquired and the sum of the assigned costs of individual tangible and identifiable intangible assets acquired less liabilities assumed.
Negative goodwill (badwill).	Occurs when the fair market value of the assets acquired is higher than the purchase price of the assets.
Organization costs.	Costs incurred in the formation of a corporation such as fees to underwriters for handling stock or bond issues, legal fees, state fees of various sorts, and certain promotional expenditures.
Patents.	Rights granted by the U.S. Patent Office which give the holder exclusive right to use, manufacture, and sell a product or process for a period of 20 years without interference or infringement by others.
Process patents.	Patents which govern the process by which products are made.
Product patents.	Patents which cover actual physical products.
Research activities.	The planned search aimed at discovery of new knowledge with the hope that such knowledge will be useful in developing a new product, service, process or technique, or in bringing about a significant improvement to an existing product or process.
Research and development costs.	The costs associated with research and development activities.
Start-up costs	Costs incurred for one time activities to start a new operation.
Specifically identifiable intangibles.	Intangibles where the costs associated with obtaining a given intangible asset can be identified as a part of the cost of that intangible asset.
Trademark or trade name.	A word, phrase, or symbol that distinguishes or identifies a particular enterprise or product. Registration with the U.S. Patent Office provides legal protection for an indefinite number of renewals for periods of 20 years each.

CHAPTER OUTLINE

Fill in the outline presented below.

(S.O. 1) Characteristics of Intangible Assets

(S.O. 2) Valuation and Amortization of Intangibles

(S.O. 3) Specifically Identifiable Intangible Assets

Patents

Copyrights

Trademarks and Trade Names

Leaseholds

Leasehold prepayments

Leasehold improvements

Capital leases

Chapter Outline *(continued)*

Franchises and Licenses

Property Rights

(S.O. 4) Goodwill

Recording Goodwill

Amortization of Goodwill

Negative Goodwill (Badwill)

Impairment of Intangibles

Reporting of Intangibles

(S.O. 6) Research and Development Costs

(S.O. 8) Presentation of Intangibles

Other Assets

Chapter Outline *(continued)*

(S.O. 9) *Accounting for Software Costs

(S.O. 10) *Valuing Goodwill

*Excess Earnings Approach

*Other Methods of Valuation

REVIEW QUESTIONS AND EXERCISES

TRUE-FALSE

Indicate whether each of the following is true (T) or false (F) in the space provided.

_____ 1. (S.O. 1) Lack of physical substance is the only characteristic of intangible assets that distinguishes them from all other assets reported on the balance sheet.

_____ 2. (S.O. 2) Cost is the basis for recording intangible assets, including acquisition price and all expenditures incurred to prepare the asset for its intended use.

_____ 3. (S.O. 2) Cost incurred internally to create intangibles are generally the basis for recording intangible assets, which are then amortized over the estimated life of the intangible asset.

_____ 4. (S.O. 2) Amortization is the systematic charge to income of the cost of an intangible asset.

_____ 5. (S.O. 2) Intangible assets are amortized over their useful lives unless the intangible has the potential to remain in existence indefinitely.

_____ 6. (S.O. 2) Immediate write-off of the cost of an intangible is not acceptable because the approach denies the existence of an asset that has just been purchased.

_____ 7. (S.O. 3) A goodwill-type intangible means that costs associated with obtaining a given intangible asset can be identified as a part of the cost of that intangible asset.

_____ 8. (S.O. 3) A patent gives the holder the exclusive right to use a product or process for a period not to exceed 20 years.

_____ 9. (S.O. 3) Long-term lease agreements ordinarily provide that any improvements made to the leased asset become the property of the party paying for the improvement at the termination of the lease.

_____ 10. (S.O. 3) Marsilius Company secured a copyright on a unique literary work. All conservative estimates indicate that the copyright will be useful for its maximum useful life; thus, this is the period over which the copyright should be amortized.

_____ 11. (S.O. 3) The cost of a franchise with a limited life should be amortized as an operating expense over the life of the franchise (but not in excess of 40 years).

_____ 12. (S.O. 4) Goodwill is recorded only when an entire business is purchased or when the portion of a business purchased is responsible for all the goodwill accumulated by the enterprise.

_____ 13. (S.O. 5) Use of the master valuation approach to measure goodwill requires an estimate of a firm's excess earning power.

_____ 14. (S.O. 5) *APB Opinion No. 17* takes the position that goodwill should be written off over its useful life or 40 years, whichever is longer.

_____ 15. (S.O. 5) Badwill arises when the fair market value of the asset acquired is higher than the purchase price of the asset.

_____ 16. (S.O. 5) The general rules that apply to impairments of long-lived assets also apply to intangibles.

_____ 17. (S.O. 5) Goodwill impairments involve a grouping of net assets.

_____ 18. (S.O. 6) As a result of *FASB Statement No. 2,* all research and development (R & D) costs should normally be charged to expense when incurred.

_____ 19. (S.O. 6) A marketing survey conducted for the purpose of determining a more efficient way to package a product is an example of R & D activities.

_____ 20. (S.O. 7) Organization costs are usually charged to an account called Organization Costs and may be carried as an asset on the balance sheet.

_____ 21. (S.O. 7) A reasonable allocation of indirect costs shall be included in research and development costs, including general and administrative costs.

_____ *22. (S.O. 9) Costs incurred in creating a computer software product should be charged to research and development expense when incurred until technological feasibility has been established for the product.

_____ *23. (S.O. 9) If computer software costs are capitalized, the basis for amortization is the lesser of (1) the ratio of current revenues to current and anticipated revenues (percent of revenue approach) or (2) the straight-line method over the remaining useful life of the assets (straight-line approach).

_____ *24. (S.O. 10) Determining the normal earning power of an enterprise requires an analysis of the earning power of similar companies.

_____ *25. (S.O. 10) When a discount rate is applied to average excess earnings in the computation of goodwill, a higher discount rate will produce a higher value for goodwill.

MULTIPLE CHOICE

Select the best answer for each of the following items and enter the corresponding letter in the space provided.

_____ 1. (S.O. 1) Which of the following is not an intangible asset?

A. Accounts receivable.
B. Patents.
C. Copyrights.
D. Franchises.

_____ 2. (S.O. 2) When intangible assets are amortized, a journal entry may be made by debiting an expense account and crediting

	The Intangible Asset	Accumulated Amortization
A.	Yes	Yes
B.	Yes	No
C.	No	Yes
D.	No	No

_____ 3. (S.O. 2) Under current accounting practice, intangible assets are classified as:

A. amortizable or unamortizable.
B. old or new.
C. specifically identifiable or goodwill-type.
D. legally restricted or goodwill-type.

_____ 4. (S.O. 2) One factor that is not considered in determining the useful life of an intangible asset is:

A. legal life.
B. expected actions of competitors.
C. salvage value
D. provisions for renewal or extension.

_____ 5. (S.O. 2) Which of the following methods of amortization is the general method of amortizing for intangible assets?

A. Sum-of-the-years' digits method.
B. Straight-line method.
C. Activity method.
D. Declining-balance method.

____ 6. (S.O. 3) On January 15, 1993, Machiavelli Corporation was granted a patent on a product. On January 2, 2002, to protect its patent, Machiavelli purchased a patent on a competing product that originally was issued on January 10, 1995. Because of its unique plant, Machiavelli does not feel that the competing patent can be used in producing a product. The cost of acquiring the competing patent should be:

A. amortized over a maximum period of 11 years.
B. amortized over a maximum period of 16 years.
C. amortized over a maximum period of 20 years.
D. expensed in 2002.

____ 7. (S.O. 3) When a company develops a trademark or trade name the costs required to develop it should generally be capitalized. Which of the following costs associated with a trademark or trade name would not be allowed to be capitalized.

A. Attorney fees.
B. Consulting fees.
C. Research and development fees.
D. Design costs.

____ 8. (S.O. 3) A large publicly held company has developed and registered a trademark during 2001. How should the cost of developing and registering the trademark be accounted for?

A. Charged to an asset account that should not be amortized.
B. Amortized over 25 years if in accordance with management's evaluation.
C. Expensed as incurred.
D. Amortized over its useful life or 40 years, whichever is shorter.

____ 9. (S.O. 3) Luther Tire Repair negotiated a 40 year lease of a 2 acre plot of land adjacent to a shopping center. On the land Luther constructed a tire repair facility with an estimated useful life of 25 years. Assuming Luther has the right to renew the lease for an additional 40 years, over what period of time should the repair facility be depreciated?

A. 40 years, the maximum length of time an intangible can be amortized or depreciated.
B. Over a period agreed upon with the lessor since the lease will probably be extended for an additional 40 years.
C. 80 years, as the repair facility is not an intangible asset and is not subject to the 40 year limit.
D. Over the 25 year life of the repair facility since it is less than the life of the lease.

_____ 10. (S.O. 3) Hooker Corporation acquired a franchise to operate a Good Pet Dog Kennel in January, 1999. The cost of the franchise was $125,000 and was estimated to have an indefinite life. Early in the year 2005, the franchise was deemed worthless due to significant law suits that caused the franchisor to go out of business. What amount of cost or expense should be charged to the income statement of Hooker Corporation for the years noted below?

	1999	2004	2005
A.	$5,000	$5,000	$ 5,000
B.	$3,125	$3,125	$ 3,125
C.	0	0	$125,000
D.	$3,125	$3,125	$106,250

_____ 11. (S.O. 3) Smith Co. bought a window franchise from Paine, Inc., on January 2, 2001, for $100,000. A highly regarded independent research company estimated that the remaining useful life of the franchise was 50 years. Its unamortized cost on Paine's books at January 1, 2001, was $15,000. Smith has decided to write off the franchise over the longest possible period. How much should be amortized by Smith Co. for the year ended December 31, 2001?

A. $ 375
B. $ 2,000
C. $ 2,500
D. $15,000

_____ 12. (S.O. 4) Goodwill:

A. generated internally should not be capitalized unless it is measured by an individual independent of the enterprise involved.
B. is easily computed by assigning a value to the individual attributes that comprise its existence.
C. represents a unique asset in that its value can be identified only with the business as a whole.
D. exists in any company that has earnings that differ from those of a competitor.

_____ 13. (S.O. 5) The amortization of goodwill:

A. is dependent upon the number of years a company expects to use the benefits it provides.
B. is the one exception where an intangible asset can be amortized for a period greater than 40 years.
C. represents as acceptable an accounting practice as does the immediate write-off method.
D. should be computed using the straight-line method unless another method is deemed more appropriate.

_____ 14. (S.O. 5) The reason goodwill is sometimes referred to as a master valuation account is because:

A. it represents the purchase price of a business that is about to be sold.
B. it is the difference between the fair market value of the net tangible and identifiable intangible assets as compared with the purchase price of the acquired business.
C. the value of a business is computed without consideration of goodwill and then goodwill is added to arrive at a master valuation.
D. it is the only account in the financial statements that is based on value, all other accounts are recorded at an amount other than their value.

_____ 15. (S.O. 5) The accounting profession does not allow the immediate write-off of goodwill. The best reason for this requirement seems to be that:

A. goodwill has a useful life like all assets and should be charged as an expense at a normal rate.
B. to write-off goodwill immediately would lead to the incorrect conclusion that goodwill has no future service potential.
C. the immediate write-off would cause net income to be much lower than it had been for the company in recent years and comparability would be distorted.
D. because the amortization of goodwill is tax deductible, an immediate write-off serves no useful purpose.

_____ 16. (S.O. 5) When the fair market value of the assets acquired in a business purchase exceed the purchase price, negative goodwill (also called badwill) arises. When negative goodwill arises, GAAP requires that it be allocated:

A. to all periods benefited on an equitable basis, not to exceed 40 years.
B. to all periods benefited on an equitable basis, and may exceed the 40 year requirement of normal goodwill.
C. to reduce proportionately the values assigned to noncurrent assets.
D. to reduce proportionately the values assigned to both current and noncurrent assets.

_____ 17. (S.O. 5) In 1999, Hume, Inc. purchased Rousseau Metals for $3 million. At December 31, 2002, the Rousseau division reported net assets of $3,300,000 (including $1,700,000 of goodwill). Hume reviewed the Rousseau division and determined that expected net future cash flows equal $2,500,000 and the fair value is estimated to be only $1,800,000. What entry should Hume record concerning the Rousseau division on December 31, 2002?

A.	No entry is needed.		
B.	Loss on impairment	1,500,000	
	Goodwill		1,500,000
C.	Loss on impairment	1,200,000	
	Goodwill		1,200,000
D.	Loss on impairment	1,500,000	
	Prorata deduction of all assets		1,500,000

_____ 18. (S.O. 6) How should research and development costs be accounted for according to *FASB Statement No. 2*, "Accounting for Research and Development Costs"?

A. Must be capitalized when incurred and then amortized over their estimated useful lives.
B. Must be expensed in the period incurred unless contractually reimbursable.
C. May be either capitalized or expensed when incurred.
D. Must be expensed in the period incurred unless it can be clearly demonstrated that the expenditure will result in the discovery of a profitable product.

_____ 19. (S.O. 6) In 2001, Descartes Corporation incurred R & D costs as follows:

Materials and facilities	$ 80,000
Personnel	110,000
Indirect costs..	25,000
	$215,000

These costs relate to a product that will be marketed in 2002. It is estimated that these costs will be recovered by the end of 2004. What amount of R&D costs should be charged against 2001 income?

A. $ 0.
B. $ 25,000.
C. $190,000.
D. $215,000.

_____ 20. (S.O. 6) Which of the following would not be considered an R & D activity?

A. Adaptation of an existing capability to a particular requirement or customer's need.
B. Searching for applications of new research findings.
C. Laboratory research aimed at discovery of new knowledge.
D. Conceptual formulation and design of possible product or process alternatives.

_____ 21. (S.O. 7) Calvin Company incurred the following cost related to the organization of the business:

Attorney's fee	$10,000
Underwriter's fee	15,000
State incorporation fee................................	7,000
	$32,000

The company wishes to amortize these costs over the maximum period allowed under generally accepted accounting principles. Assuming that Calvin Company began operation on January 1, 2002, what amount of organization costs should be amortized in 2003?

A. $4,400.
B. $2,200.
C. $ 800.
D. $ 0.

_____*22. (S.O. 9) Kant, Inc. produces and sells computer games. During 2002, Kant developed a game called "Revenge of the Accountants." The development of the game incurred $300,000 in costs before completion of a detailed program design and $200,000 after completion of the detailed program design. How much of the costs incurred in 2002 can Kant capitalize to the computer game?

A. $ 0
B. $500,000
C. $300,000
D. $200,000

_____*23. (S.O. 9) Blackstone Co. has capitalized computer software costs of $2 million and its current (first-year) revenues from sales of this product are $1 million. Blackstone anticipates earning $4 million in additional future revenues from this product, which is estimated to have an economic life of 8 years. What amount should Blackstone record as amortization expense for the current year?

A. $1,000,000
B. $ 500,000
C. $ 400,000
D. $ 250,000

_____*24. (S.O. 10) In the computation of goodwill, the excess earnings approach is often used. In this approach the computation of an entity's excess earning power is required. Excess earning power is best defined by which of the following?

A. The difference between what the firm earns and what is normal in the industry.
B. The difference between what the firm earns and what its major competitors earn for a given period of time.
C. The difference between what the acquiring company earns and what is earned by the company being acquired.
D. The difference between earnings in the most recent year and the average for the preceding five years.

_____*25. (S.O. 10) Bacon Company has determined that the excess earnings of Hobbes Company are $14,500. If Bacon is interested in purchasing Hobbes Company and agrees that goodwill should be valued by capitalizing excess earnings at 20%, the value for goodwill would be:

A. $ 2,900
B. $17,400
C. $72,500
D. $87,000

REVIEW EXERCISES

1. (S.O. 2 and 3) A patent was acquired by Grotius Corporation on January 1, 1994, at a cost of $72,000. The useful life of the patent was estimated to be 10 years. At the beginning of 1998, Grotius spent $9,000 in successfully prosecuting an attempted infringement of the patent. At the beginning of 1999, Grotius purchased a patent for $25,000 that was expected to prolong the life of its original patent for 5 additional years. On July 1, 2002, a competitor obtained rights to a patent that made the company's patent obsolete. Grotius records amortization expense directly with a credit to the Patent account.

Instructions:
Calculate the following amounts for Grotius Corporation.

a. Amortization expense for 1994.
b. The balance in the Patent account at the beginning of 1998, immediately after the infringement suit.
c. Amortization expense for 1998.
d. The balance in the Patent account at the beginning of 1999, after purchase of the additional patent.
e. Amortization expense for 1999.
f. The amount of loss recorded at July 1, 2002.

Patent Account

2. (S.O. 6 and 7) Montesquieu Pharmaceuticals Company has an extensive research and development effort designed to develop new products and new knowledge. The following costs were incurred during 2002 and are thought to be related to R & D activities; however, the accountant for Montesquieu Company is uncertain as to which costs are appropriately charged to research and development.

Machinery that will be used in R&D activities for the next six years, purchased on July 1, 2002	$240,000
Salaries for R&D personnel for 2002	126,000
Laboratory research costs	52,500
Costs associated with improving XR-33 (a high quality pain reliever)	34,000
Expenditures to support legal defense of lawsuits over Baldnomore (hair growth product)	116,000
Material and labor cost to design an oven to heat chemicals to a very high degree for testing purposes	87,000
Technical engineering support for production facility to move a new product to the manufacturing stage	23,000
Quality control efforts in the production of XR-33	28,500

Instructions:
Compute the amount of research and development expense Montesquieu Company should report for the year ending December 31, 2002.

*3. (S.O. 9) Milton Company is considering the acquisition of Spinoza Company on December 31, 2002. The current value of Spinoza's assets (excluding goodwill) is $300,000. Spinoza has obligations of $100,000 that would be assumed by Milton. Earnings during the past 5 years have remained rather stable at an average of $30,000 per year.

Instructions:
For each of the following assumptions calculate (A) the amount to be paid for goodwill and (B) the total amount to be paid for Spinoza Company.

a. Earnings are to be capitalized at 10% in arriving at the business worth.

b. A return of 8% is considered normal on net identifiable assets at their appraised value; excess earnings are to be capitalized at 10% in arriving at the value of goodwill.

c. A return of 8% is considered normal on net identifiable assets at their appraised value. Excess earnings are expected to continue for 8 years. Goodwill is to be valued by the present value method using a rate of 10%. (The present value of 8 annual payments of $1 providing a return of 10% is 5.335.)

*4. (S.O. 9) Locke Company has a net worth of $480,000 excluding goodwill at December 31, 2002. During the past five years, earnings of the company have totaled $278,000. Included in these earnings figures is a nonrecurring loss of $26,000, amortization of intangibles totaling $32,000, and an extraordinary gain of $43,000. The industry within which Locke operates considers a return of 10% of net worth to be normal for the industry. Locke determines that the average annual excess earnings is 14%.

Instructions:
Compute the price that Locke would be willing to accept from a prospective purchaser for the company.

SOLUTIONS TO REVIEW QUESTIONS AND EXERCISES

TRUE-FALSE

1. (F) In addition to lack of physical existence, the characteristics of an intangible asset are that they are not a financial instrument and are long-term in nature and subject to amortization.

2. (T)

3. (F) Costs incurred internally to create intangibles are generally expensed as incurred.

4. (T)

5. (F) According to *APB Opinion No. 17,* intangible assets must be amortized over a period not exceeding 40 years.

6. (T)

7. (F) A goodwill-type intangible may create some right or privilege, but it is not specifically identifiable.

8. (T)

9. (F) Long-term leases ordinarily provide that any improvements made to the leased property revert to the lessor at the end of the life of the lease. The lessee can make use of any improvements during the life of the lease, but they become the property of the lessor when the lease expires.

10. (F) A copyright is granted for the life of the creator plus 50 years and gives the owner, or heirs, the exclusive right to reproduce and sell an artistic or published work. However, the maximum period over which the cost of a copyright can be amortized is 40 years.

11. (T)

12. (F) Goodwill is recorded only when an entire business is purchased because goodwill is a going-concern valuation and cannot be separated from the business as a whole.

13. (F) When the master valuation approach is used to measure goodwill, it is considered to be the excess of the cost over the fair value of the identifiable net assets acquired.

14. (F) Goodwill should never be written off at the date of acquisition and the period of amortization should not exceed 40 years. Thus, goodwill should be written off over its useful life or 40 years, whichever is shorter.

15. (T)

16. (T)

17. (T)

18. (T)

19. (F) In distinguishing R & D costs from selling and administrative activities, the FASB excluded costs associated with acquisition, development, or improvement of a product from the definition of R & D activities. Performing a market survey for the purpose of improving product packaging is clearly a selling and administrative activity.

20. (F) Organization costs are to be expensed as incurred.

21. (F) General and administrative costs are only included in research and development costs if they are clearly related to research and development.

*22. (T)

*23. (F) If computer software costs are capitalized, the basis for amortization is the greater of (1) the ratio of current revenues to current and anticipated revenues (percent of revenue approach) or (2) the straight-line method over the remaining useful life of the asset (straight-line approach).

*24. (T)

*25. (F) The lower the discount rate, the higher the value of the goodwill. For example, excess earnings of $20,000 capitalized at a rate of 10% yields a goodwill valuation of $200,000 ($20,000 ÷ .10). If the same $20,000 is capitalized at a rate of 20%, the goodwill valuation is $100,000 ($20,000 ÷ .20).

MULTIPLE CHOICE

1. (A) Accounts receivable would be considered a financial instrument and therefore would not be classified as an intangible asset. B, C, and D are all examples of intangible assets.

2. (A) When intangible assets are amortized, the charges should be shown as expenses, and the credits should be made either to the appropriate asset accounts or to separate accumulated amortization accounts.

3. (C) The current classification of intangibles is either specifically identifiable or of the goodwill-type. Specifically identifiable means that costs associated with obtaining a given intangible asset can be identified as a part of the cost of that intangible asset.

4. (C) Intangible assets are amortized over their legal life or their useful life, whichever is shorter. Actions of competitors as well as renewal or extension provisions affect the useful life of an intangible asset. Salvage value is a concept related to the computation of depreciation on tangible fixed assets. Salvage value is not a factor used in determining useful life of an intangible.

5. (B) Intangible assets are generally amortized on a straight-line basis, although there is no reason why another systematic approach might not be employed if the firm demonstrates that another method is more appropriate.

6. (A) The reason for acquiring the patent on the competing product is to protect the original patent acquired on 1/15/93. The original patent will expire during 2013. Thus, the cost of the patent on the competing product should be amortized over 11 years, the time between its acquisition (2002) and the expiration of the original patent's useful life (2013).

7. (C) When a trademark or trade name is developed by a company, the costs associated with that development should be capitalized. The only cost that is not appropriately capitalized are costs related to research and development. The reason for this prohibition concerns the requirement of *FASB Statement No. 2* that research and development costs be expensed when incurred.

8. (D) A trademark is no different than any other intangible asset. The costs associated with the acquisition of a trademark are amortized over its useful life or 40 years, whichever is shorter.

9. (D) Leasehold improvements should be depreciated over the life of the improvement or the life of the lease, whichever is less. Since the repair facility has a useful life of 25 years and the lease is for a 40 year period, the facility should be depreciated over its useful life.

10. (D) During the first six years of the franchise useful life the amortization would be the cost ($125,000) divided by the 40 year maximum intangible amortization period. This would result in an annual charge to expense of $3,125 ($125,000/40) for the first six years (1996 through 2001). Thus, at the beginning of 2002, when the franchise was considered worthless, the book value of the franchise account would be $106,250 [$125,000 - ($3,125 X 6)]. When the franchise is deemed worthless, it should be written off immediately.

11. (C) *APB Opinion No. 17* states that intangible assets should be amortized over their useful lives. However, the amortization period should not exceed forty years. Therefore, Smith Corporation should record franchise amortization expense of $2,500 in 2001 ($100,000/40 years = $2,500).

12. (C) Goodwill is recorded only when an entire business is purchased because goodwill is a going-concern valuation and cannot be separated from the business as a whole. Goodwill generated internally should not be capitalized in the accounts because measuring the components of goodwill is simply too complex and associating any costs with future benefits is too difficult.

13. (D) Goodwill is an intangible asset that is amortized over a maximum of 40 years. The method used to compute the annual amortization charge is normally the straight-line method. However, another method may be selected if it is considered to provide a more relevant pattern in the write-off of goodwill.

14. (B) Goodwill is the difference between the fair market value of the net tangible and identifiable intangible assets and the purchase price of a business organization. It does not represent the entire purchase price nor is it an amount added to the purchase price to arrive at a master valuation. Also, there are many accounts that appear in the financial statements at their fair market value, so alternative D is not correct.

15. (B) The reason goodwill arises is because the future earnings potential of a purchased business is in excess of what would be considered normal. Thus, goodwill reflects the future positive results that were purchased. To write this amount off immediately would be inconsistent with the reason for its initial recording.

16. (C) *APB Opinion No. 16* takes the position that an excess of fair value over purchase price should be allocated to reduce proportionately the values assigned to noncurrent assets (except long-term investments in marketable securities) in determining their fair values. If the allocation reduces the noncurrent assets to zero value, the remainder of the excess over cost should be classified as a deferred credit and should be amortized systematically to revenue over the period estimated to be benefited but not in excess of 40 years.

17. (B) The general rules that apply to impairments of long-lived assets also apply to intangibles; however, goodwill impairments involve a grouping of net assets. In performing the review for recoverability, the sum of expected future net cash flows ($2,500,000) is less than the carrying amount of the net assets ($3,300,000); therefore an impairment loss should be measured and recognized. The impairment loss is the amount by which the carrying amount of the assets exceeds the fair value of the assets ($3,300,000 - $1,800,000 = $1,500,000). Where goodwill is associated with assets that are subject to impairment loss, the carrying amount of the associated goodwill should be eliminated before the carrying amounts of impaired long-lived assets and identifiable intangibles are reduced to their fair values.

18. (B) *FASB Statement No. 2* has standardized and simplified accounting practice in the area of R & D expenditures by requiring that all research and development costs be charged to expense when incurred. The obvious exception to this rule is when the R & D costs are contractually reimbursed.

19. (D) All R & D costs are charged to expense when incurred. Thus, the 2001 expenditures of $215,000 should be charged against 2001 income.

20. (A) R & D costs are expenditures made to develop new products or processes, to improve present products, and to discover new knowledge that may be valuable at some future date. The only alternative that does not fit the general classification of R & D expenditures is alternative A. Adapting existing capabilities to a specific requirement or need does not involve R & D.

21. (D) Organization costs are to be expensed as incurred; therefore, there should be no costs associated with the organization in 2002 that will be amortized in 2003.

*22. (D) Costs incurred in creating a computer software product should be charged to research and development expense when incurred until technological feasibility has been established for the product. Technological feasibility is established upon completion of a detailed program design or working model. Therefore, the subsequent costs incurred of $200,000 should be capitalized and amortized to current and future periods.

*23. (C) Companies are required to amortize based on the greater of (the ratio of current revenues to current and anticipated revenues (percent of revenue approach) or (2) the straight-line method over the remaining useful life of the asset (straight-line approach). The percent of revenue approach results in an amount of $400,000 ($2 million x $1 million/$5 million) and the straight-line approach results in an amount of $250,000 ($2 million x 1/8). Therefore, the greater amount of $400,000 is the amortization expense for the computer software in the current year.

*24. (A) Excess earning power is the difference between what the firm earns and what is normal for the industry. This extra earning power indicates that there are unidentifiable values (normally intangibles) that provide this increased earning power. Finding the value for goodwill is a matter of discounting these excess future earnings to the present.

*25. (C) Capitalizing excess earnings at 20% means that excess earnings would be divided by 20%. Thus, the computation would be: $14,500/.20 = $72,500.

REVIEW EXERCISES

PATENT ACCOUNT

	Date	Debit	Credit	
	1-1-94	72,000	7,200	Amortization 12-31-94 (a)
			7,200	Amortization 12-31-95
			7,200	Amortization 12-31-96
			7,200	Amortization 12-31-97
Infringement Suit	1-98	9,000		
(b) Balance	1-98	$52,200	8,700	Amortization 12-31-98 (c)
Patent Purchased		25,000		
(d) Balance	1-99	$68,500	6,850	Amortization 12-31-99 (e)
			6,850	Amortization 12-31-00
			6,850	Amortization 12-31-01
			3,425	Amortization 7-1-02
		$44,525	44,525	Loss on 7-1-02 (f)

(a) $72,000 ÷ 10 = $7,200
(c) $52,200 ÷ 6 = $8,700
(e) $68,500 ÷ 10 = $6,850

2. Depreciation of equipment to be used for six years in R&D activities

($240,000/6) /2 =	$ 20,000
Salaries for R&D personnel	126,000
Laboratory research costs	52,500
Materials & labor for oven design	87,000
Engineering support for production facility	23,000
Total R&D expense for 2002	$308,500

*3. a. (A) $30,000 ÷ .10 = $300,000 - $200,000 = $100,000
(B) $200,000 + $100,000 = $300,000

b. (A) Normal earnings: $200,000 x .08 = $16,000
Excess earnings: $ 30,000 - $16,000 = $14,000
$14,000 ÷ .10 = $140,000
(B) $200,000 + $140,000 = $340,000

c. (A)

Excess earnings:	$14,000
Present value:	5.335
Goodwill:	$74,690

(B) $200,000 + $74,690 = $274,690

*4.

Earnings past 5 years	$278,000
Less Extraordinary gains	43,000
	235,000
Plus nonrecurring loss	26,000
Adjusted 5-year earnings	$261,000
Average earnings ($261,000 ÷ 5)	$ 52,200
Normal earnings ($480,000 ÷ .10)	$ 48,000
Excess annual earnings	$ 4,200

Excess earnings capitalized at 14%:
$4,200 ÷.14 = $30,000 (Goodwill)
Selling price of business: $480,000 + $30,000 = $510,000

13

Current Liabilities and Contingencies

CHAPTER STUDY OBJECTIVES

1. Define current liabilities and describe how they are valued.
2. Identify the nature and types of current liabilities.
3. Explain the classification issues of short-term debt expected to be refinanced.
4. Identify types of employee-related liabilities.
5. Identify the criteria used to account for and disclose gain and loss contingencies.
6. Explain the accounting for different types of contingent liabilities.
7. Indicate how current liabilities and contingencies are presented and disclosed.

*8. Compute employee bonuses under differing arrangements.

CHAPTER REVIEW

1. Chapter 13 presents a discussion of the nature and measurement of items classified on the balance sheet as current liabilities. Attention is focused on the mechanics involved in recording current liabilities and financial statement disclosure requirements. Also included is a discussion concerning the identification and reporting of contingent liabilities.

Current Liabilities

2. (S.O. 1) In general, liabilities involve future disbursements of assets or services. According to the FASB, a liability has three essential characteristics: **(a)** it is a present obligation that entails settlement by probable future transfer or use of cash, goods, or services; **(b)** it is an unavoidable obligation; and **(c)** the transaction or other event creating the obligation has already occurred. Liabilities are classified on the balance sheet as **current** obligations or **long-term** obligations. **Current liabilities** are those obligations whose liquidation is reasonably expected to require use of existing resources **classified as current assets** or the creation of other current liabilities.

3. The relationship between current assets and current liabilities is an important factor in the analysis of a company's financial condition. Thus, the definition of current liabilities for a particular industry will depend upon the time period (**operating cycle or one year, whichever is longer**) used in defining current assets in that industry.

* *Note: All asterisked (*) items relate to material contained in the Appendix to the chapter.*

Accounts Payable

4. (S.O. 2) **Accounts payable** represents obligations owed to others for goods, supplies, and services purchased on open account. These obligations, commonly known as **trade accounts payable,** should be recorded to coincide with the receipt of the goods or at the time title passes to the purchaser. Attention must be paid to transactions occurring near the end of one accounting period and at the beginning of the next to ascertain that the record of goods received (inventory) is in agreement with the liability (accounts payable) and that both are recorded in the proper period.

Notes Payable

5. **Notes payable** are written promises to pay a certain sum of money on a specified future date and may arise from sales, financing, or other transactions. Notes may be classified as short-term or long-term, depending on the payment due date.

6. Short-term notes payable resulting from borrowing funds from a lending institution may be interest-bearing or zero-interest-bearing. Interest-bearing notes payable are reported as a liability at the face amount of the note along with any accrued interest payable. A zero-interest-bearing note does not explicitly state an interest rate on the face of the note. Interest is the difference between the present value of the note and the face value of the note at maturity. For example, Burke Co. borrowed $138,000 from a bank by giving the bank a one-year, zero-interest-bearing note that has a face amount of $150,000. The entry to record this transaction on Burke's books would be as follows:

Cash	138,000	
Discount on Notes Payable	12,000	
Notes Payable		150,000

The balance in the Discount on Notes Payable account would be deducted from the Notes Payable account on the balance sheet.

7. The currently maturing portion of long-term debts may be classified as a current liability. When a portion of long-term debt is so classified, it is assumed that the amount will be paid within the next 12 months out of funds classified as current assets.

Refinancing

8. (S.O. 3) Certain short-term obligations expected to be refinanced on a long-term basis should be **excluded** from current liabilities. Under *FASB Statement No. 6,* a short-term obligation is excluded from current liabilities if **(a)** it is intended to be refinanced on a long-term basis and **(b)** the ability to accomplish the refinancing is reasonably demonstrated. Both conditions must exist before the item can be excluded from current liabilities. Evidence as to the **intent** and **ability** to refinance usually comes from **actually refinancing** or **existing refinancing agreements.**

Dividends Payable

9. **Cash dividends payable** are classified as current liabilities during the period subsequent to declaration and prior to payment. Once declared, a cash dividend is a binding obligation of a corporate entity payable to its stockholders. Stock dividends distributable are reported in the stockholders' equity section when declared.

Returnable Deposits

10. When **returnable deposits** are received from customers or employees, a liability corresponding to the asset received is recorded. The classification of these items as current or noncurrent liabilities is dependent on the time involved between the date of the deposit and the termination of the relationship that required the deposit.

Unearned Revenues

11. A company sometimes receives cash in advance of the performance of services or issuance of merchandise. Such transactions result in a credit to a deferred or unearned revenue account classified as a current liability on the balance sheet. As claims of this nature are redeemed, the liability is reduced and a revenue account is credited.

Taxes

12. Current tax laws require most business enterprises to collect sales tax from customers during the year and periodically remit these collections to the appropriate governmental unit. In such instances the enterprise is acting as a collection agency for a third party. If tax amounts due to governmental units are on hand at the financial statement date, they are reported as current liabilities.

13. To illustrate the collection and remittance of sales tax by a company, assume that Bentham Company recorded sales for the period of $230,000. Further assume that Bentham is subject to a 7% sales tax collection that must be remitted to the government. If Bentham recorded the gross amount of sales and remits the required tax at the end of the period, then the $230,000 of sales includes the 7% sales tax. Thus, dividing the $230,000 by 1.07 will yield the amount of sales for the period or $214,953.27. If we subtract this amount from the recorded sales figure we arrive at the amount of sales tax due the taxing unit for the period ($230,000 - $214,953.27 = $15,046.73). The entry to record the sales tax liability is:

Sales	15,046.73	
Sales Tax Payable		15,046.73

When payment is made the Sales Tax Payable account would be debited and Cash would be credited.

14. Local government units generally collect revenue through real and personal property taxes. Such taxes should be recorded by the taxpayer as a monthly accrual during the period in which the taxes are used by the governmental unit to provide benefits to the property owner.

15. A corporation should estimate and record the amount of income tax liability as computed per its tax return. Chapter 20 discusses in detail the complexities involved in accounting for the difference between taxable income under the tax laws and accounting income under generally accepted accounting principles.

Employee-Related Liabilities

16. (S.O. 4) Amounts owed to employees for salaries or wages of an accounting period are reported as a current liability. The following items are related to employee compensation and often reported as current liabilities:

a. Payroll deductions.
b. Compensated absences.
c. Postretirement benefits.
d. Bonuses.

17. The following illustrates the concept of accrued liabilities related to payroll deductions. Assume Mill Company has a weekly payroll of $25,000 that is entirely subject to F.I.C.A. and Medicare (7.65%), federal unemployment tax (.8%), and state unemployment tax (3%). Also, income tax withholding amounts to $3,300, and employee credit union deductions for the week total $975. Two entries are necessary to record the payroll, the first for the wages paid to employees and the second for the employer's payroll taxes. The two entries are as follows:

Account	Debit	Credit
Wages and Salaries	25,000	
Withholding Taxes Payable		3,300
F.I.C.A. Taxes Payable		1,913
Credit Union Payments Payable		975
Cash		18,812
Payroll Tax Expense	2,863	
F.I.C.A. Taxes Payable		1,913
Federal Unemployment Tax Payable		200
State Unemployment Tax Payable		750

18. **Compensated absences** are absences from employment—such as vacation, illness, and holidays—for which it is expected that employees will be paid anyway. In connection with compensated absences, **vested rights** exist when an employer has an obligation to make payment to an employee even if that employee terminates. **Accumulated rights** are those rights that can be carried forward to future periods if not used in the period in which earned.

19. *FASB No. 43* requires that a liability be accrued for the cost of compensation for future absences if **all** of the following conditions are met: **(a)** the employer's obligation relating to employees' rights to receive compensation for future absences is attributable to employees' services already rendered, **(b)** the obligation relates to rights that vest or accumulate, **(c)** payment of the compensation is probable, and **(d)** the amount can be reasonably estimated. If an employer fails to accrue a liability because of a failure to meet only condition (d), that fact should be disclosed. The expense and related liability for compensated absences should be recognized in the year earned by employees. Thus, if employees are entitled to a two week vacation after working one year, the vacation pay is considered to be earned during the first year. The entry to accrue the accumulated vacation pay at the end of year one would include a debit to Wages Expense and a credit to Vacation Wages Payable.

20. The accounting and reporting standards for postretirement benefit payments are complex and discussed extensively in Chapter 21.

21. Bonus agreements are common incentives established by companies for certain key executives or employees. In many cases, the bonus is dependent upon the amount of income earned by the company. However, because the bonus is an expense used in determining net income, it must be deducted before net income can be computed. Thus, we end up with the need to solve an algebraic formula to compute the bonus. In addition, when the concept of income taxes is added to the formula, calculation of the bonus requires solving simultaneous equations. Appendix 13-A covers the recording of bonuses in greater detail.

Contingent Liabilities

22. (S.O. 5) A contingency is an existing condition, situation, or set of circumstances involving uncertainty as to possible gain (gain contingency) or loss (loss contingency) to an enterprise that will ultimately be resolved when one or more future events occur or fail to occur. Gain contingencies are not recorded and are disclosed in the notes only when the probabilities are high that a gain contingency will be realized.

23. A **contingent liability** is an obligation that is dependent upon the occurrence or nonoccurrence of one or more future events to resolve its status. When a loss contingency exists, the likelihood that the future event or events will confirm the incurrence of a liability is characterized as **probable, reasonably possible,** or **remote.**

24. If the realization of a loss contingency that could result in a liability is **probable** (likely to occur) and the amount of the loss can be **reasonably estimated,** a liability exists. This liability should be recorded along with a charge to income in the period in which the determination was made. It is important to note that **both** conditions listed above must be met before a liability can be recorded. If a loss is either probable **or** estimable, **but not both,** and if there is at least a reasonable possibility that a liability may have been incurred, then the financial statements should include the following footnote disclosures: **(a)** the nature of the contingency, and **(b)** an estimate of the possible loss, range of loss, or indication that an estimate cannot be made.

Litigation

25. (S.O. 6) When a company is threatened by legal action **(litigation, claims, and assessments)**, the recording of a liability will depend upon certain factors. Among the more prevalent are: **(a)** the period in which the underlying cause for action occurred, **(b)** the degree of probability of an unfavorable outcome, and **(c)** the ability to make a reasonable estimate of the amount of loss.

Warranties

26. A **warranty** (product guarantee) represents a promise by a seller to a buyer to make good on any deficiency of quantity, quality or performance specifications in a product. Product warranty costs may be accounted for using the **cash basis method** or the **accrual basis method.** The cash basis method must be used when (1) it is not probable that a liability has been incurred or (2) the amount of the liability cannot be reasonably estimated. Under the cash basis method, warranty costs are charged to expense as they are incurred (when they are paid by the seller). No liability is recorded under the cash basis method for future costs arising from warranties.

27. The accrual method includes two different accounting treatments: (a) the **expense warranty approach** and (b) the **sales warranty approach.** The expense warranty method is the generally accepted method for financial accounting purposes and should be used whenever the warranty is an integral and inseparable part of the sale and is viewed as a loss contingency. The sales warranty method defers a certain percentage of the original sales price until some future time when actual costs are incurred or the warranty expires. Under the expense warranty method the estimated warranty expense is recorded in the year in which the item subject to the warranty is sold. When the warranty is honored in a subsequent period, the liability is reduced by the amount of the expenditure to repair the item. For example, if 200 units are sold and the estimated warranty cost is $300 per unit, the following entry would be made for the warranty:

Warranty Expense	60,000	
Estimated Liability Under Warranties		60,000

Actual expenditures made to honor the warranty would debit the liability account and credit cash.

Premiums

28. If a company offers premiums to customers in return for coupons, a liability should normally be recognized at year-end for outstanding premium offers expected to be redeemed. The liability should be recorded along with a charge to a premium expense account.

Environmental Liabilities

29. Presently companies infrequently record any liability for potential environmental liabilities. The SEC has argued that if the amount of an environmental liability is within a range and no amount within the range is the best estimate, then management should recognize the minimum amount of the range.

Self-Insurance

30. Self-insurance is not *insurance*, but risk assumption. The conditions for accrual stated in *FASB Statement No. 5* are not satisfied prior to the occurrence of the event.

Presentation and Analysis of Current Liabilities

31. (S.O. 7) Current liabilities are reported in the financial statements at their maturity value. Present value techniques are not normally used in measuring current liabilities because of the short time periods involved. Current liabilities are normally listed at the beginning of the liabilities and stockholders' equity section of the balance sheet. Within the current liability section the accounts may be listed in order of maturity, in descending order of amount, or in order of liquidation preference.

32. Short-term obligations expected to be refinanced may be shown on the balance sheet in captions distinct from both current liabilities and long-term debt such as "Interim Debt," "Short-term Debt Expected to be Refinanced," or "Intermediate Debt." If a short-term obligation is excluded from current liabilities because of refinancing, a footnote to the financial statements should include: **(a)** a general description of the financing agreement, **(b)** the terms of any new obligation incurred or to be incurred, and **(c)** the terms of any equity security issued or to be issued.

33. Two ratios often used to analyze current liabilities are the **current ratio** and the **acid-test ratio.**

*34. (S.O. 8) **The appendix, Computation of Employees' Bonuses**, discusses in detail the amount of bonus expense that should be recorded by companies.

GLOSSARY

Accounts payable. Balances owed to others for goods, supplies, or services purchased on open account.

Accrual basis method of warranty costs (expense warranty approach). Warranty costs are charged to operating expense in the year of sale.

Accumulated rights. Obligations by an employer to an employee that can be carried forward to future period if not used in the period in which earned.

Bonus. Compensation to certain or all officers and employees in addition to their regular salary or wage.

Cash basis method of warranty costs. Warranty costs are charged to expense as they are incurred.

Cash dividends payable. An amount to be paid in cash owed by a corporation to its stockholders as a result of board of directors' authorization.

Cash rebate. A buyer receives an amount of cash by returning the store receipt, a rebate coupon, and Universal Product Code to the manufacturer.

Compensated absences. Absences from employment, such as vacation, illness, and holidays, for which employees are paid anyway.

Contingency. An existing condition, situation, or set of circumstances involving uncertainty as to possible gain (gain contingency) or loss (loss contingency) to an enterprise that will ultimately be resolved when one or more future events occur or fail to occur.

Contingent liabilities. Obligations that are dependent upon the occurrence or nonoccurrence of one or more future events to confirm either the amount payable, the payee, the date payable, or its existence.

Current liabilities. Obligations whose liquidation is reasonably expected to require use of existing resources properly classified as current assets, or the creation of other current liabilities.

Current maturities of long-term debt. The portion of bonds, mortgage notes, and other long-term indebtedness that matures within the next fiscal year.

Discount on notes payable. The difference between the present value of a zero-interest-bearing note and the face value of the note at maturity.

Federal Insurance Contribution Act (FICA) tax.	A tax by the federal government levied on both the employer and the employee based on the employee's wages used to provide old-age, survivor, and disability insurance (O.A.S.D.I.).
Hospital Insurance tax.	A tax by the federal government levied on both the employer and the employee based on the employee's wages used to provide hospital and other institutional services (Medicare).
Income tax.	A tax by a government authority on the annual income of an entity.
Income tax withholding.	The withholding from the pay of each employee the applicable income tax due on those wages as required by a government authority.
Liabilities.	Probable future sacrifices of economic benefits arising from present obligations of a particular entity to transfer assets or provide services to other entities in the future as a result of past transactions or events.
Notes payable.	Written promises to pay a certain sum of money on a specified future date and may arise from sales, financing, or other transactions.
Operating cycle.	The period of time elapsing between the acquisition of goods and services involved in the manufacturing process and the final cash realization resulting from sales and subsequent collections.
Preferred dividends in arrears.	Accumulated but undeclared dividends on cumulative preferred stock.
Premiums.	Silverware, dishes, a small appliance, a toy, or other goods given to customers in exchange for boxtops, certificates, coupons, labels or wrappers.
Printed coupons.	Items that can be redeemed for a cash discount on items purchased.
Probable.	The future event or events are likely to occur.
Property tax.	A tax by a government authority based on the assessed value of both real and certain personal property.
Reasonably possible.	The chance of the future event or events occurring is more than remote but less than likely.
Remote.	The chance of the future event or events occurring is slight.

Returnable cash deposits.	Deposits received by a company from customers to guarantee performance of a contract or service or as guarantees to cover payment of expected future obligations.
Sales tax.	A tax by a government authority on the transfer of tangible personal property and certain services.
Sales warranty approach.	The seller recognizes separately the sale of the product with the manufacturer's warranty and the sale of the extended warranty.
Social security tax.	The combination of Federal Insurance Contribution Act (FICA) tax and Hospital Insurance tax.
Unearned revenues.	Cash received by a company in exchange for future goods or services.
Unemployment tax.	A tax by a government authority on the employer based on the employee's wages used to provide unemployment insurance.
Vested right.	The obligation by an employer to make payment to an employee even if his or her employment has been terminated.
Warranty (product guarantee)	A promise made by a seller to a buyer to make good on a deficiency of quantity, quality, or performance in a product.
Zero-interest-bearing note.	A note that does not explicitly state an interest rate on the face of the note. Interest is still charged, however, because the borrower is required at maturity to pay back an amount greater than the cash received at the issuance date.

CHAPTER OUTLINE

Fill in the outline presented below.

(S.O. 1) Liability

(S.O. 2) Current Liability

Types of Current Liabilities

Accounts payable

Notes payable

Interest-bearing note

Zero-interest-bearing note

Current maturities of long-term debt

(S.O. 3) Short-term obligations expected to be refinanced

Dividends payable

Returnable deposits

Chapter Outline *(continued)*

Unearned revenues

Sales taxes

Property taxes

Income taxes payable

(S.O. 4) Employee-related liabilities

- Payroll deductions
    - Social security taxes
    - Unemployment taxes
    - Income tax withholding
- Compensated absences
- Postretirement benefits
- Bonus agreements

Chapter Outline *(continued)*

(S.O. 5) Contingencies

Accounting for Loss Contingencies

Litigation, Claims, and Assessments

Guarantee and Warranty Costs

Premiums and Coupons

Environmental Liabilities

Risk of Loss Due to Lack of Insurance Coverage

(S.O. 7) Presentation and Analysis of Current Liabilities in the Financial Statements

*(S.O. 8) Computation of Employees' Bonuses

REVIEW QUESTIONS AND EXERCISES

TRUE-FALSE

Indicate whether each of the following is true (T) or false (F) in the space provided.

_____ 1. (S.O. 1) The only requirement for an obligation to be classified as a current liability is that it be liquidated within the operating cycle or one year, whichever is longer.

_____ 2. (S.O. 2) Notes payable are only classified as short-term.

_____ 3. (S.O. 2) When a company issues a zero-interest-bearing note, the difference between the face amount of the note and the cash proceeds is most appropriately recorded as a discount on notes payable.

_____ 4. (S.O. 2) Discount on Notes Payable is an adjunct account to Notes Payable and therefore is added to Notes Payable on the balance sheet.

_____ 5. (S.O. 2) The currently maturing portion of a serial bond should not be classified as a current liability if it will be paid out of a long-term asset such as a sinking fund.

_____ 6. (S.O. 3) A short-term obligation expected to be refinanced may be excluded from current liabilities if (a) a company intends to refinance the obligation on a long-term basis, and (b) the company demonstrates an ability to consummate the refinancing.

_____ 7. (S.O. 3) When refinancing on a long-term basis is expected to be accomplished through the issuance of equity securities, it is not appropriate to include the short-term obligation in owners' equity.

_____ 8. (S.O. 3) If a short-term obligation is excluded from current liabilities because of refinancing, a footnote to the financial statements should be included disclosing the particulars of the refinancing arrangement.

_____ 9. (S.O. 3) Preferred dividends in arrears should be recognized as a liability in the balance sheet.

_____ 10. (S.O. 3) A stock dividend distributable is classified as a long-term liability because it will not be liquidated using current assets.

_____ 11. (S.O. 3) A current liability results when a company collects sales taxes from customers.

_____ 12. (S.O. 4) The amount of unremitted employee and employer social security tax on gross wages paid should be reported by the employer as a current liability.

_____ 13. (S.O. 4) *FASB No. 43* requires that a liability always be accrued for the cost of compensation for future absences of full-time employees.

_____ 14. (S.O. 4) Vested rights exist when an employer has an obligation to make payment to an employee but not if the employee is terminated.

_____ 15. (S.O. 4) If sick pay benefits accumulate but do not vest, accrual is permitted but not required.

_____ 16. (S.O. 5) The term "loss contingency," as used in accounting, refers to situations that result in a liability after the passage of a specified period of time.

_____ 17. (S.O. 5) If a loss contingency is likely to occur and its amount can be reasonably estimated, it should be recorded in the accounts.

_____ 18. (S.O. 6) One factor to consider in determining whether a liability should be recorded with respect to threatened litigation is the effect such a liability will have on a reported financial condition.

_____ 19. (S.O. 6) To report a loss and a liability in the financial statements, the cause for litigation must have occurred on or before the date of the financial statements.

_____ 20. (S.O. 6) Use of the cash basis method in accounting for product warranty costs is required when a company is unable to make a reasonable estimate of the amount of warranty obligations at the time of sale.

_____ 21. (S.O. 6) When a company offers premiums to its customers in return for coupons, the cost of the premiums should be charged to expense when the premiums are distributed to customers.

_____ 22. (S.O. 6) The number of outstanding premium offers that will be presented for redemption must be estimated in order to reflect the existing current liability and to match costs with revenues.

_____ 23. (S.O. 6) When there is an absence of insurance, a firm should estimate the amount of possible future losses and record a liability at the date of the financial statements.

_____ 24. (S.O. 7) Liabilities are generally measured by the present value of the future outlay of cash required to liquidate them.

_____ 25. (S.O. 7) Because current liabilities tend to be liquidated within a short period of time, present value techniques are not normally applied.

MULTIPLE CHOICE

Select the best answer for each of the following items and enter the corresponding letter in the space provided.

_____ 1. (S.O. 1) A liability has three essential characteristics, which of the following is not one of them?

A. It is a present obligation that entails settlement by probable future transfer or use of cash, goods, or services.
B. The obligation must be liquidated using cash, goods, or services that were earned by the entity in the performance of their normal business operation.
C. The liability must be an unavoidable obligation.
D. The transaction or other event creating the obligation must have already occurred.

_____ 2. (S.O. 2) Current liabilities are:

A. liabilities that are due and payable on the balance sheet date.
B. liabilities that may be paid out of any asset pool accumulated by the enterprise as long as payment is due within one year.
C. due within one year or one operating cycle, whichever is longer.
D. void of notes payable, as notes are always long-term.

_____ 3. (S.O. 2) On October 1, 2001, a company borrowed cash and signed a one-year, interest-bearing note on which both the principal and interest are payable on October 1, 2002. How will the note payable and the related interest be classified in the December 31, 2001, balance sheet?

	Note Payable	Accrued Interest
A.	Current liability	Noncurrent liability
B.	Noncurrent liability	Current liability
C.	Current liability	Current liability
D.	Noncurrent liability	Noncurrent liability

_____ 4. (S.O. 2) The Diana Co. issues a $208,000 6-month, zero-interest-bearing note to the Tang National Bank. The present value of the note is $200,000. The entry to record this transaction by Diana Co. would include:

A. a credit to Notes Payable of $200,000.
B. a debit to Discount on Notes Payable of $8,000.
C. a credit to Discount on Notes Payable of $8,000.
D. a debit to cash of $208,000.

_____ 5. (S.O. 2) The currently maturing portion of long-term debt should be classified as a current liability if:

A. the debt is to be converted into capital stock.
B. the debt is to be refinanced on a long-term basis.
C. the funds used to liquidate it are currently classified as a long-term investment on the balance sheet.
D. the portion so classified will be liquidated within one year using current assets.

_____ 6. (S.O. 3) An enterprise is required to exclude a short-term obligation from current liabilities if it intends to refinance the obligation on a long-term basis and:

A. the enterprise can demonstrate the ability to consummate the refinancing.
B. the obligation is not a part of normal operations.
C. it can demonstrate that a negative effect on working capital will result if it is not reclassified.
D. the interest rate on the long-term obligation is not above the prime rate.

_____ 7. (S.O. 3) Which of the following would not constitute evidence concerning the ability to consummate the refinancing of a short-term obligation?

A. Actual refinancing after the balance sheet date by issuance of a long-term obligation.
B. A statement by the board of directors that refinancing is inevitable.
C. Entering into a financing agreement that clearly permits refinancing on a long-term basis with terms that are readily determinable.
D. Actual refinancing after the balance sheet date by issuance of equity securities.

_____ 8. (S.O. 3) Hegel Corporation has $1,500,000 of short-term debt it expects to retire with proceeds from the sale of 50,000 shares of common stock. If the stock is sold for $20 per share subsequent to the balance sheet date, but before the balance sheet is issued, what amount of short-term debt could be excluded from current liabilities?

A. $1,000,000.
B. $1,500,000.
C. $ 500,000.
D. $ 0.

_____ 9. (S.O. 3) If a short-term obligation is excluded from current liabilities because of refinancing, the footnote to the financial statements describing this event should include all of the following information except:

A. a general description of the financing arrangement.
B. the terms of the new obligation incurred or to be incurred.
C. the terms of any equity security issued or to be issued.
D. the number of financing institutions that refused to refinance the debt, if any.

Items 10 and 11 refer to the following information:

The June Company, which has its fiscal year the same as the calendar year, receives its property tax bill in April each year. The fiscal year for the city and county in which June Company is located begins on April 1 and ends on the following March 31. Property taxes of $48,000 are assessed against June Company property on January 1, 2001, and become a lien on April 1, 2001. Tax bills are sent out in April and are payable in equal installments on June 1 and September 1. June Company has determined that it will recognize property tax expense in the same period in which the taxes are used by the city and county to provide benefits to the property owner and June Company accrues taxes on a monthly basis.

_____ 10. (S.O. 3) The entry by June Company on April 1, 2001 should include:

A. No entry is required.
B. A credit to Property Taxes Payable of $48,000.
C. A credit to Property Taxes Payable of $36,000.
D. A credit to Property Taxes Payable of $12,000.

_____ 11. (S.O. 3) The monthly expense accrual for June Company at April 30, 2001 should include:

A. No entry is required.
B. A credit to Property Tax Payable of $4,000.
C. A debit to Prepaid Property Taxes of $8,000.
D. A debit to Property Tax Expense of $8,000.

_____ 12. (S.O. 4) Williams Co., which has a taxable payroll of $300,000, is subject to the FUTA tax of 6.2% and a state contribution rate of 5.5%. However, because of stable employment experience, the company's state rate has been reduced to 2%. What is the total amount of federal and state unemployment tax for Williams Co.?

A. $35,100
B. $24,600
C. $12,000
D. $ 8,400

_____ 13. (S.O. 4) In accounting for compensated absences, a company following the guidance in FASB Statement No. 43 would account for the liability using the:

	Cash Basis	Accrual Basis
A.	Yes	Yes
B.	Yes	No
C.	No	Yes
D.	No	No

_____ 14. (S.O. 4) In accounting for compensated absences, the difference between vested rights and accumulated rights is:

A. vested rights are normally for a longer period of employment than are accumulated rights.
B. vested rights are not contingent upon an employee's future service.
C. vested rights are a legal and binding obligation on the company, whereas accumulated rights expire at the end of the accounting period in which they arose.
D. vested rights carry a stipulated dollar amount that is owed to the employee; accumulated rights do not represent monetary compensation.

_____ 15. (S.O. 5) A contingency is defined by *FASB Statement No. 5* as:

A. an existing condition, situation, or set of circumstances involving uncertainty as to possible gain or loss to an enterprise that will ultimately be resolved when one or more future events occur or fail to occur.
B. an existing condition, situation, or set of circumstances involving uncertainty as to a possible loss to an enterprise that will ultimately be resolved when one or more future events occur or fail to occur.
C. an event that will result in the requirement to record a liability if it can be shown that an asset is in danger of being lost to the enterprise and the company has no ability to avoid the loss.
D. an uncertain event that must have a reasonable chance of occurrence and the amount must be reasonably determinable by the company.

_____ 16. (S.O. 5) Which of the following loss contingencies is normally accrued?

A. Pending or threatened litigation.
B. General or unspecified business risk.
C. Obligations related to product warranties.
D. Risk of property loss due to fire.

_____ 17. (S.O. 5) With respect to the following loss contingencies, would a liability normally be accrued or not accrued?

	Loss Related to Receivable Collections	**Loss Related to Product Warranties**
A.	Accrued	Not Accrued
B.	Not Accrued	Accrued
C.	Not Accrued	Not Accrued
D.	Accrued	Accrued

_____ 18. (S.O. 6) Marx Company becomes aware of a lawsuit after the date of the financial statements, but before they are issued. A loss and related liability should be reported in the financial statements if the amount can be reasonably estimated, and unfavorable outcome is highly probable, and:

A. the Marx Company admits guilt.
B. the court will decide the case within one year.
C. the damages appear to be material.
D. the cause for action occurred during the accounting period covered by the financial statements.

_____ 19. (S.O. 6) If a loss is either probable or estimable, but not both, and if there is at least a reasonable possibility that a liability may have been incurred, the proper accounting treatment would be reflected by which of the following?

A. Record the loss and the related liability, but at an amount that is significantly conservative.

B. Record the loss and the related liability, but indicate in a footnote to the financial statements that this loss may not occur because one of the criteria may not be met.

C. Disclose in the footnotes to the financial statements (1) the nature of the contingency, and (2) an estimate of the possible loss or range of loss or a statement that an estimate cannot be made.

D. Do not record the contingency or make mention of it in the financial statements because it lacks meeting the required criteria.

_____ 20. (S.O. 6) During 2001 Wannstedt Co. introduced a new line of machines that carry a three-year warranty against manufacturer's defects. Based on industry experience, warranty costs are estimated at 2% of sales in the year of sale, 4% in the year after sale, and 6% in the second year after sale. Sales and actual warranty expenditures for the first three-year period were as follows:

	Sales	Actual Warranty Expenditures
2001	$ 200,000	$ 3,000
2002	500,000	15,000
2003	700,000	45,000
	$1,400,000	$63,000

What amount should Wannstedt report as a liability at December 31, 2003?

A. $ 0
B. $ 5,000
C. $ 68,000
D. $105,000

_____ 21. (S.O. 6) Nietzsche Corn Flakes Company offers its customers a silver cereal spoon if they send in 5 boxtops from Nietzsche Corn Flakes boxes and $1.00. The Company estimates that 75% of the boxtops will be redeemed. In 2002 the Company sold 450,000 boxes of Corn Flakes and customers redeemed 220,000 boxtops receiving 44,000 spoons. If the spoons cost Nietzsche Company $2.50 each, how much liability for outstanding premiums should be recorded at the end of 2002?

A. $23,500
B. $35,250
C. $58,750
D. $82,250

_____ 22. (S.O. 6) Use of the accrual method in accounting for product warranty costs:

A. is required for federal income tax purposes.

B. is frequently justified on the basis of expediency when warranty costs are immaterial.

C. finds the expense account being charged when the seller performs in compliance with the warranty.

D. represents accepted practice and should be used whenever the warranty is an integral and inseparable part of the sale.

_____ 23. (S.O. 6) Wilson Company is involved in a litigation suit concerning the clean-up of old underground oil storage tanks on property it sold to a housing development company five years ago. The attorneys for Wilson Company cannot give a best estimate for the probable liability; however, the attorneys state that the liability to Wilson Company will probably fall within a range of $2 million to $10 million. According to the SEC, what should Wilson Company record with regards to this environmental liability?

A. No entry is required.
B. A loss and liability of $10 million.
C. A loss and liability of $6 million.
D. A loss and liability of $2 million.

_____ 24. (S.O. 7) Which of the following is not acceptable treatment for the presentation of current liabilities?

A. Listing current liabilities in order of maturity.
B. Listing current liabilities according to amount.
C. Offsetting current liabilities against assets that are to be applied to their liquidation.
D. Showing current liabilities immediately below current assets to obtain a presentation of working capital.

_____ *25. (S.O. 8) The controller of De Tocqueville Corporation is entitled to a bonus of 10% of net income after bonus and tax deductions. If net income before tax and bonus amounts to $80,000 and the tax rate is 40%, what amount of bonus can the controller expect to receive?

A. $3,000.
B. $4,528.
C. $5,106.
D. $8,000.

REVIEW EXERCISES

1. (S.O. 2) The following transactions were entered into by the Dewey Appliance Company during the month of December.

A. On December 6, Dewey received a deposit from Heidegger Company for a refrigerator to be used at a charity cookout. The deposit of $3,000 will be returned when the refrigerator is returned, most likely in early January.
B. The Company recorded cash sales of $621,000 during December. This amount includes 8% sales tax that must be remitted to the state by the 15th of the following month.
C. On December 10, the Company borrowed $100,000 from the Strauss Company. The loan carries a 12% interest rate, is due in one year, and interest is due when the note is paid.
D. On December 15, the Company purchased a delivery truck for $45,000, paying $10,000 in cash and signing a one-year, 15% note for the balance.

Instructions:

a. Prepare journal entries for the transactions listed above.

b. Assuming Dewey's year-end is December 31, prepare adjusting journal entries for the transactions which require adjustment.

a.

General Journal J1

Date	Account Title	Debit	Credit

b.

General Journal J1

Date	Account Title	Debit	Credit

2. (S.O. 6) Husserl Company included a coupon in each box of its cereal. For every 10 coupons returned by a customer, Husserl offered a silver spoon. Each spoon costs Husserl 75 cents. During the first year of the offer, Husserl sold 500,000 boxes of cereal. The company estimated that 80% of the coupons would be redeemed. Husserl distributed 28,000 spoons during the year.

Instructions:

a. Compute the premium expense for the first year.
b. Compute the amount of estimated liability that Husserl should show on its year-end balance sheet for unredeemed coupons.

a. and b.

3. (S.O. 6) Herren Corporation manufactures CB radios. Each radio is sold with a two-year unconditional warranty against defects. During 2002, 280 radios were sold for $150 each. The company estimates that the warranty cost will average $20 per unit. The actual warranty costs incurred in 2002 amounted to $2,350.

Instructions:
Prepare the journal entries for the sale of CBs, the estimated warranty cost, and the actual warranty cost incurred.

General Journal

J1

Date	Account Title	Debit	Credit

*4. (S.O. 8) Lopez Corporation has a bonus agreement with its sales staff. Salespersons with more than 5 years of service share a bonus of 20% of net income after deducting income taxes but before deducting the bonus. Salespersons with less than 5 years of service share a bonus of 10% of net income after deducting income taxes and their bonus. Net income before taxes and bonus is $250,000; Lopez Corporation has an income tax rate of 40%.

Instructions:

a. Compute the amount of the bonus to be shared by the salespersons with more than 5 years of service.

b. Compute the amount of the bonus to be shared by the salespersons with less than 5 years of service.

a.

b.

SOLUTIONS TO REVIEW QUESTIONS AND EXERCISES

TRUE-FALSE

1. (F) In addition to the "operating cycle or one year, whichever is longer" criterion, one other criterion is necessary for an obligation to be classified as current. Current liabilities are obligations whose liquidation is reasonably expected to require use of existing resources properly classified as current assets or the creation of other current liabilities.

2. (F) Notes payable may be classified as short-term or long-term, depending upon the payment due date.

3. (T)

4. (F) Discount on Notes Payable is a contra account to Notes Payable and therefore is subtracted from Notes Payable on the balance sheet.

5. (T)

6. (T)

7. (T)

8. (T)

9. (F) Preferred dividends in arrears are not an obligation until formal action is taken by the board of directors authorizing the distribution of earnings.

10. (F) A stock dividend distributable is liquidated using capital stock rather than assets. Thus, a stock dividend distributable should be classified in an entity's equity section.

11. (T)

12. (T)

13. (F) A liability for the cost of compensation for future absences is required if the four following conditions are met: (a) the employee's services have already been rendered, (b) the obligation relates to rights that vest or accumulate, (c) payment is probable, and (d) the amount can be reasonably estimated.

14. (F) Vested rights exist when an employer has an obligation to make payment to an employee even if his or her employment is terminated.

15. (T)

16. (F) Contingencies result in liabilities if it is probable that a liability has been incurred and the amount of the loss can be reasonably estimated. The mere passage of time is not a criteria in determining whether a loss contingency should be recorded as a liability.

17. (T)

18. (F) Threatened litigation is a loss contingency that should be recorded as a liability if it is probable that a liability has been incurred and the amount of the loss is reasonably estimated.

19. (T)

20. (T)

21. (F) The cost of premiums should be charged to expense during the period in which the sale that gave rise to the premium is made. This method will find some of the premium cost being charged to expense when the premiums are distributed to customers. However, any portion of the estimated premium expense not charged to expense during the period of sale must be accrued at year-end so that a proper matching of revenues and expense takes place.

22. (T)

23. (F) The absence of insurance does not mean that a liability has been incurred at the date of the financial statements.

24. (F) Theoretically, liabilities should be measured by the present value of the future outlay of cash required to liquidate them. But, in practice, current liabilities are usually recorded in accounting records and reported in financial statements at their full maturity value.

25. (T)

MULTIPLE CHOICE

1. (B) A liability must meet the three characteristics noted in alternatives A, C, and D. The indication in alternative B that the obligation be liquidated using assets earned in the normal course of operations is not an essential characteristic. The funds used to liquidate a liability could come from borrowing.

2. (C) Current liabilities are obligations that mature within one year or the operating cycle, whichever is longer, and they are reasonably expected to require the use of current assets for their liquidation.

3. (C) Since these liabilities will be paid within one year from the December 31, 2001 balance sheet date, both the note payable and the related accrued interest payable should be classified as current liabilities.

4. (B) The following entry would be made by Diana Co.:

Cash	200,000	
Discount on Notes Payable	8,000	
Notes Payable		208,000

5. (D) The item would be classified as a current liability as long as it met the relevant criteria. The criteria include payment within one year or the operating cycle, whichever is longer, and payment made using assets classified as current.

6. (A) An enterprise is required to exclude a short-term obligation from current liabilities if it intends to refinance the obligation on a long-term basis and the enterprise can demonstrate the ability to consummate the refinancing. The effect on working capital and the interest rate on the long-term obligation have nothing to do with the specific requirements for reclassifying the debt from current to long-term.

7. (B) The ability to consummate refinancing of a short-term obligation is best demonstrated by actual refinancing after the financial statement date but before the financial statements are issued. A mere statement by the board of directors that it can accomplish refinancing is not sufficient to classify the short-term debt as long-term debt.

8. (A) The maximum amount of short-term debt that can be excluded from current liabilities is limited to the amount secured through the refinancing arrangement. In this case the amount is $1,000,000 (50,000 x $20).

9. (D) Alternatives A, B, and C must be disclosed in the footnotes to the financial statements. There is no requirement to indicate failures to secure financing.

10. (A) No entry is required on April 1, 2001 because the city and county have not provided benefits to June Company yet.

11. (B) June Company would make the following entry on April 30, 2001:

Property Tax Expense	4,000	
Property Tax Payable ($48,000/12)		4,000

12. (D) The computation of the federal and state unemployment taxes for Williams Co. is as follows:

State unemployment tax payment (.02 x $300,000)	$6,000
*Federal unemployment tax (6.2% - 5.4%) ($300,000)	2,400
Total federal and state unemployment tax	$8,400

*When employers display by their benefit and contribution experience that they have provided steady employment and thus receive a reduction in state unemployment taxes, they are still allowed the federal credit of 5.4% even though the effective state contribution rate is less than 5.4%.

13. (C) *FASB Statement No. 43* requires that a liability be accrued for the cost of compensation for future absences if all of the following conditions are met:

1. The employer's obligation relating to the employees' rights to receive compensation for future absences is attributable to employees' services already rendered.
2. The obligation relates to rights that vest or accumulate.
3. Payment of the compensation is probable.
4. The amount can be reasonably estimated.

14. (B) Vested rights exist when an employer has an obligation to make payment to an employee even if his or her employment is terminated; thus, vested rights are not contingent on an employee's future service. Accumulated rights are those that can be carried forward to future periods if not used in the period in which they are earned. The length of time, the legality, or compensation involved are not characteristics which identify specific differences.

15. (A) A contingency is either a gain or a loss contingency as defined by *FASB Statement No. 5.* Alternative B only provides for the loss contingency. Alternatives C and D are not at all representative of contingencies.

16. (C) To accrue a loss contingency, it must be probable that a liability has been incurred and the amount must be reasonably estimated. Alternatives B and D might in some cases be considered probable, but the amount of any loss could not be predicted with any accuracy. Alternative A is incorrect because threatened litigation might not be probable and the amount would be difficult to estimate. Obligations related to product warranties are definitely probable, and the amount is normally estimable because of the past experience of the company.

17. (D) Both of these items represent loss contingencies that would normally be accrued. In both cases the loss is probable and the amount can be reasonably estimated.

18. (D) The liability must be related to the period covered by the financial statements. The other alternatives (A, B, and C) are inconsequential to recording the liability.

19. (C) When a loss is either probable or estimable, but not both, and if there is at least a reasonable possibility that a liability may have been incurred, the disclosures noted in alternative C should be made. To record this contingency would violate *FASB Statement No. 5* as the specified criteria have not been fully met.

20. (D) Wannstedt's warranty liability at December 31, 2003, can be computed as follows:

Total credited to the warranty liability account in 2001, 2002, and 2003 (12%* x $1,400,000)	$168,000
Less: Total amount debited to the warranty liability account in 2001, 2002, and 2003	63,000
Warranty liability, 12/31/03	$105,000

*2% + 4% + 6% = 12%

21. (B)

Boxtops sold in 2002	450,000		
Estimated redemptions:		450,000 X .75 =	337,500
Boxtops redeemed in 2002			220,000
Estimated future redemptions			117,500

Liability for outstanding claims:
117,500/5 = 23,500 X ($2.50 - $1.00) = $35,250

22. (D) Accounting for product warranty costs by accruing an expense is an accepted practice that should be used whenever the warranty is an integral and inseparable part of the sale.

23. (D) The SEC argues that if an environmental liability is within a range and no amount within the range is the best estimate, then management should recognized the minimum amount of the range.

24. (C) Offsetting current liabilities against assets that are to be applied to their liquidation would be inappropriate. Such a presentation would cause working capital and current ratio-type analyses to be difficult to perform. Also, readers of the financial statements could be misled by such a presentation.

*25. (B)

B = .10 ($80,000 - B - T)
T = .40 ($80,000 - B)
B = .10 ($80,000 - B -.40[$80,000 - B])
B = .10 ($80,000 - B - $32,000 + .4B)
B = .10 ($48,000 - .6B)
B = $4,800 -.06B
1.06B = $4,800
B = $4,528

REVIEW EXERCISES

				Debit	Credit
la.	A.	12/6	Cash	3,000	
			Returnable Deposits		3,000
	B.		Cash	621,000	
			Sales		621,000
	C.	12/10	Cash	100,000	
			Notes Payable		100,000
	D.	12/15	Delivery Truck	45,000	
			Cash		10,000
			Notes Payable		35,000

		Debit	Credit
b.	Sales	46,000.00	
	Sales Tax Payable		46,000.00
	($621,000 - (621,000/1.08) = $46,000)		
	Interest Expense	666.67	
	Interest Payable		666.67
	($100,000 X .12 = $12,000)		
	($12,000/12 = $1,000 X 2/3 = $666.67)		
	Interest Expense	218.75	
	Interest Payable		218.75
	($35,000 X .15 = $5,250)		
	($5,520/12 = $437.50/2 = $218.75)		

2a.

Estimate of coupons to be redeemed (500,000 x .8)	400,000
Coupons redeemed (28,000 x 10)	280,000
Estimated coupons redeemable	120,000

First year's premium expense:	
Coupons redeemed (28,000 x $0.75)	$ 21,000
Additional redemptions expected [(120,000 ÷ 10) x $0.75]	9,000
Total premium expense	$30,000

b. Estimated year-end premium liability (12,000 x $0.75) .... $ 9,000

3. Journal Entries:

Sale of CBs (280 x $150):		
Cash or Accounts Receivable	42,000	
Sales		42,000
Estimated warranty cost (280 X $20):		
Warranty expense	5,600	
Estimated liability under warranties		5,600
Actual warranty cost:		
Estimated liability under warranties	2,350	
Cash		2,350

*4a. **Greater than 5 years of service**

B = .20 ($250,000 - T)
T = .40 ($250,000 - B)
B = .20 [$250,000 -.40($250,000 - B)]
B = .20 ($250,000 - $100,000 +.4B)
B = ($30,000 +.08B)
.92B = $30,000
B = $32,608.70

b. **Less than 5 years of service**

B = .10 ($250,000 - B - T)
T = .40 ($250,000 - B)
B = .10 [$250,000 - B -.40($250,000 - B)]
B = .10 ($250,000 - B - $100,000 +.4B)
B = .10 ($150,000 -.6B)
1.06B = $15,000
B = $14,150.94

14

Long-Term Liabilities

CHAPTER STUDY OBJECTIVES

1. Describe the formal procedures associated with issuing long-term debt.
2. Identify various types of bond issues.
3. Describe the accounting valuation for bonds at date of issuance.
4. Apply the methods of bond discount and premium amortization.
5. Describe the accounting procedures for the extinguishment of debt.
6. Explain the accounting procedures for long-term notes payable.
7. Explain the reporting of off-balance-sheet financing arrangements.
8. Indicate how long-term debt is presented and analyzed.

*9. Distinguish between and account for (1) a loss on loan impairment, (2) a troubled debt restructuring that results in the settlement of a debt, and (3) a troubled debt restructuring that results in a continuation of debt with modification of terms.

CHAPTER REVIEW

1. Chapter 14 presents a discussion of the issues related to long-term liabilities. Long-term debt consists of probable future sacrifices of economic benefits. These sacrifices are payable in the future, normally beyond one year or operating cycle, whichever is longer. Coverage in this chapter includes bonds payable, long-term notes payable, mortgage notes payable, and issues related to extinguishment of debt. The accounting and disclosure issues related to long-term liabilities include a great deal of detail due to the potentially complicated nature of debt instruments.

Long-Term Debt

2. (S.O. 1) Long-term debt consists of obligations that are **not** payable within the operating cycle or one year, whichever is longer. These obligations normally require a **formal agreement** between the parties involved that often includes certain **covenants and restrictions** for the protection of both lenders and borrowers. These covenants and restrictions are found in the **bond indenture** or **note agreement,** and include information related to amounts authorized to be issued, interest rates, due dates, call provisions, security for the debt, sinking fund requirements, etc. The important issues related to the long-term debt should always be disclosed in the financial statements or the notes thereto.

3. Long-term liabilities include **bonds payable, mortgage notes payable, long-term notes payable, lease obligations,** and **pension obligations.** Pension and lease obligations are discussed in Chapters 21 and 22, respectively.

* *Note: All asterisked (*) items relate to material contained in the Appendix to the chapter.*

Bonds Payable

4. (S.O. 2) **Bonds payable** represent an obligation of the issuing corporation to pay a sum of money at a designated maturity date plus periodic interest at a specified rate on the face value. See the glossary for terms commonly used in discussing the various aspects of corporate bond issues.

5. **Bonds** are debt instruments of the issuing corporation used by that corporation to borrow funds from the general public or institutional investors. The use of bonds provides the issuer an opportunity to divide a large amount of long-term indebtedness among many small investing units. Bonds may be sold through an **underwriter** who either (a) guarantees a certain sum to the corporation and assumes the risk of sale or (b) agrees to sell the bond issue on the basis of a commission. Alternatively, a corporation may sell the bonds directly to a large financial institution without the aid of an underwriter.

6. If an entire bond issue is not sold at one time, both the amount of the **bonds authorized** and the **bonds issued** should be disclosed on the balance sheet or in a footnote. This discloses the potential indebtedness represented by the unissued bonds.

7. (S.O. 3) Bonds are issued with a **stated rate** of interest expressed as a percentage of the **face value** of the bonds. When bonds are sold for more than face value (at a **premium**) or less than face value (at a **discount**), the interest rate actually earned by the bondholder is different from the stated rate. This is known as the **effective yield** or **market rate** of interest and is set by economic conditions in the investment market. The effective rate exceeds the stated rate when the bonds sell at a discount, and the effective rate is less than the stated rate when the bonds sell at a premium.

8. To compute the effective interest rate of a bond issue, the present value of future cash flows from interest and principal must be computed. This often takes a financial calculator or computer to calculate.

Discounts and Premiums

9. (S.O. 4) Discounts and premiums resulting from a bond issue are recorded at the time the bonds are sold. The amounts recorded as discounts or premiums are amortized each time bond interest is paid. The time period over which discounts and premiums are amortized is equal to the period of time the bonds are outstanding (date of sale to maturity date). Amortization of bond premiums decreases the recorded amount of bond interest expense, whereas the amortization of bond discounts increases the recorded amount of bond interest expense.

10. To illustrate the recording of bonds sold at a discount or premium the following examples are presented. If Aretha Company issued $100,000 of bonds dated January 1, 2002 at 98, on January 1, 2002, the entry would be as follows:

Cash ($100,000 X.98)	98,000	
Discount on Bonds Payable	2,000	
Bonds		100,000

If the same bonds noted above were sold for 102 the entry to record the issuance would be as follows:

Cash ($100,000 X 1.02)	102,000	
Premium on Bonds Payable		2,000
Bonds Payable		100,000

It should be noted that whenever bonds are issued, the Bonds Payable account is always credited for the face amount of the bonds issued.

11. To illustrate the amortization of the bond discount or premium assume the bonds sold in the example in paragraph 10 above are five-year bonds. Since the bonds are sold on the issue date (January 1, 2002) they will be outstanding for the full five years. Thus, the discount or premium would be amortized over the entire life of the bonds. The entry to amortize the bond discount at the end of 2002 would be:

Bond Interest Expense	400	
Discount on Bonds Payable ($2,000/5)		400

The entry to amortize the premium would be:

Premium on Bonds Payable	400	
Bond Interest Expense		400

Note that the amortization of the discount increases the bond interest expense for the period and the amortization of the premium reduces bond interest expense for the period.

12. When bonds are issued between interest dates, the purchase price is increased by an amount equal to the interest earned on the bonds since the last interest payment date. On the next interest payment date, the bondholder receives the entire semiannual interest payment. However, the amount of interest expense to the issuing corporation is the difference between the semiannual interest payment and the amount of interest prepaid by the purchaser. For example, assume a 10-year bond issue in the amount of $300,000, bearing 9% interest payable semi-annually, dated January 1, 2002. If the entire bond issue is sold at par on March 1, 2002, the following journal entry would be made by the seller:

Cash	304,500	
Bonds Payable		300,000
Bond Interest Expense		4,500*
*($300,000 X .09 X 1/6)		

The entry for the semi-annual interest payment on July 1, 2002 would be as follows:

Bond Interest Expense	13,500	
Cash		13,500

The total bond interest expense for the six month period is $9,000 ($13,500 - $4,500), which represents the correct interest expense for the four-month period the bonds were outstanding.

13. Bond discounts or premiums may be amortized using the straight-line method, as was demonstrated in paragraph 11 above. However, the profession's preferred procedure is the **effective interest method.** This method computes the bond interest using the effective rate at which the bonds are issued. More specifically, **interest cost for each period is the effective interest rate multiplied by the carrying value (book value) of the bonds at the start of the period.** The effective interest method is best accomplished by preparing a **Schedule of Bond Interest Amortization.** This schedule provides the information necessary for each semiannual entry for interest and discount or premium amortization. The chapter includes an illustration of a Schedule of Bond Interest Amortization for both a discount and premium situation. Also, the demonstration problem at the end of the Chapter Review section illustrates the preparation of this schedule.

14. Unamortized premiums and discounts are reported with the **Bonds Payable** account in the liability section of the balance sheet. Premiums and discounts are not liability accounts; they are merely liability valuation accounts. Premiums are added to the Bonds Payable account and discounts are deducted from the Bonds Payable account in the liability section of the balance sheet.

15. If the interest payment date does not coincide with the financial statement's date, the amortized premium or discount should be prorated by the appropriate number of months to arrive at the proper interest expense.

16. Some of the costs associated with issuing bonds include engraving and printing costs, legal and accounting fees, commissions, and promotion expenses. *APB Opinion No. 21,* "Interest on Receivables and Payables," indicates that these costs should be debited to a deferred charge account entitled, Unamortized Bond Issue Costs. These costs are then amortized over the life of the issue in a manner similar to that used for discount on bonds.

Treasury Bonds

17. **Treasury bonds** are a corporation's own bonds that have been reacquired but not canceled. They should be shown on the balance sheet at their par value as a deduction from the bonds payable issued to arrive at bonds payable outstanding.

Extinguishment of Debt

18. (S.O. 5) The extinguishment, or payment, of long-term liabilities can be a relatively straightforward process which involves a debit to the liability account and a credit to cash. The process can also be a complicated one when the debt is extinguished prior to maturity.

19. The reacquisition of debt can occur either by payment to the creditor or by reacquisition in the open market. At the time of reacquisition, any unamortized premium or discount, and any costs of issue related to the bonds, must be amortized up to the reacquisition date. If this is not done any resulting gain or loss on the extinguishment would be misstated. The difference between the reacquisition price and the net carrying amount of the debt is a gain (reacquisition price lower) or loss (reacquisition price greater).

Notes Payable

20. (S.O. 6) The difference between current notes payable and long-term notes payable is the maturity date. Accounting for notes and bonds is quite similar.

21. Interest-bearing notes are treated the same as bonds—a discount or premium is recognized if the stated rate is different than the effective rate. Zero-interest-bearing notes represent a discount on the note and the discount is amortized similar to the manner as discounts on interest-bearing notes.

22. When a long-term note is issued **solely for cash,** the **interest factor** is assumed to be the stated or coupon rate plus or minus the amortization of the discount or premium. In situations where a note is exchanged for **cash and some additional privilege,** the difference between the present value of the payable and the amount of cash loaned should be recorded as a discount on the note and as unearned revenue. This discount should be amortized by a charge to interest expense over the term of the note using the effective interest method. The unearned revenue is prorated on the same basis as the privilege that gave rise to the unearned revenue realized by the lender/customer. For example, the privilege may be a favorable merchandise purchase agreement. In this case, the unearned revenue is

prorated on the basis of the ratio between each period's sales to the lender/customer and the total sales to that customer for the term of the note.

23. When a debt instrument is exchanged for **noncash consideration** in a bargained transaction, the stated rate of interest is presumed fair unless: (**a**) no interest rate is stated, (**b**) the stated rate is unreasonable, or (**c**) the face amount of the debt instrument is materially different from the current cash price of the consideration or the current market value of the debt instrument. If the stated rate is determined to be inappropriate, an **imputed interest rate** must be used to establish the present value of the debt instrument. The imputed interest rate is used to establish the present value of the debt instrument by discounting, at that rate, all future payments on the debt instrument.

24. The imputed interest rate used for valuation purposes will normally be at least equal to the rate at which the debtor can obtain financing of a similar nature from other sources at the date of the transaction. The object is to approximate the rate that would have resulted if an independent borrower and an independent lender had negotiated a similar transaction under comparable terms and conditions.

25. **Mortgage notes** are a common means of financing the acquisition of property, plant, and equipment in a proprietorship or partnership form of business organization. Normally, the title to specific property is pledged as security for a mortgage note. Points raise the effective interest rate above the stated rate. If a mortgage note is paid on an installment basis, the current installment should be classified as a current liability.

26. Because of unusually high, unstable interest rates and a tight money supply, the traditional **fixed-rate mortgage** has been partially supplanted with new and unique mortgage arrangements. **Variable-rate mortgages** feature interest rates tied to changes in the fluctuating market rate of interest. Generally, variable-rate lenders adjust the interest rate at either one or three-year intervals.

<u>**Off-Balance Sheet Financing**</u>

27. (S.O. 7) A significant issue in accounting today is the question of off-balance-sheet financing. **Off-balance-sheet financing** is an attempt to borrow monies in such a way that the obligations are not recorded. Included in this chapter is a discussion of the off-balance-sheet financing arrangement for project financing arrangements.

28. **Project financing arrangements** arise when the following three conditions are present (**a**) two or more entities form a new entity to construct an operating plant that will be used by both parties; (**b**) the new entity borrows funds to construct the project and repays the debt from the proceeds received from the project; and (**c**) payment of the debt is guaranteed by the companies that formed the new entity. The advantage of such an arrangement to the companies that form the new entity is that neither company reports the liability on its books except to disclose that they guarantee debt repayment if the project's proceeds are not enough to repay the liability.

29. Many project financing arrangements are further formalized through the use of **take-or-pay contracts** or **through-put contracts.** In take-or-pay contracts, a purchaser of goods signs an agreement with the seller to pay specified amounts periodically in return for products or services. The purchaser must make specified minimum payments even if delivery of the contracted products or services is not taken. Through-put contracts are similar to take-or-pay contracts, except that a service instead of a product is provided by the asset under construction.

Presentation of Long-Term Debt

30. (S.O. 8) Companies that have large amounts and numerous issues of long-term debt frequently report only one amount in the balance sheet and support this with comments and schedules in the accompanying notes to the financial statements. These foot note disclosures generally indicate the nature of the liabilities, maturity dates, interest rates, call provisions, conversion privileges, restrictions imposed by the borrower, and assets pledged as security. Long-term debt that matures within one year should be reported as a current liability unless retirement is to be accomplished with other than current assets.

Analysis of Long-Term Debt

31. Long-term creditors and stockholders are interested in a company's long-run solvency and the ability to pay interest when it is due. Two ratios that provide information about debt-paying ability and long-run solvency are the **debt to total assets ratio** and the **times interest earned ratio.**

*32. When a debtor experiences financial difficulty, a creditor may grant some concession to the debtor related to the debt obligation that exists between the two parties. When such a concession is granted, it is referred to as a **troubled debt restructuring.**

DEMONSTRATION PROBLEMS

1. Buffet Company issued $250,000 of 10% bonds on January 1, 2002, due on January 1, 2012, with interest payable each July 1 and January 1. If investors desire to earn an effective interest rate of 12%, how much should they pay for the bonds?

Solution:

Maturity value of bonds		$250,000
Present value of $250,000 due in ten years at 12% interest payable semiannually (Table 6-2, 6% for 20 periods) .31180 X $250,000	$ 77,950	
Present value of $12,500 interest payable semiannually for 10 years at 12% (Table 6-4, 6% for 20 periods) 11.46992 X $12,500	143,374	
Proceeds from sale of bonds		221,324
Discount on bonds		$ 28,676

(If investors pay $221,324 for this bond issue, the effective interest rate on these 10% bonds would be 12%.)

2. Using the facts in the problem above, prepare a schedule showing the amounts that would be used in recording the first two semiannual interest payments (July 1, 2002 and January 1, 2003).

Solution:

Date	Cash Credit	Interest Expense Debt	Bond Discount Credit	Carrying Value of Bonds
1/1/02				$221,324
7/1/02	$12,500 (a)	$13,279 (b)	$779 (c)	222,103 (d)
1/1/03	12,500 (e)	13,326 (f)	826 (g)	222,929 (h)

(a)	$250,000 X 10 X 6/12	(e)	same as (a)
(b)	$221,324 X .12 X 6/12	(f)	$221,103 x .12 x 6/12
(c)	$13,279 - $12,500	(g)	$13,326 - $12,500
(d)	$221,324 + $779	(h)	$222,103 + $826

GLOSSARY

Bearer (coupon) bonds. Bonds not recorded in the name of the owner and may be transferred from one owner to another by mere delivery.

Callable bonds. Bonds that give the issuer the right to call and retire the bonds prior to maturity.

Collateral trust bonds. Bonds that are secured by stocks and bonds of other corporations.

Commodity-backed bonds (asset linked bonds) Bonds that are redeemable in measures of a commodity, such as barrels of oil, tons of coal, or ounces of rare metal.

Convertible bonds. Bonds that are convertible into other securities of the corporation for a specified time after issuance.

Debenture bonds. Bonds that are unsecured.

Deep discount bonds (zero interest debenture bonds). Bonds that are sold at a discount and do not bear an interest rate.

Effective rate (effective yield or market rate). The rate of interest actually earned by the bondholders.

Face value (par value, principal amount, or maturity value). Amount stated on the face of the bond that serves as the basis for periodic interest computations and represents the amount due at maturity.

Financial instruments. Cash, an ownership interest in an entity, or a contractual right to receive or deliver cash or another financial instrument on potentially favorable or unfavorable terms.

Income bonds. Bonds that pay no interest unless the issuing company is profitable.

Indenture. Describes the contractual agreement between the corporation issuing the bonds and the bondholders.

Junk bonds. Bonds that are unsecured and also very risky, and therefore pay a high interest rate.

Long-term debt. Probable future sacrifices of economic benefits arising from present obligations that are not payable within a year or the operating cycle of the business, whichever is longer.

Long-term notes payable. Notes payable that are not expected to be paid within a year or the operating cycle, whichever is longer.

Mortgage bonds. Bonds that are secured by a claim on real estate.

Off-balance-sheet financing.	An attempt to borrow monies in such a way that the obligations are not recorded.
Premium.	When bonds sell for more than face value.
Project financing arrangements.	When (1) two or more entities form a new entity to construct an operating plant that will be used by both parties; (2) the new entity borrows funds to construct the project and repays the debt from the proceeds received from the project; and (3) payment of the debt is guaranteed by the companies that formed the new entity.
Registered bonds.	Bonds issued in the name of the owner and require surrender of the certificate and issuance of a new certificate to complete a sale.
Revenue bonds.	Bonds that pay interest from specified revenue sources, and are most frequently issued by airports, school districts, counties, toll-road authorities, and governmental bodies.
Secured bonds.	Bonds that are backed by a pledge of some sort of collateral.
Serial bonds.	Bond issues that mature in installments.
Stated rate (coupon rate or nominal rate).	The interest rate written in the terms of the bond indenture (and ordinarily printed on the bond certificate).
Term bonds.	Bond issues that mature on a single date.
Treasury bonds.	Bonds payable that have been reacquired by the issuing corporation or its agent or trustee and have not been cancelled.
***Troubled debt restructuring.**	When a creditor for economic or legal reasons related to the debtor's financial difficulties grants a concession to the debtor that it would not otherwise consider.
Unsecured bonds.	Bonds that are not backed by collateral.

CHAPTER OUTLINE

Fill in the outline presented below.

(S.O. 2) Bonds Payable

Types of Bonds

(S.O. 4) Discount on Bonds—Straight-Line Method

Premium on Bonds—Straight-Line Method

Bonds Issued Between Interest Dates

Discount on Bonds—Effective Interest Method

Premium on Bonds—Effective Interest Method

Classification of Discount and Premium

Costs of Issuing Bonds

Treasury Bonds

(S.O. 5) Extinguishment of Debt

Reacquisition of Debt

Chapter Outline *(continued)*

Reporting Gains and Losses

(S.O. 6) Long-Term Notes Payable

Special Notes Payable Situations

Notes exchanged for cash and other rights

Notes issued for property, goods and services

Imputed interest

Mortgage Notes Payable

(S.O. 7) Off-Balance-Sheet Financing

Project Financing Arrangements

(S.O. 8) Reporting Long-Term Debt

Analysis of Long-Term Debt

*(S.O. 9) Accounting for Troubled Debt

*Impairments

*Troubled Debt Restructurings

REVIEW QUESTIONS AND EXERCISES

TRUE-FALSE

Indicate whether each of the following is true (T) or false (F) in the space provided.

_____ 1. (S.O. 1) Long-term debt is ordinarily used by an enterprise as a more or less permanent means of financing to increase the earnings available to stockholders.

_____ 2. (S.O. 1) Generally, long-term debt, in whatever form, is issued subject to various covenants or restrictions for the protection of corporate stockholders.

_____ 3. (S.O. 2) Commodity-backed bonds are redeemable in measures of a commodity such as barrels of oil, tons of coal, or ounces of a rare metal.

_____ 4. (S.O. 2) Revenue bonds are bonds whose interest rate is a function of the revenue earned by the company issuing the bonds.

_____ 5. (S.O. 2) Bonds issued by a corporation represent a means of borrowing funds from the general public or institutional investors on a long-term basis.

_____ 6. (S.O. 2) When bonds are issued by a corporation, the AICPA requires that the issue be placed with an independent underwriter.

_____ 7. (S.O. 3) When bonds are issued between interest dates, the purchaser pays for interest accrued since the date the bonds were originally issued.

_____ 8. (S.O. 3) The stated rate of interest on bonds is the rate set by the party issuing the bonds.

_____ 9. (S.O. 4) If bonds are sold at a premium, the effective rate of interest is greater than the stated rate of interest.

_____ 10. (S.O. 4) Bond discount should be reported in the balance sheet as a direct deduction from the face amount of the bond.

_____ 11. (S.O. 4) The amortization of a bond discount increases the amount of bond interest expense recorded each year.

_____ 12. (S.O. 4) Under the effective interest method semiannual interest expense is computed by multiplying the effective interest rate times a constant carrying value of the bonds.

_____ 13. (S.O. 4) The expenses associated with the issuance of bonds (printing costs, legal fees, etc.), should be added to the bond discount or subtracted from the bond premium on the date the bonds are issued.

_____ 14. (S.O. 5) Any excess of the net carrying amount over the reacquisition price is a loss from extinguishment.

_____ 15. (S.O. 6) When a zero-interest-bearing note is given in return for property, the present value of the note is measured by the fair value of the property or by an amount that reasonably approximates the market value of the note.

_____ 16. (S.O. 6) An imputed interest rate used to determine the present value of a debt instrument may change during the life of the debt if a change occurs in the prevailing interest rate.

_____ 17. (S.O. 6) Mortgage "points" raise the effective interest rate above the rate specified in the note.

_____ 18. (S.O. 7) Off-balance-sheet financing is an attempt to borrow monies in such a way that the obligations are recorded in the retained earnings statement.

_____ 19. (S.O. 7) Two reasons often cited for off-balance sheet financing are: (a) keeping debt off the balance sheet enhances the quality of the balance sheet and permits credit to be obtained more easily and (b) loan covenants often impose a limitation on the amount of debt a company may have.

_____ 20. (S.O. 7) In a project financing arrangement, a single company sets up a second company for the purpose of financing a specific project that has a maximum life of five years.

_____ 21. (S.O. 8) Long-term debt that matures within one year should be reported as a current liability, unless retirement is to be accomplished with other than current assets.

_____ 22. (S.O. 8) Disclosure is required of future payments for sinking fund requirements and maturity amounts of long-term debt during each of the next 5 years.

_____ 23. (S.O. 8) The times interest earned ratio indicates the company's ability to meet interest payments as they come due.

_____ *24. (S.O. 9) A loan is considered impaired when it is possible, based on current information and events, that the creditor will be unable to collect all amounts due (both principal and interest) according to the contractual terms of the loan.

_____ *25. (S.O. 9) In a troubled debt restructuring the noncash assets or equity interest given should be accounted for at their fair market value.

MULTIPLE CHOICE

Select the best answer for each of the following items and enter the corresponding letter in the space provided.

_____ 1. (S.O. 2) If a corporation issues a debenture bond, it means the bond:

A. is secured by stocks and bonds of other corporations.
B. matures in installments.
C. is unsecured.
D. may be converted into other securities of the corporation for a specified time after issuance.

_____ 2. (S.O. 2) Bonds that pay no interest unless the issuing company is profitable are called:

A. collateral trust bonds.
B. debenture bonds.
C. revenue bonds.
D. income bonds.

_____ 3. (S.O. 2) Bonds that are secured by stocks and bonds of other corporations are called:

A. collateral trust bonds.
B. registered bonds.
C. serial bonds.
D. treasury bonds.

_____ 4. (S.O. 2) The interest rate actually earned by a bondholder who buys the bond at a discount, as compared to the stated rate on the bond is:

	Higher	Lower
A.	Yes	No
B.	Yes	Yes
C.	No	Yes
D.	No	No

_____ 5. (S.O. 2) Bonds with par value of $500,000 carrying a stated interest rate of 6% payable semiannually on March 1 and September 1 were issued on July 1. The proceeds from the issue amounted to $510,000. The best explanation for the excess received over par value is:

A. the bonds were sold at a premium.
B. the bonds were sold at a higher effective interest rate.
C. the bonds were issued at par plus accrued interest
D. no explanation is possible without knowing the maturity date of the bond issue.

_____ 6. (S.O. 3) If bonds are issued initially at a premium and the effective interest method of amortization is used, interest expense in the earlier years will be:

A. greater than if the straight-line method were used.
B. greater than the amount of the interest payments.
C. the same as if the straight-line method were used.
D. less than if the straight line method were used.

_____ 7. (S.O. 4) King Cole Corporation markets a 10-year bond issue dated January 1, 2001. The bonds pay 9% interest semi-annually on January 1 and July 1. If these bonds are sold on September 1, 2001 how many months accrued interest must be paid by the purchaser and over how many months would any premium on the bonds be amortized?

	Months of Accrued Interest	Amortization Period
A.	8	120 months
B.	8	112 months
C.	2	120 months
D.	2	112 months

_____ 8. (S.O. 4) A bond premium should be reported in the balance sheet:

A. at the present value of the future reduction in bond interest expense due to the premium.
B. as a deferred credit.
C. along with other premium accounts such as those resulting from stock transactions.
D. as a direct addition to the face amount of the bond.

The following information applies to both questions 7 and 8. On October 1, 2002 Sinatra Corporation issued 5%, 10-year bonds with a par value of $300,000 at 104. Interest is paid on October 1 and April 1, with any premiums or discounts amortized on a straight-line basis.

_____ 9. (S.O. 4) The entry to record the issuance of the bonds would include:

A. a credit of $7,500 to Accrued Interest Payable.
B. a credit of $12,000 to Premium on Bonds Payable.
C. a credit of $288,000 to Bonds Payable.
D. a debit of $12,000 to Discount on Bonds Payable.

_____ 10. (S.O. 4) The Bond Interest Expense reported on the December 31, 2002 income statement of Sinatra Corporation would be:

A. $4,050.
B. $6,900.
C. $3,450.
D. $3,750.

_____ 11. (S.O. 4) Which of the following statements correctly depicts the nature of discounts or premiums as applied to a bond issue?

A. When bonds are issued at a discount, the seller has an advantage in that interest payments are based upon an amount less than face value.
B. The terms "discount" and "premium" are the same as loss and gain, respectively, to both buyer and seller.
C. The difference between the effective rate of interest and the market rate of interest is the reason discounts and premiums arise.
D. The net cash outflow (ignoring bond issue costs) to the seller of bonds issued at a premium will be less than the maturity value of the bonds plus total interest payments.

_____ 12. (S.O. 4) Bond issue costs, such as printing fees, legal fees, commissions, etc. are most appropriately accounted for by:

A. charging them to an expense account in the year the bonds are actually sold so there is revenue to charge them against on the income statement.
B. debiting them to Unamortized Bond Issue Costs, setting them up as a deferred charge on the balance sheet, and amortizing them in a manner similar to bond discount over the life of the bond.
C. charging them to an expense account in the year the bonds are originally dated, whether or not they are sold in that year.
D. adding them to any discount on bonds or subtracting them from any premium on bonds when the bonds are sold.

_____ 13. (S.O. 4) Bonds payable that have been reacquired by the issuing corporation or its agent or trustee and have not been canceled are known as:

A. redeemed bonds.
B. treasury bonds.
C. deregistered bonds.
D. junk bonds.

_____ 14. (S.O. 4) If bonds are held to maturity any premium or discount as well as any bond issue costs:

A. should be written off directly to a bond retirement account as the bond will be redeemed.
B. are carried forward and written off in the same manner as that used prior to the maturity date.
C. will be fully amortized as their amortization period is designed to coincide with the life of the bond issue.
D. should be used to calculate the gain or loss resulting from the maturity of the bonds.

_____ 15. (S.O. 5) When debt is extinguished before its maturity date through a refunding transaction, any difference between the reacquisition price of outstanding debt and its net carrying amount per books should be:

A. amortized over the remaining original life of the extinguished issue.
B. amortized over the life of the new issue.
C. recognized currently in income as an extraordinary loss or gain.
D. treated as a prior period adjustment.

_____ 16. (S.O. 6) When a zero-interest-bearing note is given for property, goods, or services, the present value of the note is best measured by:

A. the fair value of the property, goods, or services or by an amount that reasonably approximates the note.
B. the prime interest rate unless that rate is not applicable to the entities involved in the transaction.
C. the interest rate on similar notes being offered in the market place for similar property, goods, or services.
D. a negotiated interest rate between the issuer of the note and the owner of the property, goods, or services.

_____ 17. (S.O. 6) A debt instrument with no ready market is exchanged for property whose fair market value is currently indeterminable. When such a transaction takes place:

A. the present value of the debt instrument must be approximated using an imputed interest rate.
B. it should not be recorded on the books of either party until the fair market value of the property becomes evident.
C. the board of directors of the entity receiving the property should estimate a value for the property that will serve as a basis for the transaction.
D. the directors of both entities involved in the transaction should negotiate a value to be assigned to the property.

_____ 18. (S.O. 6) Hendrix Corporation exchanged land with a fair market value of $150,000 for Gaye Company's $226,000, zero-interest-bearing, 4-year note. If the $150,000 amount represents the present value of the note at an appropriate rate of interest, Hendrix Corporation should record the difference ($76,000) as:

A. gain on the sale of land.
B. premium on the sale of land.
C. premium on notes receivable.
D. discount on notes receivable.

_____ 19. (S.O. 7) Which of the following is not a characteristic of a project financing arrangement?

A. Two or more entities form a new entity to construct an operating plant that will be used by both parties.
B. The project must be one that neither entity could enter into on its own.
C. The new entity borrows money to finance the project and repays the debt from the proceeds received from the project.
D. Payment of the debt is guaranteed by the companies that formed the new entity.

_____ 20. (S.O. 7) When a business enterprise enters into what is referred to as off-balance-sheet financing, the company:

A. is attempting to conceal the debt from shareholders by having no information about the debt included in the balance sheet.
B. wishes to confine all information related to the debt to the income statement and the statement of cash flow.
C. can enhance the quality of its financial position and perhaps permit credit to be obtained more readily and at less cost.
D. is in violation of generally accepted accounting principles.

_____ 21. (S.O. 8) Ewell Corporation's 2000 Annual Report disclosed total liabilities of $5,400,000, total assets of $8,000,000, interest expense of $400,000, income taxes of $600,000, and net income of $1,000,000. What is Ewell's times interest earned ratio?

A. 10
B. 8
C. 5
D. 2.5

_____ 22. (S.O. 8) Long-term debt that matures within one year and is to be converted into stock should be:

A. reported as a current liability.
B. reported in a special section between liabilities and stockholders' equity.
C. reported as noncurrent.
D. reported as noncurrent and accompanied with a note explaining the method to be used in its liquidation.

_____ *23. (S.O. 9) When a creditor recognizes a loss on an impaired loan, the loss is recognized as:

A. the amount of the total expected future cash flows of the investment over the recorded carrying amount of the investment.
B. the amount of the present value of the expected future cash flows of the investment over the recorded carrying amount of the investment.
C. the amount of the recorded carrying amount of the investment over the total expected future cash flows of the investment.
D. the amount of the recorded carrying amount of the investment over the present value of the expected future cash flows of the investment.

_____*24. (S.O. 9) Garcia Company recently has experienced declining profits, liquidity problems, and an unfavorable trend in its debt to equity relationship. The company completed its negotiations in 2001 for a creditor to accept 50,000 shares of Garcia common stock in settlement of a note payable for $300,000. Market value of the shares was $200,000. In accounting for this troubled debt restructuring, the appropriate treatment for Garcia is to:

A. reduce liabilities by $300,000, increase paid-in capital by $200,000, and increase retained earnings directly for $100,000.

B. reduce liabilities by $300,000 and create a separate paid-in capital section entitled "equity of former creditors-$300,000."

C. reduce liabilities by $300,000, increase paid-in capital by $200,000, and recognize an extraordinary gain of $100,000.

D. reduce liabilities and increase paid-in capital by $300,000.

_____*25. (S.O. 9) For a troubled debt restructuring involving only a modification of terms, the gain recorded by the debtor is:

A. the excess amount of the total restructured future cash flows over the pre-restructured carrying amount.

B. the excess amount of the present value of restructured future cash flows over the pre-restructured carrying amount.

C. the excess amount of the pre-restructured carrying amount over the total restructured future cash flows.

D. the excess amount of the pre-restructured carrying amount over the present value of restructured future cash flows.

REVIEW EXERCISES

1. (S.O. 3 and 4) Turner Corporation issued $800,000 of 6% bonds at 97.5 plus accrued interest on August 1, 2002. The bonds are 9-year bonds dated December 1, 2001, and pay interest on June 1 and December 1, each year. The company's fiscal year coincides with the calendar year; straight-line amortization is used.

Instructions:
Prepare the journal entries that Turner Corporation would make on August 1, 2002, December 1, 2002 and December 31, 2002.

General Journal

J1

Date	Account Title	Debit	Credit

2. (S.O.4) The following information relates to a $200,000, 4-year, 6% bond issue by Garfunkel Co. The bonds, issued on 1-1-01, are due on 1-1-05 and pay interest on January 1 and July 1. The bonds are sold to yield 5%.

Instructions:

a. Calculate the premium on bonds for Garfunkel Co. by filling in the missing amounts below.

Maturity value of bonds payable		$200,000
Present value of $200,000 due in 8 periods at 2 1/2%, semiannual interest (Table 6-2)	______	
Present value of $6,000 interest payable semiannually for 8 periods at 2 1/2% (Table 6-4)	______	
Proceeds from sale of bonds		______
Premium on bonds		______

b. Prepare an amortization schedule for Garfunkel Co. using the effective interest method.

Schedule of Interest Expense and
Bond Premium Amortization
Effective Interest Method
6% Bonds Sold to Yield 5%

Date	Credit Cash	Debit Interest Expense	Debit Bond Premium	Carrying Value of Bonds
1-1-01				$207,171
7-1-01	$ ______	$ ______	$ ______	______
1-1-02	______	______	______	______
7-1-02	______	______	______	______
1-1-03	______	______	______	______
7-1-03	______	______	______	______
1-1-04	______	______	______	______
7-1-04	______	______	______	______
1-1-05	______	______	______	______
Totals	______	______	______	______

____

____

____

____

____

3. (S.O. 3 and 4) On July 1, 2002, the Sting Company issued $200,000 of 6%, 10-year bonds with interest dates of March 1 and September 1. The company received cash of $200,250, which included the interest accrued since the authorization date of March 1, 2002. The company maintains a policy of amortizing premiums and discounts on a straight-line basis.

Instructions:
Compute the following amounts:

a. The amount of accrued interest received by Sting Company from investors on July 1, 2002.
b. The amount of the discount or premium.
c. The amount of cash that will be paid to bondholders on September 1, 2002.
d. The amount of bond interest payable that would appear on the December 31, 2002 balance sheet.
e. The amount of bond interest expense that would be reported on the income statement for 2002.

4. (S.O. 3, 4 and 5) The following transactions are taken from the records of the Elton Corporation.

a. Bonds payable with a par value of $800,000, carrying a stated interest rate of 9% payable semiannually on March 1 and September 1, were issued on June 1, 2002, at 102.5 plus accrued interest. The bonds are dated March 1, 2002 and mature on March 1, 2012.
b. September 1 interest payment is made. (Bond premium amortization is recorded only at year end.)
c. Year-end (December 31) accrued interest on bonds payable is recorded and the bond premium is amortized using the straight-line method.
d. March 1 interest payment is made.
e. Bonds with a par value of $350,000 are purchased at 101 plus accrued interest on August 1, 2000, and retired. (Bond premium amortization is recorded only at year end.)
f. September 1 interest payment is made.
g. Year-end (December 31) accrued interest on bonds payable is recorded and the bond premium is amortized using the straight-line method.

Instructions:
Prepare journal entries for the transactions noted above.

General Journal

J1

Date	Account Title	Debit	Credit

5. (S.O.3 and 4) On October 1, 2002, Costello Company issued $600,000 par value 12%, 10-year bonds dated July 1, 2002, with interest payable semiannually on January 1, and July 1. The bonds are issued at $767,592 (to yield 8%) plus accrued interest. The effective interest method is used for amortization purposes.

Instructions:

a. Prepare the journal entry on the date the bonds are issued.
b. Prepare the year-end adjusting entry for bond interest as of December 31, 2002.
c. Prepare the entry for the interest payment on January 1, 2003.

a.

General Journal J1

Date	Account Title	Debit	Credit

b.

General Journal J1

Date	Account Title	Debit	Credit

c.

General Journal

J1

Date	Account Title	Debit	Credit

SOLUTIONS TO REVIEW QUESTIONS AND EXERCISES

TRUE-FALSE

1. (T)

2. (F) Long-term debt is subject to various covenants or restrictions. However, these covenants and restrictions are for the protection of the lenders and the borrowers.

3. (T)

4. (F) Revenue bonds are bonds whose interest is paid from specified revenue sources. Such bonds are usually issued by airports, school districts, counties, tollroad authorities, and other governmental bodies.

5. (T)

6. (F) Companies issuing bonds may choose to place privately a bond issue by selling bonds directly to a large institution, financial or otherwise, without the aid of an underwriter. The AICPA has no rules about initial bond placements.

7. (F) When bonds are issued between interest dates, the purchaser pays for interest accrued from the last interest payment date to the date of the purchase. Thus, the maximum amount of accrued interest a purchaser can be required to pay is 6 months (assuming semiannual interest).

8. (T)

9. (F) If bonds sell for more than face value, they are said to have sold at a premium. Thus, the effective rate of interest is less than the stated rate of interest.

10. (T)

11. (T)

12. (F) Under the effective interest method, the interest expense for each interest period is computed by multiplying the effective interest rate times the carrying amount of the bonds at the start of the period. The carrying amount of the bonds either increases (for bonds issued at a discount) or decreases (for bonds issued at a premium) each period by the amount of the amortized discount or premium.

13. (F) Bond issue costs are debited to a deferred charge account for Unamortized Bond Issue Costs and amortized over the life of the debt in a manner similar to that used for discount on bonds.

14. (F) Any excess of the net carrying amount over the reacquisition price is a gain from extinguishment.

15. (T)

16. (F) An imputed interest rate is determined at the time a debt instrument is issued. Any subsequent changes in prevailing interest rates are ignored.

17. (T)

18. (F) Off-balance-sheet financing is an attempt to borrow monies in such a way that the obligations are not recorded.

19. (T)

20. (F) Project financing arrangements arise when (a) two or more entities form another entity to construct an operating plant that will be used by both parties; (b) the new entity borrows funds to construct the project and repays the debt from the proceeds received from the project; and (c) payment of the debt is guaranteed by the entities that formed the new company.

21. (T)

22. (T)

23. (T)

*24. (F) A loan is considered impaired when it is ***probable***, based on current information and events, that the creditor will be unable to collect all amounts due (both principal and interest) according to the contractual terms of the loan.

*25. (T)

MULTIPLE CHOICE

1. (C) A debenture bond is an unsecured bond that is issued on the good name of the company. Alternative A describes a collateral trust bond. Alternative B refers to a serial bond, and alternative D describes a convertible bond.

2. (D) Bonds that pay no interest unless the issuing company is profitable are called income bonds.

3. (A) Bonds that are secured by stocks and bonds of other corporations are called collateral trust bonds.

4. (A) When a bond is sold at a discount the effective rate of interest is higher than the stated rate on the bond. This is due to the fact that the amount paid for the bond is less than its face amount, yet the interest earned is the same as that earned if the bond had been sold at par.

5. (C) $500,000 x .06 = $30,000 annual interest
   $30,000 ÷ 12 = $2,500 interest per month
   March 1 to July 1 is 4 months accrued interest
   4 x $2,500 = $10,000 accrued interest
   $500,000 + $10,000 = $510,000 proceeds

6. (A) Interest expense is based on the carrying value of the bonds (face value plus unamortized premium). Early in the life of the bond issue, interest expense is higher under the effective interest method because the carrying amount of the bonds includes the total premium. Under the straight-line method, the bond premium is allocated equally to each bond interest period. Studying the bond premium amortization table in the text will help demonstrate this relationship.

7. (D) The payment of accrued interest by the purchaser of the bonds is from the last interest payment date to the date of the purchase. The last interest payment date was July 1, so the accrued interest required is for July and August. The amortization of any premium or discount is over the period of time the bond issue will be outstanding. In the case of the bonds noted in the question, they will be outstanding for 9 years and 4 months (112 months).

8. (D) Premiums and discounts on bonds are liability valuation accounts. The accounting profession requires that discounts be shown as deductions from the face value of bonds and premiums must be added to the face value.

9. (B)

	Debit	Credit
Cash	312,000	
Bonds Payable		300,000
Premium on Bonds		12,000

($300,000 x 1.04 = $312,000)

10. (C) Annual Interest: $300,000 x .05 = $15,000/year

Interest: October to December ($15,000 x 3/12)	$3,750
Amortization of Premium ($12,000 ÷ 120 = $100 x 3)......................	300
Interest Expense 1999...	$3,450

11. (D) For a $100,000, 10%, 5-year bond issued at a $12,000 premium, the following cash flow applies:

Bond Proceeds...		$112,000
Bond Interest (5 years at $10,000)..............................	$ 50,000	
Maturity Value	100,000	150,000
Net Cash Outflow..		$ 38,000

12. (B) Bond issue costs should be recorded as a deferred charge and amortized against income over the life of the bond issue. There is a difference between the recommended accounting for these costs as stated in *APB Opinion No. 21* and *FASB Concepts Statement No. 3.* The method that is acceptable at the present time is the method described in *APB Opinion No. 21.*

13. (B) Bonds payable that have been reacquired by the issuing corporation or its agent or trustee and have not been canceled are known as treasury bonds. The concept is similar to treasury stock which is the entity's own stock that has been reacquired and not canceled. Treasury bonds should be shown on the balance sheet at par value--as a deduction from bonds payable issued to arrive at a net figure representing bonds payable outstanding.

14. (C) At maturity date of the bonds any premium, discount, or issue costs will be fully amortized. As a result, the carrying amount will be equal to the maturity (face) value of the bond. As the maturity or face value is also equal to the bond's market value at that time, no gain or loss exists.

15. (C) According to *FASB Statement No. 4,* gains or losses from extinguishment of debt should be reported in the income statement as an extraordinary item, net of related income tax effect.

16. (A) Present value is best measured in these circumstances by the fair value of the property, goods, or services involved in the transaction. The interest element is the difference between the face amount of the note and the fair value of the property, goods, or services.

17. (A) If the fair value of the property is not determinable and if the debt instrument has no ready market, the present value of the debt instrument must be estimated. The estimation involves approximating (imputing) an interest rate. The imputed interest rate is used to establish the present value of the debt instrument by discounting, at that rate, all future payments on the debt.

18. (D) The difference between the fair market value of the land and the face value of this zero-interest-bearing note is considered a discount on the notes. The discount should be amortized over the life of the note.

19. (B) A project financing arrangement has nothing to do with the ability of either entity involved to enter into the project on their own. The other three alternatives (A, C, and D) are relevant characteristics.

20. (C) Many companies enter into off-balance-sheet financing arrangements to enhance their balance sheet and potentially allow future credit to be obtained more readily from potential lenders. There are many off-balance-sheet financing arrangements that companies enter into which are acceptable. However, these arrangements normally have to be disclosed in the footnotes to the financial statements so investors and creditors are not completely void of information on the kinds of arrangements an entity has entered into.

21. (C) The times interest earned ratio is:

$$\frac{\text{Income before income taxes and interest expense}}{\text{Interest expense}}$$

Ewell's times interest earned ratio is computed as follows:

$$\frac{\$1{,}000{,}000 + \$600{,}000 + \$400{,}000}{400{,}000} = 5$$

22. (D) Long-term debt that matures within one year and is to be refinanced, converted into stock, or is to be retired from a bond retirement fund, should be reported as noncurrent and accompanied with a note explaining the method to be used in its liquidation.

*23. (D) Answers A and B would result in a gain to the creditor. Answer C is incorrect because the present value of the expected future cash flows should be used in calculating the creditor's loss rather than the total expected future cash flows of the investment.

*24. (C) When a transfer of noncash assets or the issuance of the debtor's stock can be used to settle a debt obligation in a troubled debt restructuring, the noncash assets or equity interest given should be accounted for at their fair market value. The excess of the carrying amount of the payable over the fair market value of the assets or equity interest transferred should be accounted for as an extraordinary gain. When equity is issued by the debtor, it is recorded in the normal manner.

*25. (C) Answers (A) and (B) would result in losses to the debtor. Answer (D) is how the creditor would account for its loss, and answer (C) is how the debtor would account for its gain.

REVIEW EXERCISES

1.

Date	Account	Debit	Credit
8-1-02	Cash	788,000	
	Discount on Bonds Payable	20,000(a)	
	Bonds Payable		800,000
	Bond Interest Expense		8,000(b)

(a) \$800,000 - (\$800,000 x .975) = \$20,000
(b) (\$800,000 x .06) x 2/12 = \$8,000

Date	Account	Debit	Credit
12-1-02	Bond Interest Expense	24,800	
	Cash		24,000
	Discount on Bonds Payable		800(a)

(a) 9 years = 108 months. 108 - 8 = 100
(\$20,000 ÷ 100) x 4 = \$800

Date	Account	Debit	Credit
12-31-02	Bond Interest Expense	4,200	
	Bond Interest Payable		4,000
	Discount on Bonds Payable		200

2.

Maturity value of bonds payable		\$200,000
Present value of \$200,000 due in 4 years at 5% semiannual interest (Table 6-2) (\$200,000 x .82075)	\$164,150	
Present value of \$6,000 interest payable semiannually for 4 years at 5% (Table 6-4) (\$6,000 x 7.17014)	43,021	
Proceeds from sale of bonds		207,171
Premium on bonds		\$ 7,171

Schedule of Interest Expense and
Bond Premium Amortization
Effective Interest Method
6% Bonds Sold to Yield 5%

Date	Credit Cash	Debit Interest Expense	Debit Bond Premium	Carrying Value of Bonds
1-1-01				\$207,171
7-1-01	\$6,000(a)	\$5,179(b)	\$821(c)	206,350(d)
1-1-02	6,000	5,159	841	205,509
7-1-02	6,000	5,138	862	204,647
1-1-03	6,000	5,116	884	203,763
7-1-03	6,000	5,094	906	202,857
1-1-04	6,000	5,071	929	201,928
7-1-04	6,000	5,048	952	200,976
1-1-05	6,000	5,024	976	200,000
Totals	\$48,000	\$40,829	\$7,171	

(a) \$6,000 = \$200,000 x .06 x 6/12
(b) \$5,179 = \$207,171 x .05 x 6/12
(c) \$ 821 = \$6,000 - \$5,179
(d) \$206,350 = \$207,171 - \$821

3. a. $4,000: ($6,000 x 4/6).
   b. $3,750: discount [($200,000 + $4,000) - $200,250].
   c. $6,000: amount of semiannual interest payment.
   d. $4,000: accrual of 4 months' interest, Sept. 1 - Dec. 31.
   e. $6,194: 6 months' interest plus discount amortization ($3,750 x 6/116).

4.

	Account	Debit	Credit
(a)	Cash	838,000	
	Bonds Payable		800,000
	Premium on Bonds Payable		20,000
	Bond Interest Expense		18,000
(b)	Bond Interest Expense	36,000	
	Cash		36,000
(c)	Bond Interest Expense	24,000	
	Bond Interest Payable		24,000
	Premium on Bonds Payable	1,196.58	
	Bond Interest Expense		1,196.58
	(($20,000 ÷ 117) X 7 = $1,196.58)		
(d)	Bond Interest Expense	12,000	
	Bond Interest Payable	24,000	
	Cash		36,000
(e)	Bonds Payable	350,000	
	Premium on Bonds Payable	7,703*	
	Bond Interest Expense ($350,000 X .09 X 5/12)	13,125	
	Cash ($353,500 + $13,125)		366,625
	Gain on Retirement ($357,703 - $353,500)		4,203
(f)	Bond Interest Expense ($450,000 X .09 X 6/12)	20,250	
	Cash		20,250
(g)	Bond Interest Expense	13,500**	
	Bond Interest Payable		13,500
	Premium on Bonds Payable	1,677.34***	
	Bond Interest Expense		1,677.34

* ($20,000 x 350/800 x 103/117 = $7,703)

** ($450,000 x.09 X 4/12)

*** Amortization per year on $450,000
($20,000 X 12/117 x 450/800) $ 1,153.84
Amortization on $350,000 for 7 months
($20,000 x 7/117 x 350/800) 523.50
$1,677.34

5a.

	Debit	Credit	
Cash	785,592		
Premium on Bonds Payable		167,592	(1)
Bond Interest Payable		18,000	(2)
Bonds Payable		600,000	

(1) $767,592 - $600,000 = $167,592
(2) $600,000 X. 12 = $72,000 X 1/4 = $18,000

b.

Date	Credit Payable	Debit Interest Expense	Debit Bond Premium	Carrying Amount of Bonds
10/1/02				$767,592
12/31/02	$18,000	$15,352	$2,648	764,944

	Debit	Credit
Bond Interest Expense	15,352	
Premium on Bonds Payable	2,648	
Bond Interest Payable		18,000

c.

	Debit	Credit
Bond Interest Payable	36,000	
Cash		36,000

Notes

Notes

Notes

Notes

Notes

Notes

Notes

Notes

Notes